The Transfer of Development Rights

The Transfer of Development Rights:
A New Technique of Land Use Regulation

Edited by Jerome G. Rose

Center For Urban Policy Research
Rutgers—The State University
New Brunswick, New Jersey

The CUPR Survey Series
Series Editors: George Sternlieb and
Virginia Paulus

Land Use Controls: Present Problems and Future Reform
Edited by David Listokin

Municipal Needs, Services, and Financing: Readings on Municipal Expenditures
Edited by W. Patrick Beaton

Models of Employment and Residence Location
Edited by Franklin J. James

Suburbanization Dynamics and the Future of the City
Edited by James W. Hughes

Readings in Urban Economics and Spatial Patterns
Edited by Michael R. Greenberg

Legal Foundations of Land Use Planning
Edited by Jerome G. Rose

Legal Foundations of Environmental Planning
Edited by Jerome G. Rose

CONTENTS

About the Editor

Jerome G. Rose has a J.D. from Harvard Law School and is a member of the New York Bar. He is Professor of Urban Planning at Livingston College, Rutgers University and Editor-in-Chief of *Real Estate Law Journal*. He is author of *The Legal Advisor on Home Ownership* (1967); *Landlords and Tenants: A Complete Guide to the Residential Rental Relationship* (1973); *Legal Foundations of Land Use Planning: Cases and Materials on Planning Law* (1974); *Legal Foundations of Environmental Planning: Cases and Materials on Environmental Law* (1974); and *New Approaches To State Land Use Policies*, with Melvin R. Levin and Joseph S. Slavet (1974).

ACKNOWLEDGMENTS

I am indebted to a number of people at Rutgers' Center for Urban Policy Research, whose assistance made this book possible. Hilary Greenfield, Librarian at the Center was particularly helpful in collecting the material and preparing it for press; Carol Rosen edited the new material written especially for this collection; Lorraine Bartu typed and retyped the manuscript with accuracy and good cheer; Mary Picarella contributed her administrative talents to the task of bringing it all together. I am especially grateful to Dr. George Sternlieb, who encouraged me to undertake this work and who made it all possible by making available to me the talent and resources of the Center.

I also wish to express my appreciation to the authors and publishers who have given permission to reprint, in whole or in part, the following material:

Carmichael, Donald M. "Transferable Development Rights As a Basis for Land Use Control" 2 *Fla. State U.L. Rev.* 35, 53-99 (1974).

Chavoosian, B. Budd, Thomas Norman and George H. Nieswand. "Transfer of Development Rights." This article is printed with the permission of the Cooperative Extension Service, Cook College, Rutgers, The State University.

Costonis, John J. "The Chicago Plan: Incentive Zoning and the Preservation of Urban Landmarks" 85 *Harvard Law Review* 574-631 (1972). Copyright 1972 by the Harvard Law Review Association.

———— and Robert S. De Voy. *The Puerto Rican Plan: Environmental Protection Through Development Right Transfer*. The Conservation Trust of Puerto Rico and Real Estate Research Corporation 1-2, 16-19, 45-48 June, 1974.

Elliott, Donald H. and Norman Marcus. "From Euclid to Ramapo: New Directions on Land Development Controls" 1 *Hofstra L. Rev.* 56, 72-78 (1972).

Gans, Ellis. *Saving Valued Spaces and Places Through Development Rights Transfer* (1974).

Goodman, William J. *Descriptive Information on Transfer of Development Rights, Accompanying Proposed Legislation* (1972).

Hagman, Donald G. "Windfalls and Wipeouts" in *The Good Earth of America; Planning Our Land Use* '(C. Hariss, ed.).

Lynch, Kevin. *Controlling the Location and Timing of Development by the Distribution of Annual Development Rights* (1973).

Maryland Senate Bill, No. 254 (1972).

Moore, Audrey. *Transferable Development Rights: An Idea Whose Time Has Come* 6-31.

Richards, David A. "Development Rights Transfer in New York City" (Note) 82 *Yale LJ* 338--372 (1972). Reprinted by permission of the Yale Law Journal Company and Fred Rothman & Company from *The Yale Law Journal*, Vol. 82, pp. 335-72.

Rose, Jerome. "A Proposal for the Separation and Marketability of Development Rights As a Technique to Preserve Open Space" 2 *Real Estate L. J.* 635-663 (1974).

———"Psychological, Legal and Administrative Problems of the Proposal to Use the Transfer of Development Rights as a Technique to Preserve Open Space" *The Urban Lawyer*, Fall, 1974. This article is reprinted by permission from Vol. 6, No. 4 (1974) issue of *The Urban Lawyer*, the national quarterly journal of urban law published by the American Bar Association, Section on Local Government Law.

———"The Mandatory Percentage of Moderately Priced Dwellings (MPMPD) Ordinance Is The Latest Technique of Inclusionary Zoning" 3 *Real Estate LJ* (1974).

Shales, Jared B. "Who Pays for Transfer of Development Rights?" 40 *Planning* 7-9 July, 1974.

Sonoma County Planning Board. *The Potential for Density Transfer in Sonoma County* 1-5, 13-18 June, 1974.

Town of Southampton. *New York Building Zone Ordinance No. 26.* adopted May 2, 1972. Section 2-10-20, 2-10-80.

Wilson, Leonard U. "Precedented-Setting Swap in Vermont" 61 *American Inst. of Architects Journal* 51-52 (1974). Reprinted with permission from *AIA Journal*, March, 1974. Copyright 1974. American Institute of Architects.

To

B. Budd Chavooshian

Whose leadership, industry, and scholarship

helped to make the T.D.R concept

‹ workable technique of land-use planning

I.
INTRODUCTION

The Transfer of Development Rights:
An Interim Review
of an Evolving Concept

JEROME G. ROSE

In May, 1974, at its 40th Annual National Planning Conference in Chicago, the American Society of Planning Officials selected the transfer of development rights (TDR) as the featured subject of discussion for its prestigious Alfred Bettman Symposia.[1] The discussion served the two-fold purpose of exposing the enthusiastic response of practicing planners to this new technique of land use regulation and also providing an opportunity for those who had been experimenting with the concept to share their findings and to reaffirm their initial observation that, as Audrey Moore[2] put it, "Transferable development rights is an idea whose time has come!"

As a result of the ASPO Conference, and subsequent coverage in professional and trade journals,[3] both planners and governmental officials have been asking for more information about this exciting idea. For this reason it would seem useful to review the history and evolution of TDR and to consider the experience of communities that have proposed or adopted the transfer of development rights as a method of land use regulation.

The legal concept underlying TDR is that title to real estate is not a unitary or monolithic right, but rather it may be compared to a "bundle of individual rights," each one of which may be separated from the rest and transferred to someone else, leaving the original owner with all other rights of ownership. This is not a new or novel idea. We have long been accustomed to the separation and alienability of such components of title as mineral rights, and mortgage liens, among others. One of the components of this "bundle of rights" is the right to develop the land. In other than agricultural or mining areas, the right to develop land tends to become the component of greatest value among the many rights of ownership. In rural areas where there is little expectation of development in the foreseeable future, the right to develop the land has lower value. In either case, though, there is legal precedent for the transfer of just that one right, the development right, leaving the owner of the land with all other rights.

Each of the various TDR programs to be discussed seeks to use the transfer of development right to achieve one or more specific goals: the New York and Chicago plans seek to preserve architectural and historical landmarks by transferring the right to develop that land more intensively to owners of other land; the New Jersey proposal seeks to preserve farmland and open space by transferring the right to develop that land to designated districts; proposals in Maryland, Fairfax County, Virginia, and Sonoma County, California, seek to use TDR as a primary method of land use regulation; the Southampton, New York ordinance seeks to provide economic incentive to build low and moderate income housing; and the British plan seeks to recover the increase in the value of private land that results from public investment.

Each of the proposals uses a variation of the transfer of development rights technique to accomplish its objective: the New Jersey proposal seeks to create a free market in which development rights may be bought and sold, subject to the economic forces of the real estate market place; the Chicago plan permits with some limitations, landmark owners to sell development rights to owners of land in designated districts, subject to the power of the city to ac quire those rights by condemnation proceedings for deposit in a "development rights bank"; under the Southampton ordinance the Town Board may authorize a transfer of residential development rights pursuant to a prescribed procedure; under the British system the government acquired all development rights in 1947 and under two programs (both now abandoned) an owner of land had to buy back his development rights before developing his property.

Under those plans that seek to create a free or partially free market for development rights, the method of calculating the number of rights to which an owner is entitled varies: under the Maryland proposal, development rights would be distributed on the basis of the *number of acres* of land owned, irrespective of value; under the New Jersey proposal, development rights would be distributed on the basis of the *proportionate value* of the owner's land to the total value of all land preserved for open space use; the Sonoma County, California proposal seeks a compromise between the *acreage method* and the *value method* by creating three concentric bands around the built-up area and assigning a value factor per acre that reflects the fact that the closer-in lands are more valuable because they are likely to be developed sooner than the farther-out lands.

These and other variations upon the basic theme will become more understandable as we examine the TDR concept in an orderly manner: *first*, by examining some of the legal precedents upon which the concept is based; *secondly*, by analyzing each of the TDR proposals; and *finally*, by evaluating the concept from a legal, administrative, economic, and practical perspective.

I. LEGAL ANTECEDENTS

A. Early American Precedents

Professor Donald M. Carmichael has recently described the early American precedents upon which the TDR proposal is based.[4] His article directs attention to the four precedents for the creation of planning districts within which the development potential of individual properties was transferred to other private owners for the purpose of fulfilling a public need. Those precedents are: (1) the early transportation systems, (2) the Milldam Acts, (3) major drainage and irrigation projects, and (4) oil and gas production regulations.

In the early 1800's it was common practice for the states to authorize private corporations to plan, construct, and maintain private toll roads. To avoid the problem of costly detours around the property of uncooperative landowners, the private corporations were given the power to acquire rights-of-way upon the payment of compensation. This same power was later given to private builders of canals and railroads. This practice established the precedent for a system by which the right to develop some part of a person's property could be transferred to another private owner, upon the payment of compensation, where such transfer is designed to meet a public need.

In another practice going back to early colonial days, the private owner of land on a stream could erect a dam to harness water power for the purpose of grinding grain. The damming of the stream would invariably result in the flooding of the land of upstream landowners, thereby depriving them of their rights to develop that land. These rights could have been protected by requiring the millowner to tear down the dam. Instead, the millowner was permitted to maintain his dam and gristmill upon payment of compensation to the upstream owner for the loss of his right to develop his flooded lands. The Milldam statutes authorizing this practice also required the miller to grind the grain of all who requested the service and paid a statutory share of flour produced as a fee. The courts upheld the Milldam statutes on the grounds that they were a reasonable police power regulation. Thus, the precedent was established for the involuntary transfer of the right of upstream owners to develop their land, without the exercise of the power of eminent domain. However, a system was established by which the millowners were required to compensate the upstream owners and were also required to submit to regulation of their operation for the protection of the public.

The early American method of administering drainage and irrigation projects carries this precedent one step further. Under this mechanism the courts were authorized to oversee the administration of a drainage or irrigation district. A majority of the property owners in the district could vote to undertake an irrigation or drainage project and impose its costs upon the participating owners in accordance with benefits received from the project. Thus, some owners might be deprived of the right to develop or use their property so that the water resources could be channeled to achieve the greatest benefit for the district. Those who received that benefit would provide the funds from which those who contributed would be compensated. Thus, a district was created in which the resources of all participants were pooled and the rights of development were reassigned within the district to achieve the maximum utilization of local resources.

The fourth early American precedent described by Professor Carmichael is the oil and gas production regulations that were designed to prevent each owner of property over a gas or oil "reservoir" or "field" from producing as fast as possible to get as much oil and gas from his property, and thereby draining as much from his neighbor's property, as he could. This practice caused rapid depletion of resources, waste, duplication, and overinvestment in drilling equipment. The states adopted statutes regulating the availability of the common fund of oil and gas resources for all of the owners of land overlying it. The United States Supreme Court upheld these regulations in a decision[5] that recognized the co-equal right of all owners to share in common resources and confirmed the legislative power to prevent waste of resources and provide for a just distribution and enjoyment of those assets among the collective owners. Professor Carmichael suggests that this precedent supports the transfer of development rights concept in that the potential for development within a planning or zoning district is similar to a reservoir of gas or oil resources. Consequently the regulation of development density, type, and timing to avoid waste and provide for a pooling of resources and an equitable system of distribution of development rights among the co-owners would be supported by the precedent of the oil and gas production regulation.

B. British and Recent American Precedents

A recent article of my own[6] reviewed the British and more recent American precedents from which the transfer of development rights concept is derived. The British used the transfer of development rights technique in an attempt to establish a system by which the increases in value of real property resulting from public action would be recovered and in which owners whose use of land was restricted would be compensated. In the Town and Country Planning Act of 1947 the British government acquired the development rights of all undeveloped land in the nation. This left the owners of land with all other rights of ownership, except the right to develop. When an owner wanted to develop his land he had to buy back the right to develop from the government by paying a development charge. The funds thus derived went into a revolving fund that was used to compensate other owners of property who were denied the right to develop.

During the period from 1947 to 1971, as the governmental leadership alternated between the Conservative and Labour parties, the program was modified frequently and ultimately abandoned. At the present time, however, the British government still owns the development rights to all land but has not been able to devise a politically acceptable system to utilize its development rights as an effective technique of land use regulation.

The article also reviewed the more recent American experience with the transfer of development rights, including such programs as: (1) eminent domain acquisition of less than a fee simple, (2) landmark preservation transfer of floor area ratio rights, and (3) incentive zoning transfer of FAR bonuses.

There is ample judicial and legislative precedent for government acquisition of less-than-the-fee simple (that is, less than the full title). A typical illustration is the condemnation of a right of way for the purpose of installing utility poles. This concept has been extended to permit government acquisition (by condemnation or purchase) of only the right to develop the land, leaving the owner with all other rights of ownership. For example, the New Jersey enabling legislation authorizes the acquisition of a "restriction on the use of land"; the California statute authorizes the acquisition of a "lesser interest or right in real property . . . through limitation of their future use"; the Vermont statute is more explicit and authorizes the acquisition of "development rights." Thus, the precedent for the transfer of development rights seems to be well established; the remaining challenge is to devise a technique by which the concept may be used effectively as a land use control device.

Such a technique was attempted in the New York City and Chicago programs, in which development rights may be transferred from landmark buildings to other lots. This transfer is made possible because urban landmark buildings usually have an excess of authorized but unbuilt floor area under the floor area ratio (FAR). The FAR is a zoning technique to regulate the physical volume (density) of a building by controlling the relation between the floor area of a building and the area of the lot on which the building stands. The consideration that the landmark owner receives for the sale of his excess FAR, that is, his development rights, compensates him for preserving the landmark. This program is described in greater detail later.

Under the plan adopted by the City of San Francisco involving the zoning transfer of FAR bonuses, the downtown is divided into four districts, each with a prescribed FAR. A builder may obtain a bonus of an increased FAR by providing such public benefits as pedestrian plazas, additional set backs, observation decks, and the like. In a strict sense, the San Francisco plan and other programs of incentive zoning, offering FAR bonuses, are not examples of the transfer of development rights because part of the fee is not separated from the title on one landowner and transferred to another landowner. Instead, the government, under its police power, artificially restricts development and then prescribes conditions under which those restrictions may be relaxed. On the other hand, these plans are similar to the transfer of development rights system in that the right to develop is specifically singled out, among the other rights of ownership, and manipulated as a device to control land use.

II. CURRENT PROGRAMS AND PROPOSALS

Planners and lawyers have begun to experiment with a variety of techniques to use the transfer of development rights for purposes of land use regulation: New York City and Chicago used it for the preservation of landmarks; in New Jersey, legislation was proposed to use TDR to preserve open space; it was proposed as a technique to preserve the ecologically fragile Phosphorescent Bay in Puerto Rico; legislation has been prepared in Maryland and proposals are being developed in Fairfax County, Virginia, and Sonoma County, California, to use TDR as a primary system of land use regulation;

Southampton, Long Island, New York has adopted an ordinance using TDR to encourage construction of moderate and low income housing; St. George, Vermont uses the transfer of development rights as a device for regulating community growth; it is being studied as one of the techniques for eliminating unconscionable profits (windfalls) or losses (wipeouts) to landowners resulting from government regulation of land use. Each of these programs will be discussed.

A. Landmark Preservation

Professor John J. Costonis, one of the leading authorities on development rights, wrote the definitive description of the Chicago plan in an article in the *Harvard Law Review* in 1972.[7] In that same year, David A. Richards described the New York City plan in a note in the *Yale Law Journal*.[8] In 1973, Donald H. Elliott and Norman Marcus described the more recent use of the transfer of development rights in New York City.[9] The programs of both cities, described in these articles, seek to preserve urban landmark buildings by permitting the landmark owner to sell his authorized but unbuilt floor area to another landowner. These unused development rights may have substantial value when attached to the transferee parcel, particularly in high density commercial zones. Once the excess floor area is transferred, the authorized floor area of the landmark lot is exhausted and may no longer be used for higher density development. Thus, the landmark owner is compensated by the sale of a valuable asset—his development rights, as computed in terms of unused floor area ratio. Once sold, the economic incentive to demolish the landmark for higher density development is removed.

Professor Costonis suggests that the Chicago plan is superior to the New York City program for a number of reasons. The primary weakness of the original New York City plan was that development rights could be transferred only to adjacent lots whereas the Chicago plan permits the development rights to be transferred to designated transfer districts where increased density could be absorbed without serious effect. Secondly, the New York plan provides for only such compensation to the landmark owner as he may derive from the sale of his development rights in the open market. The Chicago plan, on the other hand, is designed to compensate the landmark owner for the actual loss incurred in retaining the landmark. A landmark commission is authorized to determine the amount of compensation and to devise a plan for payment of compensation, including development right sale, real estate tax reduction, and additional subsidy, if necessary, funded out of a municipal development rights bank. Under the Chicago plan, the municipality would play an active role in making a market for development rights by acquiring development rights by purchase and condemnation and then selling them to owners of property where increased density would be appropriate. In spite of the care with which the Chicago plan was devised and its apparent great potential for providing a method of preserving historical landmarks,

Chicago's commissioner of development and planning has indicated that the Chicago plan will not be used in Chicago.[10] Nor has the development rights technique proven helpful in preserving landmarks in New York City.[11]

B. Open Space Preservation

The proposal to use the transfer of development rights as a technique to preserve open space is the product of a committee made up of Rutgers University faculty and members of the New Jersey Department of Community Affairs. The committee's proposal has been described in two articles written by different members of the committee. One of the articles, written by B. Budd Chavooshian and Thomas Norman, appears in *Urban Land*.[12] The other article, written by this author, appears in the *Real Estate Law Journal*.[13]

The New Jersey proposal is designed to induce owners of undeveloped land to preserve their land in open space by compensating them through the sale of their development rights to developers of other land in the jurisdiction. To make such sales possible, this proposal creates a market for development rights in which owners of developable land must buy development rights from owners of preserved open space land as a prerequisite for higher density development. The proposal seeks to create such a market in the following manner:

1. Each local government would prepare a land-use plan that specifies the percentage of remaining undeveloped land in the jurisdiction and that designates the land to remain undeveloped as preserved open space land. The land-use plan would also designate the land to be developed and would specify the uses to which the developable land may be put. A zoning law would be enacted or amended to implement this plan.

2. The planning board of each local government would prescribe the number of development rights required for each housing unit to be developed. On the basis of this numerical assignment, the planning board would then compute the number of development rights required to develop the jurisdiction in accordance with the land-use plan. The local government would issue certificates of development rights (ownership of which would be recorded) in the exact amount so determined.

3. Every owner of preserved open space land would receive certificates of development rights in an amount that represents the percentage of assessed value of his undeveloped land to the total assessed value of all undeveloped land to be preserved in open space in the jurisdiction.

4. An owner of developable land, who desires to develop his land more intensively (for example, to build apartments instead of single family residences) would have to buy additional development rights in the open market from those who have acquired such rights from either original distribution or subsequent purchase.

5. Thus, owners of preserved open space would be able to sell their development rights to owners of developable land (or real estate brokers or

speculators). In return for the compensation derived from this sale, owners of preserved open space land will have sold their rights to develop their land in the future. Their land will thus be preserved in open space and the owners will have been compensated without any capital costs to the government.

6. Development rights would be subject to ad valorem property taxation as a component of the total assessed value of the developable real property in the jurisdiction.

The most notable characteristic of the New Jersey plan is that certificates of development rights will be bought and sold in the open market in a manner similar to sales of a registered bond. The same economic forces that determine the value of land will also determine the value of the separated component of the value of land, namely, the right to develop. No governmental agency will be authorized to tinker with economic forces beyond its power. The goal of the plan is limited to the preservation of open space in accordance with sound planning principles. It does not purport to be a technique for recovering unearned increment in the value of land; it does not seek to redistribute economic resources. By limiting the purposes, the proponents of the plan sought to make it more politically acceptable.

A second innovative characteristic of the New Jersey plan is that certificates of development rights would be taxed, as a component of real estate value, in a manner similar to the other components of title. As a consequence, there would be incentive for a farmer, not wishing to speculate in real estate, to sell his certificates of development rights and thus pay property taxes only on the reduced value of his land for farm purposes. There would be incentive for the purchasers of development rights to use them quickly or sell them to long term investors or speculators in real estate, who would pay property taxes as part of the cost of such investment. This provision would tend to serve the same purpose as state farm assessment acts, but without the features of these acts that have been criticized for being more beneficial to real estate speculators than the farmers.

Another characteristic of the New Jersey plan that distinguishes it from the Maryland and other proposals is that the number of development rights distributed to owners of restricted land would be based upon the *value* of the land rather than its *acreage*. Each owner would receive the same proportion of the total number of development rights distributed as the value of his restricted land bears to the total value of all other land similarly restricted to open space use. Consequently the owner of more valuable land, regardless of acreage, would receive a greater proportion of the total number of development rights than the owner of a large tract of relatively worthless land. The value would be determined initially on the basis of assessed value with a procedure established to review the assessments based upon notice of the assessment of all other restricted land.

The fourth major characteristic of the New Jersey plan, one that distinguishes it from the Fairfax County, Virginia and other proposals, is that the system relates only to the development rights for *residential* units. The New Jersey proposal does not purport to be a primary system of land use regulation. It deals only with open space land and residential development. No development rights are required for *commercial* or *industrial* development. The drafters of the New Jersey plan purposely did not extend the system to commercial and industrial development rights to avoid the complex calculations and administration that would result. It was the consensus of the drafting committee that although there was no *logical* reason why commercial and industrial development rights could not be included, there were sufficient practical and *political* reasons why the proposal should be kept as simple and understandable as possible.

C. Preservation of Fragile Ecological Resources

Professor Costonis and Robert S. DeVoy of Real Estate Research Corporation have prepared a study for the Conservation Trust of Puerto Rico[14] in which the transfer of development rights is proposed as the technique for preserving ecologically sensitive areas from development. Under their plan, development rights are transferred from "Protected Environmental Zones" (PEZ) to sites in "transfer districts" where greater density would not only be unobjectionable but would tend to implement the island's comprehensive planning objectives.

The Puerto Rican plan has four basic components:

1. *Preparation of a PEZ Inventory:* The Planning Board would be authorized to prepare an inventory of the island's ecologically fragile areas, including but not limited to the dinoflagellates of the Phosphorescent Bay. The Board would also establish criteria and procedures for designating other areas in the future. Regulations would be promolgated that prescribe the types of development, if any, that would be permitted within those areas.

2. *Identification of Transfer Districts:* The Planning Board would designate transfer districts where development at greater density would be desirable. Designation would be based upon both planning principles and market demand. Owners of land within transfer districts would be able to develop their land up to specified densities and would be able to increase this density by purchasing development rights at a price set either by open market public bid procedures or by negotiations with the Land Administration governmental agency authorized to administer the program.

3. *Administration of the Environmental Trust Fund:* The Land Administration would administer an Environmental Trust Fund that would receive payments for development rights and would use these funds for administrative expenses and to compensate landowners who are denied a reasonable return on their land because of land use restrictions.

4. *Review and Settlement of Claims:* An aggrieved landowner in a PEZ could challenge a denial of his application to develop on the grounds that such denial deprives him of a reasonable return from his land. Among the remedies available to such a landowner would be: (1) compensation for his loss, (2) liberalization of the restriction on the use, or (3) agreement between the landowner and the Land Administration on some other alternative, such

as an exchange of the owner's land for another parcel. Where compensation is made, the owner would be required to transfer his development right to the Commonwealth, thus removing from that land all rights to develop at any time in the future.

Professor Costonis readily concedes that the transfer of development rights in the Puerto Rican plan is more metaphorical than real. He contrasts the transfers in the Puerto Rican plan to those in the Chicago plan, where there is a direct transfer of a specified quantity of development rights from one property to another property. Under the Puerto Rican plan there is *no direct transfer* in kind of the right to develop one property to another property. The Puerto Rican plan seeks to transfer the *dollar equivalent* of the loss of the right to develop in the PEZ. The Land Administration is not required to maintain a balance in the amount of development rights; it is only required to balance the dollar amounts required for compensation awards and expenses of administration. There is no private market for development rights, as in the New Jersey and Maryland proposals. In fact there is no market at all—but rather a program for funding the compensation of owners whose use of land is restricted for a public use.

The Puerto Rican plan is more like the British program under the Town and Country Planning Act of 1947, than any of the American programs. Although the ostensible purpose of the Puerto Rican plan is to preserve environmental resources, its most significant contribution may be in achieving other land use regulation objectives: (1) similar to the British program, the Puerto Rican plan recovers for the public benefit the increase in land value that results from more intensive development; (2) it addresses the other half of the windfall/wipeout inequity by compensating landowners whose use of land is restricted; and (3) it directs attention to the fairness of programs that seek to charge to each development its share of the cost of environmental despoilation.

D. As a Primary System of Land Use Regulation

The transfer of development rights may be used as the primary system of land use regulation, as a substitute for, or together with, the zoning power. Under such a system the allocation and regulation of development rights would determine the use of land and the design and density of all development. To accomplish this, development rights for all types of private development—residential, commercial, and industrial—would be issued in amounts that would provide the prescribed measure of each type of development. Such proposals have been made in Maryland, in Fairfax County, Virginia, and in Sonoma County, California.

1. *The Maryland Proposal*

Maryland State Senator William J. Goodman introduced a bill[15] in the Maryland State Senate that would use the transfer of development rights as a primary technique of land use regulation. As Senator Goodman described his proposal[16] the master plan in each political subdivision would designate the land to be developed and the use of such land. Development rights would be issued to all landowners for all private development permitted; no development would take place unless the owner has the requisite number of development rights. Once an owner of land sells all of his rights he would no longer be able to develop his land unless he reacquires the requisite number of development rights.

The Maryland plan is similar to the New Jersey plan in that a free market for the purchase and sale of development rights is contemplated. The Maryland plan goes beyond the confines of the New Jersey plan in that development rights will be issued for "commercial" uses, defined to include all private uses other than residential and agricultural. Thus, commercial and industrial development as well as residential development require development rights as a condition for governmental approval. Each owner of undeveloped land in the jurisdiction receives a proportion of the total number of development rights required for total development. Unlike the New Jersey proposal, the number of shares that each landowner receives depends upon the amount of acreage he owns. Development rights would be traded, bought, and sold until they are no longer available, at which point no further development in the jurisdiction will be possible. Thus, the amount and type of development would be regulated.

2. *The Fairfax County, Virginia Proposal*

Audrey Moore, supervisor of Annandale District, Fairfax County, Virginia has proposed the transfer of development rights as a substitute for zoning.[17] Under her proposal each jurisdiction would adopt a comprehensive plan that would establish the residential, commercial, and industrial needs of the community and would calculate the number of each kind of development rights necessary to fulfill those needs. Every property owner would receive his share of development rights based upon the proportion of the amount of land he owns to the total number of acres of land in the jurisdiction. To obtain permission to build, a landowner would have to submit, with his site plan or subdivision plan, development rights in the amount required for his proposed development.

The Fairfax County proposal has a number of interesting variations on the TDR theme: the basic features of the comprehensive plan, such as projected population, would require approval by referendum. This requirement is based upon the realization that all too frequently so fundamental a policy decision as the future population of the community is based upon planners' statistical manipulations and vagaries instead of the kind of democratic discussion and compromise upon which community support may be founded. By resolving these issues by referendum at an early stage of planning it may be possible to obtain the community acceptance and continuing approval of the plan upon which the transfer of development rights implementation program depends.[18]

The Fairfax County proposal also addresses the problem of a subsequent revision of the comprehensive plan requiring an increase in the number of development rights. In such event, the revision of the comprehensive plan will require approval by referendum. If additional development rights are needed they will be distributed to existing holders of development rights, similar to a distribution of a stock split.

One of the weaknesses of the Fairfax County proposal is the provision for allocation of development rights to landowners on the basis of acreage instead of value. The rationale for the proposed method of distribution is that "all land is buildable and eventually, given enough economic pressure, it will be developed." Nevertheless, it is easy to imagine circumstances in which the owner of large tracts of worthless swamp, mountainous, or otherwise "unbuildable" land receives a disproportionate share of development rights while the owner of a smaller tract of more valuable land receives less than his fair share. The obvious inequities that result therefrom pose serious constitutional questions under the due process and equal protection clauses.

3. *The Sonoma County, California Proposal*

Based upon a proposal originally expounded by County Supervisors Robert Theiller and Ig Vella, the Sonoma County Planning Department has prepared a pilot study of the use of "density transfer" for a 14 square mile area west of Santa Rosa, California.[19] In this study, a calculation was made of the number of "density units" (that is, development rights) needed for ultimate development within a prescribed area and for transfer from outlying areas. Purchase of development rights would be financed by a charge imposed upon developers who seek rezoning for increased density within the urban development area. By this sytem it would become possible to "sell" zoning rights rather than allow windfall profits to developers who have been able to secure zoning changes for comparatively inexpensive raw land. In addition, development could proceed only within the limits of the prescribed number of development rights created. At the same time, the funds raised by the development charge would be used to purchase the development rights of land to be preserved in open space.

The study provides a detailed analysis of the two major calculations upon which the proposal is based: (1) the number of density units needed to achieve the desired mix of residential, commercial, and industrial uses, and (2) the number of development rights that would be available from the land suitable for open space preservation.

The calculation of the number of residential, commercial, and industrial development rights needed is based upon an in-depth analysis of each of nine districts into which the study area is divided. Within each district, optimum residential development is quantified in terms of residential units; optimum commercial and industrial development is quantified on the basis of trip generation potential. The formula adopted is based upon the relationship of residential, commercial, and industrial uses upon trip generation and the concomitant urban congestion and service needs. After calculating the number of density units projected in each district, the number of density units existing under present zoning is subtracted. The difference is the number of development rights needed to achieve the desired mix of uses.

The calculation of the number of development rights that would be available from the land suitable for open space preservation is based upon the premise that only land capable of development should be allowed to sell development rights. Thus land within the flood plain zone would have no development rights to sell under this proposal. Also, in the absence of sewers in the area, land with hardpan soil conditions that could not support septic tanks would also be "undevelopable" and not entitled to development rights. The calculation is also based upon the determination that an "Open Space Preserve" shall consist of no less than 25 contiguous acres.

Based upon these premises, the Sonoma County proposal reviews each of three possible methods of calculating the number of development rights to which owners of open space land would be entitled. The New Jersey method, based upon the proportion of assessed value of the property to all open space property, is proposed as one possibility. The second method is a one-for-one exchange of density units. Under this method each eligible parcel would be entitled to a share based upon the number of density units permitted under existing zoning. The third method, in which three concentric bands would be designated around the built-up area of Santa Rosa, is based upon the premise that closer-in lands are likely to be developed sooner than land further away and therefore would tend to have a higher present value. Based upon this premise, a value factor per acre would be assigned to each band that would reflect this difference in value. After analyzing each of the three methods, the study recommends a combination of the second and third methods as most appropriate for the study area.

The method proposed for the distribution of development rights is only one of the ways in which the Sonoma County proposal differs from the New Jersey and other proposals. Unlike the New Jersey proposal, a free market for the purchase and sale of development rights is not recommended. Although there is no explicit discussion of this issue, it would appear that the proposal contemplates a "development rights bank" operated by a governmental agency in which funds are raised by development rights charges to finance the cost of purchase of development rights from owners of open space land. In addition, development rights are to be required for commercial and industrial as well as residential development. The most significant contribution of the Sonoma County proposal would appear to be the care with which the calculations are made for determining the need for and distribution of development rights.

E. As A Method of Encouraging the Construction of Moderate and Low Income Housing

In 1972 the Town of Southampton, Long Island, New York amended its old zoning ordinance[20] and provided for the transfer of development rights as a means of achieving elements of its "Community Planning Objectives."

Included in those objectives was the goal of encouraging a wide variety of housing types and, more particularly, making available purchase and rental housing within the financial means of residents who have low or lower middle incomes.

To achieve this objective, the Town Board was authorized to increase residential development density for a nonprofit corporation that guarantees to develop and maintain sales or rental housing at a cost within the means of the low or lower middle income housing market. The ordinance establishes a procedure by which an application for increased residential development density is reviewed by the Town Board and may be approved subject to review by the Planning Board and execution of a contract with provisions designed to effect the purposes of the ordinance. The ordinance limits the number of low and middle income units authorized by this procedure to four percent of the total number of dwelling units of all types in the jurisdiction. It also limits the development site density to not more than 12 units per acre.

Admittedly, the Southampton ordinance does not involve a transfer of development rights in the strict sense because the right to develop land to a prescribed density is not in fact *transferred* from one property owner to another. Rather, the program is more like the San Francisco *bonus zoning* program in which a developer may obtain a bonus of increased floor area ratio (FAR) by providing such public benefits as pedestrian walkways and malls. Nevertheless consideration of the Southampton ordinance is appropriate here because the program is a variation on the basic technique by which the right to develop land is singled out, among the other rights of ownership, and manipulated as a device to control land use. In addition, there is a great likelihood that, if the flow of federal financial assistance for housing diminishes, this technique will be considered seriously by communities as a possible method of economic assistance to provide housing for low and moderate income families.

An article in the Fall, 1974 issue of the *Real Estate Law Journal*[21] discusses some of the problems involved in the use of the Mandatory Percentage of Moderately Priced Dwellings (MPMPD) ordinance. Such an ordinance provides a housing developer with a bonus in terms of zoning density and relaxation of building code requirements in return for his agreement to build a proportion of the units within the range of the moderate or low income market. To create such a program it is necessary to adopt guiding principles by which the following issues may be resolved: (1) What percentage of the total number of units built must be allocated to the moderate/low income market? (2) What range of tenant/purchaser income needs should the mandatory percentage units be designed to meet? (3) What kind of administrative machinery is necessary to adjust rents to changing economic circumstances? (4) If dwelling units are to be sold, what administrative mechanism is necessary to retain the economic advantages for future low/moderate income purchasers?

In addition to the administrative problems, MPMPD ordinances face the legal questions of statutory authorization and constitutional validity. In the only case to date in which these issues have been raised,[22] the Virginia Supreme Court has held a Fairfax County MPMPD ordinance invalid on the grounds that the ordinance is both outside the scope of statutory authority and also violates the state constitutional provision protecting private property. Nevertheless, proponents of MPMPD ordinances have urged that their validity be upheld in other jurisdictions.

F. As A Method of Regulating the Location and Timing of Community Growth

All of the TDR programs mentioned above have at least one significant characteristic in common: they all use the transfer of development rights in a *negative* way. That is, all of the programs are designed primarily to prevent development of specified areas by directing development elsewhere. However, it is also possible to use the TDR technique to achieve the *affirmative* objective of directing development to a specified area and regulating the timing of each type of development to fulfill community needs during the development process.

Leonard U. Wilson has described the program that St. George, Vermont has adopted to control the location and rate of its development.[23] St. George is a small town with a population under 500 and total size of 2300 acres. It is located in the path of development of Vermont's largest and fastest growing urban area, Burlington. Rather than allow the town to grow in a haphazard, sprawling manner, the people of St. George have adopted a plan to achieve orderly growth. They purchased 48 acres of land on a site which will become the center of a projected village where all future growth will be focused.

The town intends to use its ownership of that parcel, together with the transfer of development rights technique, to concentrate all development in the prescribed area and to regulate the pace of development. To achieve this objective the town will require a developer to transfer to the town the development rights purchased from owners of land within the town but outside the project area. In exchange for these development rights the town will authorize equivalent development within the core village. Under the plan, the number of development rights assigned to each property equals the number of dwelling units that may be built on the property under existing zoning. Thus, a developer could purchase the development rights of 10 acres of land, zoned one dwelling unit per acre, and exchange these 10 development rights for authorization to build 10 dwelling units on land within the core village that the town will sell for such development purposes.

The net effect of this plan is that development will be concentrated in the designated area, and the owners of land outside the village will be compensated by the sale of their development rights for their loss of right to develop their own land. The rate of development of the village will be regulated by the rate at which the town issues the certificates of development rights.

Some of the problems involved in the regulation of the location and timing of development by the distribution of development rights are discussed in a paper by Professor Kevin Lynch.[24] Professor Lynch notes that local government must make two political determinations: (1) the desired locations for development, and (2) the rate of growth. The first is a more stable decision, not unlike the exercise of the zoning power where areas are designated for development and restricted development. However, under the TDR system, development can be prohibited in certain areas without outright confiscation. In addition, the more equitable distribution of the rights of development within the jurisdiction should make such locational decisions easier and less prone to :orruption, political pressures, and charges of inequity.

The determination of the *rate of growth* involves a more difficult political and planning decision. Professor Lynch suggests that to achieve both public flexibility and private predictability, the growth rate might be set annually for three to five years in the future. In addition it might be necessary for the state to regulate the local government decision with respect to residential development to assure that such decision is reasonably related to ecological, fiscal, and social constraints and particularly to the planned and budgeted expansion of public services.

Once the growth rate is determined in terms of number of residential units, Professor Lynch suggests that some amount be subtracted from that total and held by the government to be given or sold to developers of low income housing. The remainder would then be distributed annually to landowners in the jurisdiction in proportion to the number of acres they own. The recommendation to distribute solely on the basis of acreage rather than development potential under existing zoning is justified on the grounds of administrative simplicity and the desire to reduce the pressures and opportunities for windfall profits from the zoning process.

The proposal to authorize an annual distribution of development rights in accordance with rational and comprehensive planning principles might be even more useful at the regional level, Lynch suggests, where a governmental entity could set growth rates for the entire region. In addition to the planning advantages that would accrue from such allocation at a regional level the marketability of development rights would be enhanced. The paper does not address the sticky problem of virulent political opposition to any proposal involving a diminution of home rule prerogatives.

G. As a Method of Avoiding the Windfalls and Wipeouts Syndrome

Professor Donald Hagman's study for the Department of Housing and Urban Development, with the catchy title *Windfalls and Wipeouts Project*, directs attention to the double-edged problem of whether: (1) the owners of real estate should be able to keep increases in value created by society rather than themselves, and (2) society should be able to impose losses on the owners of real estate without paying damages? In one of the many publications to be produced in that study[25] Professor Hagman suggests that the answer to both questions should be "no," and he proposes a number of mechanisms for recapturing windfalls or avoiding wipeouts.

The mechanisms he proposes for windfall recapture are: (1) special assessments; (2) subdivision permission exactions; (3) subdivision cash fees in lieu of deductions; (4) development permission exactions; (5) development taxes; (6) capital gains tax; (7) transfer taxes; (8) unearned increment tax; and (9) single tax. Mechanisms to avoid wipeouts include: (1) damages for public improvement; (2) damages in nuisance; and (3) compensable regulation. Suggested as the most exciting techniques that simultaneously deal with both windfall and wipeout problems are: (1) zoning by eminent domain; (2) transfer of development rights; and (3) public ownership. Thus, although the transfer of development rights is only a small part of the *Windfalls and Wipeouts* study, TDR is recognized as a mechanism that holds great potential for resolving both aspects of the problem.

Ellis Gans has proposed[26] a plan in which the transfer of development rights is combined with a "windfall tax" similar to the one used by the British in their Town and Country Planning Act of 1947. The purpose of this proposed "tax" is to recover some of the public investment that makes high density development possible.

Under Gans' plan the local government would play an active role in the process: government would help create a market for development rights by keeping a file on willing buyers and sellers and putting them in touch with each other; it would also buy and sell development rights in competition with other purchasers; government would set the windfalls tax in an amount high enough to recover part of the increment in value while leaving sufficient profit for the developer to have an incentive to produce a better product. By "fine tuning" of both the price for development rights and the amount of the "windfalls tax" government would be able to manipulate the economic forces of the marketplace to regulate development in the public interest. Mr. Gans does not address the legal problems involved in the manipulation of a "tax" or other charge.

IV. EVALUATION OF THE PROPOSALS

Many of the proposals for the use of the transfer of development rights as a technique of land use regulation have come forth during the brief period of 1972 to 1974. It is still too early for a definitive evaluation of these proposals. Nevertheless, an interim evaluation of the psychological, legal, administrative, economic, and practical problems raised by TDR would be appropriate.

A. Psychological, Legal, and Administrative Issues

A recent article of mine[27] suggests that the introduction of TDR proposals—a "strange" new concept in the body of property law—may evoke a form of intellectual xenophobia, that is, fear of a stranger, at least in the beginning. There is a rational basis for concern on the part of planners, attorneys, and government officials about the effect of the creation of a separate market and conveyance system for development rights. Consequently, a better understanding of the concept and greater knowledge of its effect upon the existing system is essential for the adoption and success of the proposal.

The article also discusses some of the legal problems raised by TDR. A conceptual problem arises because the TDR proposal does not fit unambiguously into the definition of either the police power or the power of eminent domain. It has some of the characteristics of both traditional governmental powers but only some. The TDR proposal involves something more than police power regulation of property because the right to develop land is taken away from some owners of land. On the other hand, if it is the power of eminent domain that is being exercised it would be necessary to comply with the well established principles by which "just compensation" is defined. One such principle requires that compensation be in *money*. It is unclear whether certificates of development rights for use on other property will be held by the courts to be "compensation" within the meaning of the constitutional requirement. One recent decision held that a transfer of zoning density in New York City was not just compensation under the facts of that case.[28]

However, there are sufficient differences between the TDR proposal and the traditional exercise of the power of eminent domain to preclude a blind application of the traditional principles that limit eminent domain compensation. As a result, the validity of the TDR proposal, when challenged for failure to meet the requirements of just compensation, may very well depend upon the ability of counsel to explain, and the ability of the court to understand, the unique nature of the TDR proposal.

The criticism to which the TDR proposal is most vulnerable, the article suggests, is that the success of the program depends upon the proficiency of the planners and the integrity of the governing body responsible for its administration. To the extent that either group falters, the program may be jeopardized. The planners' projection of future market demand for land development must be reasonably accurate, and the designation of sites for specified land uses must be skillfully performed if there is to be, in fact, a market for development rights. After the planners have performed their role successfully, the governing body must withstand political pressures to modify the planners' recommendations in order to enhance personal, rather than public, objectives. It will also be necessary for the governing body to persuade the real estate industry of its intention to provide long term support of the program. The belief that the program will be abandoned at any time in the future would become a self-fulfilling prophecy because it would destroy the market for development rights.

Professor Costonis, in his excellent analysis of the legal issues involved in the transfer of development rights,[29], notes that challenges to TDR are based upon the uniformity provisions of state zoning acts and state and federal equal protection clauses, and upon substantive due process. The "uniformity" issue arises out of the provision in most zoning enabling acts that all zoning regulations "shall be uniform for each class of kind of buildings throughout each district." The question is whether different treatment of lots within a transfer district violates this provision. Professor Costonis suggests that the uniformity requirement is not violated because the courts have begun to recognize that the *individual lot* is not the most appropriate unit of development control. When cluster zoning and planned unit development ordinances were challenged, the courts have held that these ordinances met the uniformity requirement if all owners *within the district* are entitled to develop their parcels in accordance with the flexible density or use provisions of the law. That is, if the same options are available to all developers within the district, there is no violation of the uniformity clause. It is generally believed that if the transfer of development rights to an developer within a transfer district does not violate the uniformity provision, it will also not violate the equal protection clause.

The legal challenge to the TDR proposal based upon substantive due process is the argument that a program that imposes density restraints upon most landowners in a district and at the same time relaxes them for some who purchase development rights sacrifices long term public objectives for short term fiscal advantages and therefore is an arbitrary exercise of the police power violating the due process clause of the fourteenth amendment. Professor Costonis believes that this argument "misconceives the process by which bulk levels are determined and functions that they serve. As a result, it invests the numbers in the zoning code with an aura of scientific exactitude that is largely without foundation in fact." He argues that density limitations are based upon both fact determination and political judgment and that reasonable variations from the prescribed density within a prescribed range would not undermine the integrity of the planning process. Therefore, it is not an arbitrary exercise of the police power and is not a violation of substantive due process.

B. From an Economic Perspective

Jared B. Shlaes has written an article appearing in *Planning*, a publication of the American Society of Planning Officials, that discusses some of the economic issues raised by TDR. More specificially, the question raised is: who, if anyone, pays the costs of the transfer of development rights to other sites? Owners of property from whom development rights are taken do not pay the costs because they are compensated by the sale of such rights. The developers who purchase the rights do not pay the costs because as long as there is sufficient market demand for development at higher densities, those costs will be included in the rental or sales charges of the new units. The purchasers or renters of the new units do not pay the costs because they will pay no more for such space than they would pay for equivalent space either inside or outside the district. Whether that space exists by virtue of development rights or of additional land purchase is immaterial to them.

It has been suggested that it is the owners of property adjacent to the higher density development who pay the costs of TDR because they must endure larger structures within the community than would otherwise be possible without a zoning change. Mr. Shlaes argues against this position for a number of reasons. First, he asserts, such claims are speculative because in the typical urban situation entire districts are grossly overzoned to begin with. Consequently, the TDR process that permits a slight overreach of permissible densities at specific locations merely redistributes the density within the district. Furthermore, Shlaes argues, the increase in value of property adjacent to high density structures may more than offset any such costs.

He also argues that the general public does not pay the costs because tax revenues are in no way diminished; landmarks and open spaces are preserved; and the community benefits from improved planning. And so it appears to Mr. Shlaes that the benefits of a TDR program may be achievable without any costs other than the costs of administration.

C. From a Practical Planning Perspective

Audrey Moore, in her evaluation of the Fairfax County, Virginia proposal,[30] calls attention to some of the disadvantages and advantages of that proposal. The Fairfax County plan is based upon a free market for development rights. Consequently, that program does not deal with the windfalls/wipeouts problem with the effectiveness possible under the Puerto Rican or Chicago plan, where a governmental agency acquires and sells development rights at prices that recover the windfalls and compensate owners whose land use is restricted. Ms. Moore also expresses her concern for the inequities that may result if the planners err in their projections of future populations: if their population projections turn out to be lower than actual growth, then astute speculators will reap large profits; if their population projections turn out to be higher than actual growth and economic demand for land, then there will be an insufficient market demand for development rights. (It is just this reason that the Sonoma County, California proposal is based upon an in-depth analysis of (1) the number of density units needed for planned development, and (2) the number of development rights to be issued.) But the greatest problem that Audrey Moore recognizes is the lack of public understanding of the TDR concept and the fear that a change from the existing system will have an adverse effect upon their rights.

On the other hand, Ms. Moore argues that the potential advantages of the TDR proposal far outweigh its disadvantages. The system can provide a more effective control of the use of land and the timing of development than zoning; it can provide compensation to owners of land whose use is restricted; it can provide an effective mechanism for monitoring and controlling total planned growth; it can save time and expense for developers by providing certainty in the rules that determine where and how development can take place; it can preserve open space and farmland; *and it can do all of these things without any direct cost to government.*

Because of this wide array of opportunities and advantages, it is easy to understand why planners, lawyers, and public officials have indicated a growing interest in the transfer of development rights as a new technique of land use regulation.

NOTES

1. Participants in the discussion were Worth Bateman, The Urban Institute; Donald M. Carmichael, Assoc. Professor of Law, University of Colorado; B. Budd Chavooshian, Department of Environmental Resources, Rutgers University; John J. Costonis, Professor of Law, University of Illinois; Robert S. DeVoy, Real Estate Research Corporation; Ellis Gans, Marin County Planning Department; James A. Graaskamp, Associate Professor of Real Estate, University of Wisconsin; Claude Gruen, San Francisco; David G. Heeter, Vermont Environmental Board; Daniel R. Mandelker, Professor of Law, Washington University; Norman Marcus, General Counsel, New York City Planning Commission; Richard A. Miller, General Counsel, Landmarks Preservation Service; Audrey Moore, Supervisor, Annandale District, Fairfax County Board of Supervisors; David Richards, Esq., Paul, Weiss, Goldberg, Rifkind, Wharton & Garrison, New York City; Jerome G. Rose, Professor of Urban Planning, Rutgers University; Jared Shlaes, Arthur Rubloff & Co., Chicago; Sidney Willis, Assistant Commissioner, New Jersey Department of Community Affairs.

2. Audrey Moore, *Transferable Development Rights: An Idea Whose Time Has Come*, (Mimeo, 1974).

3. For example, *House & Home*, June, 1974 at 26; *Planning*, July, 1974 at 7-15; *The Urban Lawyer*, Fall, 1974.

4. Carmichael, "Transferable Development Rights As a Basis for Land Use Control," 2 *Fla. State U. L. Rev.* 55 (1974).

5. Ohio Oil Co. v. Indiana, 177 U.S. 190 (1900).

6. Rose, "A Proposal For The Separation And Marketability Of Development Rights As A Technique To Preserve Open Space," 2 *Real Estate L. J.* 635 (1974).

7. John J. Costonis, "The Chicago Plan: Incentive Zoning And The Preservation of Urban Landmarks," 85 *Harv. L. Rev.* 574 (1972).

8. Note (David A. Richards) "Development Rights Transfer in New York City,' 82 *Yale L. J.* 338 (1972).

9. Elliott & Marcus, "From Euclid to Ramapo: New Directions In Land Development Controls," 1 *Hofstra L. Rev.* 56 (1973).

10. "Chicago Plan Ruled Out in Chicago," *Planning*, July, 1974 at 8.

11. Note, *Yale L. J.*, supra note 8 at 370. But see Elliott & Marcus, supra note 9 for a discussion of New York City programs administered with some success.

12. B. Budd Chavooshian and Thomas Norman, "Transfer of Development Rights," *Urban Land*, Dec. 1973 at 12.

13. Rose, *Real Estate L. J.*, supra note 6.

14. John J. Costonis and Robert S. DeVoy, *The Puerto Rican Plan: Environmental Protection Through Development Rights Transfer*, (The Conservation Trust of Puerto Rico and Real Estate Research Corporation, June, 1974).

15. Maryland Senate Bill No. 254, January, 1972.

16. William J. Goodman, "Descriptive Material on Transfer of Development Rights," accompanying his proposed legislation. (Mimeo, 1972).

17. Audrey Moore, supra note 2.

18. This issue is discussed also in Rose, "Psychological, Legal and Administrative Problems Of The Proposal To Use the Transfer of Development Rights (TDR) As A Technique To Preserve Open Space," *The Urban Lawyer*, Fall, 1974.

19. *The Potential For Density Transfer In Sonoma County*, (Sonoma County Planning Board, Mimeo, June, 1974).

20. The Town of Southampton Zoning Ordinance of 1971, adopted May 2, 1972, Sec. 2-10-20, 2-10-30.

21. Rose, "The Mandatory Percentage of Moderately Priced Dwellings (MPMPD) Ordinance Is The Latest Technique of Inclusionary Zoning," 3 *Real Estate L. J.* (Fall, 1974).

22. The Board of Supervisors of Fairfax County v. DeGroff Enterprises, Inc., 214 Va. 235, 198 S.E. 2d 600 (1973).

23. Leonard U. Wilson, "Precedent-Setting Swap in Vermont," 61 *American Inst. of Architects Journal* 51 (1974).

24. Kevin Lynch, *Controlling the Location and Timing of Development By The Distribution of Annual Development Rights*, (Unpublished Mimeo, June, 1973). Professor Lynch wrote this paper with the understanding that it would be considered to be a tentative statement subject to modification.

25. Donald Hagman, "Windfalls and Wipeouts," in *The Good Earth of America: Planning Our Land Use* (C. Harriss, ed. 1974).

26. Ellis Gans, *Saving Valued Spaces and Places Through Development Rights Transfer*, (Mimeo, 1974).

27. Rose, *The Urban Lawyer*, supra note 18.

28. Fred F. French Investing Co. Inc. v. City of New York, (Supreme Court of New York [trial court]), 352 N.Y.S. 2d 762 (1973).

29. John J. Costonis, *Harv. L. Rev.*, supra note 7. See also, Costonis, *Space Adrift: Saving Urban Landmarks Through The Chicago Plan* at 145 to 166 (1974).

30. Audrey Moore, supra note 2 at 23-31.

II.
LEGAL
ANTECEDENTS

Early American Precedents

Transferable Development Rights
As a Basis for Land Use Controls

DONALD M. CARMICHAEL
Associate Professor of Law
University of Colorado

It is manifest from this review of our decisions that there has been a growing appreciation of public needs and of the necessity of finding ground for a rational compromise between individual rights and public welfare. The settlement and consequent contraction of the public domain, the pressure of a constantly increasing density of population, the interrelation of the activities of our people and the complexity of our economic interests, have inevitably led to an increased use of the organization of society in order to protect the very bases of individual opportunity. Where, in earlier days, it was thought that only the concerns of individuals or of classes were involved, and that those of the State itself were touched only remotely, it has later been found that the fundamental interests of the State are directly affected; and that the question is . . . of the use of reasonable means to safeguard the economic structure upon which the good of all depends.

—Chief Justice Charles Evans Hughes[1]

The Constitution did not impress upon the states in a rigid mold either the common-law fuedal system of land tenures or any of the modified and variant forms of tenure prevailing in the states in 1789. Rather it left them free to devise and establish their own systems of property law adapted to their varying local conditions and to the peculiar needs and desires of their inhabitants.

—Justice Wiley Rutledge[2]

I. Two Basic Inadequacies of Police Power Regulations of Land Use

Regulation under the police power is and will doubtless continue to be our pervasive method for governmental control of private land use decisions in this country. It has not worked well, however, due to fundamental and inherent weaknesses that may become more troublesome as new social priorities emerge.

A. The Taking Issue

Police power land use regulation typically has direct impact on seemingly disparate as the erection of milldams, the formation of drainage and irrigation ditches, and the pooling and unitization of oil and gas reservoirs. To effectuate these public purposes, coordinated involvement of numerous tracts of privately owned land was necessary. Coordinated involvement in a common purpose has consistently been held to justify very substantial modification of the rights of the affected private landowners. A brief survey of these major bodies of legal precedent will help determine whether a doctrinal base exists for the creation of planning districts within which the development potential of individual tracts may be converted into transferable development rights....

III. LEGAL PRECEDENT FOR DEVELOPMENT RIGHTS
A. Early Transportation Systems

The colonies and their successor states early made consistent practice of chartering private corporations to plan, construct and maintain toll roads or turnpikes as supplements to the few roads that could be maintained by using limited public funds.[53] It was apparent that if the corporations did not have power to lay routes as seemed best, they could be forced to detour interminably around the lands of objecting owners or be forced to pay exorbitant prices for rights-of-way. Thus, they were customarily empowered to acquire rights-of-way compulsorily, upon impartial determination and payment of compensation to the affected private landowner.[54] State regulation required the turnpike corporations to maintain the roads and controlled the fee to be charged to the public for toll road use. The public had the incontrovertible right to use the roads upon the payment of requisite fees.[55] Direct right of use by the public (hereinafter referred to as "user") was thus assured. The delegation of eminent domain power to private corporations was not litigated in early times. A mixture of public necessity, public use and ratification by longstanding custom apparently rendered the practice acceptable in contemporary eyes.

The scheme of the early enabling statutes for turnpike corporations was later duplicated by many state legislatures in authorizing the construction of canals in the late 1700's and of railroads beginning in the 1820's.[56] In both applications, private corporations were chartered to lay rights-of-way, to construct and maintain facilities to transport appropriate vessels in the case of canals and, in the case of railroads, to transport the public and its goods, upon payment of regulated fees.[57]

The power of eminent domain in the canal corporations was for the most part only a collateral issue in the very early cases,[58] and the analogy to turnpike corporations seems to have been sufficiently convincing that the judiciary had little pause in approving this power in the canal corporations.[59] Railroads presented a somewhat more difficult case, however,[60] since public user was less clear[61] and occurred only in the railroads' carriages and in accordance with their schedules of operations. This contrasted with the public's ability, on turnpikes and canals, to use their own conveyances at their own convenience and for their own purposes of profit or pleasure.[62] If this diluted public user would support eminent domain powers in the railroad corporations, why not also in theater, hotel and a host of other corporations? The power of eminent domain in the railroad corporations was nonetheless upheld. The analogy to turnpikes could be stretched this far. The direct public user was deemed sufficiently certain, the necessity of a linear right-of-way was apparent and the delegation of this transportation function from the state to private corporations was not deemed impermissible.[63]

By the mid-1830's the use of eminent domain by private transportation corporations had received initial approval in influential jurisdictions. The power was limited in its exercise to acquisition of rights-of-way and necessary appurtenant lands. Direct public user helped justify the judicial approval, but a broader concept also began to emerge. The canals and especially the railroads were major technological breakthroughs promising immense multiplier effects in opening new territory and allowing the massive rapid transport of goods, people, mails and troops in time of war.[64] None of this was lost on the courts, and the "public use" served by canals and railroads became a mixture of two doctrines. Public user was present, but second and strongly ascendant was the interpretation of "public use" as general public utility and benefit, perhaps tantamount to a felt necessity given the tremendous impetus of the times toward commercial, industrial and territorial expansion.[65]

Summary of the Relation of Legal Doctrine to Development Rights.— This brief survey of the private use of eminent domain by the early transportation corporations simply serves to trace to their beginnings the doctrines that will be developed subsequently. It is not suggested that eminent domain be used for either the creation or the acquisition of development rights. The concern of this article is with the various theories justifying the assemblage of rights in individually owned tracts, as was done to create transportation rights-of-way. This power of assemblage by eminent domain, finally questionable in the hands of the infant railroad corporations, was justified by a substantial expansion of precedent—that of public utility to bolster the sagging reality of public user. The public utility contemplated was the expected multiplier effect on state and national development if transportation technology, in the hands of its corporate promoters, were given the "forward march" with eminent domain to clear the trail. Of course the evolution of the substantive content of the "public utility" concept will be closely examined in the following sections, for this concept has changed radically over time.

B. The Milldam Acts

Of antiquity equal to that of the turnpikes was the colonial practice by which a private owner on a stream could erect a dam to harness the water power and thus create special rights in himself.[66] Almost inevitably, the lands of upper streamcourse owners were flooded by the resulting pond. Had their right to exclusive possession of their properties been inviolable, they could have sued to have the dam torn down and their properties freed of the pond's encroachment.[67] As in the case of the transportation systems, a dissident private owner would thus have had obstructionist or "holdup" rights against a beneficial resource use. From at least the early 1700's, however, in many states the upstream owners were confined by statute to actions solely for damages resulting from the flooding, thereby leaving dam, pond and energy production intact.[68]

Most early usage of this sort was to power grist mills. Millers operated under state regulation obliging them to grind the grain of all comers, in turn, as fine as could be, with exaction of a statutory share of the flour produced as the fee.[69] In this sense, public user of the mill was guaranteed as it was of the turnpikes. Public user combined with the virtually indispensible public utility of grist mills to make secure this early usage of the mill acts. Here again was the grant of the power of eminent domain to a private individual to further a resource use, with regulated participation guaranteed to the public and with compensation paid for unavoidable damages to the property of other owners.

In the earliest judicial consideration of the milldam acts, shortly after 1800, the courts relied heavily on the longstanding use and ratification of the acts by custom, admitting that, were the practice novel, it might be a dubious one.[70] Indeed, courts in a few states later confined the milldam prerogative to grist mills alone, stating that these were recognized and regulated as public utilities with public user guaranteed and that other types of mills without guaranteed public user failed to satisfy the public user requirement necessary to entitle them to powers of eminent domain.[71] In some New England states, however, courts in early cases uncritically reviewed use of the milldam acts to foster mills for a wide range of industrial use, many of them purely private to the mill proprietors and lacking the element of public user that grist mills had.[72] In these states, public user receded to nearly an irrelevance, and the multiplier effect of general-purpose mill energy on the industrial and employment base of the state was elevated to the level of adequate justification for conferring the power of eminent domain on private individuals and corporations.[73]

A variant justification began to emerge as well, however. The Massachusetts courts, perhaps troubled by the full implications of the public utility analysis, carefully examined the nature of the property right taken from the flooded upstream owner. The right was stated to be more in the nature of an easement than a fee simple absolute,[74] and it was further determined, in effect, that all riparian property was held subject to this commonly known, potentially preemptive easement that might be created under the operation of the hoary milldam acts.[75] It was well-settled that riparian owners had mutual, correlative rights in the use of the stream water as it flowed past their various properties.[76] The dammer's inchoate easement was characterized as a permissible instance of the adjustment of these mutual rights among the owners along a streamcourse.[77] This rationale is quite dubious on one level, for the adjustment of true correlative rights in a flow resource can hardly be equated with the unilateral, preemptive right in one owner to dam and consequently to flood upstream owners. A mirror-image justification exists, however. Were upstream owners able to stand firm on property rights and block or seek unconscionable reparations from a dam builder, development of the innate energy of the watercourse would consistently be deterred or blocked. This "adjustment" of rights should perhaps be understood as giving any owner, and therefore all owners equally, the opportunity to move first in erecting a dam. The first owner to exercise this right then preempted its exercise by his upstream neighbors along the level of his millpond.[78] And this preemption was necessarily accompanied by the occupancy of overflowed lands. Viewed in this somewhat tortuous light, the milldam acts were characterized in Massachusetts not as invoking the power of eminent domain, but as legitimate police power regulations for the adjustment and furtherance of rights held in common by riparian owners along a stream.[79]

When the United States Supreme Court finally considered the matter, it reviewed and upheld a New Hampshire milldam statute on the basis of the rationale developed in the Massachusetts courts. The Court analogized the affected ownership rights to those of tenants in common.[80] Statutory and common law devices existed for breaking a deadlock when tenants in common did not agree on the use of their property.[81] These precedents were cited as relevant, if not controlling, in support of the milldam acts, which were thus characterized as legitimate uses of police power regulation. Although a substantial twisting of fact is needed to compare a disagreement among co-tenants to the act of a dammer in casting pond waters onto the properties of private owners upstream, the analogy becomes more tenable if the doctrine of correlative damming rights of riparians is taken seriously.

The question of public purpose did not deter the Supreme Court. The question having been long settled in the courts and legislature of New Hampshire and by customary practice in the state, the Supreme Court considered the matter so properly resolved and determined that it presented no question of federal constitutional rights.[82] When no blatant violation of federal constitutional guarantees is presented, and the public purpose question is resolved in light of local circumstances, exigencies or custom, this posture of the Supreme Court in ratifying local practice is not unusual.

Summary of the Relation of Legal Doctrine to Development Rights. —The cluster of legal precedents surrounding the milldam acts is useful for two principal purposes. First, in several jurisdictions the perceived multiplier effect of water power on the employment and industrial base of the state served to advance the public-use-as-public-utility concept with such vigor that the multiplier effect became a sufficient justification for placing eminent domain powers in the hands of private dammers. We suggest later that proper management of land resources by use of development rights may produce major, beneficial multiplier effects. While there is no proposal that any use of eminent domain be made in this connection, it should be remembered that the multiplier effect of resource use and exigencies of that use in the case of milldams have been held sufficient to justify the private use of eminent domain in some states.

Second, the courts developed the doctrine that the milldam statutes were reasonable police power regulations for the adjustment and protection of the exercise of the correlative rights of individual owners that arose from their shared relation to a common resource. In the case of milldams, the absolute physical necessity of flooding upstream owners (and their converse ability to block dams or demand an exorbitant price) perhaps eased the application of this doctrine. Subsequently, more refined and tenuous versions of the doctrine of correlative rights in a commonly shared resource use will be discussed; it is one of the cornerstones of the proposed development rights system.

C. Major Drainage and Irrigation Projects

Although drainage and irrigation projects sought diametrically opposite physical results, they went forward under comparable legal structures and evoked similar judicial response. They will be considered together.

Drainage and irrigation required large amounts of front-end capital for the construction of facilities that would produce chiefly deferred benefits. Government could properly have paid these initial costs but did not typically do so in the 1800's, creating instead legal structures for private-sector enterprise to accomplish these ends.[83] With both drainage and irrigation, there was relatively little actual acquisition of property. Transportation systems and millponds were characterized by actual physical occupancy of affected properties. Drainage and irrigation districts also occupied property, for example, for rights-of-way, dams and reservoirs,[84] but the vast majority of properties affected were those benefited by the projects, not those occupied by them.

The legal mechanisms widely adopted to effect these projects were created by statute and were relatively straightforward in structure. Upon petition to a local court by the qualifying owners of a stated percentage of lands within a proposed district, commissioners were appointed and empowered by the court to investigate and report on the economic feasibility of the project and the territorial extent of the proposed district. One or more hearings were held to consider the economic and physical feasibility of the project, to set boundaries of the project area and to assess charges on a ratable basis against the properties within the project in accordance with the expected benefits. Notice to affected property owners was given and there was the right of appeal from contested determinations.[85]

The startling, basic premise of these acts was that a majority of property owners could by vote, under statutory authorization and court supervision, impose their vision of desirable land use on an objecting minority. The imposition was in part physical and in part financial. In the case of drainage, the majoritarian imposition caused the alteration of the physical characteristics of the lands involved. There would have been no way to exclude any interior landholdings from the effects of a lowered water table, something a rice grower, for instance, might have wished. As with the milldams, then, an unwilling owner was clearly shorn of the ability to block the project on grounds that the physical nature of his land might not be altered without his consent.[86] Within an irrigation district, by contrast, there would have been no inevitable alteration in the physical nature of property (ignoring generalized effects such as seepage and a somewhat raised water table). As a physical reality, an owner could have elected not to use any project water while continuing his nonirrigated uses without disruption.[87]

Despite the sharp difference in the inevitability of physical effects on lands caused by drainage and irrigation, compulsory charges computed on the basis of "benefits" received were assessed on all "benefited" properties within both types of districts.[88] From the perspective of physical reality, there was no compelling reason for this to have been so, at least in the case of irrigation districts. In fact the assessment process, especially as applied within irrigation districts, apparently reflected a decision grounded more in fiscal reality than in any unalterable exigency arising from the reality of resource use. An owner of lands to be drained, protesting that he did not want the physical nature of his property altered, could not block the project.[89] Short of blockage, however, he might be seeking a "free ride," that is, to receive the immediate and inevitable benefits of the drainage from which he could not be excluded, while being excused from paying any of the costs because of his protestation that he neither wanted nor would receive any "benefit." The free-rider situation does not exist as clearly in the irrigation case, since owners not desiring irrigation water could certainly have been allowed to deal themselves out by binding contract. Ambiguously in the case of drainage and more clearly in the case of irrigation, it can be asserted that the principal use of the assessment for "benefits" was to compel the assemblage of front-end capital without which the projects could not have been undertaken by private sector activity.

Two further points need mention. By statutory definition, districts could typically include only lands that would be benefited by a common form of reclamation.[90] The actual delineation of the area to be included within a district was frequently a highly judgmental matter, however. Terrain elevations and the gravity-flow characteristic of water were to some extent determinative, but with improvements in construction abilities and pumping technology, and the resultant increases in project size, choices arose and were made concerning the inclusion of major additional areas within projects.[91]

Further, determination of the value of project benefits to particular tracts was highly subjective and often precipitated intense controversy. Benefits could not be pure fiction—a desert could not be charged with a drainage assessment, nor a swamp with irrigation benefits.[92] Short of this, however, intermediate cases involving marginal benefit were quite troublesome. For example, a tract arable for many purposes under natural rainfall might receive only slight benefit from irrigation, or an owner might protest with complete sincerity that he wanted no irrigation water and would relinquish all rights to it. Within the gross structural frameworks for delimiting districts and establishing assessment rates, then, there existed many difficult individual situations in which finely tuned and totally persuasive objectivity was an elusive goal.[93]

The basic analogue adopted by the courts in approving the legal structure of these districts was the variation on taxation known as the "special assessment," through which a charge is assessed against property for a benefit peculiarly conferred on the property by a public or quasi-public expenditure.[94] The use of the doctrine in this context is a bit more startling than it may first appear. The levy of a monetary assessment may not seem like the "taking" of property that occurred with milldams and railroads. It is certainly not an immediate physical occupancy. The charge was assessed against the land, however, and in the event of nonpayment the land could be sold to satisfy the charge.[95] The special assessment had the potential to eventuate in seizure of the land of a financially hard-pressed owner. And the monetary charge (and actual physical alteration in the case of drainage) was imposed by majoritarian action. It would certainly seem an unheard-of proposition if the owners of the majority of homes in a block could elect an expensive scheme of neighborhood improvement, perhaps make alterations to a dissenting owner's property, and impose a ratable share of sizeable costs on his property, with the ability to compel sale of the property to pay the charge if necessary. Yet this, from the point of view of a dissident property owner, is just what was done under the drainage and irrigation statutes.[96] The judicial approval of these very considerable modifications of individual property rights may perhaps be best understood in light of the interaction of several factors—the definition of public "use" adopted, the peculiarities of the resource to be put to public "use" and the underlying capital funding problem.

When 5,000 acres of bog were drained or arid land irrigated, it was clear that the general public did not have the direct right of a user in the benefits created as it had in the case of turnpikes, canals, railroads and grist mills. Direct use of the benefits was confined to the owners of the affected tracts. The judicial response to this problem was that the user, to be public, need not inevitably create practical user benefits in the entire public. For instance, an isolated rural school district including but a few farm homesteads was nevertheless unarguably a public use. In the case of drainage and irrigation as well, a proper public user constituency was felt to derive from the land-related status of property owners within the district benefited by the improvement.[97] This line of reasoning was coupled with another line of analysis discussed previously—that relating to public "use" in terms of public utility and efficiency. It will be recalled that enabling statutes considered here inevitably contain explicit or implicit legislative findings that drainage and irrigation districts are conducive to the productive good of the state involved. In reviewing such statutes, courts ratified the legislative determination of public utility and added their own endorsements to the general prosperity expected to flow from the utilization of the drainage or irrigation statutes under review.[98]

The resources involved in these districts were of a peculiar character, consisting of individually owned tracts of land in roughly common situations due to topographic and hydrologic conditions. Private tracts of land otherwise unrelated were thus thrown together into a forced, cooperative unit due to their common situation and reclamation potential. Here, as in the case of the milldam acts, individual properties sharing a common resource-use potential were blocked into a unit delimited by the resource use, and individual rights in the tracts of land involved were diminished radically in furtherance of the development of the resource.[99] This common-resource or common-property theory was in fact directly adopted by the Supreme Court in major cases dealing with both drainage and irrigation districts:

> If it be essential or material for the prosperity of the community, and if the improvement be one in which all the landowners have to a certain extent a common interest, and the improvement cannot be accomplished without the concurrence of all or nearly all of such owners by reason of the peculiar natural condition of the tract sought to be reclaimed, then such reclamation may be made and the land rendered useful to all and at their joint expense. In such case the absolute right of each individual owner of land must yield to a certain extent or be modified by corresponding rights on the part of other owners for what is declared upon the whole to be for the public benefit.[100]

Parenthetically, in some of the Western States the intensely predominant value and the exigencies of the use of certain resources produced a logical conclusion of one theme previously noted—the power of eminent domain was accorded to one private individual over the lands of another for specified purposes such as conveying water and ore. The immense value and multiplier effect on the local economies from resource use and the frequent ability of a dissident landowner to effect total blockage of a neighbor's use combined to justify the conferral of eminent domain powers on private individuals.[101]

It must be noted again, however, that the inevitable effects of shared resource use and project impact diminished greatly from the case within the drainage districts to the case within the irrigation districts. In fact, it is arguable that in the case of irrigation districts the capital funding motive is clearly dominant, supported only weakly by the majoritarian nature of the action and scarcely at all by any inevitability of common resource use. In the case of the transportation systems and milldams, physical invasion of property was unavoidable and compensation was paid. Within the drainage districts, alteration of all properties and conferment of "benefit" was inevitable and charges were assessed accordingly. A dissident irrigation district owner was not allowed to avoid inclusion, however, as he clearly could have done contractually. Instead, he was made a compulsory contributor to the capitalization of the unwanted project.[102] The majoritarian winners thus not only received their vision of desirable resource use, but also they were permitted to dip into the losers' pockets to help fund the accomplishment of this vision.

Summary of the Relation of Legal Doctrine to Development Rights.—Drainage and irrigation districts furnish the first example we have encountered of the assemblage of large tracts of land, as would have to be done with the planning districts that we suggest. Public utility in the sense of multiplier effect of resources being put to use is again a dominant notion.[103] The community of interest in the resource use supports the judicial invocation of the commonly-owned property analogy. Of more immediate relevance to the consideration of development rights is the fact that ownership and use of the affected lands remained in their respective individual owners. Lands were not taken by occupancy as with railroads and milldams. In the development rights scheme, lands would likewise remain in the hands of their owners. The drainage and irrigation districts, however, by making services available, were empowered to assess and to collect a related charge commensurate with the "benefit" conferred

on individual owners. In planning districts making use of development rights, there could result benefits of greatly improved planning
analysis and control and much more equitable distribution of development entitlements. Exigencies and commonality of resource use
within the development rights districts would certainly seem as high
as those found adequate to justify the assessment processes of the irrigation districts. In contrast to assessments, however, as will be discussed later,[104] it could well be that the net monetary returns would
be higher on land developed by use of development rights than under
present practices. It would then seem that the development district
approach would find strong justification from the drainage and irrigation district precedents and in fact might be considered an even more
acceptable device than were they.

D. Oil and Gas Production Regulations

The next major body of precedent, and perhaps the most informa-
tive, arose around the development of oil and gas resources. Oil and
gas commonly occur together within a rather extensive geologic stratum (a "pool," "formation," "reservoir" or "field") that underlies
numerous surface property holdings. Oil and gas are both to some extent migratory within the pool, typically being drawn toward areas of
low pressure such as those created when pressure is lowered around
a producing well. Because of numerous factors, it is impossible to recover all oil and gas from a pool. Initial production ("primary production" or "primary recovery") typically relies on the connate pressure ("energy") within the reservoir to drive gas and some oil to
the surface. This energy is often at least partially in the form of gas
contained within the stratum in the liquid state under extreme pressure. When the gas is brought to the surface, pressure is reduced and
the gas changes from liquid to gaseous form.[105]

As connate energy from gas or other sources is depleted, production slows and then stops, with much oil and some gas left in place.
Pumping may then be used for additional recovery. The amount of
oil and gas left in place after primary recovery often depends to a
considerable extent on how wisely primary recovery operations are
conducted throughout the formation, that is, on whether the connate
energy forces are harnessed to produce as much gas and oil as possible
before their depletion. After primary recovery, relatively expensive
"secondary recovery" operations may be possible by reinjecting pres-
suring agents into the stratum to drive some of the remaining oil to
selected recovery wells. Even after secondary recovery, much oil usually remains in place.[106]

Early production practices in this country were simply an all-out race. Each property owner produced as fast as possible to get as much oil and gas from his property and to drain as much from his neighbors' property as he could. This process was assisted and goaded by the courts' early characterization of oil and gas as fugitive resources, comparable to wild animals, and not belonging to anyone until "captured," that is, reduced to possession.[107] Under the strict rule of capture, rapid production of oil and gas was not considered the taking of another's property. In fact, it made sense for one owner to produce as rapidly as possible in order to capture as much oil and gas as possible, thereby making it his property.[108] As many wells as possible would be drilled as close to property lines as possible in order to drain oil and gas from under neighboring land. Each neighbor did the same, so that boundary wells "offset" each other, from one property to the next.[109] It has been said that before regulations were imposed on the famous East Texas pool, offset wells in many areas resembled picket fences along the boundary lines. Happy mass slurp.

The results of these practices soon became quite apparent. First, connate reservoir energy was depleted with extreme rapidity, with gas often simply being vented into the atmosphere once it had served the immediate purpose of bringing the more valuable oil to the surface. The rapid depletion of reservoir energy often left trapped in place much oil that would have been produced by connate energy had the energy been released more slowly. The waste, then, was often treble—energy inefficiently expended, gas vented and oil needlessly left in place.[110] Secondly, in the early days of this century, full production so exceeded limited demand that prices plummeted and much oil was simply and intentionally spilled on the ground.[111] Finally, the widespread practice of boundary-line drilling, compelling neighbors to do the same to offset the drainage, constituted an immense over-investment in unneeded wells to the extent of an estimated $160,000,-000 in the East Texas field alone. Significantly fewer wells would have been adequate and probably much more efficient in terms of total primary recovery.[112]

The earliest oil and gas regulation cases to come to the attention of the United States Supreme Court involved efforts of the states to halt the gross waste of reservoir energy and of gas in particular. The first case arose when Indiana passed a statute forbidding either gas or oil to flow into the open air from a well for more than two days after the well was brought in.[113] Much of central Indiana overlay a reservoir containing gas and some oil, and the gas was used for cheap, clean heat and light.[114] Companies dealing solely in oil had recently entered the field, were massively and rapidly depleting the gas pressure in order to force to the surface relatively small quantities of oil and were venting the gas into the atmosphere.[115] The Supreme Court concentrated on whether a state could legitimately engage in this genre of regulation of privately owned oil and gas.[116] The Court admitted that under the common law rule of capture, each surface owner over a reservoir was at liberty to reduce to possession, without violating the rights of neighbors,[117] as much of the gas and oil as possible. However, the Court characterized the oil and gas as a common fund that did not become an individual landowner's property until captured.[118] It then approved the statute as a valid regulation of the availability of the common fund to all the owners of lands overlying it:

> But there is a co-equal right in . . . all [owners] to take from a common source of supply, the two substances which in the nature of things are united, though separate. It follows from the essence of their right and from the situation of the things, as to which it can be exerted, that the use by one of his power to seek to convert a part of the common fund to actual possession may result in an undue proportion being attributed to one of the possessors . . . or more, to the annihilation of the rights of the remainder. Hence it is that the legislative power, from the peculiar nature of the right and the objects upon which it is to be exerted, can be manifested for the purpose of protecting all the collective owners, by securing a just distribution, to arise from the enjoyment, by them, of their privilege to reduce to possession, and to reach the like end by preventing waste.[119]

The Court, therefore, held that the statutory prohibition did not constitute a taking of the property of the oil companies, although the statute's operation would likely put the companies out of business.[120] Thus, oil and gas fields were brought into the fold of resources that, because of their nature, might be pronounced by legislatures and ratified by the judiciary as creating a scheme of common relations among otherwise unrelated individual landowners. This case also provides the authoritative basis for the existence of correlative rights among the owners of land overlying an oil and gas field.[121] To the earlier list of three evils of heavy, wasteful oil and gas production, must now be added a fourth: violation of the correlative rights of other owners to share in field energy and to produce a ratable share of oil and gas.

In *Walls v. Midland Carbon Co.,*[122] the Supreme Court upheld a Wyoming statute that in practical effect forbade the use of natural gas for the manufacture of carbon black from wells within ten miles of an incorporated town or an industrial plant. The statute accomplished this by prohibiting the use of gas, within the stated ten-mile radius, for manufacturing processes in which the heat potential was not fully and actually used.[123] The statute further forbade any owner or lessee of a well to sell gas for the manufacture of carbon black.[124] The carbon black companies had been using massive amounts of gas in an inefficient process to recover carbon black and types of gasoline. Although the Court accepted the company's averment that this use was more remunerative than the prices the gas would have brought in the area for fuel purposes,[125] the statute was upheld against a variety of constitutional objections as legitimately accommodating coexisting rights by the limitation of one right so that other rights might be enjoyed, and as protecting the interests of the community.[126] The Court characterized this, and the previously approved Indiana statute, as valid interpositions of state police power to prevent both waste and disproportionate use of either gas or oil by one owner. The Court thus approved the Wyoming statute as a legitimate adjustment to preserve various rights in the resources of the state.[127] The case involved not only the relative worth of gas as a source of carbon black versus its value as a fuel source, but also the fact that the carbon black plant would have exhausted the reservoir in about three years, while consumption of the gas for fuel purposes would have lasted at least ten years.[128] The legislature thus considered not only present comparative values but also the desirability of alternative resource uses over time. The Court in approving this action noted that

> necessarily there was presented to the judgment and policy of the State a comparison of utilities which involved, as well, the preservation of the natural resources of the State, and the equal participation in them by the people of the State. And the duration of this utility was for the consideration of the State, and we do not think that the State was required by the Constitution of the United States to stand idly by while these resources were disproportionately used, or used in such way that tended to their depletion, having no power of interference.[129]

Interim Note on the Relation of Legal Doctrines to Development Rights.—A basic purpose of this article is to suggest a system by which the states can defensibly and confidently do exactly what was done in these early oil regulation statutes—give valid legal enactment to systems of stated preferences for selected uses of resources over time. The legislative preference in both cases was for gas to be used as a fuel source. This use was "preferred" over that of gas as productive energy for oil extraction in *Ohio Oil Co. v. Indiana* and over that of gas for its carbon black potential in *Walls v. Midland Carbon Co.*[130]

When the Indiana and Wyoming legislatures thus preferred one use value over another in these two instances, they resolved a conflict between alternative use values that inhered in a single resource. Because of its common-source nature, however, the gas resource under regulation had the effect of linking separately owned tracts into an interrelated web of correlative rights. Legislatively preferred resource uses create somewhat comparable linkages of separate properties in the case of rights-of-way for transportation uses,[131] of the ponds necessary for milldam energy uses[132] and of the districts necessary to support the construction of drainage and irrigation facilities.[133] Legislatures prefer and impose one of two alternative resource uses in other contexts, for example, when separately owned properties are linked by a shared externality.[134] In fact, under the analysis suggested by Professor Sax, webs of externalities inextricably link lands, waters and their resource values.[135] In specialized cases, development may create such grave, widespread external consequences that legislatures may validly prefer and impose the alternative use of nondevelopment, without compensation.[136] Such forms of onerous regulation might be characterized and justified as instances of valid legislative preferment of certain uses, in order to adjust and to protect the correlative but conflicting rights of numerous owners to avoid or impose externalities. Viewed in this light, externalities from the particular use of one resource may cause the destruction or waste of both similar and different resource values in the hands of other owners. The externality web forms a common pool.

All of this discussion relates to the development rights concept in two ways. First, the covert effect of zoning is to create a common pool of development entitlements within a zoning district. All owners within this pool would have roughly correlative entitlement to a fair share of the pooled development potential.[137] Secondly, at the present time and within the proposed development districts, preferments of particular land uses would be imposed on various tracts in the form of the regulation of development density, type and timing. These preferments would be based both on reallocation of development entitlements from the zoning pool, and on avoidance of harm to the externality web or pool. Incommensurable land values would result.[138] By use of development rights, however, an adjustment of the inequities in land value

resulting from the imposition of land use preferments could be accomplished.

Despite the approval of these statutes, and the obvious evils of
the rule of capture as an operational policy, more pervasive state
efforts to regulate the production of gas and oil came slowly. There
were, of course, major pressures against any such regulation from
industry, which was perhaps dissatisfied with the situation as it existed
but not certain that regulation would effect a cure. Two major forms
of regulation eventuated, however: pooling and unitization.[139]

Pooling seeks systematic prevention of the physical and economic
waste that occurs when each owner drills as many wells and produces as much oil and gas as he wishes. It also protects the correlative rights of landowners over a reservoir. First, based on physical
data, a determination is made of the density of wells necessary to
produce a reservoir fully and efficiently under primary recovery
methods. It may be determined, for instance, that one well in the
center of each 160-acre quarter section would adequately and wisely
produce the reservoir. Each such 160-acre tract is often referred to as
a drilling unit, and in modern practice the reservoir would be divided
into drilling units by the state oil and gas regulatory authority,
ordinarily following government survey lines. Normally, one well is
permitted near the center of each drilling unit. If A owns 320 acres,
he may find that his land has been divided into two 160-acre units,
each entitled to one well. If A, B, C and D each own contiguous 40-
acre quarter-quarters, they may find that their land has been blocked
into one 160-acre drilling unit, entitled to be developed by only one
well.[140]

Controlling the number and spacing of wells, however, is only
part of the process. Further control must be exercised over the rate of
production so that each drilling unit, and thus the entire field, produces at a controlled rate.[141] This rate should serve the multiple objectives of maximum recovery of resources under primary recovery
operations, protection of the correlative and peculiar rights of owners
under a variety of criteria, and production of that field's share of larger
production quotas established by state and federal production regulation structures. These various objectives persistently tend toward mutual inconsistency but are nonetheless brought into some rough accord so that each drilling unit is given an allowable rate of production (an "allowable").[142] This system is also referred to as proration-

ing, with each well being awarded a prorated share of field-wide production.

Unitization refers to the operation of the entire reservoir, or a major part of it, as an entity, without regard to patterns of surface ownership. Certain types of highly beneficial operations virtually require unitization. For instance, it is possible to maintain pressures within a producing stratum by reinjecting gas that is brought to the surface in the production of oil.[143] Costs and expectable returns are such, however, that typically no single owner would undertake this activity unless his neighbors did likewise or agreed to cooperate in the project in some manner. Otherwise, substantial portions of the owner's reinjection costs would inure to his neighbors' benefit (another instance of the free-rider situation).[144] Again, once primary recovery has been exhausted, it may be economically feasible to inject water along a line of wells and to establish a water flood driving oil before it across the reservoir for recovery at distant wells. Unless the reservoir is operated as a unit, water flooding may be done only piecemeal and under considerable handicap. At worst, owners of injection wells may get little return over the expenses of injection, and non-participating neighbors may reap an undeserved bonanza of oil flushed onto their properties by the water flood.[145] Often under such circumstances secondary recovery will not take place. In addition to the use of unitization to facilitate secondary recovery, primary recovery may often be optimized if the reservoir is unitized.

Either pooling or unitization on a limited basis may be effected by contract among private individuals. It is strong testimony to the efficiency of these devices that they have been arranged by private contract in the face of seemingly overwhelming practical and legal impediments.[146]

Following the particularized regulation reflected in the Indiana and Wyoming cases, the modern era of regulation began in 1919 when the Railroad Commission of Texas, that state's oil and gas conservation agency, promulgated its rule 37, requiring the spacing of wells at minimum intervals of 300 feet and no closer than 150 feet to property lines. This was upheld as a reasonable exercise of the police power to prevent unnecessary fire hazards and waste.[147] In other states, conservation agencies were granted authority to subdivide a field into drilling units, representing the maximum area that could be drained economically and efficiently by one well. The result was that when several owners held land within one unit, their interests were pooled. One received permission to drill and the others participated in the profits or losses. This system has been consistently approved by the

courts as violating neither the contractual nor fourteenth amendment rights of the complaining owner.[148]

Prorationing has likewise been upheld. Under California regulations, for instance, prorationing took the form of controlling the
gas-to-oil ratio permitted during production. As in the Indiana case,
one way to get the lion's share of oil was to produce extremely rapidly,
using a disproportionate amount of gas to bring the oil to the surface
and also to produce a low pressure point towards which oil and gas
would migrate from the properties of neighbors. Control of the production ratio of gas-to-oil was a practical way to curb this practice,
and with it the waste of gas or reservoir energy of underground oil
trapped in place by avoidable pressure differentials, and to curb the disproportionate production of one owner over others. Regulation of the
gas-to-oil ratio was approved by the Supreme Court as a valid form of
police power regulation to protect both correlative rights and the
interests of the public that resources not be wasted.[149]

Marketplace and competitive realities soon dictated more sophisticated forms of control. In the early days of oil production, a tremendous competitive edge was enjoyed in Oklahoma by oil companies
with integrated operations in which their wells connected directly to
oil pipelines and to refineries.[150] Integrated operators produced at a
rapid pace into their pipelines, and although using all of the oil and
gas they produced, they were causing waste of reservoir energy and
of the full amount of oil recoverable by primary recovery.[151] In addition, they had virtually preempted the local market.[152] In order to produce any fair share of oil, non-integrated operators were forced to
pump and then store oil in large earthen reservoirs, awaiting transportation by truck or other limited means. Leakage, spoilage and fires
resulted.[153] Responding to this situation, the Oklahoma Legislature
passed a statute prohibiting petroleum "waste," defined, in addition
to its ordinary meanings, to include economic, underground and surface waste, and waste incident to production in excess of transportation or marketing facilities or reasonable market demand. This statute
further provided that when full production from a reservoir could
be had only under circumstances constituting waste as statutorily defined, production would be reduced. Under limited production situations, each producer could take only that proportion of the limited
quantity of production possible, without causing waste, as his share
of full production bore to full production throughout the reservoir.[154]
To illustrate, assume that full reservoir production is 1,000 barrels
per day, and A's well operating at full production will produce 500
barrels per day, or 50 percent of reservoir full production. Assume

further that the rate of reservoir production possible without waste (within market demand) is only 600 barrels per day. A's well's proportionate share of the permissible production would then be reduced to 300 barrels per day, 50 percent of permitted production. Noting that the statute and administrative order being reviewed did not involve price fixing or interference with interstate commerce,[155] the Supreme Court upheld this market-demand prorationing as reasonable to protect correlative rights and to prevent waste.[156]

The body of precedent that developed around pooling practices is also regarded as essentially approving the basic readjustments of rights caused by unitization. Unitization was long advocated by some persons inside and many persons outside the industry as a highly desirable, if not indispensable, form of regulation. But it also met with considerable resistance. In the 1930's and 1940's, experiments with unitization by private contract were attempted.[157] The first compulsory unitization statute was enacted in Oklahoma in 1945 and was later upheld in the courts.[158] Others followed this lead, with 25 states enacting permissive unitization statutes (to avoid state anti-trust problems) and 19 states enacting compulsory unitization statutes.[159]

Statutes enabling compulsory pooling and those enabling compulsory unitization operate in comparable manner. Compulsory pooling statutes typically presuppose the existence of drilling or spacing units and explicitly permit voluntary pooling. If voluntary pooling does not occur, owners of interests in lands or in some cases the state regulatory agency may initiate proceedings for compulsory pooling. Typically, a petition is filed that may contain information on the proposed tract, the proposed locations of the well, an enumeration of the owners of all interests, the reasons necessitating pooling, proposed methods for bearing costs and the proposed apportionment of production. Notice is then given to all affected owners, an administrative hearing is held and a pooling order issued. Only one well will be drilled on the unit, despite the fact that many parties may have an interest in the unit, and the unit driller or "operator" is usually designated in the order, with other parties losing the right to drill on their own land. The fundamental aim is that each owner receive his just and equitable share of production.[160] Major variations exist among the states with respect to the rights of those interest owners who do not wish to pay their ratable costs of drilling a well on the unit. If a dry well is drilled, some statutes immunize nonparticipating owners from any assessment for its costs.[161] If a producing well comes in, some statutes allow owners who have previously refused to make contributions to the speculative well-drilling effort, to participate in the production of the well upon payment of a penalty fee to those who initially bore the costs of successful drilling.[162]

Compulsory unitization statutes likewise provide for initiation of proceedings by interested parties and occasionally by the regulatory agency. After filing of the petition, which contains information very similar to that contained in petitions for pooling, notice is given to all owners of interests in the lands involved and a hearing is held. As a result of the hearing, and before an order may be issued, the agency must find that unitization is necessary to effectuate the statutory purposes, that unitized operations are physically feasible, that these operations will yield more return than their costs, that they are for the common good within the affected area and that fair and equitable provisions will be made to protect the various ownership interests in the unit. In contrast to pooling orders, unitization orders must often be approved by a high percentage (two-thirds or more) of various categories of interest holders within a stated period after the entry of the order; without such ratification the order fails. The order must, of course, cover a common source of supply and it typically contains or adverts to a detailed plan of unitized operations that includes the method by which costs and production are to be allocated.[163]

Dissident owners whose interests have been compulsorily pooled or unitized are subjected to an extreme abridgment of property rights. Of course, only the oil and gas right is affected. This is a discrete and severable right, however, as development rights would be under the proposed scheme. Moreover, if oil and gas development is at least moderately profitable, this incident may be the predominately valuable attribute of the land, perhaps worth much more than the entire balance of the fee interest.[164] The right to develop oil and gas is taken from the property owner and granted to the pool operator or to the committee charged with operating a unitized field. The development right is thus typically placed in the hands of others and is communitized.[165] The owner's property interest in oil and gas under his land and his ability to seek its capture have, in fact, been converted into fractional interests ultimately expressed in the dollars-and-cents costs and profits of operations conducted by others. The decisions of the operators must, of course, conform to the specific charges contained in the orders under which pooled or unitized operations are carried out, and the decisions are appealable by dissatisfied owners.[166]

Although the individual owner may participate in the expenses and profits of development, the terms and timing may be quite onerous to particular owners. If, for instance, an owner of a pooled interest is not able to raise the necessary capital to participate in the costs of drilling, he may be relegated to the peculiar status of being his own lessor. He then receives the customary one-eighth royalty from the production attributable to his interest, and the operator of the pooled unit receives the conventional lessee's seven-eighths of production, subject to costs of production.[167] Again the pooled owner may find that an existing oil and gas lease on his property has been extended indefinitely, even in the face of nearly total inaction by his lessee, if the operator of the pool brings in a producing well on a pooled unit covering even a miniscule fraction of the owner's land.[168] An owner within an area of unitized operations may be required to surrender his wells to the unit, taking credit for their value. But if his wells are producing from two or more strata, the unit proprietors may choose to shut down production from non-unitized strata without paying any compensation.[169] Formulae for the distribution of production proceeds vary greatly and are typically based on multiple criteria that are highly judgemental, both individually and in their interactive effects. Examples of such criteria are allocation on the basis of surface acreage ownership, allocation on the basis of the number of wells in place or allowed to produce and allocation that reflects the varying richness of the deposits beneath various surface landholdings underlying a common pool.[170] These examples scarcely begin to catalogue the results that may occur from pooling and unitization.[171] The fundamental reality is that someone other than the owner makes the basic decisions about the development of a highly and sometimes preeminently valuable resource of the owner's land.

Results such as those mentioned above are frequently produced and judicially condoned by widely used systems of police power regulation of oil and gas production. Much of the basic structure of the regulatory systems, the thrust and validity of the public purposes they might serve and the degree of impact they might inflict on the rights of regulated property owners were approved by the United States Supreme Court. The statutes reviewed by these decisions were generated by notoriously chaotic and immensely destructive situations that arose within the oil and gas industry.[172] The realities of these situations and the potential enormity of the resulting resource destruction were not at all lost on the courts. The shift to the correlative-rights doctrine as a conceptual justification for the control of oil and gas production was an almost inevitable result of the pernicious consequences arising under the doctrine of capture. The shift also eased vexatious constitutional questions. Public interest of utmost gravity was involved in the prevention of the massive, multiple wastes and of the destruction of valuable, nonrenewable resources. It is possible, in fact, that public interest alone would have sufficed to justify the regulations in the eyes of the courts, without the admixture of the correlative-rights analysis.[173] In any event, the urgent necessity for these regulations clearly gave them strong momentum toward favorable review in the early Supreme Court cases. It is assertible that this momentum and the strength of the early decisions remain operative as a background reality in the judicial review of oil and gas conservation legislation to this day. This is not to say, however, that agency actions will not be promptly overturned if in excess of the statutory base of authority or that statutes unsuited to the service of legitimate conservation ends will not be stricken by the courts.[174]

Coupled with this momentum, as a reality of the judicial review process, is the complexity of the regulatory proceedings under review. Statutory policies are often individually meritorious and mutually inconsistent.[175] Regulation is accomplished after extended hearing processes. The property interests regulated are typically subdivided with as much complexity as is anywhere known under our system of laws.[176] The physical processes of oil and gas production being regulated are often obscure, highly debatable and intensely controversial.[177] Given these pragmatic considerations, it is typical for courts to approve regulations that are patently less than perfect but that have been issued as a result of the informed best judgment of the regulatory agencies.[178] This situation is similar to that existing in the delineation and assessment processes relating to drainage and irrigation districts noted earlier.[179]

Summary of the Relation of Legal Doctrines to Development Rights.—Precedents provided by oil and gas regulation mesh well with much of the doctrinal base necessary to provide legal justification for development rights. The common pool of an oil and gas reservoir is quite analogous to the common pool of development potential that already exists covertly within present zoning practices and that should be overtly institutionalized by using development rights within planning districts. It is true that present practices within the zoning pool of development potential may not be comparable to the ability of the Ohio Oil Company or the Midland Carbon Company to effect unilateral seizure of a grossly disproportionate share of resources at immediate prejudice to fellow owners and to the resource itself.[180] As noted, however, highly disproportionate treatment is accorded various owners within a zoning pool.[181] Some are relegated to extremely low-value land uses, while a few are zoned for extremely high value use. And note that these gross inequities result *from the acts of the government itself.* They are the inadvertant and collateral, but presently inevitable, results of our police power regulation of land use. By contrast, the Indiana and Wyoming cases dealt with disproportionate use resulting solely from individual rapacity. Certainly it must be as permissible for the government to redress disproportionate entitlements resulting inadvertently from its own regulatory acts, as it is for the government to redress disproportions caused by individual rapacity. This is precisely what would be possible by the use of development rights.

The prevention of waste was a major justification of oil and gas regulations. It may seem that present land development present practices, which could be controlled by the development rights approach, do not generate the intense, obvious levels of waste that early oil and gas production practices generated. Land development practices do, however, cause widespread waste with grave short- and long-term societal consequences. Development in areas of natural hazards, development of land that has high alternative values, the total amount of land consumed by development, premature development, development out of phase with provision of services and many more examples might be cited. These are categories of massive, ubiquitous waste that occur despite the present systems of landuse regulation. They would all be directly amenable to much more effective, purposive control under a development rights system than they are at present. Indeed, the use of development rights may be the best, if not the only, way to effect simultaneous control of these numerous, major, interrelated problems. A case can fairly be made, then, that waste-prevention ends served by a development rights system are not at all incommensurate with those served by the oil and gas regulatory structures we have discussed.

The impact of a development rights system on landowners is comparable to, and may in some senses be considerably less than, the impact under compulsory pooling and unitization. When oil and gas occur in any particular abundance, they may be the preeminent monetary attribute of land value.[182] Pooling implies the strong likelihood, and unitization the near certainty, that the development decision and its execution will be stripped from the owner by administrative process, albeit with rights to appeal both the administrative decision and its implementation. And we have seen situations as extreme as that where a nonparticipating owner on a drilling unit is reduced to being his own lessor, that is, to receiving a one-eighth royalty of his own minerals, while the administratively appointed lessee receives the other seven-eighths.[183] By contrast, the use of development rights should alleviate the more confiscatory aspects of present zoning practices, would leave the development and sale-of-rights decision in the owner's hands, and could well result in greater total profit from development in the typical planning district.

Finally it should be noted that each of the categories discussed above (protection of correlative rights, prevention of waste, further-ance of proper resource development) may by itself serve as a proper basis for regulation. In the case of development rights, as in the case of oil and gas regulation, however, the justifications for regulation are not isolated and unrelated. Rather, the various purposes coincide powerfully to form an extremely strong, multiple justification for the proposed regulatory structure....

NOTES

1. Home Bldg. & Loan Ass'n v. Blaisdell, 290 U.S. 398, 442 (1934).

2. Republic Natural Gas Co. v. Oklahoma, 334 U.S. 62, 89 (1948) (dissenting opinion).

53. See, e.g., Stanwood v. Pierce, 7 Mass. 458 (1811); Concord R.R. v. Greely, 17 N.H. 47, 62 (1845); Proprietors of the Third Turnpike Road v. Champney, 2 N.H. 199 (1820); State v. Town of Hampton, 2 N.H. 22, 24 (1819); Brief for Defendant at 60. Beekman v. Saratoga & S.R.R., 3 Paige Ch. 45 (N.Y. Ch. 1831) (mentioning fifteen hundred turnpike, bridge and canal corporations incorporated in New York state at that time and numerous others in other states). Normally the turnpike corporations were chartered to lay roads from one town or site to another. See, e.g., Stanwood v. Pierce, supra, concerning whether a legislatively designated tollroad terminus had properly been reached.

54. See, e.g., Callender v. Marsh, 18 Mass. (1 Pick.) 418, 428 (1823); Beekman v. Sara-toga & S.R.R., 3 Paige Ch. 45, 73-74 (N.Y. Ch. 1831). Damages were typically determined by a jury or assessed by court-appointed commissioners if the parties were unable to agree. Id. See also Barre Turnpike Corp. v. Appleton, 19 Mass. (2 Pick.) 430 (1824), for review of the procedural regularity of damage assessment proceedings.

It should be noted at this point that all of the legal structures that will be explored (transportation systems, milldams, drainage and irrigation systems, and oil and gas regulation) contain major procedural due process dimensions relating to such matters as the assessment of damages for land taken in the case of the transportation systems and milldams, assessment of betterment charges in the case of drainage and irrigation districts, and computation of entitlement to shares of production with respect to oil and gas regulations. These problems will not be considered in detail, but the reader should bear in mind that beneath the substantive doctrines covered, there have constantly lurked procedural due process tensions that have been troublesome for the administrators of these systems, and that have provoked abundant litigation.

55. One court has described the public right as follows:

A turnpike is a public road or highway, in the popular and ordinary sense of the words, and in that sense the Legislature are to be presumed to have em-ployed them. Turnpike roads are, in point of fact, the most public roads or highways that are known to exist, and in point of law, they are made entirely for public use, and the community have a deep interest in their construction and preservation. They are under legislative regulations, and the gates are subject to be thrown open, and the Company indicted and fined, if the road is not made and kept easy and safe for the public use.

Rogers v. Bradshaw, 20 Johns. 735, 742 (N.Y. Ct. Err. 1823). *See also* Newburyport Turnpike Corp. v. Eastern R.R., 40 Mass. (23 Pick.) 326, 327 (1840); Medford Turnpike Corp. v. Torrey, 19 Mass. (2 Pick.) 538 (1824); Riddle v. Proprietors of the Locks and Canals, 7 Mass. 169, 179 (1810) (argument for defendants containing statement of liabilities of turnpike corporations for failure to maintain roads in good repair); Concord R.R. v. Greely, 17 N.H. 47, 62 (1845); Scudder v. Trenton Del. Falls Co., 1 N.J.Eq. 694, 728 (1832); Beekman v. Saratoga & S.R.R., 3 Paige Ch. 45, 75 (N.Y. Ch. 1831).

56. In Proprietors of Sudbury Meadows v. Proprietors of Middlesex Canal, 40 Mass. (23 Pick.) 36, 49 (1839), the court alludes to the canal company's 1793 charter as a very early one of the sort. See the history of Potomac [Canal] Company, chartered in 1784 and later to become the Chesapeake and Ohio Canal Company, as set forth in Chesapeake & O. Canal Co. v. Baltimore & O.R.R., 17 Md. 1, 72-73 (1832). The brief in one early case states that the practice of chartering railroad corporations was begun by the states in 1824. Brief for Defendant at 63, Beekman v. Saratoga & S.R.R., 3 Paige Ch. 45 (N.Y. Ch. 1831).

Canals were first used as a circumferential system to connect the waterways north and west of Boston, and to bypass lower falls on the coastal rivers. Later, much more ambitious projects were launched to connect the Hudson River with Lake Erie and Lake Champlain, and to connect the Potomac River with the Ohio Valley. *See* cases *supra* and note 58 *infra*. Especially in these latter instances, public enthusiasm was great, as evidenced by this ebullient language used by Chancellor Kent in giving an expansive reading to the statutory powers of the New York Canal Commissioners:

> If there was ever a case in the ordinary pacific operations of government in which all petty private interests should be made subservient to the interest of an entire people, this is one. The canals were undertaken "in full confidence that the Congress of the United States, and the States equally interested with this State in the commencement, prosecution, and completion of these important works, would contribute their full proportion of the expense." We have not as yet realized the fruits of that confidence, and we are left to bear singly the whole expense, as well as to enjoy all the honor and glory of this stupendous undertaking.

Jerome v. Ross, 7 Johns. Ch. 315, 342-43 (N.Y. Ch. 1823).

57. As to canals, *see* Chesapeake & O. Canal Co. v. Key, 3 D.C. 599, 605 (1829); Riddle v. Proprietors of the Locks and Canals, 7 Mass. 169 (1810); Lebanon v. Olcott, 1 N.H. 339 (1818). It does not appear that the absolute right to use railroads upon payment of requisite charges was quite as well assured initially as it was in the case of turnpikes and canals. *But see* Brief for Plaintiff at 48-49, Brief for Defendant at 61-62, Beekman v. Saratoga & S.R.R., 3 Paige Ch. 45 (N.Y. Ch. 1831). The problem, if there was one, did not persist.

58. In one early Massachusetts case the eminent domain powers of a canal corporation were reviewed very briefly and approved on the analogy to the milldams. *See* Stevens v. Proprietors of Middlesex Canal, 12 Mass. 466, 468 (1815). In two other major, early cases, however, the conflicts were between canal corporations and other utilities, and the courts thus did not focus squarely on the private eminent domain powers of the canal corporations. Chesapeake & O. Canal Co. v. Baltimore & O.R.R., 17 Md. 1, 72-73 (1832); Proprietors of Sudbury Meadows v. Proprietors of Middlesex Canal, 40 Mass. (23 Pick.) 36, 49 (1839). *See also* Scudder v. Trenton Delaware Falls Co., 1 N.J. Eq. 694, 728 (1832), in which the propriety of a milldam corporation's power to condemn a sluiceway was subsumed in the larger question of its powers to erect a milldam to which the sluiceway was appurtenant. Early, influential New York cases construed the eminent domain powers of the state Canal Commissioners under their enabling statutes, and thus did not consider private corporate use of eminent domain. *See* Wheelock v. Young, 4 Wend. 647 (N.Y. Sup. Ct. 1830); Jerome v. Ross, 7 Johns. Ch. 315, 342-43 (N.Y. Ch. 1823); Rogers v. Bradshaw, 20 Johns. 735, 742 (N.Y. Ct. Err. 1823). *But see*

Chesapeake & O. Canal Co. v. Key, 3 D.C. 599, 605 (1829), in which the court sustained corporate use of eminent domain against a protesting owner. The condemnation proceedings were overturned due to procedural irregularities. *Id.* at 610-11. *See also* note 54 *supra.* The condemnee was one Francis Scott Key, appearing *pro se,* whose "land of the free" sentiments may have been sorely tested by this litigation.

    59. *See* cases cited note 58 *supra.*

    60. Without a brief excursion into the context of the times, it is perhaps a bit difficult to fathom the obstacles of fact, doctrine and policy presented in the early 1830's when the courts were asked to extend to the infant railroad companies the doctrinal treatment previously accorded the power of eminent domain held by turnpike and canal corporations. In this era, railroads were literally roads making use of rails, and locomotives were extremely crude, weak and unreliable. See the terms of an early railroad grant mentioned in Bloodgood v. Mohawk & H.R.R., 18 Wend. 9, 20-21 (N.Y. Ct. Err. 1837), which authorized the railroad to use any combination of power, including animals and steam or other mechanical power. Another early railroad was expected to scale the Allegheny Mountains by using one hundred stationary steam engines. *See* Chesapeake & O. Canal Co. v. Baltimore & O.R.R., 17 Md. 1, 34 (1832). Further, most early railroad charters were for short lines connecting specified towns or waterways. *See, e.g.,* routes detailed in Bloodgood v. Mohawk & H.R.R., 18 Wend. 9 (N.Y. Ct. Err. 1837); and the Massachusetts process of awarding charters for the completion of portions of the routes that would eventually link Boston with Providence, 'R.I. and with the Hudson River, as described in Boston Water Power Co. v. Boston & Worcester R.R., 40 Mass. (23 Pick.) 360, 363-65 (1839). The railroads, as considered by the courts in the earliest cases, were at best an alternative to and modest improvement over tollroads and canals. *See generally* Chesapeake & O. Canal Co. v. Baltimore & 'O.R.R., 17 Md. 1, 72-73 (1832). There is no indication in the lengthy briefs and opinions in that case whether the railroad or the canals were thought in 1832 to have the better chance of scaling the mountains and connecting the Potamac and Ohio basins.

    61. Brief for Plaintiff at 48-49, Brief for Defendant at 61-62, Beekman v. Saratoga & S.R.R., 3 Paige Ch. 45 (N.Y. Ch. 1831).

    62. *See* Beekman v. Saratoga & S.R.R., 3 Paige Ch. 45, 74 (N.Y. Ch. 1831); Bloodgood v. Mohawk & H.R.R., 18 Wend. 9, 15-16 (N.Y. Ct. Err. 1837). To make this distinction more intelligible to a modern reader, it is the 19th century public-user equivalent to the current automobile driver's resistance when told that he should utilize mass transit and leave the car at home.

    63. Baltimore & O.R.R. v. Van Ness, 4 D.C. (4 Cranch.) 595 (1835); Concord R.R. v. Greely, 17 N.H. 47 (1845); Beekman v. Saratoga & S.R.R., 3 Paige Ch. 45, 60 (N.Y. Ch. 1831); Bloodgood v. Mohawk & H.R.R., 18 Wend. 9, 20-21 (N.Y. Ct. Err. 1837) (scrutinizing closely and construing the regularity of the condemnation procedure involved).

    In the first railroad case considered in Massachusetts, the propriety of eminent domain in a railroad corporation was not raised by the condemnee. *See* Carpenter v. County Comm'rs, 38 Mass. (21 Pick.) 258 (1838). The next two cases considered involved the powers of railroad corporations vis-a-vis those of a turnpike, *see* Newburyport Turnpike Corp. v. Eastern R.R., 40 Mass. (23 Pick.) 326 (1839), and of a large dam proprietor, *see* Boston Water Power Co. v. Boston & W.R.R., 40 Mass. (23 Pick.) 360, 363-65 (1839). The propriety of the railroads' eminent domain powers was tacitly approved.

    64. In witness whereof, the following is set forth at length for fanciers of florid panygeric, 19th century variety:

    Railroads are not only of great public use in the ordinary business transactions of the citizen, but they may be more advantageously used than turnpike roads for national purposes; . . . for the transportation of mails, and the rapid dissemination of intelligence, which is the life of liberty, and more than any other mode of conveyance, they tend to annihilate distance, bringing in effect places far distant near to each other: tending in their magic influence to the extension of

personal acquaintance, the enlargement of business relations, and cementing more firmly the bond of fellowship and union between the inhabitants of the States. Next to the moral lever power of the press, should be ranked the beneficial influence of railroads in their effects upon the vast and increasing business relations of the nation, and the promoting, sustaining and perpetuating the happiness, prosperity and liberty of the people.
Bloodgood v. Mohawk & H.R.R., 18 Wend. 9, 48 (N.Y. Ct. Err. 1837).

65. In New York, the "public use as public utility" doctrine received its clearest early formulation as it concerned railroads. Public use may mean that property is possessed and used directly by the government, as was the case with the major New York canals but not with the railroads. *See* notes 56-58 *supra*. The New York courts then were obliged to formulate a manageable public-use doctrine that would legitimate the power of eminent domain in the railroads against the immediate background of cases involving that power in the state-owned canal system.

The rationale adopted was a mixture of deference to legislative judgment and acceptance of at least a moderate amount of legislatively-decreed public utility as sufficient:

[I]f the Legislature should attempt thus to transfer the property of one individual to another, where there could be no pretense of benefit to the public by such exchange, it would probably be a violation of the contract by which the land was granted by the government to the individual, or to those under whom he claimed title, and repugnant to the Constitution of the United States. But if the public interest can be in any way promoted by the taking of private property, it must rest in the wisdom of the Legislature to determine whether the benefit to the public will be of sufficient importance to render it expedient for them to exercise the right of eminent domain, and to authorize an interference with the private rights of individuals for that purpose.

Beekman v. Saratoga & S.R.R., 3 Paige Ch. 45, 73 (N.Y. Ch. 1831). To justify the exercise of the right of eminent domain, there must be a necessity, or at least an evident utility on the part of the public. Bloodgood v. Mohawk & H.R.R., 18 Wend. 9, 20-21 (N.Y. Ct. Err. 1837).

Perhaps the most thorough and useful analysis of public use as public purpose contained in 19th century case law may be found in Varner v. Martin, 21 W. Va. 534 (1883). After discussing a first class of cases in which the government acquires land by eminent domain, Judge Green continued:

The second class of cases to which I have alluded is where the property is in the direct use and occupation of a private person or of a private corporation, and the general public have only an indirect and qualified use of the property condemned, or perhaps no use probably of any kind of the property condemned, but simply derives from its use by the owner for his private purposes some indirect advantage, as by the promotion of the general prosperity of the community.

. . . I think we can show from the decisions, that a person or corporation claiming to belong to this second class, and to have legislative authority to condemn lands, must first show, that he or they are possessed of each and all of these three qualifications. First, the general public must have a definite and fixed use of the property to be condemned, a use independent of the will of the private person or private corporation in whom the title of the property when condemned will be vested; a public use which cannot be defeated by such private owner, but which public use continues to be guarded and controlled by the general public through laws passed by the Legislature; second, this *public use* must be clearly a needful one for the public, one which cannot be given up without obvious general loss and inconvenience; third, it must be impossible, or very difficult at least, to secure the same public uses and purposes in any other way than by authorizing the condemnation of private property.

If any one of these essentials are wanting, the courts will declare the act of the Legislature authorizing such condemnation of private property to be unconstitutional, because it would amount to taking private property for *private* and not for public uses.

Id. at 555-56. In this case the court held unconstitutional a statute authorizing the use of eminent domain to acquire *private* rights-of-way. See Hairston v. Danville & W. Ry., 208 U.S. 598 (1908), as an example of judicial review of an alleged use of railroad eminent domain for a private purpose. *i.e.*, to acquire a spur right-of-way to serve one factory.

66. *See, e.g.,* practices and statutes cited in Otis Co. v. Ludlow Mfg. Co., 201 U.S. 140, 151 (1906); Head v. Amoskeag Mfg. Co., 113 U.S. 9, 16-20 (1885); Talbot v. Hudson, 82 Mass. (16 Gray) 417, 426 (1860); Hatch v. Dwight, 17 Mass. 289 (1821) (involving an "ancient" milldam); Brief for Petitioner at 447-51, Great Falls Mfg. Co. v. Fernald, 47 N.H. 444 (1867); Varner v. Martin, 21 W. Va. 534, 544-46 (1883) (stating that the practice in Virginia antedates 1700).

67. *See* Head v. Amoskeag Mfg. Co., 113 U.S. 9, 16-20 (1885); Stowell v. Flagg, 11 Mass. 364 (1814), in which the effect of the Massachusetts act on common law remedies was first decided; Bates v. Weymouth Iron Co., 62 Mass. (8 Cush.) 548 (1851); Jordan v. Woodward, 40 Me. 317 (1855); Bassett v. Salisbury Mfg. Co., 47 N.H. 426 (1867). In addition to the problem of physical invasion, it is certain that the millponds were a nuisance in the neighborhood on frequent occasions. *See* Ryerson v. Brown, 35 Mich. Rpts. 333, 341 (1877). Despite the statutes, the flowage right had some substantive limitations. The flooded upstream owner could apparently construct dikes on his firm land to turn back the waters of the pond. *See* Storm v. Manchaug Co., 95 Mass. (13 Allen) 10, 13-14 (1866). The Massachusetts act was held not to authorize damming on one stream if the water impounded was to be diverted to create power on another stream. Bates v. Weymouth Iron Co., 62 Mass. (8 Cush.) 548 (1851).

68. Otis Co. v. Ludlow Mfg. Co., 201 U.S. 140, 151 (1906); Head v. Amoskeag Mfg. Co., 113 U.S. 9, 16-20 (1885); Jordan v. Woodward, 40 Me. 317 (1855); Scudder v. Trenton Del. Falls Co., 1 N.J.Eq. 694, 728 (1832). This is not to say, of course, that there was not much litigation over the application of the acts to particular factual situations. *See e.g.,* Storm v. Manchuag Co., 95 Mass. (13 Allen) 10, 13 (1866); Bates v. Weymouth Iron Co., 62 Mass. (8 Cush.) 548 (1851). Other lawsuits challenged the validity of damage assessment proceedings. *See, e.g.,* Amoskeag Mfg. Co. v. Head, 59 N.H. 332 (1879), *aff'd,* 113 U.S. 9 (1885); Ash v. Cummings, 50 N.H. 591 (1872) (common law tort action not barred until damage proceedings conducted and award paid). Failure to provide for damages caused by flooding of lands by a private corporation chartered by the state was the ground for invalidation in the celebrated case of Pumpelly v. Green Bay Co., 80 U.S. 166 (1871).

69. *See* Head v. Amoskeag Mfg. Co., 113 U.S. 9 (1885); Harding v. Goodlett, 11 Tenn. 40, 45, 53 (1832); Varner v. Martin, 21 W. Va. 534, 546-47 (1883), stating: "[O]wners of water grist-mills were by these acts made as it were public servants." Lest we feel undue sympathy for these flour-encrusted drudges, one miller per mill was exempted from military watches and warnings in early Massachusetts. Otis Co. v. Ludlow Mfg. Co., 201 U.S. 140, 151-52 (1906). In Tennessee, mill keepers were in early times exempted from militia, jury duty and the road maintenance work required of able-bodied males. Harding v. Goodlett, 11 Tenn. 40, 52 (1832).

70. The Massachusetts court stated:

I cannot help thinking that this statute was incautiously copied from the ancient colonial and provincial acts, which were passed when the use of mills, from the scarcity of them, bore a much greater value, compared to the land used for the purposes of agriculture, than at present. But with this we have nothing to do. As the law is, so we must declare it.

Stowell v. Flagg, 11 Mass. 364, 368 (1814).

Whether, if this were an original question, this legislation would be considered as trenching too closely upon the great principle, which gives security to private rights, it seems now too late to inquire, such legislation having been in full operation in this state a century and a half.

Murdock v. Stickney, 62 Mass. (8 Cush.) 113, 117 (1851). *See also* Jordan v. Woodward, 40 Me. 317, 323 (1855), expressing similar reflections. In New Hampshire, the constitutionality of the milldam acts was not squarely raised and clearly decided until Ash v. Cummings, 50 N.H. 591 (1872), in which a similar approach was taken.

71. Initially, dictum appeared in cases indicating that the use of these acts in certain cases might pose grave state constitutional questions. *See* Hay v. Cohoes Co., 2 N.Y. 159 (1849); Harding v. Goodlett, 11 Tenn. 40, 53-54 (1832). *See also* Sadler v. Langham, 34 Ala. 311 (1859). Thereafter invalidation on state constitutional grounds first occurred in three nearly simultaneous cases: Loughbridge v. Harris, 42 Ga. 500 (1871); Ryerson v. Brown, 35 Mich. Rpts. 333 (1877); Tyler v. Beacher, 44 Vt. 648 (1871). In each of these cases, the court stressed that the statutes would have authorized the use of eminent domain for general milldam purposes, and not solely for grist mills. *Ryerson v. Brown* contains a most useful discussion on the realities of resource use that might persuade the judiciary to uphold an act in one era, while invalidating it in another:

An examination of the adjudged cases will show that the courts, in looking about for the public use that was to be accommodated by the [milldam] statute, have sometimes attached considerable importance to the fact that the general improvement of mill-sites, as property possessing great value if improved, and often nearly worthless if not improved, would largely conduce to the prosperity of the state. This is especially true of the decisions in those states where water power is most abundant, and where, partly because of a somewhat sterile soil, manufactures have attracted a larger proportion than in other states, of the capital, skill and labor of the community. In this state it is doubtful if such legislation would add at all to the aggregate of property. Numerous fine mill-sites in the populous counties of the state still remain unimproved, not because of any difficulty in obtaining the necessary permission to flow, but because the power is not in demand.

. . . If the act were limited in its scope to manufactures which are of local necessity, as grist-mills are in a new country not yet penetrated by railroads, the question would be somewhat different from what it is now. But even in such case it would be essential that the statute should require the use to be public in fact; in other words, that it should contain provisions entitling the public to accommodations. A flouring mill in this state may grind exclusively the wheat of Wisconsin, and sell the product exclusively in Europe; and it is manifest that in such a case the proprietor can have no valid claim to the interposition of the law to compel his neighbor to sell a business site to him, any more than could the manufacturer of shoes or the retailer of groceries.

. . . .

If, however, the use to which the property is to be devoted were one which would justify an exercise of the power, it would still be imperative that a necessity should exist for its exercise. All the authorities require that there should be a necessity for the appropriation in order to supply some public want, or to advance some public policy; the object to be accomplished must be one which otherwise is impracticable.

The opinion then considered an earlier milldam act, upon which the statute under consideration was patterned. Ryerson v. Brown, *supra* at 337-39. Judge Campbell, concurring, stressed the changes in the state's economy:

The territory was then in a state of almost complete isolation. Until the Erie canal was completed the expense of bringing steam machinery so great a distance would have been ruinous, and in the condition of the local roads it would have been impracticable. Emigrants [*sic*] were coming in rapidly and mills were necessary for their existence. Towns could not be maintained or even built without them. Water mills were the only ones of any utility in such communities, and their necessity was urgent. They were undoubtedly as indispensable as roads, and in fact very commonly preceded them. The judgment of the legislature was in complete accordance with the facts.

. . . .

The declaration of necessity in 1824 was no more significant than the finding that no further necessity existed in 1828, and this was no doubt owing to the introduction of steam. Any stream which is capable of furnishing water power is still more capable of furnishing water for running steam machinery; and any one who has the right to use running water at his steam mill is independent of riparian owners above him.

Id. at 345-46 (Campbell, J., concurring).

These passages illustrate that, although the physical reality of resource use remained constant (a dammer necessarily flooded an upstream riparian owner), the social need for the resource use shifted. Thus the earlier grist milldam statute effective between 1824 and 1828 would apparently have been valid in that era, but in 1877, the court in the instant case invalidated a general milldam statute. Also note that the progress of technology effected a complete reversal in doctrine—the perfection of steam power eliminated the dependency on water power for milling. We asserted earlier that, in a comparable manner, the interaction of technology, population expansion and affluence have so precipitated abilities to alter and develop land that a fundamental shift in the perception of land resources and their preservation is necessary. *See* p. 43 *supra*. *Compare* Township of Burlington v. Beasley, 94 U.S. 310 (1876), *with* Osborne v. County of Adams, 106 U.S. 181 (1882), involving the propriety of issuing internal improvement bonds under state statutes in order to fund steam-powered grist mills.

72. Thus, Hatch v. Dwight, 17 Mass. 289 (1821), involved a milldam said to be ancient, from which the water power was used to power a corn and hide mill. The court took no exception to the hide mill use. Boston & Roxbury Mill Dam Corp. v. Newman, 29 Mass. (12 Pick.) 467 (1832), involved a charter for a major dam across one of the necks of Boston harbor, which was to carry a roadway on top and to tap tidal ebb and flow, thereby generating sufficient diurnal energy to support a mill with energy equivalent to 20 pairs of millstones. In holding that the corporation validly held eminent domain powers to remove encroachments in the tidal basin, the court failed to make any distinction between grist mills and the general purpose energy source at hand and instead gave its approval to the public utility of the project in the following terms:

Here was a creation of an immense perpetual mill power, as well as a safe and commodious avenue, in and over the waste waters of the ocean and adjoining to a great city.

We should be at a loss to imagine any undertaking of an individual or association of persons with a view to private emolument, in which the public had a more certain and direct interest and benefit.

Id. at 476. *See also* Jordan v. Woodward, 40 Me. 317 (1855); Brief for Petitioners at 447-51, Great Falls Mfg. Co. v. Fernald, 47 N.H. 444 (1867).

73. *See* Varner v. Martin, 21 W. Va. 534 (1883); note 65 *supra*; cases cited note 72 *supra*. The perspective from the New Hampshire bench is aptly stated in Great Falls Mfg. Co. v. Fernald, 47 N.H. 444, 460 (1867):

Our soil and climate forbid us to enter into competition with the great producing States of the Union, in the sale of such agricultural productions as are sent to the great markets of the country; we are purchasers, and not vendors, of such productions. The prosperity of the farmer mainly depends with us on having close at hand a market for such products of his farm as cannot be advantageously transported for long distances, and in which he does not come into competition with the great producers of the West. Such a market can be furnished only by his neighbors, who are engaged in mechanical and manufacturing pursuits. The farmer, therefore, has an obvious and deep interest in those pursuits; and large manufacturing establishments not only afford a market for agricultural productions, but give profitable employment to great numbers of men and women, disburse large sums of money, and create a new demand for wood, timber, and other commodities.

Similar sentiments were expressed by the New Jersey court in Scudder v. Trenton Del. Falls Co., 1 N.J.Eq. 694, 728-29 (1832):

> May we not, in considering what shall be deemed a public use and benefit, look at the objects, the purposes, and the results of the undertaking? The water power about to be created, will be sufficient for the erection of seventy mills, and factories, and other works dependent on such power. It will be located at the seat of government, at the head of tide water, and in a flourishing and populous district of country. It will be no experiment in a country like ours; and, judging from the results in other places, we may make a sufficiently accurate calculation as to the result here. Take the town of Paterson as an example. The water power there is in the hands of individuals—a company like this. They are under no obligation to lease or sell any mills or privileges to the public; and yet see the result of a few years' operation. Paterson is now the manufacturing emporium of the state, with a population of eight thousand souls. It has increased the value of property in all that district of country; opened a market for the produce of the soil, and given a stimulus to industry of every kind. May we not hope that a similar benefit may be experienced here?

Two decades after Proprietors of Sudbury Meadows v. Proprietors of Middlesex Canal, 40 Mass. (23 Pick.) 36 (1839), the canal had doubtlessly been largely supplanted by improved roads and railroads. The meadow proprietors, armed with a new special statute, wished to free their lands of the waters cast back by the canal company's dam, approved in the earlier decision. The court allowed this to be done in Talbot v. Hudson, 82 Mass. (16 Gray) 417 (1860). In commenting on the vagaries that the meadows had undergone at the hands of the proprietors operating under various special legislative acts, the court delivered the following pronouncement:

> It is certainly difficult to see any good reason for making a discrimination . . . [as to the legislative conferment of the powers of eminent domain] between different branches of industry. If it is lawful and constitutional to advance the manufacturing or mechanical interests of a section of the State by allowing individuals acting primarily for their own profit to take private property [referring to the milldam acts], there would seem to be little, if any, room for doubt as to the authority of the legislature, acting as the representatives of the whole people, to make a similar appropriation by their own immediate agents [the proprietors of the meadows] in order to promote the agricultural interests of a large territory.

Id. at 427. This, of course, illustrates precisely the troublesome ultimate extension of the doctrine of public utility as public use. The power in the hands of the meadow proprietors may be explicable by the drainage precedents to be considered next. *See* pp. 67-76 *infra*. But if any corporation *qua* corporation acts for the "public use" in the sense of generalized public utility, or is a legitimate representative of a generic segment of the economy as set over against other such segments (*e.g.*, agriculture versus manufacturing), it is most difficult to see where the limits may be drawn in conferring eminent domain powers on corporations. Indeed, as will be noted briefly later, in many western states these powers are widely conferred on corporations and individuals, albeit for limited purposes. *See* p. 75 *infra*.

74. The flowage right is characterized as an easement or servitude in Otis Co. v.

Ludlow Mfg. Co., 201 U.S. 140, 153-54 (1906); Bates v. Weymouth Iron Co., 62 Mass. (8 Cush.) 548, 555 (1851); Boston & Roxbury Mill Dam Corp. v. Newman, 29 Mass. (12 Pick.) 467, 482-83 (1832). It is clear from these cases that the dammer did not acquire the fee in lands flowed, but only the right of encroachment as long as the dam and pond existed.

75. *See* Otis Co. v. Ludlow Mfg. Co., 201 U.S. 140, 153-54 (1906); Cary v. Daniels, 49 Mass. (8 Met.) 466, 476-77 (1844).

76. *See* cases cited note 75 *supra*. This included the right to make use of its natural gravitational fall for power generation purposes.

77. *See* Otis Co. v. Ludlow Mfg. Co., 201 U.S. 140, 153-54 (1906); Bates v. Weymouth Iron Co., 62 Mass. (8 Cush.) 548, 553 (1851); Murdock v. Stickney, 62 Mass. (8 Cush.) 113, 116 (1851). In the eyes of the Massachusetts courts the milldam acts were a form of police power regulation, not of eminent domain. *See* Murdock v. Stickney, *supra*. The effect of the acts was to adjust rights that were correlative, or held in common among owners along affected portions of a stream. *See* Fiske v. Framingham Mfg. Co., 29 Mass. (12 Pick.) 68, 70-72 (1884); Bates v. Weymouth Iron Co., *supra* at 552-53. *But cf.* Talbot v. Hudson, 82 Mass. (16 Gray) 417, 426 (1860), indicating that the Massachusetts act could be considered an exercise of the power of eminent domain; the case is cited to this effect in Head v. Amoskeag Mfg. Co., 113 U.S. 9, 19 (1885). *See also* discussion, note 79 *infra*.

78. The case in which this rationale was firmly adopted was Cary v. Daniels, 49 Mass. (8 Met.) 466, 477 (1844):

It seems to follow, as a necessary consequence from these [physical principles of damming] . . . that in such case, the proprietor who first erects his dam for such a [milling] purpose has a right to maintain it, as against the proprietors above and below; and to this extent, prior occupancy gives a prior title to such use. It is a profitable, beneficial, and reasonable use, and therefore one which he has a right to make. . . . For the same reason, the proprietor below cannot erect a dam in such a manner as to raise the water and obstruct the wheels of the first occupant. He had an equal right with the proprietor below to a reasonable use of the stream; he had made only a reasonable use of it; his appropriation to that extent, being justifiable and prior in time, necessarily prevents the proprietor below from raising the water, without interfering with a rightful use already made; and it is therefore not an injury to him. Such appears to be the nature and extent of the prior and exclusive right, which one proprietor acquires by a prior reasonable appropriation of the use of the water in its fall; and it results, not from any originally superior legal right, but from a legitimate exercise of his own common right, the effect of which is, *de facto*, to supersede and prevent a like use by other proprietors originally having the same common right.

Note from the above excerpt that due to physical reality, the dam had a preemptive effect both upstream and down. A downstream owner was precluded from erecting a dam that would push water against the dam of an upstream owner, thereby pro tanto reducing the vertical fall of water available to the upstream dammer for water power purposes. The dammer likewise preempted vertical fall along the level of his millpond as far as it extended upstream. Viewed in this light, the "property" subjected to prior appropriation was perhaps the vertical fall of water, with the flowage of land then viewed as a subordinate incident of the appropriation. No compensation was payable under the act for destruction of that portion of the market value of riparian lands attributable to adaptability for mill purposes. Fuller v. Chicopee Mfg. Co., 82 Mass. (16 Gray) 43 (1860).

For a compendious and detailed statement of the effects and operations of the Massachusetts act, see Brief for Plaintiff at 141-47, Otis Co. v. Ludlow Mfg. Co., 201 U.S. 140 (1906).

79. *See* Head v. Amoskeag Mfg. Co., 113 U.S. 9, 21-23 (1885). This characterization in *Head* had the important consequence of enabling the Supreme Court to deal with the case as involving an exercise of the police power. *See* note 77 *supra*. The Court explicitly refrained from treating the case as one involving the power of eminent domain, Head v. Amoskeag, *supra* at 20-21; by so doing the Court avoided the need to determine the propriety of the delegation of eminent domain to private individuals under the public-use-as-public-utility rationale. Going beyond the narrowly stated basis of the case (adjustment of rights held in common), it seems unquestionable that the police power may be exercised for the general adjustment of private rights on grounds of public utility and benefit, whereas these grounds are a highly suspect basis for the bestowal of eminent domain powers on individuals and corporations. *See* note 73 *supra*.

80. Head v. Amoskeag Mfg. Co., 113 U.S. 9, 21-23 (1885).

81. *Id.*; *see* notes 73, 77, 79 *supra*.

82. Head v. Amoskeag Mfg. Co., 113 U.S. 9, 20-26 (1885); *see* Otis Co. v. Ludlow Mfg. Co., 201 U.S. 140, 151 (1906).

83. Drainage of marshes and overflowed lands was a practice in the Eastern States from very early times. *See, e.g.*, statutes and practices discussed in Willson v. Black Bird Creek Marsh Co., 27 U.S. (2 Pet.) 245 (1829) (involving a Willson drainage corporation); Proprietors of Sudbury Meadows v. Proprietors of Middlesex Canal, 40 Mass. (23 Pick.) 36 (1839); Hoagland v. Wurts, 41 N.J.L. 175, 179 (1879) (terming special legislation for the drainage of meadows "a branch of legislation that has existed in this state from the earliest times"); Coster v. Tide Water Co., 18 N.J.Eq. 54, 69 (1866) (mentioning that the court had been referred to hundreds of private drainage acts in New York and New Jersey); Belknap v. Belknap, 2 Johns. Ch. 463 (N.Y. Ch. 1817); Phillips v. Thompson, 1 Johns. Ch. 130 (N.Y. Ch. 1814). In tidal areas and along some of the inland rivers, drainage was accomplished by building levees to repel the onslaught of tides or floods. United States v. Lynah, 188 U.S. 445 (1903) (involving a levee); Eldridge v. Trezevant, 160 U.S. 452 (1896) (involving Louisiana levee practices); Willson v. Black Bird Creek Marsh Co., *supra*; Coster v. Tide Water Co., *supra*. Widespread irrigation arose only as the West was settled, and then largely west of the 100th principal meridian. *See, e.g.*, Lake Koen Navigation, Reservoir & Irrigation Co. v. Klein, 65 P. 684 (Kan. 1901), discussing a statutory scheme indicating legislative intent to authorize irrigation in Kansas west of the 99th meridian.

84. *See, e.g.*, the following cases involving powers in a district to condemn a right-of-way for the conveyance of water: O'Neill v. Leamer, 239 U.S. 244 (1915); Merrill v. Southside Irrigation Co., 44 P. 720 (Cal. 1896); to condemn a portion of an existing irrigation canal: Portneuf Irrigating Co. v. Budge, 100 P. 1046 (Idaho 1909); to condemn bottomland for a reservoir: Lake Koen Navigation, Reservoir & Irrigation Co. v. Klein, 65 P. 684 (Kan. 1901); Paxton & Hershey Irrigating Canal & Land Co. v. Farmers' & Merchants' Irrigation & Land Co., 64 N.W. 343 (Neb. 1895). In usages such as these, of course, the districts held powers of eminent domain and proceeded under them. When drainage involved the land of but a few individuals, infliction of impact outside of the drainage area, as by interfering with the water supply of established mills, raised troublesome problems of the private use of eminent domain. *See* Belknap v. Belknap, 2 Johns Ch. 463 (N.Y. Ch. 1817) (decided on ultra vires grounds); but such powers were granted in the special act under review in Phillips v. Thompson, 1 Johns. Ch. 130 (N.Y. Ch. 1814).

85. *See generally* the statutory structures under review, and statutes and cases cited in Lake Shore & M.S. Ry. v. Clough, 242 U.S. 375 (1917); O'Neill v. Leamer, 239 U.S. 244 (1915); Fallbrook Irrigation Dist. v. Bradley, 164 U.S. 112 (1896); Wurts v. Hoagland, 114 U.S. 606 (1885); Hagar v. Reclamation Dist. No. 108, 111 U.S. 701 (1884); *In re* Bonds of Madera Irrigation Dist., 28 P. 272 (Cal. 1891); Lake Koen Navigation, Reservoir & Irrigation Co. v. Klein, 65 P. 684 (Kan. 1901); Coomes v. Burt, 39 Mass. (22

Pick.) 422 (1839); Lundberg v. Green River Irrigation Dist., 119 P. 1039 (Utah 1911). All of these cases contain review of various aspects of due process requirements surrounding the formation of districts and the levy of betterment assessments.

86. This was assumed, *sub silentio*, in Wurts v. Hoagland, 114 U.S. 606 (1885); Hagar v. Reclamation Dist. No. 108, 111 U.S. 701 (1884). The author has found no case in which physical alteration of drained land was raised and treated as an issue separate from larger questions of the validity of overall public purposes served by drainage projects. An owner's denial that he was receiving any benefits, *see* note 87 *infra*, did not raise the issue. Physical alteration offsite, such as reduced water flow to milldams, was treated in a few cases. *See, e.g.,* Belknap v. Belknap, 2 Johns. Ch. 462 (N.Y. Ch. 1817); Phillips v. Thompson, 1 Johns. Ch. 130 (N.Y. Ch. 1814). The closest approach to direct discussion of the issue is that of Beasley, C.J., in Hoagland v. Wurts, 41 N.J.L. 175, 177-79 (1879):

> If the law in question were defensible alone on the ground that it is an emanation of the legislative power in its ordinary exercise, I should be constrained to yield my assent to . . . [the contention that the statute is invalid]. There is nothing that I know of in the nature of legislation that could stand as a warrant for such an enactment. To make this evident, all we have to do is to realize fully the character of the authority thus assumed. The purpose of the law is to enable one set of land owners to compel another set to co-operate, against their will, to drain that body of meadow land in which they have separate interests. The persons thus coerced manifestly suffer an invasion of their ordinary proprietary rights. Why should they thus be forced either to improve their own land or help to improve the land of others? . . .
>
> . . . .
>
> But, nevertheless, I think this act, with respect to its general scope and operation, is to be vindicated. The right to appoint methods for the drainage of meadows has been a branch of legislation that has existed in this state from the earliest times, and has been so frequently exercised and acknowledged, that it has become a part of the local common law.

The physical necessity of draining the land of all owners within a drainage district is mentioned in Fallbrook Irrigation Dist. v. Bradley, 164 U.S. 112, 163-64 (1896).

87. The dissident owner's asserted right to do precisely this was reviewed in Fallbrook Irrigation Dist. v. Bradley, 164 U.S. 112 (1896). Mrs. Bradley's property was susceptible of beneficial use without the necessity of water for irrigation and had for several years been used for beneficial purposes other than cultivation by irrigation. *Id.* at 166. It was nonetheless assessed for irrigation benefit in the amount of $51.31, and when Mrs. Bradley refused to pay the assessment, the land was sold to collect the amount. *Id.* at 121-23.

Contrasting the necessity of physical invasion in the case of milldams and the necessity of physical alteration in the case of drainage districts, Mrs. Bradley argued that she was being compelled to take and pay for water whether she wanted it or not, without any physical necessity for the compulsion. Brief for Appellees at 137-39, Fallbrook Irrigation Dist. v. Bradley, *supra*. The Supreme Court did not agree:

> If land which can, to a certain extent, be beneficially used without artificial irrigation, may yet be so much improved by it that it will be thereby and for its original use substantially benefited, and, in addition to the former use, though not in exclusion of it, if it can then be put to other and more remunerative uses, we think it erroneous to say that the furnishing of artificial irrigation to that kind of land cannot be, in a legal sense, a public improvement, or the use of the water a public use.

Id. at 167. In so holding, the Supreme Court relied heavily on an earlier California case that approved the inclusion of the city of Modesto within an irrigation district although many improved properties within the city would assertibly receive no benefit

from the availability of irrigation water. Board of Directors of Modesto Irrigation
Dist. v. Tregea, 26 P. 237 (Cal. 1891). The Supreme Court interpreted as includable
within the irrigation district all lands that *in their natural state* were susceptible of
receiving benefits from irrigation. Fallbrook Irrigation Dist. v. Bradley, 164 U.S. 112,
164-67 (1896), *citing* Board of Directors of Modesto Irrigation Dist. v. Tregea, 26 P. 237,
241-42 (Cal. 1891). Thus, under statutory mandate by the California Legislature, as
approved by the courts, the physical reality that an owner could have refused to participate in an irrigation district gave way to the legal reality that he could not do so.
Interestingly, the Supreme Court bolstered this approach by noting that an owner,
having been compelled to take a share of irrigation project water and pay for the
benefits thereby conferred, was at liberty to sell or assign any irrigation water in excess
of his needs and thus to offset or perhaps to recoup the amount of the assessment. Fallbrook Irrigation Dist. v. Bradley, 164 U.S. 112, 162-63 (1896). This is comparable to the
ability of a property owner to sell development rights.

88. *See generally* notes 85 & 87 *supra.*
89. *See* note 87 *supra.*
90. *See* note 85 *supra.*
91. *See, e.g.,* Board of Directors of Modesto Irrigation Dist. v. Tregea, 26 P. 237, 244
(Cal. 1891), in which the decision was belatedly made to exclude 28,000 acres from
the originally proposed 108,000-acre district. In this case an offer of proof was made,
which the court held was correctly rejected, that the inclusion of Modesto within the
district was a gerrymander to assemble enough favorable votes from city residents to
override the opposition of outlying farmers to the formation of the district. *Id.* at 243.
92. *See, e.g.,* Myles Salt Co. v. Iberia Drainage Dist., 239 U.S. 478 (1916), in which
the drainage district for a low lying coastal area attempted to embrace and to assess
for drainage betterments a geologically anomalous "island" that rose to a height of 175
feet above the plain, suffered from excessive drainage and erosion under natural circumstances, and happened to be the most valuable single piece of property within the
district. The Supreme Court struck down the inclusion and assessment of the "island"
within the district in the following language:

It is to be remembered that a drainage district has the special purpose of the
improvement of particular property and when it is so formed to include property
which is not and cannot be benefited directly or indirectly, including it only
that it may pay for the benefit to other property, there is an abuse of power
and an act of confiscation.

Id. at 485.

On a broader level, the determination that lands within the district would benefit
from the proposed system of drainage or irrigation was a jurisdictional one—it was
one of the threshhold questions that required an affirmative answer before a drainage
or irrigation district could be created under the typical statute. *See* Lake Shore & M.S.
Ry. v. Clough, 242 U.S. 375 (1917); Fallbrook Irrigation Dist. v. Bradley, 164 U.S. 112,
175-78 (1896).

93. Perhaps the best general statement is to be found in Hagar v. Reclamation
Dist. No. 108, 111 U.S. 701, 705 (1884):

The expense of such works may be charged against parties specially benefited,
and be made a lien upon their property. All that is required in such cases is
that the charges shall be apportioned in some just and reasonable mode, according
to the benefit received. Absolute equality in imposing them may not be reached;
only an approximation to it may be attainable. If no direct and invidious dis-
crimination in favor of certain persons to the prejudice of others be made, it is
not a valid objection to the mode pursued that, to some extent, inequalities may
arise.

In a specific situation, the Supreme Court of California, in Board of Directors of
Modesto Irrigation Dist. v. Tregea, 26 P. 237, 242 (Cal. 1891), had this to say:

If this objection was good ground for excluding the city from the district, it is probable that no district could ever be successfully organized; for, in the nature of things, an irrigation district must cover an extensive tract of land, and, no matter how purely rural and agricultural the community may be, there must exist here and there within its limits a shop or warehouse covering a limited extent of ground that can derive no direct benefit from the use of water for irrigation.

It is assertible that the courts foresaw and moved to forestall a plethora of suits on the merits by individuals whose lands had been assessed by drainage and irrigation districts. In any event, the judicial approach of the United States Supreme Court was: (1) to give initial broad review to the validity of the purposes and general structure of the districts, see, e.g., Fallbrook Irrigation Dist. v. Bradley, 164 U.S. 112 (1896); Wurts v. Hoagland, 114 U.S. 606 (1885); Hagar v. Reclamation Dist. No. 108, 111 U.S. 701 (1884); (2) to decide additional cases that related specifically to assessment procedures and theories, see, e.g., Houck v. Little River Drainage Dist., 239 U.S. 254 (1915); O'Neill v. Leamer, 239 U.S. 244 (1915); (3) to stake the outer limits of permissible inequities in assessments, see, e.g., Myles Salt Co. v. Iberia Drainage Dist., 239 U.S. 478 (1915); and (4) thereafter to leave the matter with inferior courts with a strong presumption of administrative regularity in proceedings within the districts, see, e.g., Houck v. Little River Drainage Dist., 239 U.S. 254 (1915).

94. Hagar v. Reclamation Dist. No. 108, 111 U.S. 701, 704-06 (1884). See also Houck v. Little River Drainage Dist., 239 U.S. 254, 264-65 (1915); Fallbrook Irrigation Dist. v. Bradley, 164 U.S. 112, 176-78 (1896); excerpt from *Hagar*, note 93 *supra*. But cf. Wurts v. Hoagland, 114 U.S. 606, 611, 614 (1885), in which the Supreme Court appears to adopt the rationale, developed in the New Jersey courts, that statutes authorizing the formation of drainage districts by majority action of the affected landowners were based on the police power and not on the power of taxation, despite the ability of the districts to assess each owner for betterments. See also the excerpt from *Wurts*, note 86 *supra*. A second species of drainage statute used in New Jersey chartered private corporations to drain marshes, thereby producing general public benefit as well as special private benefit to landowners within the drained areas. In reviewing the powers of these chartered drainage corporations the New Jersey courts had held that private inholders could not constitutionally be assessed for costs of improvements in amounts greater than the actual benefits conferred on their properties. Costs greater than the amount of private benefits conferred were required to be levied on the public at large, on the theory that these costs had created only public benefit. Tide-water Co. v. Coster, 18 N.J.Eq. 518, 526-31 (N.J. Ct. Err. 1866). This was, of course, an application of taxation doctrines.

95. See, e.g., Fallbrook Irrigation Dist. v. Bradley, 164 U.S. 112 (1896); Hagar v. Reclamation Dist. No. 108, 111 U.S. 701 (1884), both of which involved actions by landowners to block the forced sale of their property to satisfy betterment charges assessed by the districts within which the properties were situated.

96. For a comparable judicial characterization of the results, see excerpt quoted note 86 *supra*.

97. O'Neill v. Leamer, 239 U.S. 244 (1915); Fallbrook Irrigation Dist. v. Bradley, 164 U.S. 112, 160-63 (1896); Hagar v. Reclamation Dist. No. 108, 111 U.S. 701, 704-06 (1884); In re Madera Irrigation Dist., 28 P. 272 (Cal. 1891). The analysis of public benefits versus private benefits that arose in New Jersey courts, see note 94 *supra*, involved a massive drainage project in the flat coastal plains of that state. See Tide-water Co. v. Coster, 18 N.J.Eq. 518, 520-21 (N.J. Ct. Err. 1866). The project involved a marsh covering about one-fourth of Hudson County and several thousand acres in Union County, New Jersey. This marsh was comparatively useless and undevelopable in its natural condition, and it was exceedingly difficult to construct roads and railroads across the marsh to connect the towns on its borders. *Id.*

98. Drainage could, of course, typically be justified as protecting public health. *See* Leovy v. United States, 177 U.S. 621 (1900).

> We think that the trial court might well take judicial notice that the public health is deeply concerned in the reclamation of swamp and overflowed lands. If there is any fact which may be supposed to be known by everybody, and, therefore, by the courts, it is that swamps and stagnant waters are the cause of malarial and malignant fevers, and that the police power is never more legitimately exercised than in removing such nuisances.

Id. at 636.

In Hagar v. Reclamation Dist. No. 108, 111 U.S. 701, 704 (1884), the Supreme Court coupled community prosperity with community health as legitimate ends that might be served by drainage. Then in Wurts v. Hoagland, 114 U.S. 606, 613 (1885), reliance on the public health justification was omitted, and the rationale of the beneficial development of commonly-situated properties was espoused. The Court next used the dual rationales of commonly-situated property and public utility in Fallbrook Irrigation Dist. v. Bradley, 164 U.S. 112 (1896). In upholding the state legislature's determination of public utility, the Court stated:

> While the consideration that the work of irrigation must be abandoned if the use of the water may not be held to be or constitute a public use is not to be regarded as conclusive in favor of such use, yet that fact is in this case a most important consideration. Millions of acres of land otherwise cultivable must be left in their present arid and worthless condition, and an effectual obstacle will therefore remain in the way of the advance of a large portion of the State in material wealth and prosperity. To irrigate and thus to bring into possible cultivation these large masses of otherwise worthless lands would seem to be a public purpose and a matter of public interest, not confined to the landowners, or even to any one section of the State.

Id. at 161.

99. In the final analysis, the substantive power of the drainage and irrigation districts to block up similarly situated lands seems to be based on the police power. The special assessment analogy provided the necessary doctrinal base for the assessment of betterment charges. *See* note 94 *supra*. It was solely relied upon in Hagar v. Reclamation Dist. No. 108, 111 U.S. 701 (1884), and no mention was made therein of the common resource or common property theory. Head v. Amoskeag Mfg. Co., 113 U.S. 9 (1885), did not reach the Court until the following year.

In *Head* the Court clearly adopted the common property analogies and cited drainage district cases as invoking this rationale for regulation. *Id.* at 21-26.

In Wurts v. Hoagland, 114 U.S. 606 (1885), the Court incorporated into its conceptual scheme the New Jersey doctrine that drainage statutes authorizing majoritarian action by landowners within a district were based on the police power. *See* note 94 *supra*. As the Court had done earlier in *Head*, the Court in *Wurts* posited the existence of a generic category of resources that due to commonality of situation and exigency of development might be validly subjected to the peculiar genre of police power regulation under review. 114 U.S. at 611, 614.

In Fallbrook Irrigation Dist. v. Bradley, 164 U.S. 112, 163 (1896), the Court swept irrigation districts into this generic category of resources. Taking these cases together, it is fair to say that this category of resources is subject to regulation under a specialized branch of the police power that permits the use of elements of eminent domain or special assessment if necessary to accomplish the purposes at hand and to achieve rough equity among the various property owners involved. *See* p. 77 *infra*.

100. Fallbrook Irrigation Dist. v. Bradley, 164 U.S. 112, 163 (1896); *accord*, Wurts v. Hoagland, 114 U.S. 606, 614 (1885); note 99 *supra*.

101. *See, e.g.*, Strickley v. Highland Boy Gold Mining Co., 200 U.S. 527 (1906) (upholding a Utah statute authorizing acquisition of private right-of-way to carry ore);

Clark v. Nash, 198 U.S. 361 (1905) (upholding a Utah statute that permitted one individual to acquire a right-of-way across lands of another where necessary to convey irrigation water); Oury v. Goodwin, 26 P. 376 (Ariz. 1891) (private right-of-way for irrigation); Dayton Gold & Silver Mining Co. v. Seawell, 11 Nev. 394 (1876) (private mining right-of-way). The following excerpt gives a flavor of the spirit and realities of the times in which these acts were passed and upheld:

> Mining is the greatest of the industrial pursuits in this state. All other interests are subservient to it. Our mountains are almost barren timber, and our valley lands could never be made profitable for agricultural purposes except for the fact of a home market having been created by the mining developments in different sections of the state. The mining and milling interests give employment to many men, and the benefits derived from this business are distributed as much, and sometimes more, among the laboring classes than with the owners of the mines and mills. The mines are fixed by the laws of nature, and are often found in places almost inaccessible. . . . Now it so happens, or, at least, is liable to happen, that individuals, by securing a title to the barren lands adjacent to the mines, mills or works, have it within their power, by unreasonably refusing to part with their lands for a just and fair compensation, which capital is always willing to give without litigation, to greatly embarrass if not entirely defeat the business of mining in such localities. . . . Nature has denied to this state many of the advantages which other states possess; but by way of compensation to her citizens has placed at their doors the richest and most extensive silver deposits ever yet discovered. The present prosperity of the state is entirely due to the mining developments already made, and the entire people of the state are directly interested in having the future developments unobstructed by the obstinate action of any individual or individuals.

Id. at 409-10. To allay a nagging sense of *deja vu*, see the comparable rationale expressed as to the New Hampshire milldam act, note 73 *supra*.

102. Fallbrook Irrigation Dist. v. Bradley, 164 U.S. 112, 165-70 (1896).

103. We should note the radical reversal in perceptions of the social value of resources, as between the materials covered in notes 83-102 *supra*, and the extremely recent resource-preservation cases at notes 29-34 *supra*. The perception that underlies the milldam cases, the drainage and irrigation districts cases and the private right-of-way cases from the Western States was that land and natural resources were being wasted unless they were promptly developed and thus made part of the productive capital stock of society. The perception in the recent preservation cases is that society is best served over the productive long haul if at least certain types of critical land resources (*e.g.* wetlands) are saved from development and left to fulfill their vital natural functions. The rapidity and extent of this policy shift are best illustrated by the situation described in Candlestick Properties, Inc. v. San Francisco Bay Conservation & Dev. Comm'n, 89 Cal. Rptr. 897 (Ct. App. 1970). The marshland there involved had been included in a drainage and reclamation district created in 1955 under legislative finding that "compelling economic necessity exists for the reclaiming . . . of tidelands . . . [which] now serves no useful purpose for industry, commerce or navigation." *Id.* at 901. That is a fair statement of the dominant philosophy of the 19th and first half of the 20th centuries in this nation. Yet the marshland was now included within the jurisdiction of the Commission, whose 1965 enabling statute described the Bay as "the most valuable single natural resource of an entire region" and mandated the protection of "the present shoreline and body of San Francisco Bay to the maximum extent possible." *Id.* at 900-01. See discussion of the impact of this rapid reversal of policies on the broadly held expectations of landowners, pp. 43-46 *supra*. The author's conviction of the need for these new policies, coupled with concern at the diminution of values and disappointments of landowners expectations that will result, are two of the principal motivations for writing this article.

104. *See* pp. 102-03 *infra*.

105. *See generally* 1 H. WILLIAMS & C. MEYERS, OIL AND GAS LAW §§ 101-04 (1959) [hereinafter cited as H. WILLIAMS & C. MEYERS].

106. *See generally* 1 R. MYERS, THE LAW OF POOLING AND UNITIZATION, VOLUNTARY-COMPULSORY §§ 2.01-.05 (2d ed. 1967) [hereinafter cited as R. MYERS]; 6 H. WILLIAMS & C. MEYERS § 901. Primary recovery is ordinarily thought of as that production yielded solely by the connate energy of the reservoir. Secondary recovery is thought of as commencing after primary recovery has stopped, or nearly so. The line between the two is not always clear, however, because some of the same techniques may be used in both phases of production. For instance, injection of substances to maintain or stimulate reservoir energy may occur during primary recovery (*e.g.*, reinjection or "cycling" of gas produced, or certain types of water injection), and may also be used during secondary recovery operations (*e.g.*, certain types of water injection). Pressure maintenance during primary recovery may raise the same needs for unitization that are the hallmark of conventional secondary recovery operations.

107. *See* State v. Ohio Oil Co., 49 N.E. 809 (Ind. 1898); Townsend v. State, 47 N.E. 19 (Ind. 1897); Westmoreland & Cambria Natural Gas Co. v. DeWitt, 18 A. 724 (Pa. 1889). This bizarre characterization was produced by two factors. First, because of the limited technical information of the times, the courts apparently thought that oil and gas were literally as migratory as wild game or underground water. Second, given this perception, the courts were obliged to fit oil and gas into one of the available common law classifications of property rights, and the category of property rights in wild animals was early selected as a controlling analogy. *See* State v. Ohio Oil Co., *supra*; Townsend v. State, *supra*; Westmoreland & Cambria Natural Gas Co. v. DeWitt, *supra*.

108. *See* cases cited in note 107 *supra*. That is to say, no party had individual property rights in oil and gas until it had been captured by bringing it to the surface and reducing it to possession and control. While in repose under an owner's land, oil and gas were a part of the land and in some inchoate sense "belonged" to the owner. *See* Brown v. Spilman, 155 U.S. 665, 669-70 (1895). If drawn away by a neighbor's well on his property and reduced by him to possession, they then became the property of the neighbor as captor. *See* note 116 *infra*.

109. *See* note 108 *supra*. Indeed, there was often no other rational choice in the matter, for when a new field came in, a frenzied rush usually occurred to capitalize on the early, high-energy phase of the field's production, called "flush" production. All owners were compelled to join the race and sell the oil for whatever price it would fetch, or lose the bulk of the producible oil under their properties to drainage from neighbors. *See* Ely, *The Conservation of Oil*, 51 HARV. L. REV. 1209, 1220-21 (1938). A contemporary observer gave this description:

> When once man has started things, this property is mobile, so that the contest cannot be a leisurely procedure in the courts but of necessity becomes a strenuous fight on the ground, with drilling rigs and crews racing to reach the oil first and to reduce to actual possession the elusive and fugitive property. The ordinary workings of the economic law of supply and demand find no chance in the business of producing petroleum. The decision to drill does not wait on market reports; demand for the product is rarely a factor in influencing the development of oil property—simply the desire to get the oil before someone else gets it. Thus, as in no other activity, the oil industry throws financial conservatism and business sagacity to the winds and indulges in the primitive instincts of the chase.

Work, *Conservation's Need of Legal Advice*, 52 REPORTS OF THE AM. BAR ASS'N 570 (1927).

110. *See generally* Ely, *supra* note 109, at 1218-22, depicting and documenting production practices and their consequences. There the estimate is made that rapid, unregulated production may leave trapped in place between 75% and 90% of the oil, much of which might have been produced by wisely conducted primary recovery operations. *Id.*

at 1220. For a review of production practices and their consequences, see Sterling v. Constantin, 287 U.S. 378, 388-92, 396-98 (1932) (upholding injunction restraining Governor of Texas and military officials from enforcing military orders restricting production from plaintiff's oil wells in East Texas field, martial law having been declared for this purpose); Champlin Ref. Co. v. Corporation Comm'n, 286 U.S. 210, 226-32 (1932); Bandini Petroleum Co. v. Superior Court, 284 U.S. 8, 16-18 (1931); Walls v. Midland Carbon Co., 254 U.S. 300, 310-14 (1920); Ohio Oil Co. v. Indiana, 177 U.S. 190, 201, 211 (1900).

111. See Ely, *supra* note 109, at 1213-14, describing the drop in oil prices from ninety cents to ten cents per barrel when the East Texas field was brought in and commenced production at the rate of a million barrels per day in 1930-1931. *See also* Champlin Ref. Co. v. Corporation Comm'n, 286 U.S. 210, 226-32 (1932); Hardwicke, *Legal History of Proration of Oil Production in Texas*, 56 TEX. BAR ASS'N REPORTS 99, 104-05 (1937); discussion, note 107 *supra*. The reality was that huge quantities of oil commanding very low prices could not be stored above ground economically. In the race for production during the early phase of a field's operations, however, the choices were simple: a man could let the neighbors drain his property, or he could produce as rapidly as possible, as the neighbors were doing, store oil as best he could temporarily, sell as much as possible and dump the rest. As noted in Champlin Ref. Co. v. Corporation Comm'n, *supra* at 226-32, some Oklahoma operators in those fields, not having pipeline connections, were forced to store their production in earthen reservoirs or let it run at large.

112. Ely, *supra* note 109, at 1232-33. The author also cites estimates of between 4,000 and 5,000 unnecessary wells drilled annually in that era, at a drilling cost of between $80 and $100 million. *Id.*

113. Ohio Oil Co. v. Indiana, 177 U.S. 190, 190-92 (1900).

114. *Id.* at 192-95.

115. *Id.* at 195-97.

116. The Court held oil and gas to be "private property" in a peculiar sense. It conducted a brief review of the common law doctrine, developed in Indiana and other states, that analogized oil and gas to wild animals. *Id.* at 203-08; *see* note 107 *supra*. It was settled, however, that wild animals were public things subject to the absolute control of the state, which could allow, regulate, or wholly forbid their capture. Geer v. Connecticut, 161 U.S. 519 (1896). The Court in *Ohio Oil* noted not only this, but the further distinction that while all members of the public were empowered to capture wild animals, that is, to reduce a portion of this peculiar public property to possession by capturing an animal, in the case of oil and gas only the owners of land overlying a reservoir had the right to capture the oil and gas beneath their lands. 177 U.S. at 209. In this sense, the surface owners within an oil and gas field were held to have the exclusive right to reduce to possession the underlying oil and gas. On this basis, then, oil and gas in place were held to be private property—a pool resource, subject to the exclusive, composite right of all overlying surface owners to reduce the resource to possession, but the individual property of no one surface owner until reduced to possession by that owner. *Id.*

117. 177 U.S. at 204-06.

118. *Id.* at 209-10.

119. *Id. See generally* 1 H. WILLIAMS & C. MEYERS §§ 204.4, 204.6-.7; Kuntz, *Correlative Rights in Oil and Gas*, 30 MISS. L.J. 1 (1958).

120. 177 U.S. at 199, 211-12.

121. *See generally* 1 H. WILLIAMS & C. MEYERS §§ 204.4, 204.6-.7; Kuntz, *supra* note 119. There exists some slender precedent under the capture doctrine for entitlement of owners to ratable shares of production, as suggested in Union Gas & Oil Co. v. Fyffe, 294 S.W. 176 (Ky. 1927), and to prevent totally preemptive drainage by a neighbor, Ross v. Damm, 270 N.W. 722 (Mich. 1936), but it was the correlative rights doctrine

that furnished a firm basis for judicial adjustment of rights among owners within
a field. When applied by the courts, the doctrine has been used to prevent gross wast-
ing of extracted oil and gas, the impairment of the productive capacity of the reservoir
as a common source of supply, malicious depletion of the common source of supply
and violation of the right of others to a fair opportunity to produce oil and gas. *See*
Ohio Oil Co. v. Indiana, 177 U.S. 190 (1900); Manufacturers' Gas & Oil Co. v. Indiana
Natural Gas & Oil Co., 57 N.E. 912 (Ind. 1900); Louisville Gas Co. v. Kentucky Heating
Co., 77 S.W. 368 (Ky. 1903). *See generally* Kuntz, *supra* note 119. The doctrine may offer
additional grounds for an action by one landowner against another to recover damages
caused by the negligent waste of oil and gas. *See* Elliff v. Texon Drilling Co., 210 S.W.2d
558 (Tex.), *on remand*, 216 S.W.2d 824 (Tex. Civ. App. 1948); 62 Harv. L. Rev. 146 (1948);
27 Texas L. Rev. 349 (1949). *See also* Louisville Gas Co. v. Kentucky Heating Co., 111
S.W. 374 (Ky. 1908).

122.   254 U.S. 300, 309-10 (1920). In the interim the Court had sustained a New
York statute that in effect forbade the pumping of percolating, naturally carbonated
waters for the purpose of extracting and selling the gas, when the de-gassed water
was then wasted. Lindsley v. Natural Carbonic Gas Co., 220 U.S. 61, 77 (1911).

123.   254 U.S. at 309-10.

124.   *Id.*

125.   *Id.* at 310-11, 323.

126.   *Id.*, stating that the case fell within that licit category of state regulation to
prohibit an extravagant, wasteful or disproportionate use of natural gas that had
previously been approved in Ohio Oil Co. v. Indiana, 177 U.S. 190 (1900), and
Lindsley v. Natural Carbonic Gas Co., 220 U.S. 61 (1911).

127.   254 U.S. at 323-25.

128.   *Id.* at 321. Midland's facilities were built to be portable, raising the spectre
of a peripatetic carbon black company moving about the state, depleting gas fields
as it went.

129.   *Id.* at 324. The Court also acknowledged that the *Ohio Oil Co.* case had
likewise contained tacit recognition that a state could by statute give preference to
the long term use of natural gas as a heat source over its short term use as an energy
source to raise oil, and thus inferentially over the heat potential of the oil thus
raised. *Id.*

130.   Because of the particularized nature of the resource uses pursued by the
Ohio Oil Co. and Midland Carbon Co., the legislative preferment of the fuel value
of the gas resource apparently forced the companies out of the business of using the
gas for their chosen purposes. Thus most of the value of their specialized on-site
production facilities was destroyed. By contrast, the other gas producers were protected
in their extraction of the gas as a fuel resource, and they retained full and perhaps
enhanced use of their production facilities. The legislative preferment of one use
of a common pool resource was thus an inevitable preferment of the established
expectations and investment of one user group over those of another. The preferment
may have been rational, beneficial and economically efficient, but these facts are not
responsive to the question, "Why shouldn't the losers in such situations be compensated?" This problem is explored extensively in Sax I; Michelman, *supra* note 6, at 1193-
1201, 1236-44; and Sax II, where variations on the issue are raised.

131.   *See* pp. 53-57 *supra*.

132.   *See* pp. 58-66 *supra*.

133.   *See* pp. 66-67 *supra*.

134.   The classic example is Miller v. Schoene, 276 U.S. 272 (1928), in which one
farmer's cedar trees, which served as host for but were not harmed by cedar rust,
were ordered destroyed, essentially without compensation, to prevent destruction of
nearby apple orchards from communication of the rust.

135.   Sax II at 151-61.

136. *Id.* at 151-61, 167-71; *see* pp. 41-44 *supra.*

137. *See* pp. 39-41 *supra.*

138. *See* pp. 39-46, 48-50 *supra.*

139. *See generally* 1 R. MYERS §§ 1.02, 8.01

140. *Id. See generally* 5 W. SUMMERS, THE LAW OF OIL AND GAS § 951 (1966) [hereinafter cited as W. SUMMERS]; 6 H. WILLIAMS & C. MEYERS §§ 902-07, 923-24. The basic structure was approved in Patterson v. Stanolind Oil & Gas Co., 305 U.S. 376 (1939).

Interestingly, from a development rights perspective, the first pooling acts were municipal ordinances, passed and upheld as exercises of the zoning power, by which municipalities sought to confine oil and gas wells to a density of one per city block, or less. *See* Marrs v. City of Oxford, 24 F.2d 541 (D. Kan. 1928), *aff'd,* 32 F.2d 134 (8th Cir.), *cert. denied,* 280 U.S. 573 (1929). The Oxford ordinance required that all lot owners within the block be allowed to participate in the proceeds of production on a ratable basis, and in direct effect made the right to develop oil and gas a transferable development right within a market place defined as one city block. 24 F.2d at 544. The ordinances were held valid as a legal curbing of nuisances, 24 F.2d at 546-47; 32 F.2d at 139-40, and as adjusting and protecting correlative rights. 24 F.2d at 548-49, 32 F.2d at 140. *See also* Adkins v. City of West Frankfort, 51 F. Supp. 532 (E.D. Ill. 1943) (ordinance generally upheld, but invalidated because of provision imposing absolute liability on operator regardless of legal liability for any harm caused); Tysco Oil Co. v. Railroad Comm'n, 12 F. Supp. 195 (S.D. Tex. 1935); Sovereign Oil Corp. v. Fenton, 114 P.2d 18 (Cal. Ct. App. 1941); Thompson v. Johnson-Kemnitz Drilling Co., 145 P.2d 422 (Okla. 1943).

141. *See generally* 5 W. SUMMERS § 951; 6 H. WILLIAMS & C. MEYERS §§ 902-07, 923, 925.

142. *See generally* 1R. MYERS §§ 1.01(6)-(7); 6 H. WILLIAMS & C. MEYERS §§ 970; 7 *id.* 14-16, 474-75; Comment, *Proration in Texas: Conservation or Confiscation?,* 11 Sw. L.J. 186 (1957). The simplest method to allocate production among various tracts is one based upon surface acreage. *See, e.g.,* Humble Oil & Ref. Co. v. Welborn, 62 So. 2d 211 (Miss. 1953), and statutes reviewed therein. This formula is perhaps too simple to reflect accurately the variations in richness and recoverability of oil and gas deposits over a field. Frequently, therefore, complex formulae are used in an attempt to reflect two or more factors. In Woody v. State Corporation Comm'n, 265 P.2d 1102 (Okla. 1954), the court upheld a formula that allocated 50% of production on a per-acreage basis, and 50% of production on the basis of the saturated hydrocarbon pore space underlying various tracts. Obviously the allocation might have been made on a 60/40 or even 90/10 basis. Where all tracts have previously been developed, allocation may be based on records of prior production. Commissioner v. Belridge Oil Co., 27 T.C. 1044, *aff'd,* 267 F.2d 291 (9th Cir. 1959). There are some reported instances of formulae that are designed to change after a certain amount of production has been obtained, so that some parties receive a larger share of early production (*e.g.,* first one million barrels), and a smaller share thereafter, *see, e.g.,* Kingwood Oil Co. v. Bell, 244 F.2d 115 (7th Cir. 1957). Extremely imaginative approaches to such formulae are often taken when either pooling or unitization is being accomplished by private contract between several producers. State regulatory agencies may have some latitude to use multiple factors in formulae, *see, e.g.,* Humble Oil & Ref. Co. v. Welborn, 62 So. 2d 211 (Miss. 1953); Woody v. State Corporation Comm'n, *supra,* but agency orders must finally mesh with the general and specific statutory criteria under which the agencies operate. *See, e.g.,* Continental Oil Co. v. Oil Conservation Comm'n, 373 P.2d 809 (N.M. 1962) (agency order invalid as lacking factual base required by statute). For a discussion of the possibility of allocating development rights using complex formulae such as the ones discussed here, see pp. 100-01 *infra.*

143. This process, known as "recycling," is described in 1 H. WILLIAMS & C. MEYERS § 104. Water produced from wells may also be recycled. *Id.*

144. *See, e.g.,* Union Pac. R.R. v. Oil & Gas Conservation Comm'n, 284 P.2d 242 (Colo. 1955), in which the Colorado regulatory agency, not having power to order unitization, apparently sought to force it nonetheless by ordering that gas produced with the oil from a particular reservoir must be returned to the reservoir and in effect must be recycled. The order was stricken down as ultra vires, but unitization would undoubtedly have followed had it been upheld.

145. For examples of secondary recovery operations pursued without unitization. see Tidewater Oil Co. v. Jackson, 320 F.2d 157 (10th Cir. 1963), and Railroad Comm'n v. Manziel, 361 S.W.2d 560 (Tex. 1962). Such situations arise when owners of sufficient tracts decide to pursue secondary recovery operations within their extensive landholdings, operating some of their wells for injection and some for recovery. For a description of difficulties that holdouts caused to an attempted unitization program, see Prutzman, Fletcher, Miller, Cage, Keith & Winn, *Chronicle of Creating a Fieldwide Unit,* in SOUTH-WESTERN LEGAL FOUNDATION, FIFTH NATIONAL INSTITUTE FOR PETROLEUM LANDMEN 77, 126-27 (1964), *cited in* 6 H. WILLIAMS & C. MEYERS § 910, at 88-89. *See generally* 6 H. WILLIAMS & C. MEYERS §§ 901, 905, 912.

146. The potential benefit of such operations is illustrated in Western Gulf Oil Co. v. Superior Oil Co., 206 P.2d 944, 946 (Cal. Ct. App. 1949), in which it was estimated that recycling would yield 61 million barrels (valued at more than $166 million) more than could be expected from conventional production. Despite this fact, defendants in that action successfully resisted plaintiff's efforts to coerce them into the recycling activities by litigation, there being no compulsory unitization statute available. *Id.* at 952.

Cases such as the above illustrate the difficulties of achieving voluntary unitization, even when it seems an act of financial insanity to resist it, although the possibility of exorbitant exactions by nonparticipating holdout owners always lurks in the background of such cases. Despite such difficulties, the major treatises recount numerous examples of voluntary unitization and give samples of the legal documents by which such agreements are governed. *See generally* 1 R. MYERS §§ 2.06, 3.01, 4, 6.01, 8.02; 5 W. SUMMERS §§ 952-53, 955-72; 6 H. WILLIAMS & C. MEYERS §§ 904, 910-11, 921, 938.

147. Railroad Comm'n rule 37, November 26, 1919, as amended, was upheld in Brown v. Humble Oil & Ref. Co., 83 S.W.2d 935, *rehearing denied,* 87 S.W.2d 1069 (Tex. 1935). For a summary history of the rule, see Hardwicke, *Oil-Well Spacing Regulations & Protection of Property Rights in Texas,* 31 TEXAS L. REV. 99 (1952). The rule has spawned much litigation and commentary. *See generally* H. WILLIAMS, R. MAXWELL & C. MEYERS, CASES AND MATERIALS ON THE LAW OF OIL AND GAS 640-82 (1964).

148. *See* Panhandle E. Pipe Line Co. v. Isaacson, 255 F.2d 669 (10th Cir. 1958); Patterson v. Stanolind Oil & Gas Co., 77 P.2d 83 (Okla. 1938), *appeal dismissed,* 305 U.S. 376 (1939). For compendious listings of the state statutes and discussions of their impact, see 1 R. MYERS §§ 6.01, 8.01; 5 W. SUMMERS §§ 1000-51; 6 H. WILLIAMS & C. MEYERS §§ 905.1-.2, 934.

149. *See* Bandini Petroleum Co. v. Superior Court, 284 U.S. 8, 21-22 (1931).

150. Champlin Ref. Co. v. Corporation Comm'n, 286 U.S. 210, 226-28 (1932).

151. *Id.* at 233.

152. *Id.* at 226-30.

154. *Id.* at 223-26; OKLA. STAT. ANN. tit. 52, § 273 (1969).

155. 286 U.S. at 232-35; *see* Williams v. Standard Oil Co., 278 U.S. 235 (1929).

156. 286 U.S. at 233-34. Other Supreme Court decisions further expanded the scope of regulations for gas and oil allocation. *See, e.g.,* Railroad Comm'n v. Rowan & Nichols Oil Co., 310 U.S. 573 (1940); Hunter Co. v. McHugh, 11 So. 2d 495 (La. 1942), *appeal dismissed,* 320 U.S. 222 (1943). *But cf.* Thompson v. Consolidated Gas Utilities Co., 300 U.S. 55 (1937).

157. *See generally* 1 R. MYERS §§ 1.02, 8.01, 8.02.

158. OKLA. STAT. ANN. tit. 52, §§ 286.1-.17 (1969). The law's validity was upheld in Palmer Oil Corp. v. Phillips Petroleum Co., 231 P.2d 997 (Okla. 1951), *appeal dismissed sub nom.* Palmer Oil Corp. v. Amerada Petroleum Corp., 343 U.S. 390 (1952).

159. For compilations of state statutes, see 1 R. Myers §§ 6.01-.07, 8.02; 2 *id.* §§ 15.11-.17; 5 W. Summers §§ 1000-51, 1053 (the last section contains excerpts from a useful report describing the implementation and frequency of use of the statutes in various states, based upon reports issued by state governors in the mid-1960's); 6 H. Williams & C. Meyers §§ 911-12, 934.

160. *See generally* 1 R. Myers §§ 8.01, 9; 6 H. Williams & C. Meyers §§ 905, 940-48.

161. The problem of the non-contributing co-owner may be caused by the co-owner's financial inability to contribute his share, or a financially able co-owner may for a variety of reasons prefer that his fellow owners use their money and none of his in what he may regard as a speculative drilling venture. Typical statutes that immunize a non-contributing co-owner from a ratable share of the expenses of drilling a dry well provide that the ratable share of his expense may only be deducted from production actually achieved by a well. *See, e.g.,* Colo. Rev. Stat. Ann. § 100-6-4 (1963). Similar state statutes are cited in 6 H. Williams & C. Meyers § 905.2.

162. *See* 6 H. Williams & C. Meyers § 905.2; pp 92-93 *infra.*

163. *See generally* 1 R. Myers §§ 8.02, 9; 6 H. Williams & C. Meyers §§ 912-13, 940-48.

164. *See* note 146 *supra;* 39 Can. B. Rev. 275, 282-83 (1961), discussing litigation over a quarter section of Canadian land that overlay $5,000,000 of oil and gas. Devotees of *The Beverly Hillbillies* will need no substantiating citations.

165. To this point there has been no discussion of the formidable complexity into which the ownership interests in oil and gas are customarily subdivided, but now there will be limited discussion in order to clarify the text. Typically, a property owner does not himself develop oil and gas, but leases the minerals to an operator for development. The customary lease is for a primary term of a few years, with a provision for indefinite extension as long as oil and gas production may last. Most leases contain various provisions to prod the lessee (often called the "operator") to explore for and develop the oil and gas. The lease usually provides that the owner will receive a royalty of one-eighth of all oil and gas produced, free and clear of production costs, which the lessee bears. *See generally* 1 H. Williams & C. Meyers § 202. Prior to granting a lease, the landowner does not ordinarily expect to undertake actual physical development of the oil and gas but does expect to determine when and if these resources will be developed, who the lessee will be and what provisions the lease will contain. These latter expectations are the ones that may be very substantially affected by pooling or unitization. Assume that lands owned by *A*, *B* and *C*, are included within a pooled unit, that *A* has leased his oil and gas to *AL* (lessee of *A*), that *B* had leased to *BL* and that *C* has not leased his lands. Assume that *AL* has been designated unit operator and expects to begin development promptly. A very sketchy delineation of the impact on the rights of the parties would be the following: *A*'s lessee continues as operator, but under duty to conduct operations with the interests of all parties in mind. 6 H. Williams & C. Meyers §§ 990-92. *B* and *BL* are relegated to the sidelines, with some limited voice in, and the ability to seek review of, administrative orders and the operating decisions made by *AL*. *Id.* §§ 941, 946, 948, 950-57, 976, 990-92. *C*, presently without a lessee, might become an operator by contributing to well-drilling costs, but if he does not wish to do this, he may be forced to become a lessor of *AL*. *See* Anderson v. Corporation Comm'n, 327 P.2d 699 (Okla. 1957). He otherwise enjoys the same limited decision-making and the appeal rights as *B* and *BL*.

Unitization frequently involves many tracts and consequently causes the extreme diminution of an owner's control over his resources. Although his right to seek review is preserved, he has become only one among many owners who participate in the development decisions that are eventually made. *See generally* 6 H. Williams & C. Meyers §§ 948, 976. A significant exception exists if the statute being used is the type that allows dissident owners to avoid participating in a unitization program for the lands that surround them. In this case, the rights of the non-unitized holdouts must be protected, often with considerable reduction in the total effectiveness of the unitization plan. *Id.* §§ 934, 937. Further, not all states have compulsory unitization statutes. Texas being a notable example.

166. *See* note 165 *supra.*

167. Anderson v. Corporation Comm'n, 327 P.2d 699 (Okla. 1957).

168. Panhandle E. Pipe Line Co. v. Isaacson, 255 F.2d 669 (10th Cir. 1958); Clovis v. Pacific Northwest Pipeline Corp., 345 P.2d 729 (Colo. 1959).

169. West Edmond Hunton Lime Unit v. Stanolind Oil & Gas Co., 193 F.2d 818 (10th Cir. 1951), *cert. denied,* 343 U.S. 920 (1952). It is not uncommon for several oil-rich strata to exist at varying depths underneath a tract, like the layers of frosting in a layer cake. A well may then be completed to produce from two or more strata simultaneously. If only one stratum is unitized, the well owner may wish to continue production from the non-unitized stratum that is also being tapped by his well. Permission to do so was denied in the principal case, and the unit operators were allowed to close down production from the non-unitized stratum.

170. *See, e.g.,* Jones Oil Co. v. Corporation Comm'n, 382 P.2d 751 (Okla.), *cert. denied,* 375 U.S. 931 (1963); Chenoweth v. Pan American Petroleum Corp., 382 P.2d 743 (Okla. 1963); note 142 *supra.*

171. For an exhaustive analysis of myriad further consequences, see 1 R. MYERS §§ 10, 13, 14; 6 H. WILLIAMS & C. MEYERS §§ 950-64, 980-84.

172. *See generally* notes 109-12 *supra.*

173. An alternative proposition is that most of the oil and gas regulations examined might have been sustained solely on the basis that they protected correlative rights, without the admixture of the public interest justification. Either proposition elicits the same response—it is difficult to delineate the fracture line between protecting correlative rights and protecting broader public interests. To the extent that distinct "public interest" components exist in the oil and gas regulatory systems examined, they often seem to consist of an extension of policies that give generalized protection to correlative rights. If this be so, it may be traced to the process by which correlative rights are defined.

The doctrine of correlative rights has no inherent normative content. Until some benchmarks of permissible resource use or individual entitlement are supplied, the lowest common denominator of individual greed seems a perfectly appropriate operative norm. Once this standard is rejected as unsatisfactory, however, it is difficult to imagine any substitute norm that is not conducive toward long-term public interests, if these are defined in terms of resource conservation. "Public interest" itself must of course be fleshed in with substantive content, not an inconsiderable problem.

One authority has suggested:

[T]he correlative rights of owners in a common source of [oil and gas] supply include: (1) the right against waste of extracted substances, (2) the right against spoilage of the common source of supply, (3) the right against malicious depletion of the common source of supply, (4) the right to a fair opportunity to extract oil or gas.

Kuntz, *Correlative Rights in Oil and Gas,* 30 MISS. L.J. 1, 2 (1958).

The standards are incomplete, however. They lack any solid referents in terms of acceptable uses, production processes and consumptive rates for the common resource. These referents must be supplied by the courts, the legislature or perhaps by consensus among the owners involved. The referents, in the form of standards or rules, will then comprise the substantive content of the correlative rights of the owners. However supplied, and whatever their substantive content, the rules governing the exercise of correlative rights inevitably have a highly contextual aura about them. The context from which they derive and to which they must apply is that of numerous owners exercising rights in a resource. The owners in a sense constitute a mini-public. Specific regulation of their exercise of correlative rights is thus pro tanto "public" in its focus from the outset and simply cannot be shorn of this "public" content. Thus between regulations to adjust correlative rights and regulations that safeguard general "public" interest, there is a troublesome blurring of a commonly shared thrust toward resources conservation.

At the extreme ends of the regulatory spectrum, public interest and correlative rights may be in sharp conflict. Permitting the exercise of correlative rights by "flush" production would violate any public policies of resource conservation, whereas regulations to preserve the resource by forbidding its production would "adjust" correlative rights only in the sense of denying their exercise. Short of such extremes, it is clear that regulations frequently constrain the exercise of correlative rights much further than the owners would have done on a purely consensual basis. Also, some regulations are characterized by a special sensitivity toward correlative rights, as in Champlin Ref. Co. v. Corporation Comm'n, 286 U.S. 210 (1932). In that case, a simple prohibition against earthen storage and oil spillage would have prevented the major waste involved, but with considerable violence to the correlative rights of the nonpipelining operators, who would have subsequently been closed. Despite such instances, however, in the middle ground of moderate production regulation it seems that the furtherance of public interests and the generalized adjustment of correlative rights often tend to coincide considerably.

It is our thesis, of course, that the use of development rights would in comparable manner tend simultaneously toward the adjustment of correlative rights, which assertibly exist within, but are unaccounted for by, our present zoning system, and toward the furtherance of broad public interests in land use. See pp. 84-85 supra; pp. 104-06 infra.

174. See, e.g., Thompson v. Consolidated Gas Co., 300 U.S. 55 (1937) (statute not in furtherance of conservation interests or correlative rights); Continental Oil Co. v. Oil Conservation Comm'n, 373 P.2d 809 (N.M. 1962) (agency order invalid as lacking factual base required by statute). See generally 6 H. WILLIAMS & C. MEYERS § 948.

175. For discussion of tension and overlap between the protection of correlative rights and the furtherance of conservation interests, see note 174 supra.

176. See note 165 supra.

177. See, e.g., Railroad Comm'n v. Rowan & Nichols Oil Co., 310 U.S. 573 (1940). The Supreme Court there observed:

> The record is redolent with familiar dogmatic assertions by experts equally confident of contradictory contentions. These touch matters of geography and geology and physics and engineering. No less is there conflict in the evidence as to the solidity of respondent's apprehension that there will be drainage of the oil beneath its surface by neighboring wells. The Commission's experts insist that threat, if existent at all, is speculative, and that the Commission's power of continuous oversight is readily available for relief if real danger should arise in the future.
>
> Plainly these are not issues for our arbitrament.

Id. at 583.

178. The Supreme Court has stated:

> The state was confronted with its general problem of proration and with the special relation to it of the small tracts in the particular configuration of the East Texas field. It has chosen to meet these problems through the day-to-day exertions of a body specially entrusted with the task because presumably competent to deal with it. In striking the balances that have to be struck with the complicated and subtle factors that must enter into such judgments, the Commission has observed established procedure. If the history of proration is any guide, the present order is but one more item in a continuous series of adjustments. It is not for the federal courts to supplant the Commission's judgment even in the face of convincing proof that a different result would have been better.

Id. at 583-84.

179. *See* discussion and authorities cited at notes 87-96 and accompanying text *supra.*

180. *See* notes 110-29 and accompanying text *supra.*

181. *See* pp. 35-53 *supra.*

182. *See* notes 146 & 167 *supra.*

183. *See* pp. 92-93 *supra.*

British and Recent American Precedents

A Proposal for the Separation and Marketability of Development Rights as a Technique to Preserve Open Space

JEROME G. ROSE

Introduction: Alternate Techniques of Preserving Open Space

The history of American land-use policy has been a history of land *development*.[1] From the Northwest Ordinance of 1787 to the Homestead Act of 1862 to the large-scale FHA mortgage insurance programs in aid of home ownership after World War II, the objective of land-use policy has been the *development* of land to meet the shifting patterns of national migration. During the nineteenth century, opportunities for land ownership and development were used to encourage the migration to the Western states. During the last half of the nineteenth century, intensive land development was encouraged to provide for the aggregations of population in the cities. In the middle of the twentieth century, our land-use policy encouraged the development of land to create suburban communities around those cities. Currently a new migration of population appears to be emerging from metropolitan areas to nonmetropolitan areas in Vermont, Virginia, Colorado, California, Washington, and attractive regions of other states.[2] Encouraged by manufacturers of second homes, the recreation industry, the hotel-motel industry, the road-builders[3] and real estate industry, this migration may create a surge of demand for land deevlopment beyond the regulating ability of existing techniques of land-use control.

An examination of existing techniques of regulating land development to preserve open space is useful to determine the limits of effectiveness of those techniques.[4] Some techniques are in general use; others are proposals that have not been widely adopted. Considered together, the following constitute the current state of the art of open space preservation: (1) police power regulation (e.g. zoning and subdivision control); (2) compensable regulation; (3) public acquisition of the fee; and (4) public acquisition of less than the fee (e.g. conservation easements).

Police Power Regulation

Police power regulation is based upon the principle that, in a society governed by law, everyone must submit to reasonable regulation of his liberty and property to prevent the abuse of these rights by those who are unskillful, careless or unscrupulous.[5] The police power is exercised by the government "to promote and protect the health, safety, morals, comfort and general welfare of the people."[6] Based upon this power, states have delegated to local government the power to regulate the use of property and "to impair the owner's rights therein to some *reasonable extent* without compensation because the legislature, acting under the police power of the state, deems the free exercise of such rights detrimental to the public interests." [Emphasis added.][7]

The difficulty in relying upon the police power to preserve open space is the lack of objective standards for determining whether the property use restriction is reasonable under the circumstances.[8] In determining the reasonableness (and therefore the validity) of a land-use regulation, a court must weigh the evidence relating to the public interest and the rights of the property owner. As a result of this comparative evaluation, the court may determine that the public interest is so slight or the deprivation of the owner is so great that the regulation is unreasonable under the circumstances and therefore is invalid as a violation of substantive due process.[9] Based upon this reasoning, courts have held invalid zoning ordinances restricting land use to flood storage and open space,[10] parking lot purposes,[11] school and recreational use,[12] and greenbelt and park purposes.[13] Similarly, subdivision regulations have been held invalid, in spite of a substantial public interest, where the owner is denied reasonable use of his property.[14]

In *Morris County Land Improvement Co. v. Parsippany-Troy Hills Tp.*,[15] a leading case on the issue of zoning regulation for flood-detention purposes, the court conceded that the determination of whether the ordinance is a valid regulation or an invalid taking is always a matter of degree. It stated, however, that "there is no question that the line has been crossed when the purpose and practical effect of the regulation is to appropriate private property for a flood-water basin or open space."[16] The court stated that public *acquisition* (with compensation) rather than *regulation* (without compensation) was required to provide land for open space.

To the extent that this principle continues to be adopted by the courts, police-power regulation will not provide an effective technique for preserving open space.

Compensable Regulation

To overcome the constitutional objection to the harsh effect of depriving an owner of the use of his property restricted to open space purposes, Professors Jan Krasnowiecki and James Paul proposed a system by which owners would be compensated for part of their losses.[17] Under their proposal, an owner would be compensated for the loss of the development value of his property at the time the controls were imposed. For example, an owner of agricultural land with a market value of $1,000 before it is restricted to open space use would be entitled to compensation of $400 if the market value of his land is reduced to only $600 when restricted to agricultural or other open spaces use. The proposed compensation represents the development value of the property "taken" from the owner by the police-power restriction upon the use of his property. The owner would not be eligible for compensation until he sells the property because, until the sale, he would have not incurred any loss. To prevent fraudulent claims for excessive compensation, the proposal includes a requirement for an administratively controlled public sale.

The Krasnowiecki and Paul proposal is based upon a skillful and imaginative combination of the police power and the eminent domain power. The harshness of police-power restriction is softened by compensation for the loss of the development value. The high cost of acquisition under the eminent domain power is reduced by limiting the public cost to the development value at the time of regulation. In spite of these advantages, compensable regulation has not been utilized as an effective technique for preserving open space for a number of reasons. The primary reason is that the American public does not seem prepared to accept a program that denies a property owner the speculative value of his property; i.e., the value based upon the expectation, whether real or fancied, that the value will continue to increase with time. Secondly, the public and the legal profession are not sufficiently comfortable with the concept of development rights and are fearful of unknown consequences of the concept upon the real estate market. Thirdly, the proposal requires a relatively complex system of governmental administration that would tend to impede the alienability of property. Consequently, the effectiveness of compensable regulation as a technique for preserving open space remains untested.

Public Acquisition of the Fee

The power of the federal and state governments to acquire property for park and recreational purposes is well established.[18] A number of states, including New Jersey,[19] New York,[20] Massachusetts,[21] California,[22] and Wisconsin[23] have authorized state or local government acquisition of land for recreational, conservation, or open-space purposes. There is little doubt about the effectiveness of this technique to preserve open space—when it can be implemented. The primary impediment to the use of public acquisition of the fee is the lack of funds available for this purpose. Voter reluctance to approve programs or bond issues that will result in increased taxation is a serious obstacle. The numerous federal programs of financial assistance for local government acquisition of land[24] have not overcome this problem because the federal appropriations under these programs can fill only a very small portion of the need.

In addition to the lack of financial resources, there are other objections to the public acquisition of lands for open-space preservation: (1) When title is transferred from private to public ownership, the property is removed from the tax rolls and the remaining property owners in the jurisdiction must bear a proportionately larger share of the tax burden. (2) There exists in many areas of the nation strong political opposition to government ownership and management of land. (3) Many farmers and other landowners are unwilling to relinquish possession of their land even for a fair consideration. (4) Although preservation of open space is a commendable objective, the high costs of land acquisition would divert substantial public resources from other objectives of higher priority, such as education and housing. Taken together, these factors have created a formidable obstacle to the widespread use of public acquisition of land for open space preservation.

Public Acquisition of Less Than the Fee: Conservation Easements

In 1959, William H. Whyte, Jr. proposed a method of preserving open space by authorizing governments to acquire only the owner's right to develop the land, leaving him with all other rights of owner-ship, including the right of continued possession.[25] Whyte called this right a "conservation easement" because the purpose of its ac-quisition by government is to conserve the environmental amenities of land, air, soil, open space, and historic areas. After acquisition of the conservation easement by the government, the owner con-tinues to own and use his land, subject only to the right of the government to prevent its development. The easement runs with the land and binds all subsequent purchasers.

Public acquisition of the conservation easement rather than the fee simple (entire title) has a number of advantages: (1) The cost of acquisition of a conservation easement is less than the cost of the fee. The value of a conservation easement would be the difference between the value of the land without any restriction on development and the value of the land restricted to agricultural or other open space uses. Consequently, in rural areas, outside the in-fluence of demand for urban development, the conservation ease-ment could be acquired at very low cost. (2) There would be less opposition from farmers to the acquisition of conservation ease-ments because they would be able to remain in possession and use their land for farming purposes. (3) The land would remain on the tax rolls and, at the time of acquisition, would not impose any appreciable burden upon other property owners. The property tax would be imposed upon the assessed value of the land restricted to agricultural or open space use. Therefore, property taxes would not increase as development values rise and would not make the land too costly to maintain for farming purposes. As the demand for development in the area increases, the owners of developable land will reap the benefits of increased value and will pay taxes upon a higher assessed value.

In spite of these apparent advantages, public acquisition of con-servation easements has not been an effective technique of pre-serving open space. As one critic put it, "A policy of taking conservation easements is undesirable, potentially unfair, and legal-ly dangerous." [26] It has been argued that conservation easements are not effective where they are used to make significant changes in existing land use or where real estate speculation has affected the market value of the land.[27] Because of these difficulties, the National Park Service discontinued the acquisition of scenic ease-ments and reported: "On the basis of 20 years of experience, such easements breed misunderstandings, administrative difficulties, are difficult to enforce, and cost only a little less than the fee." [28]

Thus, it seems clear that each of the existing techniques of preserving open space has one or more serious limitations that makes it incapable of preventing the development of land in the amount and locations necessary to enhance the quality of life in metropolitan areas. New and imaginative techniques must be devised, refined, and perfected for this purpose. It is the thesis of this report that the separation and marketability of development rights may provide the legal instrumentality by which open space may be preserved in a manner that is consistent with constitutionally protected property rights and the realities of municipal finance.

Precedent for Transferability of Development Rights

The transfer of development rights as a means of controlling the use and development of land is not without precedent. Almost three decades of British experimentation in land-use control has been based upon this concept. In the United States, there are numerous illustrations of judicial recognition of its existence and sanction of its validity. Examination of these precedents will be useful to an understanding of the concept.

The British Experiment [29]

In the late 1930's and early 1940's, the British Parliament, concerned with the need to decentralize and disperse industries and industrial population, redevelop congested urban areas, and decrease the vulnerability of population and industry to air attack, created three committees to study and report on these problems and their solution. Extensive studies by these committees resulted in three now famous reports: (1) the *Barlow Report*,[30] (2) the *Uthwatt Report*,[31] and (3) the *Scott Report*.[32] Together, these reports proposed land-use planning on a national scale, recommended that private rights in land be subjected to the public welfare, and that the use of land by private owners be restricted to accomplish this objective.[33]

Of the three reports, the *Uthwatt Report* made the most significant contributions to the field of land use regulation in its conceptualization of the problem and its recommendations for solution. The Uthwatt Report defined and emphasized the importance of several new land-use concepts, including (1) *betterment* and (2) *floating value*.

Betterment is defined as an increase in the value of land that results when government undertakes public works or other improvements on adjacent or nearby land. This concept includes "the principle that persons whose property has clearly increased in market value by an improvement effected by local authorities should specially contribute to the cost of the improvement." [34] *Betterment charge* is the term describing the exaction by which government recoups this increment in market value.

Floating value is defined as the potential increase in value of all undeveloped land in an area. In the early stages of development of an area, it is practically impossible to predict with any certainty the exact parcels of land upon which the floating value will settle. However, public control of land use results in shifting of floating value from some land to other land.

After analyzing the nature and implications of these concepts the Uthwatt committee recommended, inter alia, that:

(1) A system be established to "recoup the betterment" from landowners who are "unjustly enriched" by increases in value of their land resulting from government action and to compensate landowners from whose land the "floating value" had been shifted by governmental action; and

(2) The rights of development in all land lying outside built-up areas (with certain exceptions) be vested immediately in the government and that fair compensation be paid for those rights. Thereafter the land could not be developed without the consent of the government and the repurchase of the development right.

The Uthwatt committee believed that these (and other) recommendations would achieve the benefits of government control of land use without government nationalization (i.e., ownership) of the land. The device proposed to accomplish this objective was the separation of the development right from the other rights of ownership of land and the transfer of that right to government.

Parliament adopted these recommendations in the Town and County Planning Act of 1947[35] (hereinafter called the 1947 Act). Under this law, the British government took over the development rights of all undeveloped land. This left the owners of land with all other rights of ownership, except the right to develop.[36] When an owner wanted to develop his land he had to buy back the right to develop from the government by paying a development charge.

The 1947 Act provides for compensation to landowners for the value of the development right at the time of the taking in 1947. The amount of the compensation was set at the value of the land in excess of "existing uses" as defined in the statute. A 300-million-pound revolving fund was created from which compensation would be paid and into which the betterment charges would be deposited.

In spite of the hopes and best intentions of planners and legislators, it is generally conceded that the system did not work well in practice,[37] primarily because owners "refused to develop their land or sell it for anything less than its full market value." [38] Buyers, who would have to pay a development charge in an amount equal to the difference between the current market value and the 1947 "existing-use" value would be willing to pay for land no more than the 1947 "existing-use" value. It soon became apparent that the price that sellers demanded and the price that developers could pay for land was so far apart that the marketability of land had been destroyed. Consequently, Parliament abolished the development charge in the Town and Country Planning Acts of 1953 and 1954.[39] This legislation did not return the development rights to the land owners. The law only eliminated the charge previously exacted for permission to develop. The development rights remained separated from the rest of the rights of land ownership.

Then in 1967, in an extremely intricate and complex[40] piece of legislation,[41] the development charge was reinstated at 40 percent of the development value (not unlike our capital gains tax) and remained in effect until 1971 when it was abolished once again.[42]

The British experience with development rights has been something less than a resounding success. The development rights are still separated from the balance of the title and have been retained by the British government. Thus far, the British have been unable to devise an effective system by which the separation and marketability of development rights may be used as a land use control device.

American Experience

American experience with development rights transfer is less specific, more diverse, less systematized, and more recent than the British. Nevertheless, the development rights transfer concept has been used in the United States in the following programs: (1) eminent domain acquisition of less than a full fee; (2) landmark preservation transfer of FAR rights; (3) incentive zoning transfer of FAR bonuses.

Eminent Domain Acquisition of Less Than the Fee

There are both judicial and legislative precedents for government acquisition of less-than-the-fee simple.[43] One of the original proponents of government acquisition of less-than-the-fee simple used the phrase "conservation easement" to describe the part of the title acquired by government.[44] The use of the word easement to describe this legal right was an unfortunate choice of nomenclature because of numerous technical common law restrictions on easements. For example, there are the following common law principles: (1) The law will not recognize the creation of new kinds of easements.[45] (2) The benefits of easements are generally not assignable.[46] Where assignable may not be separated from the land benefited therefrom.[47] In spite of these common law rules, American courts have recognized the right of government agencies to acquire less than the full fee under varied circumstances. For example, the Minnesota Supreme Court upheld the "taking" of the right to build certain classes of buildings in areas where such restriction was necessary to assure a fit and harmonious surrounding for residential use.[48] In California, a court upheld the condemnation of the right of joint use of utility line poles. The court conceded that there was no precise legal designation for the right being acquired but said that, wherever a substantial right of use exists, that right is subject to the power of eminent domain.[49] In New York, a court upheld the condemnation of interests in strips of land next to a highway that left the owner of the fee with little more than the right to use the land for ornamental courtyards only. The court held that the city could limit its taking to only that legal interest required to meet the public need.[50]

The legislatures of several states have begun to recognize the advantage of acquiring interests in land less than the full fee. The New Jersey Green Acres Land Acquisition Act of 1961 provides:

"Without limitation of the definition of 'lands' herein, the commissioner may acquire, or approve grants to assist a local unit to acquire . . . (b) an interest or right consisting, in whole or in part, of a *restriction on the use* of land by others including owners of other interests therein. . . ."[51] [Emphasis added.]

Notice that the New Jersey statute describes the right to be taken in negative terms, i.e., authorization is granted to acquire a "restriction on the use of land." This self-conscious discomfort with the concept also appears, but to a lesser extent, in the wording of the California statute:

"Any county or city may acquire, by purchase, gift, grant, devise, lease or otherwise, and through the expenditure of public funds, the fee, *or any lesser interest or right* in real property in order to preserve, *through limitation of their future use,* open spaces and areas for public use and enjoyment." [52] [Emphasis added.]

On the other hand, authors of the Vermont statute seem to have overcome any insecurity with this new concept and have expressly recognized development rights in their eminent domain enabling legislation:

"The legislative body of a municipality or a department, as the case may be, shall determine the types of rights and interests in real property to be acquired, including licenses, equitable servitudes, profits, rights under covenants, easements, *development rights,* or any other rights and interests in real property of whatever character." [53] [Emphasis added.]

As American planners and attorneys became familiar with the concept of the transferability of development rights, they began to experiment with techniques by which the concept may be used as a land-use control device. This effort has moved in two directions to date: (1) preservation of landmarks and (2) incentive or bonus zoning.

Transfers of FAR Rights to Preserve Historic Landmarks

One student of urban affairs has compared urban landmarks to the ocelot and the snow leopard because all are "imperiled species." [54] Attempts to preserve urban landmarks by police-power prohibition of their demolition have been held to violate the constitutional protection against unreasonable deprivation of property.[55] On the other hand, municipal resources are chronically insufficient to fund the acquisition of urban landmarks through the eminent domain power. This dilemma has provided the incentive for some cities, including New York City and Chicago, to experiment with the transfer of development rights as a means of preserving urban landmarks.[56]

The New York City ordinance provides:

"The City Planning Commission may permit *development rights* to be transferred to adjacent lots from lots occupied by landmark buildings . . . and may permit in the case of residential developments or enlargements, the minimum required open space or the minimum lot area per room to be reduced on the basis of such transfer of development rights." [57] [Emphasis added.]

The New York City transfer of development rights system is based upon the fact that the value of real estate in many parts of the city depends upon the intensity of development permitted under the zoning law and the fact that urban landmarks usually have an excess of authorized but unbuilt floor area under the floor area ratio (FAR) provisions. The FAR is a zoning technique to regulate the physical volume (density) of a building by controlling the relation between the floor area of a building and the area of the lot on which the building stands.[58]

Expressed as a formula:

$$\text{FAR } (5) = \frac{\text{Floor Area } (50{,}000 \text{ sq. ft.})}{\text{Lot Area } \quad (10{,}000 \text{ sq. ft.})}$$

Thus, a building to be constructed in a zoning district with an FAR of five could have five times more floor space than lot area. Consequently, an owner of a lot of 10,000 square feet could build no more than 50,000 square feet of floor space. If that parcel happens to be in an area with sufficient economic demand for more intensive development, e.g., high-rise office construction, the owner would seek to find ways to increase the floor area of his proposed building. The New York City ordinance permits landmark owners to sell the authorized but unused floor area of their landmark site to adjacent lotowners. Consequently, the owner of an adjacent lot may purchase the unused floor area from the landmark owner. The consideration for this transfer of development rights compensates the landmark owner for preserving the landmark. Once the landmark owner transfers the development rights (i.e., authorized but unused floor area), the incentive to demolish the landmark is reduced because of the limited floor area authorization still remaining for use on the landmark site.

The New York City system of development right transfer has been neither widely used nor successful in preserving the city's landmarks.[59] The Chicago ordinance seeks to improve upon this system by a more ambitious and comprehensive program. Under the Chicago plan:[60] (1) Transfers of development rights are not limited to adjacent properties. Transfers are permitted to any property within specially created development rights transfer districts. (2) An attempt is made to compensate the landmark owner for the actual cost of preserving the landmark structure, including the right to transfer up to 100 percent of the FAR, and real estate tax reduction and special municipal subsidies, where necessary. Nevertheless, the primary incentive in the transfer of development rights from one land owner to another. The Chicago plan stops short of a general bonus system for favored improvements.

Incentive (Bonus) Zoning

The logical extension of the New York City and Chicago programs, where development rights are transferred from one owner to another, is a general bonus system where an FAR bonus is created by the municipality. The City of San Francisco has adopted this system. Under the plan, the downtown is divided into four districts, each with a prescribed FAR. A builder may obtain a bonus of an increased FAR, within prescribed limits, by providing public benefits such as: (1) improved accessibility (e.g., rapid transit access; rapid transit proximity; parking access); (2) improved pedestrian movement (e.g. multiple building entrances, sidewalk widening, shortening walking distances); (3) pedestrian amenities (e.g., a plaza); (4) light and air for streets (e.g., additional setbacks or low coverage on upper floors); or, (5) view enhancement (e.g., an observation deck).[61]

In a strict sense, the San Francisco plan and other programs of incentive zoning offering FAR bonuses are not examples of the transfer of development rights because a part of the fee is not separated from the title of one landowner and transferred to another landowner. Instead, the government, under its police power, artificially restricts development and then prescribes conditions under which those restrictions may be relaxed. On the other hand, the San Francisco plan is similar to the transfer of development rights system in that the right to develop is specifically singled out, among the other rights of ownership, and manipulated as a device to control land use. For this reason, awareness of the incentive bonus system, as well as the landmark preservation system and the British experiments is helpful in understanding the newer proposals to use the transfer and marketability of development rights as a means of preserving open space.

Proposed Legislation to Utilize Development Rights Marketability and Transfers to Preserve Open Space

The first legislative attempt to create a comprehensive system in which the marketability and transfer of development rights are used to regulate land use was introduced in the Maryland Senate in 1972 by State Senator William Goodman.[62] At the same time, in New Jersey, a committee made up of Rutgers University faculty and members of the New Jersey Department of Community Affairs were independently engaged in a similar project.[63] The provisions set forth below are excerpts, *with modifications* of the legislative proposal that emerged from that committee.[64] This draft does not purport to be a complete or final draft of a legislative proposal. It is designed primarily as a device to draw attention to the possibilities for the use of the concept and to the problems which require solution.

Summary of the Legislative Proposal[65]

The proposed legislation seeks to utilize the separability and transferability of development rights as the basis of a technique to induce owners of undeveloped land to preserve their land in open space. The owners of preserved open space are compensated for their deprivation of use by the sale of development rights to developers of other land in the jurisdiction. To make these sales possible, it is necessary to establish a system that creates a market for development rights in which owners of developable land must buy development rights from owners of preserved open space land as a prerequisite for development.

The legislation is designed to create such a market in the following manner:

(1) Each local government would prepare a land-use plan that specifies the percentage of remaining undeveloped land in the jurisdiction and that designates the land to remain undeveloped as preserved open space land. The land-use plan would also designate the land to be developed and would specify the uses to which the developable land may be put. A zoning law would be enacted or amended to implement this plan.

(2) The planning board of each local government would prescribe the number of development rights required for each housing unit to be developed. On the basis of this numerical assignment, the planning board would then compute the number of development rights required to develop the jurisdiction in accordance with the land-use plan. The local government would issue certificates of development rights (ownership of which would be recorded) in the exact amount so determined.

(3) Every owner of preserved open space land would receive certificates of development rights in an amount that represents the percentage of assessed value of his undeveloped land to the total assessed value of all undeveloped land in the jurisdiction.

(4) An owner of developable land, who desires to develop his land more intensively (e.g., apartments instead of single family residence) would have to buy additional development rights, on the open market, from those who have acquired such rights from either original distribution or subsequent purchase.

(5) Thus, owners of preserved open space would be able to sell their development rights to owners of developable land (or real estate brokers or speculators). In return for the compensation derived from this sale, owners of preserved open space land will have sold their rights to develop their land in the future. Their land will thus be preserved in open space and the owners will have been compensated without any capital costs to government.

(6) Development rights will be subject to ad valorem property taxation as a component of the total assessed value of the developable real property in the jurisdiction.

NOTES

[1] Two notable exceptions to this generalization are the Conservation Movement during the administration of Theodore Roosevelt and the Greenbelt Movement during the administration of Franklin D. Roosevelt.

[2] *See* Note, "Protection of Environmental Quality in Nonmetropolitan Regions By Limiting Development," 57 Iowa L. Rev. 126 (1971), particularly footnotes 4 to 14 for citations of articles describing this migration in different regions.

[3] *Id.* at 127.

[4] In general *see* Note, "Techniques for Preserving Open Spaces," 75 Harv. L. Rev. 1622 (1962); Eckert, "Acquisition of Development Rights: A Modern Land Use Tool," 23 U. Miami L. Rev. 347 (1969); Eveleth, "Appraisal of Techniques to Preserve Open Space," 9 Vill. L. Rev. 559 (1964); Beuscher, "Some Legal Aspects of Scenic Easement," 1 Land Use Controls 28 (1967); Krasnowiecki and Paul, "The Preservation of Open Space in Metropolitan Areas," 110 U. P. L. Rev. i79 (1961).

[5] Fruend, *The Police Power* (1904).

[6] La Salle Nat'l Bank v. Chicago, 5 Ill. 2d 344, 350, 125 N.E.2d 609, 612 (1955).

[7] Robinson v. Town Council of Narragansett, 60 R.I. 422, 434, 199 A. 308, 313 (1938).

[8] For a general discussion of this topic *see* Heyman & Gilhool, "The Constitutionality of Imposing Increased Community Costs on New Suburban Residents Through Subdivision Exaction," 73 Yale L.J. 119 (1964) Sax, "Takings and the Police Power," 74 Yale L.J. 36 (1964); Netherton, "Implementation of Land Use Policy; Police Powers vs. Eminent Domain," 3 Land and Water L. Rev. 33 (1968); Comment, "Control of Urban Sprawl or Securing Open Space: Regulation by Condemnation or Ordinance?" 50 Calif. L. Rev. 483 (1962).

[9] *See* Rose, *Legal Foundations of Urban Planning: Cases & Materials on Planning Law* 46 (1973).

[10] Morris County Land Improvement Co. v. Parsippany-Troy Hills Tp., 40 N.J. 539, 193 A.2d 232 (1963).

[11] Vernon Park Realty v. Mount Vernon, 307 N.Y. 493, 121 N.E.2d 517 (1954).

[12] City of Plainfield v. Borough of Middlesex, 69 N.Y. Super. 136, 173 A.2d 785 (L. Div. 1961).

[13] Greenhills Home Owners Corp. v. Village of Greenhills, 202 N.E.2d 192 (Ohio Ct. App. 1964), rev'd 5 Ohio St. 2d 207, 215 N.E.2d 403 (1965), *cert. denied* 385 U.S. 836 (1967); *see* Kusler, "Open Space Zoning: Valid Regulations or Invalid Taking," 57 Minn. L. Rev. 1 (1972).

[14] Baker v. Planning Board, 353 Mass. 141, 228 N.E. 831 (1967). (The court held that a planning board could not disapprove a subdivision plan so that the town could continue to use the owner's land as a water storage area.)

[15] Note 10 *supra*.

[16] *Id*. at 555.

[17] Krasnowiecki and Paul, note 4 *supra;* see also Krasnowiecki and Strong, "Compensable Regulations for Open Space," 29 Journal of the American Institute of Planners 87 (1963).

[18] Shoemaker v. United States, 147 U.S. 282 (1893).

[19] N.J. Stat. Ann. § 13:8A-1 (1961).

[20] N.Y. Conservation Law §§ 1-0701, 1-0708 (1960 *as amended* 1964).

[21] 1B Mass. Laws. Ann. Ch. 40 § 8(c) (1961).

[22] Calif. Gov't Code 12 §§ 6950-6954 (1959), § 7000 (1963).

[23] Wis. Stat. Ann. § 23.09(16).

[24] E.g., the Open Space Program in Title VII of the Housing Act of 1961, §§ 701-06, 42 U.S.C.A. §§ 1500-1500(e) (Supp. 1961); the Federal Land and Water Conservation Program, 16 U.S.C. §§ 4601-5 (Supp. V. 1970); the Cropland Adjustment Act, 7 U.S.C. § 1838 (1971); the Watershed Protection and Flood Prevention Act, 16 U.S.C. §§ 1001-09 (1964) *as amended* (Supp. V. 1970).

[25] Whyte, Securing Open Space For Urban America: Conservation Easements (Urban Land Inst. Tech. Bull. No. 36, 1959).

[26] N. Williams, Land Acquisition For Outdoor-Recreation—Analysis of Selected Legal Problems, 48 (U.S. Outdoor Recreation Resources Review Comm. Study Report No. 16, 1963).

[27] *Id*. at 45.

[28] H. R. Rep. No. 273, 87th Cong. 1st Sess. 1961, as cited in Eveleth, note 4 *supra*, at 566-567.

[29] American students of British land-use planning have observed and reported on developments in the British experiment in land-use planning over the years. The following, in chronological sequence, is a bibliography of those reports: D. Pooley, The Evolution of British Planning Legislation (Legislative Research Center, University of Michigan Law School, 1960);

Mandelker, "Notes from the English: Compensation in Town and Country Planning," 49 Calif. L. Rev. 699 (1961); D. Heap, An Outline of Planning Law (4th ed. 1963); D. Heap, Introducing the Land Commission Act (1967); Heap, "The Taxation of Development Value in Land: The English Bill for a Land Commission," Trends (ASPO 1967); Thomas, "Land Planning and Development Values in Postwar Britain," Trends (ASPO 1967); Garner, "Introduction to English Planning Law," 24 Okl. L. Rev. 457 (1971); Garner & Callies, "Planning Law in England the Wales and in the United States," 1 Anglo-American L. Rev. 434 (1972); Hagman, "Planning Blight, Participation and Just Compensation: Anglo-American Comparisons," 4 The Urban Lawyer 434 (1972); Moore, "Planning in Britain: The Changing Scene," 1972 Urban Law Annual 89.

30 Royal Commission on the Distribution of the Industrial Population, Report Cmd. No. 6153 (1940).

31 Expert Committee on Compensation and Betterment, Final Report, Cmd. No. 6386 (1942).

32 Committee on Land Utilization in Rural Area, Report Cmd. No. 6378 (1942).

33 *See* Pooley, *supra,* note 29 at 27.

34 House of Lords Paper (159) at 1894 quoted in the Uthwatt Report, ¶ 259 at 104; *see* Pooley, note 29 *supra,* at 17.

35 10 & 11 Geo. 6, c. 51.

36 "Indeed, after July 1, 1948, ownership of land carries with it nothing more than the bare right to go on using it for its existing purpose. The owner has no right to develop it, that is to say, has no right to build on it and no right to change its use." Heap, *An Outline of Planning Law* 12 (1963).

37 Town and Country Planning in Britain (Central Office of Information Reference Pamphlet No. 9, 1962).

38 Pooley, note 29 *supra,* at 84.

39 1 & 2 Eliz. 2, c.16; 2 & 3 Eliz. 2, c.72.

40 "I would be the last person to say I understand the Bill", a statement made by the Lord Chancellor on December 6, 1966 during the House of Lords debate on the Land Commission Bill, as cited in D. Heap, Introducing the Land Commission Act (1967).

41 Land Commission Act, 1967, c.1.

42 Land Commission (Dissolution) Act of 1971; see Moore, note 29 *supra,* at 91, 93.

43 Weissburg, "Legal Alternatives to Police Power: Condemnation and Purchase, Development Rights, Gifts," in *Open Space and The Law* (F. Herring ed. 1965); N. Williams, *Land Acquisition for Outdoor Recreation—Analysis of Selected Legal Problems* (U.S. Outdoor Recreation Resources Review Comm. Study Report No. 16, 1963).

44 Whyte, note 25 *supra.*

[45] Keppell v. Bailey, 2 Myl. & K. 517, 535, 39 Eng. Rept. 1042, 1049 (Ch. 1834).

[46] 2 American Law of Property §§ 8.78-8-83 (Casner ed. 1952).

[47] 2 American Law of Property supra at § 8.73; see Eveleth, note 4 supra, at 568 for additional authorities cited therein.

[48] See State ex rel. Twin City Bldg. & Inv. Co. v. Houghton, 144 Minn. 1, 174 N.W. 885 (1919), 176 N.E. 159 (1920).

[49] Sacramento Municipal Util. Dist. v. Pacific Gas & Elec. Co., 72 Cal. App. 2d 638, 165 P.2d 741 (Dist. Ct. App. 1946).

[50] In the Matter of the City of New York, 57 App. Div. 166, 68 N.Y. Supp. 196, aff'd. mem. 167 N.Y. 624, 60 N.E. 1108 (1901).

[51] N. J. Stat. Ann. § 13:8A-12 (1961).

[52] Cal. Gov't. Code § 6950.

[53] Vt. Stat. Ann. tit. 10, § 6303(b) (Supp. 1971).

[54] Costonis, "The Chicago Plan: Incentive Zoning and the Preservation of Urban Landmarks," 85 Harv. L. Rev. 574 (1972).

[55] See People ex rel. Marbro Corp. v. Ramsey, 28 Ill. App. 2d 252, 171 N.E. 246 (1960); In re Opinion of the Justices, 333 Mass. 773, 128 N.E.2d 557 (1955).

[56] See Costonis, note 54 supra; see also Note, "Development Rights Transfer in New York City," 82 Yale L. J. 338 (1972).

[57] New York City Zoning Ordinance, art. VII, ch. 4, §§ 74-79 (1971).

[58] For a more detailed discussion of the system, see Note, "Building Size, Shape and Placement Regulations: Bulk Control Zoning Reexamined," 60 Yale L. J. 506 (1951).

[59] For a discussion of the reasons for its failure see Costonis, supra, note 54 and Note, "Development Rights Transfer in New York City," note 56 supra.

[60] San Francisco Planning Code, §§ 122-122.4.

[61] See Sversky, "San Francisco: The Downtown Development Bonus System," and Ruth, "Economic Aspects of the San Francisco Zoning Ordinance Bonus System," both in The New Zoning: Legal Administrative and Economic Concepts and Techniques, N. Marcus & M. Grove, Eds. (1970).

[62] S. 254, Senate of Maryland; introduced, read first time and referred to the Committee on Economic Affairs, January, 1972.

[63] Members of this committee were: T. Airola, R. Binetsky, R. Ginman, T. Hall, J. Jager, T. Norman, E. Reoch and J. Rose.

[64] Many of the provisions set forth herein contain modifications made by this author and may not be in accord with the corresponding provisions in the final draft submitted by the committee. For a more detailed report of the work of this committee, see B. Chavooshian and T. Norman, Transfer of Development Rights; A New Concept in Land Use Management (Mimeo,

Leaflet No. 492, Cooperative Extension Service, Cook College, Rutgers University, 1973).

[65] *See* Rose, "Proposed Development Rights Legislation Can Change the Name of the Land Investment Game," 1 Real Estate L. J. 276 (1973).

III.
CURRENT
PROGRAMS
AND
PROPOSALS

As A Method of Preserving Landmarks
The Chicago Plan:
Transfers of Designated Districts

The Chicago Plan:
Incentive Zoning and the Preservation
of Urban Landmarks

JOHN J. COSTONIS
Professor of Law
University of Illinois

Present legal methods for preserving America's architectural landmarks are being shown to be only minimally effective in preserving landmarks located in high development sections of the nation's cities. Professor Costonis examines the economic and legal reasons for the ineffectiveness of these ordinances. He then proposes an alternative approach — the Chicago Plan — which promises to be a more effective solution to the landmark problem. After discussing in detail the features of the Plan, Professor Costonis goes on to examine and rebut the various legal challenges that might be brought against the Chicago Plan.

"[T]he issues really being raised concern the relationship of the city's past to its present, and what new construction gives a city in functional, societal and architectural, as well as economic, terms. Questions are being asked everywhere about institutional attitudes toward development objectives and the effect of rigid investment patterns. Ultimately, the problem is the quality of the urban environment and who is responsible for it."
— Ada Louise Huxtable [1]

URBAN landmarks merit recognition as an imperiled species alongside the ocelot and the snow leopard. Over fifty per cent of the 12,000 buildings listed in the Historic American Buildings Survey, commenced by the federal government in 1933, have since been razed.[2] The threat to the remainder continues undiminished as the recent loss of Chicago's Old Stock Exchange Building [3] and the precarious status of New York's Grand Central Terminal attest.[4] If this trend is not reversed, the nation at its bicentennial in 1976 will mourn the loss of an essential part of its architectural and cultural heritage rather than celebrate the visible evidence of its past.

The demise of so many cherished buildings is a peculiarly

American phenomenon. In part it reflects the national penchant for identifying change with progress, even at the cost of destroying the nation's links with its past. More fundamentally, however, it is the product of a system that vests the initiative for most urban development decisions in private property owners, whose choices, predictably enough, are shaped by the necessities of the real estate market. The stubborn reality underlying the landmarks dilemma is that landmark ownership in downtown areas of high land value is markedly less profitable than redevelopment of landmark sites. Hence there is an incessant trade-off — injurious to the urban environment — of buildings of unique architectural distinction for glass and steel towers that are crammed with as much rentable floor area as local zoning permits and as the market will absorb.

Over the last decade, American cities have adopted a variety of incentive zoning programs in a determined attempt to expand their leverage over private land use decisions.[5] By modifying the economics of downtown development, these programs encourage development decisions that would normally be precluded by the harsh realities of the marketplace. Where successful, they have enabled cities to channel development in accordance with municipally selected urban design policies. Although these programs differ widely among themselves, they are all premised upon a trade between the city and the developer. The city relaxes its zoning bulk restrictions,[6] thereby allowing the developer to build more profitably by including more rentable floor area in his project than the prevailing zoning otherwise permits. In return the developer must either provide a public amenity, such as a plaza, at his own expense or make a cash payment that will enable the city to finance the purchase of a public improvement.

How does the city derive the additional floor area that it allocates to the developer? If the city seeks an amenity, it simply creates the floor area *ex nihilo* and bestows it upon the developer as a so-called "zoning bonus." The amount of the bonus is calculated to equal or slightly to exceed in value the cost that the developer incurs in providing the amenity. The case is more complicated where the city seeks to retain buildings, such as landmarks, that enrich its character. Recognizing that these buildings often fail to exhaust the floor area authorized for their sites under local zoning, the city allows their owners to sell their unused floor area to developer-owners of other sites, a practice commonly referred to as the "transfer of development rights." The cash carrot that results, it is hoped, will induce owners of the "underimproved" sites to forego demolition of their buildings.

Zoning bonus programs have been enthusiastically received by private developers and by municipal governments.[7] The response to these programs in New York City, the nation's most innovative practitioner of incentive zoning,[8] is illustrative. Almost every major office or commercial development erected in Manhattan's central business district since adoption of the New York bonus provisions in 1961 has included bonus space.[9] The City has employed bonuses to enhance its Broadway theater,[10] Lincoln Center,[11] and Fifth Avenue retail [12] districts. It is currently banking upon bonuses to induce private developers to provide a coordinated network of physical facilities to service the traffic generated by its 10,000,000 square foot World Trade Center.[13] And it has even proposed that bonuses be enrolled in the effort to encourage the production of moderate and low income housing.[14]

Development rights transfer programs, on the other hand, have fared poorly. Again the New York experience is instructive. Although that city adopted a transfer program in 1968 [15] that was designed to preserve its landmark buildings, the program has not as yet figured in a single executed transaction.[16] A number of reasons account for its failure to win the confidence of landmark owners, real estate developers, and title insurers, as well as at least one member of the New York City Planning Commission.[17] Inadequate analysis of the economic burdens of landmark ownership and of the urban design consequences of development rights transfers have hampered the program. Onerous administrative controls of dubious necessity have dampened the enthusiasm of the private sector for the program. And wholly apart from the merits of the New York program itself has been the uneasiness of its prospective participants concerning the underlying legality of the transfer mechanism.

The object of this article is to offer a development rights transfer proposal, referred to herein as the Chicago Plan,[18] that will provide an effective foundation for municipal landmark preservation efforts. The article contains three sections. The first details the economic causes behind the grave attrition of America's urban landmarks and reviews the conventional legislative responses of the nation's cities to this threat. The second analyzes the use of development rights transfers to preserve urban landmarks, examining the structure and deficiencies of the New York transfer program and then the content of the Chicago Plan. The third addresses the issues that are likely to arise in a comprehensive legal challenge to the validity of the Chicago Plan.

I. The Problem: The Vanishing Urban Landmark

A. *Economics and Landmark Ownership*

The history of Chicago's Old Stock Exchange Building illustrates the economic vulnerability of urban landmarks. It was located in Chicago's Loop, an area in which most of the city's other architectural gems are concentrated and, ominously, an area of skyrocketing land values. Its height of thirteen stories exhausted less than one-third of the approximately forty-five stories authorized for its site under present zoning regulations. Hence, it realized a mere fraction of the rental income that a modern office tower would have returned if located on the same site. Its mechanical systems, interior space, and exterior walls were in need of substantial renovation. Even with refurbishing, moreover, the annual maintenance costs of the seventy-eight year old building would probably have exceeded those of its modern steel and glass competitors. Typical of other turn-of-the-century buildings, its interior space was carved up with courts, columns and other structural features that diminished its appeal to large corporate tenants.[19]

Chicago's zoning bonus program intensified the Exchange's vulnerability. Like the programs of other cities, it is intended to encourage the provision of plazas, arcades, and other amenities. By awarding enormous premiums for projects occupying a half block or more,[20] however, the program has brought development on small lots to a standstill, and hastened the amalgamation of existing smaller holdings into assemblages that can exploit the program to best advantage. Ironically, therefore, the Exchange was as much the victim of the city's own zoning regulations as of the speculative motives of the building's owners.[21]

If the Exchange's owners had been forced to maintain the Exchange as a landmark, they would thus have suffered several economic disadvantages. They would have been prevented from redeveloping the site or capitalizing on the site's premium value for assemblage purposes. Designation might also have precluded the owners from internal modernization of the Exchange that would have increased its return by increasing its operating efficiency. They would also have been unable to obtain mortgage financing on terms competitive with those extended to the owners of properties unencumbered by landmark designation. Finally, profitable operation of the landmark might have been eventually endangered as the building continued to age and the net income from operation progressively declined.[22]

B. Municipal Preservation Ordinances:
An Inadequate Response

In light of these factors, the conventional municipal ordinance [23] offers scant hope of achieving the preservation of threatened urban landmarks. The typical ordinance calls for the designation of individual landmarks, such as the Exchange, and of entire historic districts, such as New Orleans' Vieux Carré.[24] The ordinance enumerates the cultural, aesthetic, and historic criteria that the city landmark commission, often with the advice of the city planning commission, must take into account in proposing designation of individual buildings or historic districts.[25] Actual designation, however, generally rests with the legislative body.[26]

After designation, permits for demolition or significant alteration of individual landmarks or of buildings within historic districts require the approval of the landmarks commission.[27] If the commission withholds its consent, it then has a grace period [28] in which to devise a compromise plan acceptable to the landmark owner that will safeguard the structure. If the owner rejects the plan, some ordinances authorize the commission to deny the permit outright regardless of economic hardship [29] while others require approval in such cases.[30] In most cities, however, the landmark commission has no power after this grace period to stay the demolition or alteration of a landmark, but can only recommend that the legislature acquire or condemn the threatened building.[31]

These ordinances have proven useful in preserving both buildings that are within historic districts and landmarks that are outside of high land value areas. These structures usually hold little interest for speculators because they tend to be smaller, easily maintained residential structures located in low density zones. In fact, at times owners of buildings within historic districts will welcome designation for the prestige it lends to the neighborhood and for its beneficial impact upon land values there.[32] Few owners of these buildings litigate permit denials because the prospects for financial gain through demolition or alteration seldom offset the costs and delays of a legal challenge.[33]

The picture differs dramatically for landmarks located on downtown parcels. The gap between the income potential of these parcels as presently developed and as improved to their most profitable use is such that few owners — speculators or otherwise [34] — warmly embrace designation. The typical response of an owner who contemplates redeveloping his site is to force the city's hand by demanding that it either acquire the property outright or issue a demolition permit forthwith.[35]

The city's options when the gauntlet is thrown down are not enviable. Even those landmark commissions that have the power to deny a demolition or alteration permit are unlikely to do so. The constitutionality of provisions authorizing such denials is dubious;[36] moreover, political pressures from downtown developers make such an action by the commission improbable in many cities. On the other hand, condemnation is also unlikely.

Other demands of greater priority preclude most cities from expending the enormous sums required for the acquisition of downtown properties.[37] Nor would the city's costs end with acquisition. The building may require substantial refurbishing in addition to ordinary maintenance. Removing it from the municipal tax roll will deny the city not only the increased taxes that the proposed project would yield,[38] but also the taxes currently being returned by the landmark property. In addition, redevelopment of the landmark site with a modern structure may benefit the general economic health of the city by revitalizing an entire block or district.[39]

II. The Search for an Alternative Economic Framework: Landmark Preservation Through Development Rights Transfers

Conventional preservation ordinances have failed to safeguard urban landmarks because they ignore the economic realities that lie at the heart of the landmarks dilemma. Owners will not and cities cannot shoulder the full costs of preservation. Resolution of this dilemma requires enlarging the present economic framework to include other participants who will themselves assume a major share of these costs. The most obvious solution, of course, would be to spread the costs of preservation to all taxpayers within the city by a general levy. But political obstacles rule out this approach at the present time:[40] the corollary to the refusal of American cities to spend for preservation [41] is their unwillingness to tax for this purpose.

If preservation efforts are to have any chance of success, therefore, another basis of cost allocation must be found that does not threaten to drain the city's general revenues. New York City's effort to redistribute these costs through development rights transfers constitutes a giant step in this direction.[42] To date, however, that effort has not borne fruit. An examination of the reasons for its lack of success has given rise to the rather different transfer proposal discussed in this article. The following paragraphs summarize the New York transfer program, catalog its defects, and then turn to a detailed examination of the Chicago Plan.

A. Transfers Under the New York Zoning Resolution

New York landmark owners may transfer the authorized but unbuilt floor area of their landmarks to adjacent lots in certain districts within the city. The "authorized but unbuilt floor area" that may be transferred is determined by multiplying the lot area of a landmark by a factor, known as a floor area ratio (FAR), that differs for the city's various bulk districts.[43] From this product is subtracted the floor area already exhausted by the landmark. An adjacent lot is defined as one that is contiguous to or across a street or intersection from a landmark lot; it may also be one of a series of lots that connect with the landmark lot, provided that all of these lots are in single ownership. Although in most zones the floor area of the transferee lot may not be increased by more than twenty per cent above its authorized level, no limit is set for transferee lots in high density commercial zones. Transfers may be made to one or several lots until the excess floor area is exhausted. Once transferred, the excess floor area is irrevocably withdrawn from the authorized floor area of the landmark lot.

Procedures for obtaining approval of a proposed transfer are complex. First, the New York Landmark Commission must examine the plans for the development which will utilize the transferred development rights in order to determine whether the new development's materials, design, scale, and location are compatible with the landmark. The owners of the landmark and the transferee lot must then apply to the New York Planning Commission for preliminary approval of the transfer. Accompanying this application must be a site plan for both lots showing the proposed development of the adjoining lot, a program for continuing maintenance of the landmark, and a report of the Landmark Commission detailing the effect of the proposed transfer upon the landmark. The Planning Commission must then decide whether the transfer will have unduly detrimental effects on the occupants of buildings in the vicinity of the transferee lot and whether the proposed maintenance program will in fact result in preservation of the landmark. If the Planning Commission recommends approval, the application then goes to the Board of Estimate, which has final authority to grant or deny the application. The difficulties of obtaining transfer approval are further complicated by the power of the Planning Commission in certain instances to condition approval of the transfer upon provision of an amenity by the development rights purchaser; in these cases, the Planning Commission must approve the purchaser's submission for the amenity as well.

Despite the ingenuity evident in its conception, the New York initiative contains at least five drawbacks that have crippled its effectiveness as a vehicle for a comprehensive municipal preservation program. Heading the list is the absence of a rational incentive structure for inducing landowners to agree to preserve their landmarks. By limiting development rights transfers to adjacent lots, the program imposes severe restraints upon the potential market for these rights. Existing zoning in New York and other cities already permits developers to shift unused floor area to contiguous parcels.[44] Hence, the plan is useful only when a developer can be found who happens to own a lot located across a street or an intersection from a landmark or when a landmark owner who owns a series of lots that connect with the landmark lot desires to build on one or more of those lots. Under the plan, moreover, the market value of the rights is controlled wholly by the vagaries of construction activity within the immediate vicinity of the landmark. Thus, while the transfer of, for example, two hundred thousand square feet of floor space may command a premium if the landmark adjoins the site of a projected skyscraper, that space may be worthless if no construction is contemplated on the sites adjacent to the landmark. Nor does the plan offer a secure basis for predicting that the income received from the transfer of development rights in any given instance will equal or exceed rather than fall short of the economic burdens of landmark ownership. As pointed out earlier,[45] these burdens are attributable to a variety of factors in addition to the unused development potential of the landmark site. Physical and functional obsolescence, assemblage value, and impairment of mortgageability and feasibility of renovation are only some of these additional factors. In a limited number of instances, moreover, the landmark may already utilize virtually all of the floor area authorized for its site.[46] Finally, the New York plan fails to provide supplementary funding for those cases in which development rights sales do not promise full compensation.

The second weakness of the New York plan lies in its labyrinthine procedures governing the issuance of transfer permits. The maze of discretionary approvals based upon vague aesthetic, planning, and urban design criteria are hardly calculated to attract the voluntary participation of developers and landmark owners. These permits, moreover, are issued *after* formal designation has occurred. Yet the battle to safeguard threatened buildings of landmark quality is often lost at the designation stage itself. Owners of proposed landmarks typically oppose designation in response to their quite reasonable fears concerning its economic impact. Local governing bodies, too, have proven reluctant to designate buildings of unquestioned landmark status, as the Exchange debacle itself illustrates.[47] This reluctance may stem either from the potent political influence of downtown realtor and developer groups, who generally oppose meaningful preservation programs,[48] or from a concern for the eventual fiscal consequences that designation would entail for the city.[49] If approval of an equitable incentive package, including an appropriate transfer authorization, were included in the designation process, it seems likely that the resistance of landmark owners and local governing bodies would lessen.

A third difficulty with the plan is its reliance upon the voluntary participation of landmark owners. They may balk, because they question the legality of the plan or the marketability of the development rights, because they are developers who wish to proceed with redevelopment of the landmark site, or for any number of other reasons. Without their participation, of course, the prospects for preservation revert to their former unhappy state.

Fourth, it can be questioned whether the New York initiative adequately insures that the landmarks of participating landowners will in fact be preserved. Relying essentially upon the transfer of some or all of a landmark's floor area for this purpose is unnecessarily risky. Under the New York plan a landmark owner apparently retains the right to demolish his landmark and replace it with a building of equivalent bulk if he decides that redevelopment would be more profitable.[50] In addition, a subsequent increase in the FAR of the district in which the landmark is located would rekindle speculative interest in the property; by recreating the excess floor area that had previously been transferred, it would give the owner an incentive to replace his landmark with a larger structure. The New York plan also lacks a mechanism that precisely defines the obligations assumed by the present and future owners of the landmark in consequence of the transfer authorization and that affords the city an effective remedy for the breach of these obligations.

Finally, the adjacency limitation of the New York plan needlessly produces a number of unfortunate urban design consequences. First, mammoth concentrations of bulk within the compass of a block or less [51] might lead to an excessive demand for municipal services and to traffic congestion in the vicinity of the landmark. Second, a landmark building might be suffocated in adjacent superdensity, the visual enjoyment of a landmark being blotted out by the tall buildings around it. New York has responded to these risks by encasing development rights transfers in the straightjacket of administrative controls discussed above. But these controls have served only to deaden the enthusiasm of landmark owners and developers whose participation in the plan is absolutely essential to its success.

B. The Chicago Plan

1. An Overview. — The discussion of the plight of the Old Stock Exchange Building touched upon four characteristics that are fairly common among urban landmarks throughout the United

States. First, most utilize only a fraction of the floor area authorized for their sites under modern zoning. Second, most landmarks
are currently able to operate at a profit;[52] their imperilment
stems from the greater value of their land as the site of large
office or commercial structures.[53] Third, endangered landmarks
tend to be grouped in one or more reasonably compact areas of
the city, usually in high land value commercial and service districts. Finally, municipal facilities and supportive services are
also most heavily concentrated in these districts. This network
of public facilities and services enables these districts to absorb
large numbers of people with greater efficiency than other areas
of the city.

The Chicago Plan attempts to avoid the drawbacks of the
New York plan through recognition of these factors. Briefly,
the Plan would operate as follows. The city council, upon recommendation of the landmark and planning commissions, would
establish one or more "development rights transfer districts,"[54]
which would roughly coincide with the areas where downtown
landmarks are concentrated. Upon designation of his landmark
or at any time thereafter, the landmark owner would be entitled
to transfer its development rights to other lots within the transfer
district in which the landmark is located and to receive a real
estate tax reduction reflecting the reduced value of his property.
Transfers may be made to one or more transferee lots provided
that the constructive lot area of any transferee lot is not increased
by more than fifteen per cent.[55] Transfers would be subject to
additional planning controls set forth in the municipality's preservation ordinance. In return for this transfer authorization, the
owner would be required to convey to the city a "preservation
restriction," which would bind him and future owners of the
landmark to maintain it in accordance with reasonable standards
and to refrain from demolishing or altering it without the city's
permission.

Should a landmark owner reject the transfer option, the city
would step in and condemn a preservation restriction and the
landmark's development rights, though, in exceptional cases, the
city might choose to condemn the landmark property in fee. Acquisition costs and other expenses of the program would be funded
through a municipal "development rights bank." The bank would
be credited with development rights that have been condemned
from recalcitrant owners, rights donated by owners of other landmarks, and rights transferred from publicly owned landmarks.
The city would sell these pooled development rights as necessary
to meet program costs, subject to the same planning controls that
apply to private owners.

As outlined above, the Chicago Plan redistributes preservation costs equitably and realistically. Transfer authorizations — or cash awards, if the city is forced to condemn the property — and tax relief compensate the landmark owner for his losses. Eliminating the property's development potential by acquisition of the preservation restriction decreases the value of the site and extinguishes speculative interest in it. Landmarks will remain in private hands as vital commercial or office buildings instead of undergoing mummification as museums. Hence, the city avoids outlays for fee acquisition, restoration, and maintenance, and may continue to tax the landmark property, although at a lesser rate. Moreover, these tax losses will be more than offset by increased tax yields from the larger buildings authorized by the transferred development rights. And, in return for their financial contribution to the landmarks program, downtown developers receive full value in the form of governmental licenses to build larger structures than local zoning otherwise permits.

In addition to safeguarding threatened landmarks, the Chicago Plan promises to expedite downtown development generally by easing the difficulties of land assembly. Developers who have assembled all but a small fraction of a unified tract would be permitted to fill out the remainder by purchasing development rights from landmark owners or from the municipal development rights bank. This privilege would be subject, of course, to appropriate safeguards — again set out in advance in the preservation ordinance — concerning light, air and other design features of these projects. At the present time, developers often obtain bulk variances on spurious legal grounds [56] or spend months or years trying to acquire the additional strip needed to make their project economically feasible.[57]

2. The Elements of the Chicago Plan: A Closer Examination. — a. The Incentive Package. — Unlike the New York program, the Chicago Plan is designed to compensate the landmark owner for the actual losses that he suffers. Prior to proposing designation of a landmark, the landmark commission will obtain an appraisal of the property that details the economic consequences of designation. The appraisal will also enumerate any structural defects, restoration or rehabilitation problems, or unique maintenance problems that further intensify the burdens of private ownership. The commission will then devise a package to compensate the owner that will include an authorization to transfer up to one hundred per cent of the landmark's lot area and an appropriate real estate tax reduction. Transfers under the Chicago Plan will be measured in terms of lot area rather than floor area,[58] since the introduction of zoning bonuses and other complications into modern zoning codes makes lot area, rather than floor area, the factor that developers use to calculate the size and volume of projected developments.[59] An additional subsidy, funded out of the municipal development rights bank, may be included to cover losses not met by the package and to deal with special difficulties affecting the building.

The real estate tax reduction, an integral element of the Chicago Plan, should prove especially attractive to landmark owners.[60] The impact of a real estate tax reduction can be dramatic because real estate taxes are the largest single item in the cost of operating downtown buildings.[61] A study recently undertaken in Chicago, for example, concluded that a twenty-five per cent reduction in the assessed valuation of downtown office buildings would result in a tax saving equal to twice the average repairs and maintenance budget for such properties.[62] These savings alone will compensate the owners of many landmarks for their losses.[63] Since tax reductions under the Plan will be geared to the drop in appraised value that landmark properties suffer as a result of permanent designation, these reductions can be expected to equal or exceed the twenty-five per cent figure in a large number of instances.

b. Preservation Restriction. — Under the Chicago Plan, municipalities will obtain a preservation restriction in landmark properties except in the rare case when fairness requires that the city acquire a property in fee.[64] The advantages of less-than-fee acquisition are substantial. By this means, government limits its interference with private ownership, yet secures the preservation of landmarks. The latter continue in their original use or in an adaptive reuse that serves the space needs of the downtown area. The condemnation award will be reduced; maintenance and restoration costs are borne by the owner aided, in appropriate cases, by subsidies from the development rights bank; and the landmark property remains on the tax rolls.

Other advantages of preservation restrictions may also be cited. The preservation restriction enables landmark owners to qualify for federal [65] and state [66] income tax and local [67] real estate tax benefits that they might not otherwise enjoy. It also allows for more precise regulation of the obligations of landmark ownership. While these obligations can also be defined to some extent by general ordinance, as in New York, the interests of the city and the landmark owner are better served by an instrument that has been carefully tailored to take account of the peculiarities of individual properties. Finally, the preservation restriction offers accurate notice to mortgagees, purchasers, and other interested parties of the encumbrances attaching to the landmark property.[68]

c. The Development Rights Transfer District. — The adjacency restriction is a principal culprit in the failure of the New York initiative to win the support of the real estate industry and of landmark owners. It severely impairs the marketability of development rights. It scatters density throughout the city on the capricious principle of how closely proposed developments border on landmarks. And it necessitates burdensome design review procedures to insure that landmark buildings are not overwhelmed by adjacent behemoths.[69]

The Chicago Plan dispenses with the adjacency requirement by permitting transfers to any property within the development rights transfer district in which the landmark is located. This approach promises to avoid the economic and planning difficulties that have crippled the New York plan. The market for development rights under the Chicago Plan should prove more lucrative than the market under the New York plan on two counts. First, transfer districts are likely to encompass the high land value areas of the city since, as already noted,[70] threatened urban landmarks tend to be grouped in such areas. It can be assumed that municipalities will capitalize on this advantage in drawing the boundaries of their development rights transfer districts. Second, the marketability of development rights will not be dependent upon the vagaries of construction activity on sites immediately adjacent to landmarks. They will be governed instead by the general vigor of the construction and real estate markets in the particular municipality's central commercial and service areas.

The area-wide approach, as conceived under the Chicago Plan, also promises to minimize the undeniable risk of urban design abuse that attends any incentive zoning program. It will do so by means of controls that govern the establishment of development rights transfer districts and that regulate transfers that subsequently take place within these districts. Prior to recommending the establishment of any district, the municipal landmark and planning commissions will prepare a study of the area in question that inventories the number and type of prospective landmarks there; that estimates the amount of floor area — over and above that already authorized for the area under present zoning — that might be transferred upon designation of the landmarks; and that details the capacity of the area's public services and facilities to absorb this additional density. In addition, the planning commission will review the compatibility of the proposed district with the municipality's comprehensive plan and its detailed plan, if any, for the area. This study and the accompanying recommendation of the two agencies will provide the basis for the local governing body's decision to establish the district and to determine its boundaries.

Once established, transfer districts will be protected from undue concentrations of density in at least three respects. First, an upper bound on the amount of lot area that may be transferred within a district is fixed by the number of designated landmarks there. That number is not likely to be excessive in absolute terms: Chicago's architecturally-rich Loop area, for example, will probably have no more than thirty designated landmarks. Nor will all of the landmarks within a district incur substantial depreciation upon designation. Measured against the size of the district and its capacity to absorb density, therefore, the total amount of transferable density is likely to be marginal.[71]

Second, most if not all of the floor area that will be added to new projects under the Chicago Plan will already have been authorized by existing zoning. The main thrust of the Plan, therefore, is upon the redistribution of previously authorized floor area rather than upon the creation of wholly new floor area as in the case of zoning bonuses. Hence, the Plan will occasion little or no net increase in presently authorized density of the district.[72]

Third, the proposal envisages that transfers will be restricted to selected use and bulk districts — essentially high density commercial and apartment zones — within the development rights transfer district, and that no transferee site may be increased by more than fifteen per cent of its actual lot area. These limitations will further minimize the possibilities of urban design abuse. Preliminary indications are that the principal buyers of development rights will be developers of smaller interior lots in commercial zones that cannot practicably utilize zoning bonuses and of lots devoted to high-rise apartment developments.[73] Such shifts in density are unlikely to distort the cityscape within the transfer district. With the advent of the skyscraper and the absence of stringent height limitations, the American cityscape has assumed a distinctly irregular form best exemplified by the Manhattan skyline. Sprinkling an additional four to six stories on lots in these centrally located districts will make little difference in such a setting.[74]

d. *The Role of the Municipality.* — The municipality's role under the New York plan is both too little and too great. It is too little because the city must expend its own scarce revenues to safeguard threatened landmarks if the development rights carrot fails to entice landmark owners. And it is too great because the plan's labyrinth of discretionary approvals tends to discourage owners and developers from electing to participate in the program at all.

The Chicago Plan directly addresses both of these problems.

As to the first, it enables the municipality to finance a vigorous preservation program without dipping into general revenues. Sales of development rights from the municipal development rights bank should provide the financial basis for effective public intervention in whatever form individual cases may require.

Development rights credited to the bank will derive from three sources. The principle source will be landmark owners who decline the transfer option and insist that the city pay them a cash award for their losses.[75] The bank will receive an increment of lot area in such cases equal to the value of the award but in no event greater than one hundred per cent of the landmark site. A second source will be other landmark owners who donate lot area. That such donations will be forthcoming is highly probable in view of the tangible federal, state, and local tax benefits that donors will enjoy and, perhaps more importantly, in light of the central role that private philanthropy has traditionally played in the American preservation movement. The third will be the city itself, which is likely to own a fair number of the community's landmarks. The bank would be credited in the last two instances with increments of lot area proportional to the authorized but unbuilt floor area of the landmarks.

The lion's share of the city's preservation costs will be covered by the sale of condemned development rights. But additional funds will be necessary for subsidies and for the relatively infrequent cases in which the transfer authorization-tax reduction package fails to provide adequate compensation. Donated development rights and those provided by the city should provide an ample cushion in these cases.

The Plan also seeks to simplify the administrative procedures governing development rights transfer authorizations. The problem here is to strike a correct balance between preventing urban design abuse through proper planning controls and facilitating the marketability of development rights by freeing them of onerous restrictions. Under its program New York has little choice but to err on the side of the former. Because every transfer shifts bulk to a site adjacent to a landmark, its aesthetic impact on the landmark must be examined on an individualized basis and in terms of highly subjective criteria. Moreover, the New York program provides no assurance beforehand that the physical services and facilities in the landmark's immediate area will be able to absorb the additional density resulting from the transfer. This uncertainty, too, necessitates case-by-case review.

The Chicago Plan largely avoids both problems by permitting transfers throughout development rights transfer districts. Few, if any, transfers under the Plan will be to sites adjacent to landmarks because the number of potential transferee sites is vastly expanded and because most cities already permit such transfers as of right under conventional zoning provisions. Except in the rare cases when such transfers occur, therefore, no need for design review exists. Further, development rights transfer districts are selected expressly upon the basis of the capacity of their public services and facilities to absorb any increased density that may be allocated within them under the Plan. Preselecting the districts in this way also enables the city to dispense with case-by-case review. The remaining controls envisaged under the Plan, such as the limitations concerning bulk and use districts to which transfers may be made and the permitted increases in the size of transferee lots, will be set forth in advance in the preservation ordinance and need not, therefore, be administered on a discretionary basis. An additional advantage of the Chicago Plan is that it telescopes into a single proceeding the separate proceedings in New York. By this means, it will tend to reduce the resistance of owners and city councils to the formal designation of landmark buildings.[76]

   e. Implementation of the Chicago Plan. — The Chicago Plan employs zoning techniques to advance preservation objectives; thus it could be implemented either as a zoning or as a preservation measure. This choice will determine whether municipal authority to adopt the Plan should originate in state zoning or state preservation enabling legislation and whether the zoning or the preservation ordinance should be the primary tool for its implementation at the municipal level. It may also shape the relative influence of the local planning and landmark commissions in administering the Plan.

   The American Law Institute's Model Land Development Code [77] offers an ideal solution. Intended to serve as a comprehensive state enabling act to empower local communities to regulate land use and development, the Code treats zoning [78] and preservation [79] as two categories of this regulatory power. It thereby recognizes the close ties of technique and objective that zoning and preservation share,[80] but does not ignore their separate identities. It envisages adoption at the local level of a single Land Development Ordinance [81] to be administered by a single Land Development Agency.[82] Under this arrangement, the Plan could serve as one component of the Ordinance, which is intended to address a variety of land use concerns on a coordinated basis. "Ultimate responsibility" [83] for administering the Ordinance — and thus the Plan — would rest with the Agency, an entity that most resembles the municipal planning commission. But landmark commissions would likely play an influential role as well in view of the Code draftsmen's suggestion that the Agency "delegate the administration of historic and other special preservation regulations to specialized bodies expert in architecture and planning." [84]

The Code, unfortunately, is still adrafting, and resort must be had to a less satisfactory approach. Two alternatives are suggested by the existing legislative framework that governs zoning and preservation matters. First, the Plan might be treated essentially as a preservation undertaking: authority to adopt it would appear in the state preservation enabling act; its mechanics would be detailed in the local preservation ordinance; and its administration would be vested primarily in the municipal landmark commission. The second alternative, on the other hand, would emphasize the Plan's hybrid character by according an increased role to the state zoning enabling act and to the local zoning ordinance and planning commission.

The first of these routes was generally followed in Illinois.[85] That state's preservation enabling act was amended in 1971 to empower municipalities to implement all features of the Plan, including establishment of a development rights bank, acquisition of preservation restrictions and transfer of development rights.[86] As a precautionary measure, the "purposes" section of the state zoning enabling act was also revised to reflect that preservation of historic buildings is a proper objective of zoning.[87] Local communities will implement the Plan through their preservation ordinances,[88] but must revise the definition of "zoning lot" in their zoning ordinances to include the constructive lot area which owners are authorized to transfer under the Plan as well as actual lot area.[89] The respective responsibilities of the landmark and planning commissions assume the form outlined earlier in this article.[90]

The second approach has been chosen in New York. Provisions implementing the New York program appear in the city's zoning ordinance,[91] which assigns the dominant administrative role to the planning commission.[92] Since no amendatory legislation was sought at the state level, the city apparently concluded that its state zoning enabling act already empowered it to adopt these provisions.

Although either approach is workable, the Illinois route seems preferable because it permits coordinated treatment in a single statutory enactment of the property, condemnation, and land use features of the Plan. In addition, it recognizes that zoning and the regulation of individual landmarks are actually separable manifestations of the police power.[93]

NOTES

The author wishes to acknowledge the invaluable assistance of Messrs. Jared Shlaes and John F. Hartray, Jr., with respect to the economics and urban design elements of the study discussed in this paper. He also expresses his gratitude to the National Trust for Historic Preservation and the Chicago Chapter Foundation of the American Institute of Architects for their financial support in this endeavor. Of course, the author remains solely responsible for any inaccuracies or distortions that the study may contain.

[1] Huxtable, *Bank's Building Plan Sets Off Debate on 'Progress,'* N.Y. Times, Jan. 17, 1971, § 8, at 1, col. 2.

[2] *See* Conti, *Preserving the Past*, Wall St. J., Aug. 8, 1970, at 1, col. 1.

[3] The Old Stock Exchange Building was the work of Louis Sullivan and Dankmar Adler, two of the most accomplished practitioners of the internationally renowned Chicago School of Architecture. A precursor of the modern skyscraper, it has been favorably compared with the great palaces of Renaissance Italy in terms of its historic import. *See* Huxtable, *The Chicago Style — On Its Way Out?*, N.Y. Times, Nov. 29, 1970, § 2, at 27, col. 1. The Chicago Landmark Commission, on two separate occasions during the period 1970–71, urged that the Exchange be accorded formal landmark status, but the Chicago City Council on both occasions refused to accept the Commission's recommendation. A permit for the building's demolition was issued in October 1971. *See* Huxtable, *Non-Fables for Our Time*, N.Y. Times, Nov. 14, 1971, § 2, at 22, col. 4.

[4] The New York Central Railroad, as owner of the site of the Grand Central Terminal, sought in the early sixties to lease the air rights over the Terminal to a developer who intended to erect a second Pan-Am type building there. The New York City Landmarks Commission, however, refused to approve the project on the ground of its aesthetic incompatibility with the facade of the Terminal, a designated landmark. The New York Central responded by threatening to overturn the Commission's action in the courts, but bankruptcy of its successor company, the Penn Central Company, and the softening of the New York City office space market have relieved the pressure on the Terminal, at least for the time being. *See* Address by Norman Marcus, First Conference on Legal Techniques in Preservation, in Washington, D.C., May 2, 1970 (sponsored by National Trust for Historic Preservation) [hereinafter cited as Marcus].

[5] *See* THE NEW ZONING: LEGAL, ADMINISTRATIVE, AND ECONOMIC CONCEPTS AND TECHNIQUES 125–238 (N. Marcus & M. Groves eds. 1970) [hereinafter cited as NEW ZONING]; Comment, *Bonus or Incentive Zoning — Legal Implications*, 21 SYR. L. REV. 895 (1970); *cf.* URBAN LAND INSTITUTE, NEW APPROACHES TO RESIDENTIAL LAND DEVELOPMENT: A STUDY OF CONCEPTS AND INNOVATIONS (Tech. Bull. No. 40, 1961).

[6] Some communities might also relax use and tower coverage requirements and coordinate variance procedures for the miscellaneous minor adjustments that are necessitated by the grant of incerased floor area. *Cf.* Svirsky, *San Francisco: The Downtown Development Bonus System*, in NEW ZONING 139, 142–43.

[7] *But see* note 229 *infra*.

[8] For a review of the various incentive zoning programs that have been adopted or considered in New York City, see Burks, *City Wants Air Rights to Hop, Skip and Jump*, N.Y. Times, Apr. 26, 1970, § 8, at 1, col. 1; Gilbert, *Saving Landmarks*, HIST. PRESERVATION July–Sept. 1970, at 13; Marcus.

[9] NEW ZONING 201.

[10] NEW YORK, N.Y., ZONING RESOLUTION art. VII, ch. 1, § 81–00 *et seq.* (1971). This provision creates a Special Theater District that includes the area

between 40th and 57th Streets and 6th and 8th Avenues. Developers owning parcels within the District who agree to include a legitimate theater in their projects may receive an increase of up to 20 per cent in the floor area authorized for their parcels under prevailing zoning. *See* Weinstein, *How New York's Zoning Was Changed to Induce the Construction of Legitimate Theaters,* in NEW ZONING 131. Plans for the construction of five theaters pursuant to the provision have been announced. *See* N.Y. Times, May 19, 1970, at 39, col. 2.

[11] NEW YORK, N.Y., ZONING RESOLUTION art. VIII, ch. 2, § 82-00 *et seq.* (1971).

[12] NEW YORK, N.Y., ZONING RESOLUTION art. VIII, ch. 7, § 87-00 *et. seq.* (1971). This provision created a Fifth Avenue Retail District encompassing Fifth Avenue between 38th and 59th Streets. It mandates that the two lower floors of any building constructed within the District be used for retail purposes. Developers who elect to provide more than the minimum retail space will be given additional floor area to be used for apartments or hotel accommodations.

[13] NEW YORK, N.Y., ZONING RESOLUTION art. VIII, ch. 6, § 86-00 *et seq.* (1971), creates a Special Greenwich Street Development District encompassing a 29 square block area between the World Trade Center and Battery Park. The District regulations include a map and a manual which prescribe a firm area network of circulation features consisting of open and covered arcades, pedestrian bridges, subway connections, elevated plazas, and the like. Developers building within the District will be required to provide some of these features and may elect to provide others. In return for these features and for payment of sums into a subway improvement fund, developers will receive increases in the floor area authorized for their lots and may also be allowed to build towers that cover a greater amount of lot area than the zoning would otherwise permit.

The District differs in two respects from New York's existing special districts. First, the desired features have been previously mapped so that every lot owner knows beforehand which mandatory and optional features he must or may provide in return for the increased floor area. Second, the area plan is so specific and the schedule of bonuses so precise that developers need not negotiate with the Planning Department, submit their development plans for site and design review, or secure a special permit, all of which are a part of the approval procedure under the regulations applicable to the other districts. *See* N.Y. Times, Dec. 6, 1970, § 8, at 1, col. 1. *See also* Huxtable, *Concept Points to 'City of the Future,'* N.Y. Times, Dec. 6, 1970, § 8, at 1, col. 3.

[14] The New York Planning Commission proposed the establishment of a Special Development District on New York's Lower East Side that would contain 2,355 apartments, of which 1,837 would be luxury class and 418, low income class. Developers were to be given the option either of providing 15 per cent of the units in their buildings for low income rental or of paying $15.30 per square foot of the lot area of their parcels into a special fund to be used to acquire public housing sites. They would have received an additional floor area authorization in return. But the proposal appears to have died as a result of opposition of community residents who saw it as a "give-away" to developers and as a disguised means of displacing low income persons in the area. *See* N.Y. Times, May 13, 1970, at 40, col. 1.

[15] *See* N.Y. Times, Oct. 7, 1969, at 34, col. 4; NEW YORK, N.Y., ZONING RESOLUTION art. VII, ch. 4, §§ 74-79, 74-791 to -793 (1971).

[16] One transfer has almost taken place. All of the formalities relating to the transfer of the excess floor area of the Amster Yard, a designated landmark, have been completed, but the transaction has been stalled by the softening of the New York office space market. *See* Huxtable, *City Landmark Gets a Chance for Survival,* N.Y. Times, Aug. 2, 1970, § 8, at 1, col. 1; Marcus.

[17] *See* p. 628 *infra.*

[18] Prior to the demolition of Chicago's Old Stock Exchange Building, the National Trust for Historic Preservation and the Chicago Chapter Foundation of the American Institute of Architects commissioned the author and Jared Shlaes, a real estate consultant, to devise a transfer proposal that would safeguard the Exchange and Chicago's remaining architectural landmarks. The product of this study appeared as a report entitled Development Rights Transfers: A Solution to Chicago's Landmarks Dilemma (Chicago Chapter Foundation of the American Institute of Architects & National Trust for Historic Preservation, May 13, 1971) [hereinafter cited as Chicago Report]. The Chicago Report contains a summary legal and economic analysis of the proposal discussed in this article. It also includes draft amendments to the Illinois Historic Preservation and Zoning Enabling Acts and to the Chicago Zoning Code that would permit implementation of the proposal. See Chicago Report apps. I, II & III. The proposed amendments to the state legislation have since been adopted. See Ill. Pub. A. No. 77–1373 (Ill. Leg. Serv., Aug. 31, 1971), amending ILL. REV. STAT. ch. 24, § 11–13–1 (1969); Ill. Pub. A. No. 77–1372 (Ill. Leg. Serv., Aug. 31, 1971), in part to be codified at ILL. REV. STAT. ch. 24, § 11–48.2–1A, in part amending ILL. REV. STAT. ch. 24, § 11–48.2–2 & –6 (1969).

[19] The competitive disadvantages suffered by urban landmarks should not be overstated, however. A review of income and operating expense data for Chicago office buildings revealed that, while maintenance-related expenses

> do tend to increase with the age of the building, [they] do not increase at such a rate as to impose unreasonable burdens upon older buildings as such.
> . . . .
> It is not apparent from national averages that buildings over 40 years old suffer from any striking competitive disadvantage; indeed, they net more per square foot than buildings 25–40 years old on a national basis, perhaps because of special characteristics of buildings constructed during the depression and war years 1930–45. Net income before depreciation and capital charges for buildings over 40 years old is approximately 78% of the national average for all buildings but tends to approach $1.60 per square foot, indicating that these older buildings, while somewhat penalized by their age, are by no means functionally obsolete.

Chicago Report 21. See E. SHULTZ & W. SIMMONS, OFFICES IN THE SKY 88 (1959) [hereinafter cited as OFFICES].

[20] An example serves to illustrate the extent of these bonuses. CHICAGO, ILL., MUNICIPAL CODE, ZONING ORDINANCE ch. 194A, art. 8.5–6(5)(c) (1970) provides:

> On any zoning lot, for each floor above the ground floor which is set back from one or more lot lines, a premium equal to 0.4 times the open area of the lot at the level of such floor divided by the gross lot area may be added to the permissible floor area ratio . . . .

The "floor area ratio" (FAR) is an integer prescribed by the ordinance for each bulk district, which, when multiplied by the area of the zoning lot, gives the amount of floor area that may be included in a building erected on that lot. Thus, if the district FAR is 10, the maximum floor space of a building erected on a 10,000 square foot lot is 100,000 square feet. However, if the developer of this 10,000 square foot site decided to leave 50% of his lot open when he constructed a building upon it, he would be entitled under the above-quoted provision to 140,000 square feet of floor space. He would receive a premium of 0.4 times 0.5 times the number of initial floors he was entitled to build (0.4 x 0.5 x 20), bringing the FAR to 14. While the above-quoted provision theoretically has equal application to large and small lots, in practice only large projects can benefit from it. There is little economic advantage in building tall buildings with a small base since too much of the space on each floor is devoted to nonrentable uses, such as elevator and support constructions.

[21] See note 229 infra.

[22] The economic consequences of designation are not entirely negative. Its

prestige factor could operate to attract stable, high quality tenants and to reinforce pride of ownership which would be reflected in the marketplace. *See Hearings Before the Commission on Chicago Architectural and Historical Landmarks Concerning the Designation of the Monadnock Building as an Official Chicago Landmark* 90 (Apr. 1970) (on file with the Commission on Chicago Historic and Architectural Landmarks). Moreover, designation makes space in a landmark attractive to tenants who wish to avoid relocation and other vagaries of the development process.

[23] State and local landmarks legislation and programs are reviewed in J. MORRISON, HISTORIC PRESERVATION LAW (1965); J. PYKE, LANDMARK PRESERVATION (Citizens Union Research Foundation, Inc., 1970); Wilson, *The Response of State Legislation to Historic Preservation*, 36 LAW & CONTEMP. PROB. No. 3 (to be published); Wolfe, *Conservation of Historic Buildings and Areas — Legal Techniques*, in 2 ABA SECTION ON REAL PROP., PROBATE, & TRUST LAW PROCEEDINGS 18 (1963); Note, *The Police Power, Eminent Domain and the Preservation of Historic Property*, 63 COLUM. L. REV. 708 (1963); Note, *The Landmark Problem in New York*, 22 N.Y.U. INTRAMURAL L. REV. 99 (1967); Comment, *Landmark Preservation Laws: Compensation for Temporary Taking*, 35 U. CHI. L. REV. 362 (1968).

[24] *See, e.g.*, CHICAGO, ILL., MUNICIPAL CODE § 21-64(a) (1970); Mobile, Ala., Ordinance 87-036, Mar. 20, 1962; NEW ORLEANS, LA., CODE § 65-6 (1956).

[25] *See, e.g.*, CHICAGO, ILL., MUNICIPAL CODE § 21-64(b) (1970); NEW YORK, N.Y., ADMIN. CODE ANN. ch. 8-A, § 207-1.0h & k (1971).

[26] *See, e.g.*, CHICAGO, ILL., MUNICIPAL CODE § 21-64(f) (1970). The New York ordinance allows the Landmark Commission to designate landmarks; its decision, however, may be overridden or modified by the Board of Estimate. *See* NEW YORK, N.Y., ADMIN. CODE ANN. ch. 8-A, § 207-2.0f(2) (1971).

[27] *See, e.g.*, CHICAGO, ILL., MUNICIPAL CODE § 21-64.1 (1970); NEW YORK, N.Y., ADMIN. CODE ANN. ch. 8-A, §§ 207-4.0 to -8.0 (1971); CHARLESTON, S.C., CODE §§ 51-28 to -30 (1966).

[28] The usual period is 180 days. *See, e.g.*, Mobile, Ala., Ordinance 87-036, Mar. 20, 1962 (6 months); CHARLESTON, S.C., CODE § 51-30(4) (1966). *But see* Los Angeles, Cal., Ordinance 121,971, Apr. 30, 1962 (up to 360 days).

[29] *See, e.g.*, NEW ORLEANS, LA., CODE § 65-10 (1956); CHARLESTON, S. C., CODE § 51-30 (1966).

[30] *See, e.g.*, Mobile, Ala., Ordinance 87-036, Mar. 20, 1962.

The New York City Landmarks Ordinance contains a unique provision that authorizes outright denial of a permit for alteration or demolition in the case of designated landmarks whose owners either receive state or local tax relief or obtain a "reasonable return" — identified as a 6% return on the assessed valuation of the property. NEW YORK, N.Y., ADMIN. CODE ANN. ch. 8-A, §§ 207-1.0q, 207-8.0 (1971). By setting the return at this relatively low rate, *see* Comment, *The Landmark Problem in New York, supra* note 23, at 107, and requiring the landmark owner to come forward with rather precise evidence establishing the economic burden entailed by designation, the ordinance enables the city's Landmark Commission to exert considerably greater leverage in dealing with landmark owners than commissions in other cities enjoy.

[31] *See, e.g.*, CHICAGO, ILL., MUNICIPAL CODE § 21-64.2 (1970); CHARLESTON, S.C., CODE § 51-30(7) (1966).

[32] *See, e.g.*, N.Y. Times, May 27, 1970, at 35, col. 3; Chicago Sun-Times, Oct. 22, 1970, at 3, col. 2.

[33] In 1970, the author surveyed preservation agencies in 12 representative cities to obtain their appraisals of the efficacy of their ordinances. The agencies were generally enthusiastic about their success in administering historic districts, but

many suggested that nonlegal factors, such as those mentioned in the text, accounted for their success.

The agencies were far less sanguine about their efforts in safeguarding individual landmarks. All noted that their city governments assigned a relatively low priority to historic preservation, especially if the latter necessitated the expenditure of general revenues. Few instances of the use of eminent domain or the purchase of threatened properties on behalf of these agencies were reported. Although at least four of the cities are authorized by state law to accord real estate tax abatement to official landmarks, moreover, only one city was actually doing so.

[34] The stakes are so high where downtown properties are concerned that even those institutions that want to "do the right thing," such as museums, churches and service organizations, also balk at designation. *See The Chicago Style*, note 3 *supra*.

[35] The position of the Building Managers of Chicago (BMA) is representative of the views of most downtown building owners and managers in the United States. In the BMA's view:

> [W]e can see no way to accomplish [the preservation of urban landmarks] unless the City, State or Federal Government purchase the property in question, spend large amounts of money toward rehabilitation and be [*sic*] prepared to operate the property, possibly at a loss.
>
> . . . .
> . . . [T]he more we study the subject . . . the more we are convinced that the only solution is for a Government agency to purchase the building and maintain it. The willingness of some Government agency to purchase should be ascertained *before* proceedings are instituted to designate a building as a landmark so as to avoid unnecessary harm to the owner.

Letter from Richard M. Palmer, President, BMA, to Samuel A. Lichtmann, Chairman, Commission on Chicago Historical and Architectural Landmarks, Aug. 6, 1970. For similar views in New York, see N.Y. Times, May 27, 1970, at 35, col. 3; N.Y. Times, Apr. 29, 1970, at 27, col. 3.

[36] Courts have consistently held that landmark preservation statutes may not impose undue economic hardships on landmark owners, and that in cases of undue economic hardship the city must either acquire the building or permit its demolition. *See, e.g.*, People *ex rel.* Marbro Corp. v. Ramsey, 28 Ill. App. 2d 252, 171 N.E. 246 (1960); *In re* Opinion of the Justices, 333 Mass. 773, 128 N.E.2d 557 (1955); *cf.* note 93 *infra*. Thus, the imposition of permanent landmark status on a building that is currently unprofitable seems clearly unconstitutional. On the other hand, the constitutionality of ordinances such as New York's, *see* note 30 *supra*, that do allow permanent designation if the landmark is returning a net profit of 6% of assessed valuation is less clear. While "undue economic hardship" is perhaps not normally thought to apply to ownership of buildings that return a profit, it is certainly arguable that in cases where the landmark owner is forced by designation to forego a vastly more profitable sale of his site the foregone opportunity constitutes such a hardship. *See* Comment, *The Landmark Problem in New York*, *supra* note 23, at 104.

> [37] The Committee feels that the aesthetic value of the Old Stock Exchange Building does not exceed the relative cost and, in this day of demand to meet urgent financial needs in other areas, the City of Chicago cannot afford the luxury of a building as a landmark that, though it may be treasured for historic value and architectural originality, is too far deteriorated to warrant the cost of rehabilitation. The Committee is confident that the people of the City of Chicago would want better application of their tax dollars for we are convinced of a resultant dollar deficiency if rehabilitation were attempted — the building would become known as Chicago's White Elephant.

Committee on Cultural and Economic Development, Special Report Relative to Designation of the Old Stock Exchange Building 6 (August 1970) (advising the

Chicago City Council to reject the Landmark Commission's recommendation that the Old Stock Exchange be designated).

[38] The differences between the taxes presently received on the Old Stock Exchange and a new 45-story tower on its site, for example, are estimated at $640,000 per year. *See* Conti, *supra* note 2.

[39] Lewis Hill, Commissioner of the Chicago Planning Department and a member of the Landmark Commission, voted against designation of the Old Stock Exchange on the ground that:

> It remains my judgment that the designation of this building will not contribute to the strengthening of LaSalle Street as the great economic center of the mid-west.

Letter from Lewis W. Hill to Samuel A. Lichtmann, Chairman, Commission on Chicago Historical and Architectural Landmarks, March 17, 1971.

[40] *See* note 33 *supra*.

[41] *See id*; cf. Elliot, *Introduction* to NEW ZONING at xv (cities lack capital required to maintain or enhance amenity level of urban areas).

[42] NEW YORK, N.Y., ZONING RESOLUTION art. VII, ch. 4, §§ 74–79, 74–791 to –793 (1971). The discussion in the following two paragraphs of the text is based on the provisions of these statutes.

[43] For a detailed evaluation of the FAR system, see OFFICES 280–82; Note, *Building Size, Shape, and Placement Regulations: Bulk Control Zoning Reexamined*, 60 YALE L.J. 506 (1951).

[44] The New York Zoning Resolution defines the term "zoning lot" to include the following:

> (c) A tract of land, located within a single *block*, which at the time of filing for a building permit . . . is designated by its owner or developer as a tract all of which is to be used, *developed,* or built upon as a unit under single ownership. A zoning lot, therefore, may or may not coincide with a lot as shown on the official tax maps of the City of New York or on any recorded subdivision plat or deed.
> For the purposes of this definition, ownership of a *zoning lot* shall be deemed to include a lease of not less than 50 years duration, with an option to renew such lease so as to provide a total lease of not less than 75 years duration.

NEW YORK, N.Y., ZONING RESOLUTION art. I, ch. 2, § 12–10 (1971). *See* CHICAGO, ILL., MUNICIPAL CODE, ZONING ORDINANCE ch. 194A, art. 3.2 (1970). Under these provisions a developer may increase the authorized floor area on the project site by obtaining a long-term lease on an underimproved or vacant adjacent site, designating both that site and the project site as a single "zoning lot," and shifting the unused floor area from the former to the latter.

One hundred thousand square feet of excess floor area authorized for the site of the Appellate Division Courthouse, a New York landmark, were transferred to an adjacent project site pursuant to § 12–10 and without the aid of § 74–79, the landmark transfer provision, which, at the time of the transaction, was not applicable to publicly owned landmarks. A developer, desiring to incorporate the additional floor area into his project on the adjacent site, leased the landmark property for a 50-year period with a 25-year renewal option, then subleased it back to the City reserving the 100,000 square feet of floor area. The operative clause of the lease provides:

> Section 4.01. (a) Tenant is hereby given the right, prior to or during the Demised Term, to combine the zoning lot of the Demised Premises with the zoning lot of the Adjoining Premises, so as to obtain a combined Floor Area Ratio . . . for the zoning lots of the Demised Premises and the Adjoining Premises; however, as a result of such combination of zoning lots, Tenant shall not obtain more than one hundred thousand (100,000) square feet of floor area from the zoning lot of the Demised Premises.

Lease between the City of New York and 41 Madison Company § 4.01(a), Apr.

10, 1970. *See* Sher, *'Air Rights' Lease, Zoning*, 164 N.Y.L.J. Oct. 9, 1970, at 1;
N.Y. Times, Apr. 16, 1970, at 34, col. 1. Sher notes that the method is "used
commonly by private developers." Sher, *supra*, at 2.

[45] *See* pp. 579–80 *supra*.

[46] An example is the Monadnock Building, Chicago's last and tallest skyscraper of masonry construction, which was designed by John Root.

[47] *See* note 3 *supra*.

[48] *See* note 35 *supra*.

[49] *See* pp. 583–84 & notes 37–39 *supra*.

[50] Mr. Frank Gilbert, Secretary of the New York Landmarks Preservation
Commission, suggests that development rights transfers would discourage but not
prohibit the destruction of the landmark:

> [W]hen completed, [a development rights transfer] reduces much of the
> economic pressure to tear down the landmark since it *could be replaced
> only by another building with the same amount of floor space.*

Gilbert, *supra* note 8, at 14 (emphasis added).

The absence of an express requirement that a landmark owner convey an
interest in the property obligating himself and future owners not to demolish or
alter the landmark also points in this direction. Either § 74–791, which calls for
a "program for . . . continuing maintenance," or § 74–793, which requires filing
at the county registry of "[n]otice of the restrictions upon further development"
of the landmark and transferee lots might be construed to include the conveyance
of a preservation restriction. NEW YORK, N.Y., ZONING RESOLUTION art. VII,
ch. 4, §§ 74–791, –793 (1971). But both are extremely vague. Significantly, no
such restriction was contemplated in the Amster Yard transaction, discussed in
note 16 *supra*.

[51] The magnitude of density is enormous in the case of certain New York
landmarks. For example, the excess development rights of the United States
Customs House are 789,800 square feet, an amount equal to the floor area of the
60-story Woolworth Building. *See* Burks, *supra* note 8, at 9, col. 5.

[52] *See* notes 19 & 22 *supra*.

[53] The impact of rising land values on existing downtown development has
been described as follows:

> In our big cities of a half million or more population, [the] demolition of
> older structures was made economically feasible by parabolic increases in
> land values. *As a matter of fact, there are very few parcels of land in our
> largest cities which have not had as many as three different structures on
> them in the last hundred years* . . . . Our megalopolitan cities have grown
> so fast, however, that we have seen 25-year periods . . . where the land
> value has increased so rapidly that it has become economic to demolish even
> a fairly new building in order to use the land more intensively — to exploit
> to its highest and best use the new land value created in a short span of time.

Nelson, *Appraisal of Air Rights*, 23 APPRAISAL J. 495 (1955) [hereinafter cited as
Air Rights] (emphasis added).

[54] A development rights transfer district should not be confused with the
traditional historic district referred to at p. 581 *supra*. Unlike the historic district, it serves as a marketing area for development rights and contains only
a small number of buildings of significant architectural or historic character in
relation to the total number of buildings within its boundaries. In addition, the
municipal landmark commission reviews only those applications for alteration or
demolition that relate to designated individual landmarks within a transfer district. In contrast, the commission engages in building permit review with respect
to all buildings within historic districts.

[55] The figure of 15% was concurred in by municipal planners and architects
in Chicago who viewed it as low enough to protect against the risk of urban design
abuse, but not so low as to deprive the plan of economic appeal for landmark

owners. Other cities may wish to increase or decrease this figure on the basis of their peculiar urban design needs and preferences.

[56] *See* authorities cited in note 201 *infra*.

[57] *See Air Rights* 497. The author is personally familiar with a number of land assemblies in Chicago that required from four to six years to complete.

[58] The Chicago Plan uses the same technique — combination of the lot area of the landmark and project sites — that was used in the Appellate Division Courthouse transaction. *See* note 44 *supra*. It does *not* entail the transfer of "air rights." The latter are a property interest in a three-dimensional location in space. Development rights, on the other hand, are simply a governmental license to build a defined amount of floor area as measured by the amount of lot area that has been constructively "transferred" to the project site.

[59] Another difference between the New York and Chicago Plans concerns the permanence of a development rights transfer. Transfers of development rights are "irrevocable" in New York. *See* NEW YORK, N.Y., ZONING RESOLUTION art. VII, ch. 4, § 74–792 (4) (1971). Under the transfer proposal, on the other hand, landmark owners may be authorized by the municipal landmark commission and city council to purchase additional development rights to use on their sites if their buildings are destroyed by natural or other casualty occurrences beyond their control.

[60] Real estate tax relief is not included in the New York plan as such. The New York Landmarks Act, N.Y. GEN. MUN. LAW § 96(a) (McKinney Supp. 1970) and the Preservation of Landmarks and Historical Districts Ordinance, NEW YORK, N.Y., ADMIN. CODE ANN. ch. 8–A, § 207–8.0a(2) (1971) both authorize tax abatement. But the latter has not yet been extended to New York landmark owners, either generally or in conjunction with development rights transfers.

[61] OFFICES 123.

[62] Chicago Report 22.

[63] *Id.* at 15.

[64] This will be the case when the economic burdens of landmark ownership, as a result of an individual landmark's structural unsoundness, functional obsolescence or other cause, rise to such a level that its profitable operation is impossible.

[65] A preservation restriction may help to ensure that donors of development rights to the development rights bank receive a federal charitable deduction. *See* INT. REV. CODE OF 1954, § 170; Rev. Ruling 64–205, 1964–2 CUM. BULL. 62. *See also* R. BRENNEMAN, PRIVATE APPROACHES TO THE PRESERVATION OF OPEN LAND ch. 5 (1967) [hereinafter cited as BRENNEMAN]. Presently under consideration is a change in the federal income tax laws that would liberalize guidelines for qualifying donations of preservation restrictions as charitable deductions. Address by Kenneth Gemmill, First Conference on Legal Techniques in Preservations, in Washington, D.C., May 2, 1970 (sponsored by National Trust for Historic Preservation).

[66] Twenty-six states have a personal income tax base that is derivative of the federal income tax base. Hence, charitable deductions taken under the latter may be included under the former as well. Address by Kenneth Gemmill, *supra* note 65.

[67] The existence of a preservation restriction would have probative value in showing a lower appraisal value of property. *See, e.g.*, ILL. REV. STAT. ch. 24, § 11–48.2–6 (1969); N.M. STAT. ANN. § 4–27–14 (Supp. 1971).

[68] The adequacy of existing recording indexes for this purpose, however, has been questioned on two grounds. First, the absence of an index specifically devoted to public restrictions complicates title searches on landmark properties. Second, in the absence of special legislation, recorded preservation restrictions are subject to termination pursuant to state obsolete restrictions and marketable title acts. *See* note 167 *infra*.

[69] The adoption of the adjacency restriction in New York, despite these drawbacks, was motivated by a desire to fit development rights transfers into the legal rationale that purportedly justifies the award of zoning bonuses. *See* Marcus. The latter, it will be recalled, are granted in return for an amenity. Located on the same lot as the oversize building, the amenity, it is claimed, "digests" the building's extra floor area by providing additional light and air or by facilitating the movement of traffic generated by the building. This rationale thus answers the concern of city planners that the increased intensity of use resulting from the granting of zoning bonuses will be absorbed by the amenity for which the bonus was given. *See generally* DEPARTMENT OF CITY PLANNING, SAN FRANCISCO DOWNTOWN ZONING STUDY, FINAL REPORT (1966); Ruth, *Economic Aspects of the San Francisco Zoning Ordinance Bonus System*, in NEW ZONING 159; Svirsky, *supra* note 6. Landmarks, too, are viewed as amenities in the form of so many "light and air parks." *See* Marcus. But they obviously cannot be located on the same lot as the building to which their excess floor area has been transferred. If they are to digest this additional density, it is thought, they must be as close to the building as possible. Hence, the origin of the adjacency restriction.

While the adjacency restriction thus fits within the digestion rationale, the advantages of this rationale may be more apparent than real. It has not received express judicial approval. Moreover, the rationale seems more metaphorical than legal in content since it is difficult to conceive of an operational test that indicates how much light and air is needed to "digest," let us say, 50,000 additional square feet of office space. In addition, the digestion rationale is demonstrably inadequate as an explanation for some types of incentive zoning. Amenities such as theaters, *see* note 10 *supra*, or retail stores, *see* note 12 *supra*, will actually increase traffic at the project site.

[70] *See* p. 582 *supra*.

[71] It is estimated that the transfer of some 300,000 feet of lot area, coupled with appropriate tax reductions, will be sufficient to fund a preservation program for the landmark buildings in Chicago's Greater Loop area. *See* Chicago Report 20. Because the scope of the program is so limited, concern that a city will be engulfed in surplus density is misplaced. But proposals have been made that would escalate development rights transfers to a level that might produce this result. For example, Ira Duchan, New York City Commissioner of Real Estate, has suggested that excess floor area be transferable to nonadjacent sites from *any* building or facility owned by the city. *See* Burks, *supra* note 8.

[72] Under the New York plan, no net increase in density can occur because transfer of only the authorized but unused floor area is allowed from any landmark site. *See* p. 584 *supra*. A net increase is theoretically possible under the transfer proposal, however, because transfers of up to 100% of a landmark's lot area may be authorized in appropriate cases. But data compiled in the Chicago Report indicate that a net increase in the density of a transfer district is highly improbable. Relatively few landmarks are likely to incur such grave depreciation that only a full 100% transfer authorization over and above real estate tax relief will promise to compensate their owners fairly. *See* Chicago Report 12–15. In fact, tax relief alone will be sufficient to compensate landmark owners in many cases. *Id.* at 21–22. Nor should it be anticipated that all of the lot area pooled in the municipal development rights bank will be put on the market. On the contrary, only an amount necessary to provide supplementary funding for the municipal preservation program will be transferred. *Id.* at 20.

[73] *See* Chicago Report 16–19.

[74] As described in the text, development rights transfer districts would roughly coincide with geographic areas of the city in which urban landmarks are concentrated. In this way an urban design tradeoff is achieved: bulk within the district

is redistributed in exchange for the increased amenity resulting from the presence of low density structures there. Moreover, the bulk restrictions of the traditional bulk zones within the district are left unchanged.

A second approach is conceivable under which transfer districts would coincide with areas that, though presently zoned to relatively low densities, are expected to undergo intensive development soon. Whether or not these areas contain landmarks would be irrelevant. In rezoning them to the greater densities warranted by development expectations, densities permitted as of right would be deliberately skewed to levels falling somewhat short of the total amount of density that the market could absorb and that would be consistent with community health and safety. Developers within these areas would be permitted to purchase the remaining density increments from landmark owners, wherever located, or from the municipal development rights bank.

A proposal for restoring the Georgetown Waterfront Historic District has been advanced along these lines. Premised on the expectation that the stringent height limitations presently in force in downtown Washington will be removed, it would enable owners of property within the Historic District to sell development rights to developers within the downtown Washington area, the receipts of these sales being used to upgrade the Historic District. *See* Von Eckardt, *Getting Charm and Height*, Wash. Post, Feb. 27, 1971, § C, at 1, col. 5.

Unlike the Chicago Plan, this alternative method is open to serious due process challenges. As will be shown later, the existence of the Chicago Plan casts no doubt on the underlying reasonableness of the bulk restrictions that remain in effect on nontransferee lots in the development rights transfer district, *see* pp. 628-31 *infra*. Under the alternative, however, communities have conceded that the bulk levels permitted as of right in the transfer district are below those that would pose a threat to public health and safety.

That the landowners may nevertheless obtain what the courts may deem a "reasonable return" on their property is not a sufficient answer to this objection. In addition to meeting the reasonable return criterion, communities adopting these programs must also convince the courts that the development potential of private property may be regulated under the police power to raise funds or otherwise provide compensation for public improvements that government is unable to finance through general tax revenues. That question will be resolved affirmatively only if the courts are prepared frankly to extend the general welfare concept in the incentive zoning context to include fiscal as well as regulatory objectives. Whether the courts will take this step at the present time is unclear.

[75] Some commentators have intimated that an award of development rights alone may be sufficient to meet the constitutional requirement of just compensation that incentive zoning programs may trigger. Professor Mandelker, for example, speaks of zoning bonuses as "a *de facto quid pro quo* for corresponding increases in development costs." Mandelker, *The Basic Philosophy of Zoning: Incentive or Restraint?*, in NEW ZONING 16. Norman Marcus has suggested that the availability of the transfer option might make it more difficult for landmark owners to establish that landmark restrictions deprive them of a reasonable return on their property. *See* Marcus. While this view may be acceptable in some jurisdictions, *see generally* Haar & Hering, *The Determination of Benefits in Land Acquisition*, 51 CALIF. L. REV. 833 (1963), it is open to two objections in others. First, the jurisdiction may require that compensation for the interest taken be in cash. *See, e.g.*, 3 P. NICHOLS, NICHOLS' THE LAW OF EMINENT DOMAIN § 8.2 (3d rev. ed. 1970) [hereinafter cited as NICHOLS]; Department of Pub. Works v. Caldwell, 301 Ill. 242, 133 N.E. 642 (1921). Those jurisdictions that do permit special benefits to be set off against the interest taken might nevertheless regard

development rights as having too uncertain a value to merit recognition as a form
of special benefits.

76 *See* pp. 587–88 *supra.*

77 ALI MODEL LAND DEVELOPMENT CODE (Tent. Draft No. 2, 1970).

78 *Id.* Art. 2.

79 *Id.* §§ 2–208 to –209.

80 Municipal preservation efforts have been upheld as a manifestation of local
zoning powers. City of Santa Fe v. Gamble-Skogmo, Inc., 73 N.M. 410, 415,
389 P.2d 13, 17 (1964). They have been deemed "auxiliary to the general zoning
power" in states having independent preservation enabling acts. Rebman v. City
of Springfield, 111 Ill. App. 2d 430, 440, 250 N.E.2d 282, 287 (1969). Many municipalities incorporate some or all of their preservation measures in their zoning ordinances. *See, e.g.,* NEW YORK, N.Y., ZONING RESOLUTION art. 1, ch. 1, § 11–121;
art. 2, ch. 1, § 21–00; art. 2, ch. 3, § 23–69; art. 7, ch. 4, §§ 74–71, 74–79 (1971);
CHARLESTON, S.C., CODE ch. 51, art. III (1966). Some state legislatures have
expressly authorized municipalities to pursue historic preservation objectives under
the zoning power. *See, e.g.,* MO. REV. STAT. § 89.040 (1971); NEB. REV. STAT.
§ 19–903 (1970). And numerous preservation enabling acts contain provisions
expressly keyed into local zoning procedures. *See, e.g.,* N.H. REV. STAT. ANN. §
31:89–b (1970) ("All [historic] districts and [preservation] regulations shall be
established in relation to the comprehensive plan and the comprehensive zoning
ordinance of the city, or town"); R.I. GEN. LAWS ANN. § 45–24.1–7 (1971)
(denials of building permits by the historic district commission appealable to
zoning board of appeals).

81 ALI MODEL LAND DEVELOPMENT CODE § 2–101 (Tent. Draft No. 2, 1970).

82 *Id.* § 2–301.

83 *Id.* § 2–209, Note at 52.

84 *Id.* § 2–209, Note at 52.

85 *See* Ill. Pub. A. No. 77–1372 (Ill. Leg. Serv., Aug. 31, 1971), *in part to be
codified at* ILL. REV. STAT. ch. 24, § 11–48.2–1A, *in part amending* ILL. REV.
STAT. ch. 24, § 11–48.2–2 & –6 (1969).

86 *Id.*

87 *See* Ill. Pub. A. No. 77–1373 (Ill. Leg. Serv., Aug. 31, 1971), *amending* ILL.
REV. STAT. ch. 24, § 11–13–1 (1969). Other state zoning enabling acts containing
a similar provision are listed in note 80 *supra.*

88 *See* Chicago Report app. III.

89 *Id.*

90 *See* pp. 591–92, 595 *supra.*

91 *See* NEW YORK, N.Y., ZONING RESOLUTION, art. VII, ch. 4, § 74–79 *et seq.*
(1971).

92 *See* p. 585 *supra.*

As A Method of Preserving Landmarks
The New York Plan:
Transfers to Adjacent Properties

Development Rights Transfer
in New York City

DAVID A. RICHARDS, ESQ.

When the Equitable Building in lower Manhattan was completed in 1915, its formidable bulk cast a shadow over seven acres[1] and brought realtors and reformers together behind the nation's first comprehensive zoning ordinance.[2] The tension between their conflicting desires—to encourage the intensive development of tax-generating property, and yet to limit urban congestion—has shaped the city's zoning ever since.[3] Today the New York City Planning Commission is forging a new zoning tool, heated by the demand for office space and tempered by the recognition of the adverse consequences of unreasonably intensive land use. That tool is, in the parlance of planners, development rights transfer.[4]

"Development rights" is planning shorthand for the amount of floor area that may be developed on a given lot. Frequently, older buildings such as landmarks and townhouses do not fill the imaginary, three-dimensional envelope of space permitted by the zoning ordinance. These low-rise buildings are said to possess "authorized but unused" or "excess" development rights. By allowing the constructive "transfer" of these rights from smaller structures to the sites of new apartments or office towers, the Planning Commission intends both to preserve the landmarks and townhouses and promote the construction of office buildings and luxury apartments, with their greater assessed valuation.

Theoretically, development rights transfer does not add to the overall congestion of a district: The new floor area permitted by the transfer has all been "authorized" by the area's original bulk regulations. This fiction conveniently ignores the fact that the rights transferred were hitherto "unused," and thus did not add to the district's needs for light, air, open space, transportation, and utilities. By encouraging the intensification of actual—as opposed to hypothetical—urban density, development rights transfer may well cast a new shadow over New York.

The use and potential abuse of this technique is of considerable import to other American cities. Just as the pioneering ordinance of 1916 had significant influence throughout the United States and was widely emulated,[5] so also has New York's plan for development rights transfer in aid of landmark preservation already attracted national attention.[6] It seems reasonable to expect that the Planning Commission's variations on the theme will also be emulated. A critical analysis now may avoid the making of the same zoning mistakes "over and over again . . . because we do not have knowledge of what is applicable across-the-board and what is unique in each community."[7]

I.   The Concept of Development Rights

A.   *Law and Order for Buildings*: *The 1916 Zoning Resolution*

To understand why development rights transfer may constitute a retreat rather than an advance in city planning, a brief review of zoning controls on building size is in order. The common law bequeathed to the American colonies two competing principles governing a landowner's right to build skyward. The better-known is the common law right to build upwards without legal limitation. Blackstone, elaborating on Coke,[8] tied the ownership of the land surface to the ownership of the superjacent space:

> Land hath also, in its legal signification, an indefinite extent, upwards as well as downwards. *Cujus est solum, ejus est usque ad coelum* (whoever has the land possesses all the space upwards to an indefinite extent), is the maxim of the law; upwards, therefore, no man may erect any building or the like to overhang another's land . . . .[9]

That this maxim was not absolute is demonstrated by the fact that the first reference to it in English case law is a note to a 1586 case, *Bury v. Pope*,[10] a suit for "stopping another's lights." The Law of Ancient Lights gave a right of action to a landowner who was cut off from sunlight by the erection of a building on his neighbor's land, if the first landowner had uninterruptedly enjoyed that access for twenty years or more.[11] However, this right to light has not fared well in competition with the right to build. The plaintiff in *Bury v. Pope* lost his suit, and the champions of light in the United States have been no more successful.

In 1838, in *Parker & Edgarton v. Foote*,[12] New York's highest court became the first state court to reject the right to light,[13] noting that "it cannot be applied in the growing cities and villages of this country, without working the most mischievous consequences."[14] This frontier desire to improve newly-cleared land to the fullest was approved in the treatises of the "American Blackstone," James Kent. In his *Commentaries on American Law* (1826-1830), Chancellor Kent cited Coke for the proposition that land "has an indefinite extent, upwards as well as downwards, so as to include every thing terrestrial, under or over it."[15]

The extent of "upwards" could afford to be "indefinite" because the actual height of buildings, at least until 1860, was severely limited by the available technology. Without elevators, six stories was the limit of the most athletic tenants, and above the third floor rents decreased.[16] Without steel frame construction, the thickness of masonry walls had to increase in direct proportion to their height.[17]

The development of steel skeleton construction[18] and the invention of the elevator[19] largely removed these constraints,[20] yet the law offered no substitute. In 1865, New York was still a city of relatively low structures, four to five stories high.[21] However, in 1870, when the first building to incorporate an elevator in its original design rose to seven stories, one of the top floors was soon leased at twice the rental of the city's best office accommodations.[22] The lesson was not lost on New York's builders, who were to transform lower Manhattan from a horizontal to a vertical city in less than two generations.[23]

Aesthetic considerations aside, there are three major reasons for building high: a need for concentration of certain functions in close association; a shortage of land; and simple prestige.[24] On the southern tip of the island of Manhattan all three factors exist. Continued growth in the nation's trade and industry demanded the close proximity of brokers, bankers, lawyers, and corporate officers.[25] Their demand for space has in turn doubled and tripled property values in the business center.[26] Moreover, it was at least partly for the prestige of owning the largest commercial office building in the world that General duPont erected the infamous Equitable Building, which helped provoke the passage of the first New York City Zoning Resolution.[27]

The 1916 Resolution was based on the conclusions and recommendations of the Heights of Buildings Commission, a body created by the Board of Estimate and Apportionment in 1913.[28] Their report articulated the twin themes which have dominated planning policy in New York's central business districts to the present: the preservation of property values[29] and the encouragement of office buildings.[30] Control was to be maintained through height,[31] setback,[32] and area limitations on building size. These regulations established what came to be called the "zoning envelope," an imaginary three-dimensional mold representing the maximum bulk to which a building might be developed under the proposed regulations.[33] Significantly, nothing was said about specific limits on population density, nor about the relation of building size to the capacities of traffic arteries or mass transit services.

As enacted, the 1916 Resolution established five classes of height districts, based on street width.[34] Towers could rise to any height as long as they covered at their base not more than twenty-five per cent of the lot area and observed certain given setbacks from the streets.[35] The 1916 Resolution also introduced a bonus provision, allowing a builder to add height if he provided open space beyond that required by the applicable district ordinance.[36]

Unfortunately, the planning philosophy of the Resolution was not as straightforward as its technique. "It is too big a city, the social and economic interests involved are too great to permit the continuance of the *laissez faire* methods of earlier days," the accompanying report proclaimed; but several pages later "economic interests" had triumphed over "social" ones: "No limit can be set to the growth and expansion of the city."[37]

B. *Recidivism and Reform*: *The 1961 Zoning Resolution*

Within a decade planners were observing that the 1916 height and area regulations were inadequate.[38] Height zoning, while altering the form and indirectly limiting the bulk of skyscrapers, still permitted the crowding together of towering structures and encouraged separate buildings which overshadowed their districts.[39]

Between 1925 and 1931, Manhattan's office space increased by ninety-two per cent, and the next two years added yet another fifty-six per cent, including the Empire State Building and Rockefeller Center. The Grand Central area alone saw seventy new office buildings erected between 1921 and 1946.[40] Belatedly, planners noted the obvious: Subway traffic at express stops increased roughly in proportion to the increase in rentable floor space. As a solution, the nation's foremost expert on building height and setback regulations suggested in 1931 that "it might well be good business to provide the additional transit facilities as needed."[41]

Belatedly, too, New York City's planners calculated the building capacity of the 1916 Resolution. They found that if the city were developed to the densities permitted by the zoning envelope, its residential districts alone would house seventy-seven million people; the commercial districts would embrace a working population of three hundred and forty-four million.[42] Planning control was reasserted in 1944, when the height and area regulations of the more intensive districts were lowered to those in effect for the next most restrictive district. But the Planning Commission did not depart from the basic mechanics of the original Resolution and continued to regulate building size through height, setback, and area restrictions.[43]

As density controls, these techniques were indirect and inefficient. Students of New York's bulk zoning came to realize that height and setback restrictions were almost entirely devices to insure adequate light and air, which only incidentally limited the concentration of the working population.[44] Admittedly, a city planner could determine the maximum building size allowable on each lot, translate this into square feet of floor space, divide that figure by an estimate of floor space per employee, and arrive at the maximum working population of an area.[45] But this is not an easily reversible computation. One cannot use a desired density to generate an ideal height and setback configuration. Furthermore, the aim of all these calculations may be thwarted by a builder who lowers ceiling heights and thereby squeezes more stories into the permitted height of the building.[46]

Direct regulation of density was possible, however, through the Floor Area Ratio (FAR) technique. This ratio is an index figure which expresses the total allowable floor area of a building as a multiple of the area of its lot.[47] A 10,000 square foot lot, in a district where the FAR was twelve, would thus be limited to a maximum of 120,000 square feet of floor space. The latter figure is thus a constant control on the density of the lot. The builder can double the height of his building (provided he does not exceed the absolute height limitation of the district), but then can build on only half the lot, in order to stay within the maximum square footage of the FAR zoning envelope.

The FAR device had been incorporated into the zoning ordinance for the city's lowest density residential districts as early as 1940,[48] but was bypassed in the general rezoning of 1944. Not until the Resolution of 1961, after seventeen years of political maneuvering and two major reports by architectural consultants, were FAR controls extended to the city's commercial areas.[49] By that time, attention had turned from the need for FAR controls in the congested central business districts to the determination of their upper limits.

By fixing the maximum office floor space that can be erected in a city's downtown districts, FAR regulations limit the growth of business. Developers argued that setting the FAR too low would make it almost impossible to erect buildings big enough for the largest companies. The builders also complained that, because of the FAR limit, the taller the building erected, the smaller its floor plan will be, the less efficient office space it will provide, and the more space its elevators will use.[50]

Consultants hired in 1956 for the rezoning attempted to balance the builders' desires with the predictable needs of the city. The consultants took account of the size of the future national economy, New York's share of national office construction, future office employment, anticipated floor space per employee, and the amount of office space constructed since World War II. Their projections, extrapolated through 1975, indicated that there was likely to be an annual increase of about three million square feet of rentable space. Allowing for demolitions, more space per worker in existing buildings, and a somewhat higher vacancy rate, this amount of new construction would provide space for an additional 185,000 office workers by 1975.[51]

The amount of additional land needed to provide for this new office space naturally depended upon the FAR level. If the FAR were ten, 162 acres would be necessary, while a ratio of fifteen would permit the same intensity of development on 108 acres. The consultants' studies of post-World War II office buildings, erected under the old height and setback regulations, produced an average FAR of fifteen. Since developers had been building profitably at that level, and the 108 acres required to accommodate the projected increase in floor space at that level was "a modest amount relative to total commercial land available in the Central Business District" (Manhattan, south from 59th Street), the Planning Commission established fifteen as the FAR in its highest density commercial districts under the 1961 Resolution.[52]

New York's builders and realtors objected strenuously to any reduction in bulk regulations in the new zoning ordinance.[53] To win their support for the 1961 Resolution [54] the planners incorporated two further features which undermined the limitation on building bulk represented by the FAR of fifteen. The first was a bonus device[55] which granted a developer a twenty per cent increase in permitted floor area in exchange for a plaza surrounding his building.[56] A builder might therefore increase his FAR from fifteen to eighteen simply by covering less of his lot and putting more of his permitted bulk into a tower.

The second innovation was a liberalization in the definition of the zoning lot to which the FAR figure was applied. The 1961 Resolution defines the term "zoning lot" to include not only the project site, but also any other parcel located within the same city block owned by the developer. For the purpose of this definition, ownership of all or part of a zoning lot includes control through a lease of at least seventy-five years.[57] By leasing an adjacent underdeveloped or vacant parcel on a long-term basis and designating it as part of his total "zoning lot," a developer can add the authorized but unbuilt bulk of the leased parcel to the bulk of his project site.

The developers' enthusiastic adoption of this embryonic form of development rights transfer has been an important factor in prompting the city to adopt additional transfer provisions. To their use and abuse, this Note now turns.

II. The Transfer of Development Rights

In 1968, the Planning Commission enacted its first major development rights transfer regulation for a specific class of structures. This regulation (Section 74-79 of the zoning ordinance) was intended to supplement existing programs for landmark preservation, by permitting the owner of a landmark to transfer his authorized but unused floor area to adjacent parcels for development.[58]

Landmarks were endangered both by the zoning ordinance's encouragement of new office buildings and by urban economics. Older buildings not only enhanced the city's character through their historic associations and architectural distinction;[59] they also provided wells of light and air amid the skyscrapers. Yet their economic return could never approach that of the office towers which might replace them, so the urge to demolish was overwhelming.[60]

The intensive development of New York office space that began with the birth of the skyscraper in the late nineteenth century took its toll: In Manhattan today there is not a single building dating back to the seventeenth century and only nine going back to the eighteenth.[61] In the twentieth century, successive waves of skyscraper construction were equally destructive of the city's architectural heritage. The office boom of the late 1950's[62] was particularly devastating.[63] Although the New York Community Trust, a private organization, initiated a program of mounting bronze plaques on landmark structures,[64] the preservation of such buildings was only the incidental result of a long-term tenancy or holdout owner.

In 1956, the state legislature had amended the General City Law

to permit the acquisition or control of buildings having special aesthetic interest or value,[65] but the city failed to act until pressured by
citizens' preservation groups.[66] In April 1965, the city council enacted the Landmarks Preservation Law,[67] which created the Landmarks Preservation Commission. That Commission can designate
any appropriate structure or site as a landmark; it can also name any
area of the city possessing special historical, aesthetic, or architectural
interest as an historic district. Both designations are made only after a
public hearing, and must be approved by the city's Board of Estimate,
a group composed of elected officials.[68]

The Commission is not required to consider the hardships landmark designation may impose on the owner of the building, even
though he may not demolish it or alter its exterior without Commission approval.[69] In practice, however, witnesses at the designation
hearings do testify on the loss in property values expected from
designation.[70] After designation, the owner may appeal the Commission's refusal to grant permission for alteration or demolition
only on the ground that he is not receiving a fair return from his
landmark.[71] The statute defines this reasonable return as a net annual return of six per cent of the assessed valuation of the building
and its site.[72] If the landmark owner proves to the Commission's
satisfaction that he cannot realize this return without alteration or
demolition, the Commission then works with him to devise a plan
for preservation, which provides the required return. In devising
such a plan, the Commission has the power, with the approval of the
Board of Estimate, to grant partial or complete exemption from, or
remission of, taxes.[73]

By mid-1969, some 285 structures had been designated as landmarks.[74] Of this number, only one could not be saved from demolition.[75] This overwhelmingly successful program of preservation has
been achieved without resort to the tax relief possible under the
preservation laws.[76] Yet it was allegedly to supplement these tax
abatement provisions that the Planning Commission enacted Section
74-79, allowing transfer of landmarks' unused development rights.[77]
It should be recalled that the 1961 Resolution already permitted the
transfer of potential development rights to a *contiguous* parcel, provided that both areas were under the same ownership in the same
designated "zoning lot."[78] But this meant that no merger would be
possible where (1) all the sites contiguous to a landmark were already
fully developed, (2) the neighboring buildings were themselves landmarks, or (3) the planners had elected to preserve a state of "underdevelopment" in the immediate vicinity of the landmark, as was the

case with certain midblocks of brownstones.[79] Moreover, the requirement that the lots be under common ownership imposed an additional barrier.

The 1968 amendment sought to remove these restrictions by
broadening the definition of "contiguous" to include lots across the
street or intersection from the landmark, and by permitting transfers
between separately owned zoning lots. In the 1968 provision, however, the transferee lot was only permitted a twenty per cent increase
in floor area through the transfer. The new law allowed a landmark
owner to sell portions of his unused development rights to several
adjacent owners, but he could not sell the same portion more than
once. The development rights of the landmark's zoning lot were for-
ever reduced by the amount of rights sold, and notice of the restrictions upon further development had to be filed in the appropriate
land records office. Finally, approval of the transfer was conditioned
upon a finding by the Planning Commission:

> (a) that the permitted transfer of floor area or minor variations
> in the front, height and setback regulations will not unduly in-
> crease the bulk of any new development, density of population
> or intensity of use in any block, to the detriment of the occupants
> of buildings on the block or nearby blocks, and (b) that the
> [required] program for continuing maintenance will result in
> the preservation of the landmark.[80]

In its statement accompanying the rights transfer amendment, the
Planning Commission cited the provision's "multiple benefits."

> The owner of a designated landmark building can realize an
> economic gain by selling his unbuilt, but allowable, develop-
> ment rights; the buyer of these rights, in return, can acquire
> additional floor area he would otherwise not have; the neighbor-
> hood, meanwhile, can retain an essential amenity, a revitalized
> landmark, plus new development harmonious with the charac-
> ter of the area and of a quality unobtainable under previous
> conditions; the City, most importantly, can benefit by new tax
> revenues from what was previously untaxable.[81]

The Commission's concluding remark clearly identifies development
rights transfer as primarily a method of fiscal[82] rather than aesthetic
zoning. It also suggests that the amendment would provide a good
excuse for not utilizing the tax relief provisions originally enacted to
compensate the landmark owner.[83] But whatever its fiscal advantages, the new provision proved inadequate in dealing with the "Grand
Central Terminal Crisis,"[84] a plan to build a fifty-five story office

building over the Terminal, a designated landmark, which would bring 12,000 more workers into the area.[85]

A. *Grand Central and Grander Transfers: The 1969 Amendment*

In the nineteenth century, the public outcry against the noise, smoke, and danger of the first trains had caused the city to move progressively northward the boundary below which locomotives could not run into Manhattan; thus, 42nd Street became the ultimate location of the present Grand Central Terminal. In 1875, a disastrous passenger train collision forced the New York Central Railroad to acquire several acres of valuable uptown property in order to widen its narrow tunnel. By 1902, the right-of-way had been redesigned and put underground to carry 600 trains a day. Above them, Park Avenue was carried on steel posts, as were nine cross streets similarly bridging the railyard.[86]

The cost of these improvements was met largely by the sale of air rights[87] over the covered tracks to permit the building of commercial structures along Park Avenue. As hotels, clubs, apartment houses, and office buildings rose over the forty-eight-acre railyard, it became one immense realty holding under single ownership. Meanwhile, "Grand Central City" grew into the transportation transfer center of the metropolis, bound to the rest of New York not only by surface streets but also by the old elevated lines and the new subways constructed concurrently with the station.[88]

In this way, the common carrier became uncommonly wealthy. Its monumental and sumptuous Terminal, completed in 1913, cost $75 million—$225 million in today's dollars.[89] In time, the value of the land occupied by the Terminal increased enormously, but the railroad business declined. This combination naturally led the New York Central to consider possible means of realizing at least some of the value of the terminal site. The Terminal represented a FAR of 1.5 in a district with a maximum FAR of eighteen.[90] In September 1967, the New York Central first proposed to build a skyscraper containing some two million square feet of floor space over the Terminal waiting room;[91] in January 1968, the new Penn Central leased that unused space to a private developer for fifty years at a minimum annual return of $3 million.[92] The erection of a building of such magnitude in an area which already suffered from extreme congestion made city planners shudder. But, given the generous FAR ceiling of the 1961 Resolution, the proposed building was completely within the zoning law and needed no variance or approval from the Planning Commission.[93]

After more than a year of controversy and the presentation of two alternative plans by the architect, the Landmarks Preservation Commission finally blocked construction by ruling, in late 1968, that the proposed development had an exterior effect on the Terminal, which had been designated a landmark only one month before plans for the building had been announced.[94] This ruling meant that the proposed building could not be erected without exhausting the Commission's various ameliorating procedures.[95] The Penn Central's counsel had announced that the railroad would go to court to challenge the constitutionality of the landmarks legislation,[96] and the negative ruling triggered a suit against the city for $8 million a year until permission to build was granted.[97]

The Terminal presented a situation where a massive amount of development rights were available to be transferred in an area in which all the "adjacent" lots, as then defined, were already intensely developed. The 1968 amendment noted above was thus of no assistance in solving the Grand Central problem.

In reaction to the proposed tower, the Planning Commission moved in mid-1968 to acquire greater control over the construction in the immediate areas of the city's three major transportation centers— Grand Central, Pennsylvania Station, and the Long Island Railroad complex in Queens. Within these districts, if established, the Commission would have the discretionary power to restrict the bulk of any new building to eighty per cent of the size otherwise permitted under the zoning law. The Commission members

> made no secret of the fact that they consider the heavy development on the East Side of Manhattan in recent years to have overburdened the transportation facilities—rail, rapid transit, vehicular and pedestrian—in the vicinity of Grand Central.[98]

The plan could have rendered the Grand Central office tower project economically infeasible.[99] After public hearings, the proposal failed to gain the approval of the Commission and the Board of Estimate and was indefinitely tabled.[100] How hard the planners fought for their transportation district program is not clear, but they had proposed it only two months after enacting the first landmark development rights transfer provision. Having rubbed that genie out of the lamp, with all the promises of new construction permitted by transfer, it was certainly easier for the Commission to modify an expansive measure rather than to fight for a restrictive one.

The modification finally adopted by the Planning Commission, with one eye on enhancing its position in the Penn Central suit,[101]

was to amend Section 74-79. The amended transfer provision defined "adjacent" sites in the highest density commercial districts to
include

> a lot . . . which is across a street and opposite to another lot or
> lots which except for the intervention of streets or street inter-
> sections form a series extending to the lot occupied by the land-
> mark building. All such lots shall be in the same ownership.[102]

This amendment, announced October 7, 1969 (the same day the
railroad's suit was filed), allowed the Penn Central to distribute the
Terminal's "excess" development rights among the properties it controlled around the Terminal and up Park Avenue. One such prospective transferee lot was the Barclay Hotel on Lexington Avenue between 48th and 49th Streets, five blocks away from the Terminal.
With this amendment, development rights could be not merely "si-
phoned off" to nearby parcels, but jumped over entire city blocks.[103]
The 1968 provision had limited development rights transfer to a
twenty per cent increase in FAR on the transferee lot. Because the
Terminal had such a great unused development rights potential, that
limitation would have demanded several transferee redevelopments.
Such widespread redevelopment in the densely-built district around
the Terminal was hardly likely. For this reason the 1969 amendment
revoked the twenty per cent restriction with regard to the highest-
density commercial districts (those with a FAR maximum of eighteen).
The transfer of *all* of the unused development rights to *one* lot was
thus permitted. As the Planning Commission's counsel later observed,
this was a practical decision based on the railroad's eagerness to convert its development rights into revenue-producing office space as
rapidly as possible.[104]
The Commission had one further rationale for lifting the twenty
per cent restriction: the "prevalence of non-complying buildings [in
excess of FAR eighteen] in the area," making "one more extra-large
building . . . relatively innocuous."[105] The planners must have been
redefining "innocuous" as well as "adjacent lot": nothing else can
explain the Commission's obliviousness to the transportation chaos
which it was permitting through such a massive transfer of development rights.[106]
If the original rights transfer resolution could be characterized as
fiscal zoning,[107] this brief history reveals the 1969 amendment of that
resolution to be a classic case of spot zoning:[108] an amendment enacted solely for the benefit of one landowner which was not in accordance with a comprehensive plan.[109] Permitting development rights

transfer of such magnitude from the Terminal to a single transferee lot, given the appalling state of transit facilities in the Grand Central area, is the very antithesis of rational planning. Under the statute, that single transferee lot could have a FAR of 34.5,[110] almost twice the current permissible maximum. Fortunately for those who work or travel in the district, none of the Terminal's development rights have as yet been transferred.[111] If it does happen, the owners of buildings to be overshadowed by the transferee project might well have the legal opportunity, on a spot zoning theory, to cut their new neighbor down to size.[112]

B. *Public Landmarks and Private Levies: The 1970 Amendment*

Although roughly one-quarter of New York's designated landmarks were publicly-owned[113] when the original rights transfer amendment was adopted, that provision applied only to privately-owned landmarks. Transfers from publicly-owned landmarks, however, could conceivably be made under the 1961 Resolution's definition of "zoning lot" *if* the landmark site was contiguous to the developer's parcel and was under his "control."[114] In fact, the first transfer of development rights from a public landmark used this provision.

In the fall of 1969, an owner of land adjacent to the Appellate Division Courthouse, a city-owned landmark with Corinthian columns and rooftop statuary, proposed to construct an office tower containing approximately a half million square feet; applicable FAR limitations for the district permitted the construction of only 400,000 square feet. To aid the builder, the city took advantage of its power to lease municipally-owned buildings for up to ninety-nine years.[115] The developer leased the courthouse for fifty years with a twenty-five-year renewal option; he then subleased it back to the city, reserving the one hundred thousand square feet of floor area he needed for his office project. Since the developer now had a lease for seventy-five years, he was deemed to be the owner of the courthouse lot and could combine it with his own to produce more floor space under the district's FAR.[116] The city's gain averaged $46,000 per annum—a total for the lease term of $3,450,000.[117] None of this was marked for maintenance of the courthouse or improvement of the transit systems serving the huge new office building. Not long thereafter, the Planning Commission amended Section 74-79 to bring publicly-owned landmarks under its provisions. This 1970 amendment requires a finding by the Commission,

[t]hat in the case of landmark sites owned by the City, State or Federal Government, transfer of development rights shall be con-

tingent upon provision by the applicant of a major improvement
of the public pedestrian circulation or transportation system in
the area.[118]

Clearly, in the future, public benefits were to be extracted as the
price of transfer by levying upon the private builder who would
utilize the development rights. As the Commission's General Counsel
later explained:

> The additional requirement in the case of development rights
> transfers from public landmarks was an attempt to recognize the
> additional obligation borne by the public in supporting its own
> landmarks. Transfer of air rights over public landmarks must
> therefore accommodate the notion of the private transferee de-
> veloper providing a major improvement in the public pedestrian
> circulation or transportation system in the area. Developments
> incorporating formerly publicly owned air rights are therefore
> held to a higher amenity standard than those utilizing privately
> owned and transferred air rights. Presumably this negates any
> thought that the city might sell air rights solely to bolster the
> municipal treasury.[119]

This admirable objective is, however, tarnished by the circumstances surrounding the amendment. The new provision was added,
not as an abstract principle determined after deliberate consideration, but in response to one specific development project. The amendment was the product of a proposal involving the massive but squat
United States Custom House, which faces Bowling Green at the foot
of Broadway. Under the zoning regulations, the Custom House's permitted zoning envelope contains 1,134,000 square feet of floor space,
of which only 344,200 square feet have been developed. The building's
unused development rights, 789,800 square feet, represent a floor area
roughly equal to that of the Woolworth Building. A neighboring developer wanted to replace his fifteen-story building with a new project,
perhaps as high as fifty stories, using the Custom House's development rights. The Planning Commission obliged him by again amending Section 74-79.[120] The Commission held that the 1970 amendment meant that in return for approval of the Custom House transfer, the builder had to make a substantial contribution to increasing
the underground access and corridors to the adjacent Bowling Green
subway station and to contribute to a fund for or take a direct part in
preserving the Custom House.[121]

Whether the Commission might have won a "higher amenity
standard"[122] from the builder is now a moot question, for the transaction was never consummated.[123] The provision, nevertheless, re-

mains on the books as clear evidence of the Commission's eagerness to accommodate potential developers.[124]

C. *The Battle of the Brownstones*

Although the original rights transfer provision had allowed transfer to "residential developments or enlargements,"[125] all of the transfers actually contemplated or proposed through the fall of 1970 had involved only office buildings. But the provision recognized that new, high-rise luxury apartments would also generate greater tax revenues and was designed to encourage them. Furthermore, no conceptual bar limited the applicability of development rights transfer to landmarks alone. Hundreds of older buildings failed to fill the FAR envelope permitted under the 1961 Zoning Resolution, and very few were designated landmarks.

It was therefore not surprising that in 1970 the Planning Commission formulated a zoning amendment which would have allowed builders of high-rise apartments to exceed their FAR restrictions by purchasing and utilizing the unused development rights of smaller townhouses.[126]

The proposal met determined opposition, however, and the Commission retreated. Six weeks after proposing the amendment, the Commission announced that it had decided to "either drop the item or continue the matter to a future hearing in order to reformulate it."[127] The full history of the proposal suggests that its abandonment was a rare example of a politically expedient decision that was also wise.

The upper East Side of Manhattan, for which the amendment was primarily designed,[128] is bounded by the East River, Central Park, 59th, and 96th Streets. Its residential population (200,200)[129] roughly equals that of Austin, Texas.[130] As the planners conceded, this area had seen the greatest concentration of private residential construction in the city, built upon some of the nation's most expensive real estate.[131] To allow developers a return on their investments, the 1961 Resolution permitted a living density that would be the highest in the world: A builder can cover every square inch of the site in constructing up to 363 four-room apartments per acre.[132]

Since the 1961 Resolution, such zoning (R-10) has been limited to the wide north-south avenues and major cross-town streets in Manhattan's luxury residential areas. In these areas, the authors of the official *Plan for New York City* in 1969 found that,

buildings of great bulk are tolerable. The high level of services and transportation access and the relative roominess of the apartments are compensation for the high degree of stacking. . . . To fill up whole neighborhoods with this kind of building, however, would clearly be wrong. The service load, for one thing, would be intolerable.

There would be neither space nor sense of space. Most of the buildings would be in perpetual shadow.

The creation of such luxury tenement districts would be an act of cannibalization. The smaller scale of the side streets is one of the major reasons why New York's most pleasant neighborhoods are pleasant—and why big towers on the avenues and corners can do as well as they do. The towers borrow space and sunlight from the lower buildings on the side streets.[133]

To preserve these midblock wells of light and air, the Planning Commission in 1961 had placed the side streets of the upper East Side under the protection of lower density zoning (R-8), permitting a maximum of only 247 apartments per acre.[134]

The Commission released its residential transfer amendment in November 1970. It proposed to permit the transfer of unused development rights from buildings in the midblock R-8 districts to R-10 lots fronting the avenue, where both the R-8 and R-10 districts were located within the same city block. The amended provisions might also be applied to the transfer of development rights within a single zoning lot divided by a boundary between an R-8 district and an R-10 district. The amendment borrowed the original percentage limitation of the 1968 transfer law: The builder of the high-rise might not exceed his FAR limit by more than twenty per cent.

The proposal also required that the transferee developer increase the amount of open plaza space on his site by as much as he increased the floor space of his building. Since apartment developers are not ordinarily required by the zoning ordinance to provide such open space for the public, this provision represented another application of the planners' long-standing policy to encourage open space by permitting buildings to exceed the otherwise applicable FAR limit. Another provision allowed an avenue developer to purchase any deteriorated side block property, raze it, and add the square footage to that of his avenue property, although this could be done only with the Commission's approval. As with the landmarks provision, transfers would be "irrevocable" and recorded, so that the transferred rights could no longer be developed on the transferor lot.[135]

The success of prior development rights transfer amendments hinged on two factors: the paucity of sites—all landmarks—which would be affected, and the absence of any organized constituency which would have to live with the results. In the battle of the brownstones, however, people who would have to contend with the increased density and building bulk resulting from development rights transfer on a scale never before proposed, had a voice. Their response to the planners was resoundingly negative.[136]

In defeating the Commission's amendment, the upper East Side residents cast grave doubt upon the master plan's rosy portrait of the "high level of services and transportation access" and other amenities claimed to be available for their neighborhood. Their arguments were presented by William Diamond, a former Housing Commissioner in the Lindsay administration, who now chaired Community Planning Board 8, the city's citizens' advisory panel responsible for the upper East Side.[137]

First, transfer of development rights to avenue-front apartments would increase the *actual* population density of the area, and thus the burden on district services and amenities, even though the *permissible* density under FAR ceilings remained constant. While the upper East Side's population had grown by over 15,000 since 1960, there had been no increase in the amount of public open space for community residents.[138] The overcrowding on the district's one subway line was notorious;[139] and the automobiles of the new residents would add not only to the congestion in the streets but also to the pollution in the air.[140] Moreover, the huge new buildings would themselves increase that pollution through their heating, cooling, power generation, and refuse disposal.[141]

Secondly, the amendment, by allowing a developer to buy any side street property "for which it is found that continued preservation and maintenance would have been or would be unfeasible or unsafe,"[142] might encourage owners on side blocks to permit their dwellings to deteriorate. "We would have introduced a new element, deterioration for profit, into the already sad decline of livable housing in this city," Diamond later declared.[143] The absorption of the development rights of these demolished buildings by luxury high-rises would also change the character of the neighborhoods by driving away the middle class, unable to afford the new rents.[144]

Finally, those midblock wells of light which the city plan had vowed to preserve[145] were again threatened. Apartment buildings in the R-10 zones along the avenues, generally limited to thirty stories, might go as high as forty-two under the amended rights transfer scheme.[146] Ironically, forty-two stories was precisely the height of the old Equitable Building which had darkened the streets of the financial district and helped provoke New York's first zoning resolution so many years before.[147]

The Commission had declared that its proposed amendment had two objectives: to stop further redevelopment of the midblocks by keeping them at their present scale, and to increase the potential number of dwelling units in new buildings on the avenue.[148] At the press conference announcing the proposal, preservation was emphasized as the primary aim.[149] But one year later, following the defeat of this amendment, the planners were proposing a temporary FAR bonus for upper East Side sites zoned partially R-8, partially R-10,[150] which suggests that their first priority was indeed construction. Again, development rights transfer had been good camouflage for an exercise in fiscal zoning. The only opponents of the plan were the people who would have had to live with the results.

III.   The Impact of Development Rights Transfer

A.   *A Solitary Success—Perhaps*

With all the sound and fury generated by the rights transfer amendments since 1968, it might be thought that several builders would have rushed to take advantage of them and thereby contributed to the preservation of several New York landmarks. In reality, only one such transfer has been completely processed by the Commission, and it has yet to be consummated by construction of the new office building which is to absorb the landmark's development rights. This transaction demonstrates both the unreliability of development rights transfer as a preservation device and the folly of employing the technique without regard to the impact on existing facilities.

Amster Yard is a designated landmark group of nineteenth-century, one- to four-story brick residences built around a garden courtyard. Its lot between East 49th and 50th Streets had several thousand square feet of unused development rights. The owner of the adjacent lot proposed to build a forty-story office tower. The permitted zoning envelope for the tower allowed the development of 544,122 square feet. By purchasing an additional 30,967 square feet in development rights from Amster Yard, the developer could build two stories above the normal limit of forty. Alternatively, he could build larger, more desirable tower floors averaging 14,000 instead of 12,000 square feet—a distinct commercial advantage worth at least a $30,000 a year additional profit.[151]

In exchange, the developer made a number of design concessions, including the use of materials and colors sympathetic to the scale and style of the landmark and a covered shopping arcade on three sides of the new structure. The landmark owner or his trustee administrator were to be paid $494,731 over fifteen years for the transferred rights. Of that sum, $100,000 was to be put in trust for the landmark's maintenance.[152]

"Although processed and tied with a ribbon"[153] since the summer of 1970, the Amster Yard transfer has never been used because the market for new office space in New York is currently quite weak.[154] An estimated fourteen million square feet of office space has been added to the market by buildings completed between 1970 and 1972. The Planning Commission has estimated that in 1973 as much as thirty-four million of a total of 225 million square feet will go unrented. Only 2,904,000 square feet of new office space was rented in 1971—the lowest amount in the last decade.[155]

Thus, the initial defect in any program designed to preserve landmarks through development rights transfer is that it cannot work unless a builder *wants* those development rights, regardless of the distance he can transfer them.[156] An eminently more reliable method of landmark preservation was and is available under the city's Landmarks Preservation Law,[157] and that legislation should continue to save more architectural monuments than development rights transfer schemes ever will.

The second flaw in the landmarks version of the device is that any rights transferred are most likely to flow to areas which are already highly congested due to those private economic advantages of concentration which make transfer attractive in the first place.[158]

The proposed office tower adjacent to Amster Yard has a prime location, and so development rights transfer making possible two extra floors would be profitable for the builder. But the structure will bring about 3600 more workers into the Grand Central area,[159] where the present strain on surface and subway transportation is already intolerable according to both the master planners and those who travel there. About 200 of those workers will occupy the floor space transferred from Amster Yard. That is, to be sure, a small number compared with the 2000 who would be brought in by the exploitation of the unused development rights of the U.S. Custom House.[160] But in either case, given the sorry state of mass transit in New York and all the attendant ills to which a densely-developed city is heir, the wisdom of encouraging an increase in congestion through development rights transfer is at best doubtful.

B. *The Larger Failure*

The development rights transfer technique has not proven help-

ful in preserving landmarks in New York, and its utilization in a
residential context was seen by the citizens affected as a threat to
the character and viability of their midblock neighborhoods. Almost
assuredly, in order to spur construction and generate increased tax
revenues, the Planning Commission will formulate other versions of
the device. The city's Real Estate Commissioner has proposed widespread transfer of development rights from municipal fire houses,
police stations, and schools, both to adjacent sites and to properties
farther away. The Planning Commission has yet to permit this, but
the siren song of growth may prove irresistible.

But certain conclusions from New York's experience with the
technique are already clear, and these are worth pondering by any
city contemplating its adoption. First, development rights transfer
is not a *necessary* device for saving landmarks, where the municipal
landmarks commission has other preservation powers and is willing
to employ them.[161] Second, it is not a *reliable* device for landmark
preservation, because it depends on the local market for new office
space. This market may well be glutted through overbuilding or,
ironically, through the extensive utilization of other FAR bonus provisions in the municipal zoning ordinance.[162] Third, it is not even a
serviceable device over the long run, unless the city intends to abandon
effective limits on the intensity of development. Only new and bigger
office towers and apartments can absorb the transferred rights, and
this necessarily means increased residential and employee densities.[163]

Finally, development rights transfer is a *pernicious* device in today's
congested cities. Whether from landmarks, midblock brownstones,
or municipal buildings, unused rights will always flow to those areas
where the commercial advantages of concentration make transfer
economically attractive. If this existing concentration is attended by
its usual effects—if the subways and buses are overloaded; the streets,
clogged; the air, polluted; and the few remaining open spaces, in the
perpetual shadow of surrounding office or apartment towers—then
development rights transfer can only make life more miserable.

In the final analysis, debate on the merits of development rights
transfer is really an argument about the optimal size of buildings
in the central city. Forty years ago, one commentator cast the controversy in such terms:

Conclusive quantitative proof of the desirability of these things
[sunlight, air, etc.] is almost impossible, as is also the setting up
of any unqualified standard for safety and well-being below which
we should not go. The general indications would lead to the belief that, while sunlight, air, outlook, privacy, the avoidance of

a sense of "shut-in-ness" and of actual congestion are highly desirable, we are not able to set up a minimum which, let us say, if curtailed by 10 percent would spell disaster or if augmented by 10 percent would spell relative happiness and prosperity.[164]

Because conclusive proof is still lacking, proponents of transfer schemes can argue with some conviction that this new zoning practice "is defensible in planning terms."[165] But whatever the planning terms, the results of urban concentration are increasingly intolerable in human terms, and a zoning device aimed at increasing that concentration deserves censure rather than praise.

In sum, development rights transfer will be justified only where planning administrators condition its use on the establishment of open space and services which adequately satisfy the needs of the existing population. And even if the planners can meet such conditions, they should still consider the critique of New York's "new zoning" made by an administrator of the New York State Office of Planning Services:

> The one philosophical point implicit in the 1961 Resolution is that the attainment of zoned capacity is undesirable, unnecessary and unwarranted. The envelope that was created was to provide some reasonable expectation of flexibility within the framework of planning considerations. The idea of every parcel being developed to its maximum either directly or through transfer of development rights, while becoming increasingly popular as a sophisticated expression of laissez-faire, is essentially a perversion of all that planning has traditionally stood for. The major thrust behind much of the new incentive zoning is growth, albeit related to economics. Growth, too, is the major characteristic of cancer.[166]

NOTES

1. At forty-two stories, the Equitable Building represented a thirty-five million dollar investment for its builder, General Thomas duPont. One hundred thousand people entered the building daily and thirteen thousand worked in its 1,250,000 square feet of rentable office space. The Equitable Building cut off the sunlight from the fronts of buildings as tall as twenty-one stories, and practically all of the surrounding owners got reductions in their tax assessments when they proved a loss of rents due to the light and air taken by their massive new neighbor. S. TOLL, ZONED AMERICAN 71 (1969).

2. Woodbury, *The Background and Prospects of Urban Redevelopment in the United States*, in THE FUTURE OF CITIES AND URBAN REDEVELOPMENT 641 (C. Woodbury ed. 1953).

3. On the conflicting ends of the 1916 New York Resolution, see S. TOLL, *supra* note 1, at 184-85; for a similar conclusion regarding the 1961 Resolution see S. MAKIELSKI, THE POLITICS OF ZONING 106 (1966).

4. The same device has been called "air rights transfer" by both reporters and lawyers. *See, e.g.,* Burks, *City Wants Air Rights to Hop, Skip, and Jump,* N.Y. Times, April 26, 1970, § 8, at 1, col. 1; Conti, *Groups Fight to Stop Leveling of Landmarks by Urban Developers,* Wall St. J., Aug. 10, 1970, at 1, col. 1; Marcus, *Air Rights Transfers in New*

York City, 36 LAW &͏ CONTEMP. PROB. 372, 374 (1971). However, the technique does *not* entail the transfer of "air rights."

The latter are a property interest in a three-dimensional location in space. Development rights, on the other hand, are simply a governmental license to build a defined amount of floor area as measured by the amount of lot area that has been constructively "transferred" to the project site.

Costonis, *The Chicago Plan: Incentive Zoning and the Preservation of Urban Landmarks*, 85 HARV. L. REV. 574, 592 n.58 (1972).

5. *See* E. BASSETT, ZONING 8 (1940); H. JAMES, LAND PLANNING IN THE UNITED STATES FOR THE CITY, STATE, AND NATION 239 (1926).

6. On June 31, 1971, the U.S. Department of Housing and Urban Development announced that the National Trust for Historic Preservation had been commissioned to study the uses of the development rights transfer approach to save historic buildings. Professor John J. Costonis, the author of the article cited in note 4 *supra*, is the project director. Letter from Roger Holt, Assistant for Legal Services, Department of Field Services of the National Trust for Historic Preservation, to author, Jan. 26, 1972, on file at *Yale Law Journal*.

7. H. PERLOFF, A NATIONAL PROGRAM OF RESEARCH IN HOUSING AND URBAN REDEVELOPMENT AND A SUGGESTED APPROACH 20 (Washington, Resources for the Future, Inc., 1961), quoted in Sussna, *Bulk Control and Zoning: The New York City Experience*, 43 LAND ECONOMICS 158 (1967).

8. And lastly, the earth hath in law a great extent upwards, not only of water, as hath been said, but of ayre and all other things, even up to heaven; for *cujus est solum ejus est usque ad coelum* . . . .

COKE ON LITTLETON, Lib. 1, Ch. 1, § 1, at 42 (1628), quoted in R. WRIGHT, THE LAW OF AIRSPACE 16 n.20 (1968).

9. 2 W. BLACKSTONE, COMMENTARIES *18. For a detailed history of the maxim, see Klein, *Cujus Est Solum Ejus Est. . . . Quousque Tandem?*, 26 J. AIR L. & COM. 237 (1959). For the subsequent development of the maxim in England, see R. WRIGHT, *supra* note 8, at 11-13.

10. Cro. Eliz. 118, 78 Eng. Rep. 375 (Ex. 1586). The court held that it was not a nuisance for a landowner to build a house which shut off the light of another whose house had been erected thirty or forty years before, since it was the complaining landowner's "folly to build his house so near to the other's land." *Id.*

11. This doctrine, which is said to be the earliest attempt to assure a minimum standard of light to the ground story of all buildings, dates back to the reign of Richard Coeur de Lion in 1189. The practice of centuries was embodied in statute in the Prescription Act, 2 & 3 Wm. 4, c. 71 § 3, at 448 (1832). *See* G. FORD, BUILDING HEIGHT, BULK AND FORM 62 (1931).

12. 19 Wend. 309 (N.Y. 1838).

13. For collections of American cases on this point, see 3 R. POWELL, THE LAW OF REAL PROPERTY 485 (1970); 4 H. TIFFANY, THE LAW OF REAL PROPERTY 556 (3d ed. 1939).

14. 19 Wend. at 318.

15. 3 J. KENT, COMMENTARIES ON AMERICAN LAW *401. On the acceptance of the maxim *usque ad coelum* in America, see R. WRIGHT, *supra* note 8, at 31-65.

16. E. SCHULTZ & W. SIMMONS, OFFICES IN THE SKY 19 (1959) [hereinafter cited as OFFICES].

17. S. TOLL, *supra* note 1, at 49-50.

18. On the innovation known variously as the steel-frame building cage, or skeleton construction, see S. GIEDION, SPACE, TIME AND ARCHITECTURE 204-08 (5th ed. 1967). The ten-story Home Insurance Company Building in Chicago, completed in 1885, was the first American steel-frame structure. OFFICES, *supra* note 16, at 35-38.

19. Elisha Otis demonstrated the world's first safe elevator at the New York Crystal Palace Exposition in 1853. Otis would dramatize his new device's reliability by having himself pulled aloft, and then cutting the hoist rope: Quickly coming to a stop, he would announce to the crowd, "All safe, gentlemen!" S. TOLL, *supra* note 1, at 47-48. Nevertheless, it took developers several years to appreciate the possibilities of the elevator in commercial office buildings.

20. Other technical innovations also facilitated the rapid development of skyscrapers. Edison's advances allowed electricity to be distributed to virtually every street in Manhattan, and by the time New York's first steel-frame building was constructed, electric rather than gas illumination was the rule. Plate glass was mass produced by 1881. Finally, one historian has suggested that the telephone was also vital to the growth of the skyscraper. *See* S. TOLL, *supra* note 1, at 51.

21. Weisman, *New York and the Problem of the First Skyscraper*, J. OF THE SOC'Y OF ARCH. HISTORIANS, Mar. 1953, at 15.

22. This was the Equitable Building:

The history of this lower Manhattan building and its successor on the site brackets the beginning and end of the skyscraper's pre-zoning era. By disclosing the possibility of elevators in office buildings, the first Equitable Building started the breakout from the traditional five-story maximum. The following Equitable Building carried the development of the skyscraper to such intolerable extremes that, beyond any other structure, it may be isolated as the one building which was a final cause of zoning law.

S. TOLL, *supra* note 1, at 48.

23. In 1894, the cross atop Trinity Church lost its title as the highest point in New York, and the same year *Harper's Weekly* proclaimed "The Age of Skyscrapers." In 1896, the words "sky line" were used for the first time. J. KOUWENHOVEN, THE COLUMBIA HISTORICAL PORTRAIT OF NEW YORK 394 (1953). For a list of the names and heights of New York's office towers through 1915, just prior to the passage of the city's first zoning ordinance, see OFFICES, *supra* note 16, at 64-72.

24. Gregory, *Thoughts on the Architecture of High Buildings*, in SYMPOSIUM ON THE DESIGN OF HIGH BUILDINGS 345 (S. Mackey ed. 1962). *Cf.* L. SULLIVAN, *The Tall Office Building Artistically Considered*, in KINDERGARTEN CHATS AND OTHER WRITINGS 202 (1947).

25. By 1900, the port of New York was unloading nearly two-thirds of all American imports and sending on forty per cent of our exports. Because of the city's trade leadership, most banks kept reserve deposits there, and this accumulation of funds in turn made New York the security trading center of the nation. By 1900, sixty-nine of the country's 185 largest industrial combinations had their headquarters in the city. OFFICES, *supra* note 16, at 55-57.

26. *Id.* at 57. Indeed, between 1875 and 1925, land values increased so rapidly that it became economically prudent to demolish even fairly new buildings in order to use the land more intensively. *See* Nelson, *Appraisal of Air Rights*, 23 APPRAISAL J. 495 (1955), cited in Costonis, *supra* note 4, at 589 n.53. As city planner George Ford explained in his classic study:

As business increases, not in arithmetical proportion to population but according to a power of the increase in population, the intensity of business is greater in the larger cities. This causes a more rapid rise in land values of those cities and consequently quicker obsolescence of their office buildings.

G. FORD, *supra* note 11, at 123-24.

27. On the construction of the second Equitable Building and the opposition to it, see C. RODGERS, NEW YORK PLANS FOR THE FUTURE 163-64 (1943); S. TOLL, *supra* note 1, at 68-71; OFFICES, *supra* note 16, at 75-81. Besides the owners and tenants of office buildings in the congested financial district, there were two other groups which supported a comprehensive zoning resolution. Urban reformers wanted to insure adequate light and air to the crowded tenements of the lower East Side. *See* Williams, *The Evolution of Zoning*, 15 AM. J. OF ECON. & SOC. 253 (1956). And the merchants on Fifth Avenue, who had seen their business dwindle as the fashionable district was inundated by the garment workers from the lofts on the nearby side streets, hoped low height limits would insure that their customers would not be disturbed by strange tongues, dress, and odors. *See* S. TOLL, *supra* note 1, at 158-59.

28. NEW YORK CITY HEIGHTS OF BUILDINGS COMMISSION, REPORT TO THE COMMITTEE ON THE HEIGHT, SIZE AND ARRANGEMENT OF BUILDINGS OF THE BOARD OF ESTIMATE AND APPORTIONMENT OF THE CITY OF NEW YORK (1913) [hereinafter cited as 1913 REPORT]. The purpose of the Commission was announced in the opening statement of the *1913 Report*:

There is a growing sentiment in the community to the effect that the time has come when effort should be made to regulate the height, size and arrangement of buildings erected within the limits of the City of New York; in order to arrest the seriously increasing evil of the shutting off of light and air from other buildings and from the public streets, to prevent unwholesome and dangerous congestion both in living conditions and in street and transit traffic and to reduce the hazards of fire and peril to life . . . .

Id. at 1.

On the *1913 Report*, see S. MAKIELSKI, *supra* note 3, at 20-23; S. TOLL, *supra* note 1, at 143-71.

29. Height and court restrictions should be framed with a view to securing to each district as much light, air, relief from congestion and safety from fire as is consistent with a proper regard for the most beneficial use of the land and as is practicable under existing conditions as to improvements and land values.

1913 REPORT, *supra* note 28, at 67. The Commissioners demonstrated so much concern for "safeguarding of existing and future investments and the encouragement of an appropriate and orderly building development," *id.* at 68, that protection of health and life became almost secondary.

30. Although the concern with office skyscrapers had brought the Commission into being, the *1913 Report* revealed that not those buildings but department stores and hotels had the greatest average heights. Nevertheless,

> the much greater proportion of high office buildings and their concentration in a few areas make the determination of a maximum rule applicable to all buildings very largely a question of determining what rule will be most appropriate for office buildings in the areas of maximum congestion.

1913 REPORT, *supra* note 28, at 17.

31. At this time New York was virtually without any direct controls over height, save for apartment and tenement houses which were held to one and a half times the width of the widest abutting street. However, Chicago, Baltimore, Washington, Boston and a number of other American cities had direct controls over building height by 1913. *See* S. TOLL, *supra* note 1, at 155. The Supreme Court had reviewed Boston's height control regulations, holding that it was constitutional to enact such controls. Welch v. Swasey, 214 U.S. 91 (1909). A decade after the passage of the New York Resolution, the Court held that comprehensive zoning, going beyond mere height regulations, was also a constitutional exercise of the police power. Village of Euclid v. Ambler Realty, 272 U.S. 365 (1926).

32. Setback regulations require that a building, after rising from the street or lot line a certain height, must be set back from that line at some fixed ratio, for example, one foot for each three feet of height. The setback regulation is responsible for the distinctive pyramid effect of buildings in downtown New York and other large cities.

33. George B. Ford, architect and secretary to the Commission (and later author of the leading study of building bulk regulations, *see* note 11 *supra*, carved soap models of the possible envelopes of skyscrapers in order to visualize their height and setback configurations. E. BASSETT, AUTOBIOGRAPHY 125 (1939), cited in S. TOLL, *supra* note 1, at 165.

34. The height districts (designated as districts A through E) were the "one-times," "one-and-quarter-times," "one-and-half-times," "two-times," and "two-and-half-times" districts. Where the height map showed a "one-times" district, the height of a new building could generally not be greater than one times the street width (which of course meant the actual width of the street). G. FORD, NEW YORK CITY BUILDING ZONE RESOLUTION 6-15 (New York Title & Mortgage Co. 1917), cited in Sussna, *supra* note 7, at 158 n.10. The Commissioners' Plan of New York City of 1811, which established New York's gridiron pattern, had provided for broad thoroughfares. That plan laid out a dozen north-south avenues, each 100 feet wide. Crossing these at right angles every 200 feet were 155 streets, each sixty feet wide, running east-west between the two rivers. *See* J. REPS, THE MAKING OF URBAN AMERICA 296-99 (1965).

35. CITY OF NEW YORK, BUILDING ZONE PLAN 19 (1916), cited in Sussna, *supra* note 7, at 159 n.11.

36. The amount of prescribed open space for a lot became progressively greater in the five height districts A through E. But if property owners in C and D districts set aside, in addition to other required open space, ten per cent of the lot area for the joint recreational space of the plot, they could build according to the requirements of B and C districts. *Id.* at 22-24, cited in Sussna, *supra* note 7, at 160 n.16.

37. NEW YORK CITY COMMISSION ON BUILDING DISTRICTS AND RESTRICTIONS, FINAL REPORT 9, 46 (Supp. ed., The City Club of N.Y. 1916).

38. Horowitz, *Bassett on Density Zoning*, ZONING DIGEST, Aug. 1963, at 194, 195.

39. C. RODGERS, *supra* note 27, at 168; S. TOLL, *supra* note 1, at 204.

40. In the same period, only twenty new buildings rose in the former center of skyscraper construction, the financial district, while eighteen new ones were completed in the Times Square area. OFFICES, *supra* note 16, at 153.

41. G. FORD, *supra* note 11, at 46.

42. Ackerman, *Population Expectations, Zoning, Appraisals, and Debt*, 49 AMERICAN CITY, Oct. 1934, at 49, 50. During the Planning Commission campaign for the passage of the 1961 Zoning Resolution, the Commission chairman cited slightly smaller figures: "The city that our present zoning would permit is a nightmare of 55 million residents and 250 million workers." Felt, *Preface* to VOORHEES, WALKER, SMITH & SMITH, ZONING NEW YORK CITY at vi (1959) [hereinafter cited as ZONING NEW YORK CITY]. The difference may be explained by changed assumptions on the nature of new development, family size, trends in floor space per worker and other such variables. While the comparable residential figure under the 1961 Zoning Resolution is for a population of 10,900,000, ZONING NEW YORK CITY, *supra*, at 5, the potential working population capacity of the central business district was not published, if indeed ever calculated. "In any event that issue is really academic since the problem is not what the theoretical capacity was or is, but rather some realistic approach to what legitimate needs are and how best to balance these." Letter from Edwin Friedman, Assistant District Director for Metropolitan

New York, State of New York Executive Department of Planning Services, to author, Feb. 25, 1972, on file at *Yale Law Journal*.

43. NEW YORK CITY PLANNING COMMISSION, REPORT ON AMENDMENTS OF THE ZONING RESOLUTION OF THE CITY OF NEW YORK AFFECTING HEIGHT AND AREA 16 (1944). The persistent use of the old tools of regulation is revealed by a comparison of zoning textbooks written before and after the 1944 amendments. *See* G. SMITH, THE LAW AND PRACTICE OF ZONING 458-60, 462-69 (1937); L. SQUIRE, ZONING IN NEW YORK 18, 31 (1948).

44. Williams, *Deficiencies of Zoning Law and Legal Decisions,* in AM. SOC'Y OF PLANNING OFFICIALS, PLANNING 1950, at 164 (1951); Toll, *Zoning for Amenities,* 20 LAW & CONTEMP. PROB. 266 (1955); Vladeck, *Large Scale Developments and One House Controls,* 20 LAW & CONTEMP. PROB. 255 (1955); Note, *Building Size, Shape and Placement Regulations: Bulk Control Zoning Reexamined,* 60 YALE L.J. 506, 514-15 (1951).

45. *See* Toll, *supra* note 44, at 273.

46. ZONING NEW YORK CITY, *supra* note 42, at 49.

47. AM. SOC'Y OF PLANNING OFFICIALS, FLOOR AREA RATIO (Planning Advisory Service Report No. 111, 1958), provides a discussion of the device.

48. *See* Note, *supra* note 44, at 518 n.50. Four years later, the floor area ratio technique was described as "a comparatively recent concept." AM. PUB. HEALTH ASS'N, PLANNING THE NEIGHBORHOOD 40 (1948), cited in Toll, *supra* note 44, at 274 n.27. In 1955 one commentator observed that the floor area ratio regulation had, up to that time, appeared in but one case, decided in Ohio in 1925, in which there was dictum approval. Toll, *supra* note 44, at 274 n.27. The date of the case indicates the long dormancy of the technique.

49. S. MAKIELSKI, *supra* note 3, at 71-106.

50. *See, e.g.,* OFFICES, *supra* note 16, at 280-81. *Offices* was written under the sponsorship of the National Association of Building Owners and Managers (now the Building Owners and Managers Association International) in 1959, and was published just as the technique was gaining popularity among city planners. *See* AM. SOC'Y OF PLANNING OFFICIALS, *supra* note 47.

51. ZONING NEW YORK CITY, *supra* note 42, at 10-11.

52. *Id.* at 11. For a compilation of the present FAR ceilings in the central business districts of fourteen other major American cities, see AM. SOC'Y OF PLANNING OFFICIALS, CBD ZONING CONTROLS IN SELECTED CITIES (Planning Advisory Service Information Report No. 180, 1963). These ranged from a maximum FAR of 8 in Philadelphia to a maximum of 32.1 in Minneapolis. By contrast, the FAR ceiling in London's commercial districts is 4.5. Kahn, *Real Estate With A British Accent,* REAL ESTATE REV., Fall 1971, at 72, 73.

53. *See* S. MAKIELSKI, *supra* note 3, at 133-34, 137-38.

54. [T]he FAR limits were arrived at empirically, based on the fact that two-thirds of post-war office construction took place at FAR's of less than 18, the maximum proposed under the 1961 legislation. The final numbers were to some extent arrived at pragmatically as a result of a consensus of interests within the City. Letter from Norman Marcus, General Counsel, New York City Planning Commission to author, Mar. 2, 1972, on file at *Yale Law Journal*.

55. For the initial use of the bonus device in New York City's zoning, *see* p. 344 *supra*.

56. "The slight increase in maximum permitted bulk resulting from this bonus is well justified by the benefits of increased open space." ZONING NEW YORK CITY, *supra* note 42, at 127. Despite this explanation, other reasons for the FAR bonus were not aesthetic but political and economic. *See* note 54 *supra*. This twenty per cent floor area bonus provision has since proven to be "one of the most widely used features of New York City's 1961 zoning resolution." Barnett, *Case Studies in Creative Urban Zoning,* in THE NEW ZONING: LEGAL, ADMINISTRATIVE, AND ECONOMIC CONCEPT: AND TECHNIQUES 125, 127 (N. Marcus & M. Groves eds. 1970) [hereinafter cited as THE NEW ZONING].

57. The New York City Zoning Resolution defines the term "zoning lot" to include the following:

(c) A tract of land, located within a single *block*, which at the time of filing for a building permit . . . is designated by its owner or developer as a tract all of which is to be used, *developed*, or built upon as a unit under single ownership.

A *zoning lot,* therefore, may or may not coincide with a lot as shown on the official tax maps of the City of New York, or on any recorded subdivision plan or deed.

For the purposes of this definition, ownership of a *zoning lot* shall be deemed to include a lease of not less than 50 years duration, with an option to renew such lease so as to provide a total lease of not less than 75 years duration.

NEW YORK, N.Y., ZONING RESOLUTION art. I, ch. 2, § 12-10 (1971).

Although the concept of the "zoning lot" was first explicitly introduced by the 1961

Zoning Resolution, there were attempts to utilize it in the prior Resolution. Without express authorization, however, the courts refused to accept it. Letter from Norman Marcus, note 54 *supra*. However, in 1972 the New York Court of Appeals gave its blessing to what General Counsel Marcus called the "contiguous lot assemblage siphoning principle," even where the parties to the lease evidenced no express intention to reach that result. In that case the defendant's lease of the plaintiff's property, executed in 1953, had a minimum term of twenty-one years with options to renew for additional periods until the year 2052, and the defendant owned contiguous parcels in fee. The Court of Appeals held that he was entitled to full utilization of the leased parcel's development rights, absent a provision in the lease precluding their transfer—despite the fact, unmentioned by the court, that such a transfer was not even possible until the adoption of the 1961 Zoning Resolution, eight years after the lease was signed. Newport Associates, Inc. v. Solow, 30 N.Y.2d 263, 332 N.Y.S.2d 617, 283 N.E.2d 600 (1972).

For examples of the "zoning lot" concept in other cities' ordinances, see CHICAGO, ILL., MUNICIPAL CODE, ch. 194A, art. 3.2 (1970); AM. SOC'Y OF PLANNING OFFICIALS, GLOSSARY OF ZONING DEFINITIONS 12-13 (Planning Advisory Service Report No. 233, 1968).

58. New York City Planning Commission, Minutes 302 (May 1, 1968).

59. J. PYKE, LANDMARK PRESERVATION 2-3 (Citizens Union Research Foundation, Inc., 1970) [hereinafter cited as LANDMARK PRESERVATION].

60. For example, the construction of Lincoln Center during the late 1950's made the venerable Carnegie Hall expendable, and its owners subsequently announced their intention to raze the historic Hall and replace it with a modern office tower. Given the economics of midtown Manhattan, the Hall's owners were undoubtedly correct in asserting that they could realize more income from a commercial building located on the same site. Only when area businessmen and landlords joined the chorus of protest, because they depended upon the continued presence of the Hall, was the building saved through purchase by a quasi-public corporation. LANDMARK PRESERVATION, *supra* note 59, at 3.

61. *Id.* at 15.

62. *See* Jacobs, *New York's Office Boom*, ARCH. FORUM, Mar. 1957, at 104.

63. "The list of casualties included Pennsylvania Station, the Metropolitan Opera House, and the Singer and Guaranty Trust buildings on lower Broadway and the Brokaw mansions. In addition, during this time at least two other landmarks, the Times Tower and the Black Starr building on Fifth Avenue, were transformed by the placement of contemporary facades over the old skeletons." LANDMARK PRESERVATION, *supra* note 59, at 15.

64. *Id.*

65. *See* N.Y. GEN. CITY LAW § 20 (25-a), (McKinney 1968). The "Bard Law," named after its sponsor, Albert S. Bard, enabled the cities to adopt "[i]n any such instance such measures, [which] if adopted in the exercise of the police power, shall be reasonable and appropriate to the purpose, or if constituting a taking of private property shall provide for due compensation which may include the limitation or remission of taxes." *Id.* Such measures include provision for the "protection, enhancement, perpetuation or use [of landmarks], which may include appropriate and reasonable control of the use or appearance of neighboring private property within public view, or both." *Id.*

66. LANDMARK PRESERVATION, *supra* note 59, at 15; NEW YORK CITY PLANNING COMMISSION, PLAN FOR NEW YORK CITY, VOL. I: CRITICAL ISSUES 152 (1969) [hereinafter cited as CRITICAL ISSUES].

67. 2 NEW YORK, N.Y., CHARTER AND ADMINISTRATIVE CODE ch. 8-a (1971).

68. For a description of the Landmarks Preservation Commission's powers and functions, see Wolf, *The Landmark Problem in New York*, 22 N.Y.U. INTRA. L. REV. 99 (1967). *See also* LANDMARK PRESERVATION, *supra* note 59, at 16-24.

69. *See* 2 NEW YORK, N.Y., CHARTER AND ADMINISTRATIVE CODE ch. 8-a, § 207-5.0, a.(1) (1971).

70. *See, e.g.,* Burks, *Owners of Woolworth Building Call Landmark Law 'Onerous,'* N.Y. Times, Apr. 29, 1970, at 27, col. 3.

71. *See* 2 NEW YORK, N.Y., CHARTER AND ADMINISTRATIVE CODE, ch. 8-a, §§ 207-8.0, a.(1)-(2) (1971).

72. *See id.*, § 207-1.0, q. The statute provides that "net annual return" shall be the excess of earned income from the property over operating expenses, excluding mortgage interest, amortization, and allowances for obsolescence and reserves, but including a specified allowance for depreciation.

73. *Id.*, § 207-8.0, a.(2); *see* LANDMARK PRESERVATION, *supra* note 59, at 19.

74. They included forty-three residences, eighty churches and related buildings, sixty-nine public buildings, fifty industrial and commercial structures, seven cemeteries,

one bridge, and one tree. Although these officially designated landmarks could be found in every borough and every kind of neighborhood, the majority were in Manhattan. CRITICAL ISSUES, *supra* note 66, at 152.

75. LANDMARK PRESERVATION, *supra* note 59, at 18-19.

76. *See* Costonis, *supra* note 4, at 592 n.60.

77. *See* note 58 *supra*.

78. *See* p. 348 *supra*.

79. Address by Norman Marcus, Counsel of the New York City Department of City Planning, at the First Conference on Legal Techniques in Preservation, Washington, D.C., May 2, 1971, at 3. (Mimeo, copy on file at *Yale Law Journal*.) A modified version of this address was later published. *See* Marcus, *supra* note 4.

80. NEW YORK, N.Y., ZONING RESOLUTION, art. VII, ch. 4, § 74-792 (1971).

81. New York City Planning Commission, Minutes 303 (May 1, 1968). Preservation organizations greeted the transfer provisions enthusiastically. *See, e.g.,* Gilbert, *Saving Landmarks: The Transfer of Development Rights,* HISTORIC PRESERVATION, July-Sept. 1970, at 13.

82. "Fiscal zoning" is any act which encourages developments adding more in property taxes than they cost in public services. In its usual context, the term refers to jurisdictions which seek industrial and commercial uses and luxury housing. *See* NATIONAL COMMISSION ON URBAN PROBLEMS, BUILDING THE AMERICAN CITY 212 (1969). But it also embraces any practice which aims to produce tax revenues in excess of the cost of public services needed to encourage the development—and here, the only costs are the administrative expenses of the Planning Commission's approval of the development rights transfer, since the adequacy of public services in the area of transfer is not an explicit prerequisite for that approval. Former New York City Planning Commission member Beverly Spatt has publicly denounced development rights transfer as fiscal zoning. *See* Burks, *Planners Seek to Shift Custom House Air Rights,* N.Y. Times, Apr. 9, 1970, at 56, col. 4.

83. *See* p. 351 *supra*.

84. *See* address by Norman Marcus, *supra* note 79, at 6.

85. Fowler, *Grand Central Tower Will Top Pan Am Building,* N.Y. Times, June 20, 1968, at 1, col. 4.

86. OFFICES, *supra* note 16, at 52-54; Haskell, *The Lost New York,* ARCH. FORUM, Nov. 1963, at 107.

87. These were air rights in the classic sense of a property interest in a three-dimensional location in space. None of the buildings constructed on air rights leased or purchased from the New York (now Penn) Central receives ground rights from its legal possession of the air above the street level. These superimposed structures have no basements, and buy electricity, steam and hot water from the railroad. Trustees of Penn Central Transportation Company, Debtor, Proposed Sale of Mid-Manhattan Properties: General Memorandum 13-14, Aug. 11, 1971 (on file at *Yale Law Journal*).

88. Haskell, *supra* note 86, at 109.

89. *Id.*

90. Shipler, *Landmarks Zoning Change Proposed,* N.Y. Times, Oct. 7, 1969, at 34, col. 4.

91. Fowler, *Grand Central May Get A Tower,* N.Y. Times, Sept. 21, 1967, at 1, col. 4.

92. Fowler, *Breuer To Design Terminal Tower,* N.Y. Times, Feb. 24, 1968, at 30, col. 3.

93. Huxtable, *Architecture: Grotesquerie Astride A Palace,* N.Y. Times, June 20, 1968, at 37, col. 3.

94. N.Y. Times, Aug. 7, 1967, at 31, col. 6.

95. Shipler, *Landmarks Panel Bars Office Tower Over Grand Central,* N.Y. Times, Aug. 27, 1969, at 1, col. 4. The Landmarks Preservation Commission's procedures after denial of a petition for alteration are described at pp. 350-51 *supra*.

96. Shipler, *New Tower Sought For Grand Central,* N.Y. Times, Apr. 11, 1969, at 1, col. 7.

97. The following press accounts provide a running history of the litigation: N.Y. Times, Sept. 5, 1969, at 40, col. 1; Tomasson, *Penn Central Sues City in Fight to Build Grand Central Tower,* N.Y. Times, Oct. 8, 1969, at 51, col. 2; Waggoner, *Officials Called in Terminal Suit,* N.Y. Times, May 21, 1972, at 17, col. 1; Waggoner, *An Impressive Battery of Legal Talent Joins the Battle To Save Grand Central Terminal From Destruction,* N.Y. Times, July 30, 1972, at 18, col. 1.

98. Fowler, *Plan Board Seeks Wider Control of Rail Center,* N.Y. Times, July 3, 1968, at 70, col. 5. *See also* Bennett, *City Urged to Bar Terminal Tower,* N.Y. Times, July 14, 1968, at 45, col. 1.

The almost total blockage of surface traffic movement in the central business districts, disregard of limited parking regulations, and extensive double-parking have long been problems. In 1969 about 50,000 cars were towed off the streets. *See*

Ascher, *Welcome to New York*, 36 PLANNING: A NEWSLETTER OF THE AM. SOC'Y OF PLANNING OFFICIALS 21, 24 (1970).

Before the publication of the master plan in 1969, one noted planner questioned the lack of realism in the 1961 Resolution with regard to vehicular traffic and off-street parking. Sussna, *Parking and Zoning: A Case Study*, 21 TRAFFIC Q. 435, 440 (1967). Even Douglas L. Elliman, one of the city's major realtors, advocated keeping private automobiles out of Manhattan rather than encouraging any increase. N.Y. Times, Feb. 14, 1972, at 32, col. 5.

Following Rome's adoption, in the spring of 1972, of a plan to eliminate mass-transit fares and ban private motor vehicles from that city's center, spokesmen for Mayor Lindsay said that while the idea was attractive, especially as a way of discouraging the use of automobiles in New York, there was no source of financing for such an endeavor. The Lindsay administration has considered banning private motor vehicles from the city's center, and a few temporary pedestrian malls have been created on Madison Avenue and other thoroughfares. But the suggestion of a permanent ban has brought angry protests from merchants and businessmen, and no action has been taken. *See* N.Y. Times, April 1, 1972, at 27, col. 8.

99. *See* Fowler, *supra* note 98.

100. N.Y. Times, Nov. 28, 1968, at 36, col. 3. Ironically, the high FAR ceiling awarded the Grand Central Terminal area by the 1961 Resolution helped generate the economic threat to the landmark. The permitted FAR of the Terminal's zoning lot is eighteen, the Terminal itself being deemed a plaza which entitles the owner to a twenty per cent bonus above the regular district FAR ceiling of fifteen. *See* Shipler, *supra* note 90. Without those extra FAR rights, which had been added to the 1961 Resolution for political rather than planning reasons, *see* note 54 *supra* and accompanying text, the builder would have been in the same position that the Planning Commission hoped to put him with its "special transportation center districts"—that is, unable to afford to erect atop the landmark an office building any smaller than the full FAR eighteen envelope would permit.

101. Shipler, *supra* note 90.

102. NEW YORK, N.Y., ZONING RESOLUTION, art. VII, ch. 4, § 74-79 (1971). On "'owner-ship" of a zoning lot, see note 57 *supra*.

103. In his analysis of the New York plan of landmark development rights transfer, Professor Costonis criticizes the ordinance on the ground that transfer can only take place between contiguous lots. Costonis, *supra* note 4, at 586-87. But in this reading of the New York statute, Costonis seems to have missed the point that transfer over a greatly enlarged area—the keystone of his own "Chicago Plan"—was possible in New York more than two years before he published his own rights transfer proposal. Nor was Professor Costonis the first to suggest that development rights "hop, skip, and jump" from one lot to another some distance away. This was proposed by New York City Real Estate Commissioner Ira Duchan in April 1970. *See* Burks, *supra* note 4.

104. Marcus, *supra* note 4, at 375.
The Commission was ultimately more concerned with the realistic possibility that development rights would be transferred than with bowls of light and air when it amended the original development rights transfer sections to permit transfer across properties within a common chain of ownership.
Letter from Norman Marcus, *supra* note 54.

105. Marcus, *supra* note 4, at 375.

106. Before seeing any plans, the Planning Commission announced that, before clearing the project, it would have to be satisfied that the new tower would not overwhelm the Grand Central district with more office workers than its transportation and services could sustain. Fowler, *supra* note 91. The concern was justified, if later effectively abandoned. In the Grand Central area, 80,000 people emerge from the concrete between 8:00 and 9:00 A.M.; and 200,000 surface in the course of a day. Huxtable, *Slab City Marches On*, N.Y. Times, Mar. 3, 1968, § 2, at 22, col. 1. The Penn Central's new skyscraper would have brought another 12,000 people into the area. Fowler, *supra* note 85. Yet the same 12,000 would be overloading the same area even if the Terminal's development rights were dispersed among several railroad-owned lots or transferred in one great block under the amended provision for transfer.
The Commission knew the extent of this strain. In its *Plan for New York City*, the master planners noted:
The last major improvement in the subway system was completed in 1935. The subways are dirty and noisy. Many local lines operate well beneath capacity; but many express lines are strained way beyond capacity—in particular the lines to Manhattan, now overloaded by 39,000 passengers during peak hours.
CRITICAL ISSUES, *supra* note 66, at 48. The Lexington Avenue express—the only subway

line serving the area in which the Terminal development rights would be transferred—
carries 170 persons per car during the rush hour. *Id.*
107. *See* p. 352 *supra.*
108. *See* R. ANDERSON, ZONING LAW AND PRACTICE IN NEW YORK STATE, § 5.03, at 85
(1963); Comment, *Spot Zoning and the Comprehensive Plan,* 10 SYRACUSE L. REV.
303 (1959).
109. The *Plan For New York City* did not consider permitting development rights
transfers of the magnitude permitted by the 1969 amendment to Section 74-79, even
though the "Grand Central dilemma" is briefly discussed. CRITICAL ISSUES, *supra* note
66, at 152.
110. This figure is reached by adding the eighteen FAR, permitted under the
district limit, to the three FAR (twenty per cent) bonus for providing a plaza and
the 16.5 FAR transferred from Grand Central Terminal.
111. After filing its suit against the city, *see* p. 354 *supra,* the Penn Central
went bankrupt. On June 2, 1971, the bankruptcy trustees offered for sale virtually
all of the railroad's mid-Manhattan property. *See* Bedingfield, *Pennsy Will Sell 23
Valuable Sites in Mid-Manhattan,* N.Y. Times, June 3, 1971, at 1, col. 8.
   The only bid on the Terminal's development rights was made by the current
lessee of the air rights, UGP Properties, Inc. UGP made package bids for either
the Roosevelt Hotel or the Biltmore Hotel along with the Terminal development
rights in order to bring itself under the language of the landmark development
rights transfer provision and add to the maximum floor area permitted on the lot
cleared by the demolition of either hotel. The bankruptcy trustees, who had vowed
they would not sell the properties at "fire sale prices," rejected these bids: However
fair the bids for the hotels standing alone, UGP had offered only $3.5 million for
the fee to the development rights which they were leasing for $3 million a year for the
next half-century. Wall St. J., Oct. 18, 1971, at 6, col. 2; *id.,* Nov. 16, 1971, at 11, col. 1.
Although the trustees have since recommended the rejection of nine unexpired leases
of its mid-Manhattan properties, the UGP lease on the Grand Central air rights
was not among them. *Id.,* Jan. 17, 1972, at 14, col. 2.
112. New York's planners have at least acknowledged this legal problem, although
not in the Grand Central Terminal context and not explicitly in terms of the spot
zoning objection. In his address to the National Trust for Historic Preservation, Norman
Marcus asked rhetorically:
   Over how many blocks can the benefit of a preserved landmark be rationalized?
   Does, for example, the property owner on East End Avenue buried in the shade
   of an overbulk new apartment house benefit from the preservation of a landmark
   on Fifth Avenue over a mile away?
Address by Norman Marcus, *supra* note 79, at 13. *See also* Marcus, *supra* note 4, at 378.
   Professor Costonis has attempted to construct a legal foundation for transfer of development rights over a wide area. *See* Costonis, *supra* note 4, at 620-31. There have, however,
been no legal tests of the development rights transfer amendments and proposals discussed in this Note, since none have been transferred. *See* pp. 367-68 *infra.* The aim of
this study is not to decide the legality of development rights transfer, but rather to question its utility as a preservation method and its rationality as a zoning device in central
business districts which are already heavily congested.
113. CRITICAL ISSUES, *supra* note 66, at 152.
114. *See* p. 348 *supra.*
115. 1 NEW YORK, N.Y., CHARTER AND ADMINISTRATIVE CODE, ch. 15, § 384(b) (1963).
116. As quoted in Sher, *"Air Rights" Lease, Zoning,* N.Y.L.J., Oct. 9, 1970, at 1,
the operative clause of the lease provides:
   Section 401.(a) Tenant is hereby given the right, prior to or during the Demised
   Term, to combine the zoning lot of the Demised Premises, with the zoning lot
   of the Adjoining Premises, so as to obtain a combined Floor Area Ratio (as defined in the Zoning Resolutions and the Laws of the City of New York) for the
   zoning lots of the Demised Premises and the Adjoining Premises; however, as a
   result of such combination of zoning lots, Tenant shall not obtain more than
   one hundred thousand (100,000) square feet of floor area from the zoning lot of
   the Demised Premises.
117. The rent would be $35,000 a year for the first twenty years, and $50,000 for
the remaining fifty-five years, or $3.50 and $5.00 a year per square foot of ground
area, respectively. According to Real Estate Commissioner Ira Duchan, who supervised
the transaction, office rents in that area at the time of transfer were approximately
$7.00 and higher, and based on these figures, the developer would need to increase
his tenants' rents for 520,000 square feet of office space by less than seven cents per
square foot for the first twenty years, and less than ten cents per square foot for the
last fifty-five years, to cover his rental payments to the city for the privilege of

adding 100,000 square feet to his structure. *See Whether Hot or Cold . . . Air Rights Loom Today*, CITY TITLE INS. CO. RECORD, June 1970, at 1.

118. NEW YORK, N.Y., ZONING RESOLUTION, art. VII, ch. 4, § 74-792, 5.(c) (1971).

119. Letter from Norman Marcus, *supra* note 54.

120. "The zoning law change was specifically carpentered to fit the building plan at No. 1 Broadway . . . ." Burks, *supra* note 4, at col. 2. *See also* Dissenting Report of Commissioner Beverly Moss Spatt, in 4 New York City Board of Estimate, General Proceedings 3281-83 (1970). Other details of the Custom House development rights transfer are given in Burks, *Planners Seek to Shift Custom House Air Rights*, N.Y. Times, April 9, 1970, at 56, col. 4.

121. *See* Burks, *supra* note 120.

122. *See* p. 360 *supra*.
The planners' belated concern for the impact of development rights transfer on the transit system serving the area was well-founded. In the same year that the Commission hoped to approve the Custom House transaction, more than 14,000,000 riders used the single, narrow platform of the Bowling Green subway station. Realistically, no "higher amenity" could have been extracted from that single builder which would have countered the added strain of two thousand new workers arriving daily at that station. Dissenting Report of Commissioner Beverly Moss Spatt, *supra* note 120, at 3282.

123. This occurred for the same reason that no other development rights transfers have been manifested in new office buildings, *i.e.*, the weak market for new office floor space in New York. *See* Strachen, *The "Morning After" In New York Is Today*, REAL ESTATE REV., Fall 1971, at 46; Horsley, *Office Leasing Picture Dampens Building Plans*, N.Y. Times, Feb. 6, 1972, § 8, at 1, col. 1; Oser, *Vacancy Rate High in Midtown Offices, id.*, July 9, 1972, § 8, at 1, col. 5; Brown, *Rates of Occupancy in Office Structures Continue 2-Year Drop*, Wall St. J., Aug. 16, 1972, at 1, col. 6.

124. The new amendment provoked a resounding dissent from Planning Commissioner Beverly Moss Spatt, who said she did not believe the city should be "selling" zoning rights of public landmarks. Commissioner Spatt wrote:
This leasing is accomplished without referring the matter to the Planning Commission and, in actuality, makes today's text change meaningless and superfluous. Leasing and selling air rights in such an ad hoc manner is nothing but spot zoning. It can only lead to an unplanned future—to chaos.
Dissenting Report of Commissioner Beverly Moss Spatt, *supra* note 120, at 3283.
In an interview during the hearings preceding the amendment's adoption, she asked, "If we sell the air rights over the Custom House the first time, what will be next? The Public Library on 42nd Street? And the museums?" Burks, *supra* note 120, at col. 7. A Commission spokesman said later that the development rights over the Public Library might indeed be transferred in some future project. Mrs. Spatt, despite an energetic campaign, was not reappointed to the Commission when her term expired at the end of 1970. N.Y. Times, Jan. 1, 1971, at 32, col. 2.
The Custom House transfer proposal was a display of both bad planning and chutzpah. The federal government was and is the fee owner of the Custom House, and usually takes umbrage when the city designates a federal structure as a landmark which cannot be altered or enlarged. With the amendment of May 1970, which would have made the Custom House transfer possible, the Planning Commission seemed to propose bartering away development rights belonging to the federal government. The Executive Director of the Landmarks Preservation Commission "conceded a possible conflict of interest with the Federal Government in the Custom House case." Burks, *supra* note 4, at 9, col. 4.

125. NEW YORK, N.Y., ZONING RESOLUTION, art. VII, ch. 4, § 74-79 (1971), reads in pertinent part:
[T]he City Planning Commission may permit development rights to be transferred to adjacent lots from lots occupied by landmark buildings . . . and may permit in the case of residential *developments* or *enlargements*, the minimum required *open space* or the minimum *lot area per room* to be reduced on the basis of such transfer of development rights . . . .

126. New York City Planning Commission, Rep. CP-21420, in Calendar of the City Planning Commission of the City of New York, Nov. 18, 1970, at 3-8.

127. Knowles, *East Siders Claim High-Rise Victory*, N.Y. Times, Jan. 1, 1971, at 1, col. 2, at 32, col. 5.

128. The change would have applied along the whole East Side, as well as to a smaller area on the West Side abutting Central Park. *See* Knowles, *supra* note 127, at 1, col. 2. That the fashionable upper East Side was the real target of the proposal may be deduced from the Commission's rezoning of fifteen tracts in that area to permit more high-density apartment projects just over a year after the development rights plan was defeated. *See* N.Y. Times, Feb. 13, 1972, at 50, col. 1.

129. N.Y. Times, Feb. 13, 1972, at 50, col. 1. The same area's population during the working week is 350,000. Testimony of William J. Diamond, Chairman of Manhattan Community Board No. 8 on the Master Plan 1, Feb. 8, 1972 (mimeo, on file at *Yale Law Journal*).

130. CRITICAL ISSUES, *supra* note 66, at 115.

131. *Id.* at 140. The land cost of Manhattan private high-rise construction has gone from a range of $30-$70 per square foot in 1960 to the range of $60-$125 per square foot in 1970. NEW YORK CITY DEPARTMENT OF CITY PLANNING, INFILL ZONING 5 (1972) [hereinafter cited as INFILL ZONING].

132. CRITICAL ISSUES, *supra* note 66, at 141. To understand what these high densities mean, one need only compare the population per square mile of the most densely zoned areas in Manhattan with that of selected high density districts in other major cities in the world: Manhattan, 71,145; Paris, 69,368; Tokyo, 63,800; Mexico City, 61,864; London, 34,315; Moscow, 30,400. The population per square mile of the entire city of New York is 25,452. *Id.* at 37. Higher population densities do exist. According to its latest census, Calcutta has a density of 102,000 per square mile. G. MOORHOUSE, CALCUTTA 89 (1972).

133. CRITICAL ISSUES, *supra* note 66, at 141.

134. The Commission came under great pressure to remap these areas to R-10 density: Builders claimed the prices of R-8 tracts were so high that only through rezoning could they be profitably developed. CRITICAL ISSUES, *supra* note 66, at 20-21. In the 1969 master plan, the Commission correctly rejected this as a circular argument, even though it deplored the drop in construction of new apartments. *Id.* at 20-21, 141. Private housing construction of multiple dwelling units in Manhattan dropped from 5,837 in 1966 to 1,062 in 1970, largely as the result of the rise in the costs of construction and interest. INFILL ZONING, *supra* note 131, at 5, 38.

135. New York City Planning Commission, *supra* note 126.

136. Undaunted by its reversal, the Planning Commission later proposed to allow public institutions to increase their size by permitting development rights transfer from smaller, outlying buildings. The Commission argued that the proposed resolution would not alter the total density permitted an institution, but would permit greater flexibility in its deployment. Once again Community Planning Board 8's Chairman, William Diamond, challenged the proposal on the grounds that it would remove light and air now available to nearby apartments. Van Gelder, *Air Rights Issue Pressed By Board*, N.Y. Times, Sept. 19, 1971, at 54, col. 4. This scheme was then abandoned in favor of a proposed amendment which calls for the "updating of regulations pertaining to large-scale community facility developments, giving the [City Planning] Commission and the Board of Estimate the power to modify bulk regulations." Under the proposal, such institutions would not have to apply to the Board of Appeals and Standards in order to alter the size and location of new or existing construction. Goodman, *Planners Vote to Ease Zoning Rules for Community Institutions in the City*, N.Y. Times, April 6, 1972, at 39, col. 1. Thus, just as its development rights transfer plan for the mid-block brownstones was defeated by community opposition, the Planning Commission has moved to exercise other powers which will yield the same result: increased bulk in the buildings which were originally to have been the transferees of unused development rights.

The Commission's most recent proposal was presented at a public hearing on a developer's plans to replace Tudor City Park, two small, private oases on 42nd Street near First Avenue, with two new luxury apartment towers. Among the several zoning amendments drafted by the Commission staff to effect a compromise between the builder's goals and the local residents' desires was one proposing the establishment of Special Park Districts, within which the unused development rights of privately owned open spaces might be transferred to lots within the central business district. The transferee lots could be used for either residential or commercial purposes, and would be limited to a ten per cent overage on the normal FAR; the future use of the transferor lots would be limited to "park-related passive recreation for the general public." The specific purpose of the proposal is to "promote the most desirable use of land in this area and thus to conserve the value of land and thereby protect the City's tax revenues." New York City Planning Commission, Rep. CP-22128, in Calendar of the City Planning Commission of the City of New York, Oct. 4, 1972, at 7. At the hearing the Commission reached no decision on the matter. See Clines, *Planning Unit Approves Forest Hills Compromise*, N.Y. Times, Oct. 5, 1972, at 51, col. 1.

137. Community Planning Boards, set up officially under the new City Charter, operate at a local but not necessarily a neighborhood level. See NEW YORK CITY PLANNING COMMISSION, C/P/D: COMMUNITY PLANNING DISTRICTS, BOUNDARIES AND PROCEDURES FOR MODIFICATION (1968). There are twelve such boards in Manhattan, sixty in the city as a whole. Each board has fifty members. Its effectiveness is dependent on the

care with which the Borough President names members, the degree of consideration he gives board recommendations, and the spirit on the board itself.

138. Testimony of William J. Diamond, *supra* note 129, at 5.

139. In 1951 the voters approved a $500 million bond issue which they believed would finance a new subway under Second Avenue. Under a little-noted clause in the law, the money was instead utilized for urgently needed rehabilitation of signal systems and rolling stock on existing lines. The voters authorized $2.5 billion in state borrowing for improved transportation once more in 1967. *See* Ascher, *supra* note 98, at 23. In 1969, the master planners were still counting on "the projected Second Avenue subway" which would "greatly improve access to east midtown, the lower east side, and downtown, and by doing so take the pressure off the now badly overcrowded Lexington Avenue line." CRITICAL ISSUES, *supra* note 66, at 16. In October 1972, ground was finally broken for the first part of the Second Avenue line, which is to be completed in the fall of 1975. This segment is north of the areas for which development rights transfer devices have been proposed. There is no firm estimate of completion date for the southern portion of the line. *See* N.Y. Times, Oct. 28, 1972, at 35, col. 4.

140. Residents of the East Side call their district "asthma alley" because it has the highest rate of air pollution of any area in the city. Testimony of William J. Diamond, *supra* note 129, at 5.

Recently, City officials conceded that one of the metropolis' key air pollutants—suspended particulate matter, or dirt—had increased seven per cent over the past three years despite stepped-up control efforts. Bird, *City Air Found 7% Dirtier Than in '69*, N.Y. Times, Feb. 9, 1972, at 20, col. 4.

141. In hearings on the selective rezoning discussed at note 128 *supra, see also* IN-FILL ZONING, *supra* note 131, at 38-40, Board 8 Chairman Diamond substantiated this charge by making public a letter, part of which reads:

I believe an unfortunate and environmentally unacceptable precedent is being set by the rezoning of the fifteen R-8 areas in Manhattan to higher density R-10.

It is clear to us now that, unless we change our strategy, there will be areas of the City in which we will be unable to meet the Federally mandated 1975 air pollution standards for stationary type pollutants—sulfur dioxide and particulates. The areas likely to not meet standards include . . . eastern and northern Manhattan. Thus, the City should not increase the pollution burden in these areas by increasing housing density nor should it promote more people moving into these unhealthy areas rather than to less polluted areas of the city.

. . . We should gain concessions from the [builder] as to his methods of heating, cooling, power generation and refuse disposal.

. . .

The impact of 700 additional housing units on the eastern Manhattan air pollution problem is small to be sure, but the precedent is troubling.

Letter from Fred C. Hart, Acting Commissioner of the New York City Department of Air Resources, to Donald Elliot, Chairman of the New York City Planning Commission, Jan. 31, 1972, on file at *Yale Law Journal*.

Obviously, development rights transfer on the scale to be encouraged by proposed amendment 74-89 would have involved many more than the 700 units which aroused the Department of Air Resources' concern here.

142. New York City Planning Commission, *supra* note 126, at 7.

143. Knowles, *supra* note 128, at 32, col. 5.

144. [The neighborhood groups] fought it primarily to avoid relocation. They predicted that the proposal would generate the formation of assemblages of sites and result in ultimate elimination of ethnic and economic diversity from the old rent-controlled structures. This controversy has underscored the likelihood that a broadened air rights transfer provision, if applied to old rent-controlled housing, would cause relocation and social exclusivity.

Marcus, *supra* note 4, at 378. East Side residents repeated these arguments in combatting the Planning Commission's proposal to rezone selected sites a year later. *See* N.Y. Times, Feb. 13, 1972, at 50, col. 1.

145. *See* p. 363 *supra*.

146. Knowles, *supra* note 127.

147. *See* note 1 *supra* and accompanying text.

148. Marcus, *supra* note 4, at 378.

149. Weisman, *supra* note 128:

The principle of transferring air rights has been used before, mostly to allow owners of landmarks . . . to sell the rights over their structures as a compensation for not being able to demolish them.

Yesterday's proposal, however, was said to be the first time the principle was suggested to preserve the quality of a whole neighborhood.

150. *See* INFILL ZONING, *supra* note 131, at 38-40; N.Y. Times, Feb. 13, 1972, at 50, col. 1.

151. Conti, *supra* note 4, at 15, col. 5; Huxtable, *City Landmark Gets A Chance For Survival*, N.Y. Times, Aug. 2, 1970, § 8, at 1, col. 1.

152. Huxtable, *supra* note 151.

153. Address by Norman Marcus, *supra* note 79, at 9.

154. Marcus, *supra* note 4, at 376. Professor Costonis notes this as the reason for the delay of the Amster Yard Transfer. Costonis, *supra* note 4, at 578 n.16. However, in his indictment of the inefficiency of the "New York plan" for preserving landmarks through development rights transfer, *id.* at 586-89, he never mentions the factor on which development rights transfer in *any* city must depend: the metropolitan market for new office building space or high density residential developments. The market is, in turn, the product of a combination of factors, including the costs of land, labor, and money; and no mere loosening of the "straightjacket of administrative controls" in New York, in favor of the arguably more flexible "Chicago plan," is going to remove the market impediment to landmark preservation through development rights transfer.

The market for commercial space is currently severely depressed in several major cities, including Chicago (with a vacancy rate of over ten per cent and ten million more square feet of office space coming on the market by 1975), Boston (vacancy over eight per cent), Pittsburgh (over twenty-five per cent), Dallas (over twenty-five per cent), Houston, San Francisco, Los Angeles, Atlanta, St. Louis and Minneapolis. *See* articles by Horsley, Oser, and Brown, *supra* note 123. And of course, until this excess base is absorbed, the construction of new buildings incorporating landmark development rights can only mean increasing the density levels of these downtown areas.

155. Horsley, *supra* note 123. This oversupply has its roots in the fevered rental market of the late 1960's. From the mid-1940's through 1966, rental rates for new space in prime locations moved upward slowly, from $4.50 per square foot to $6.50. But in 1968 rates jumped to $8.50, and by 1969, rentals for 1971 occupancy were going for $10 per square foot. This rise in rentals was due to the shortage of space brought about by the rise in employment, which began to move up in 1965 much faster than before. *See* Carruth, *Manhattan's Office Building Binge*, FORTUNE, Oct. 1969, at 114, 115.

Where in 1968, some 4,980,000 square feet of office space came on the market, 1969 produced 11,980,000 square feet, 1970 added another 8,651,000, and the city-wide construction completion figure for 1971 was 14,869,000 square feet—the largest figure for any year in the postwar era. The city's rate of absorption of office space, which reached a peak of 9.9 million square feet in 1969, did not keep pace with this rate of development, and in 1970 only 6.2 million square feet were leased. Horsley, *supra* note 123.

156. This objection applies not only to Section 74-79 as amended, but also to Professor Costonis' "development rights transfer districts," which would be those areas where landmarks are concentrated. *See* Costonis, *supra* note 4, at 590.

157. *See* pp. 350-51 *supra*.

158. *See* p. 342 *supra*.

159. The Planning Commission has "nothing so neat as a table of conversion" for translating floor space into number of employees, but rather feels the figures in the 1961 zoning study are still "useful as rules of thumb." Letter from Norman Marcus, *supra* note 54. That study shows an average of 157 square feet per office worker in 1955 with a projected trend upwards to 190 square feet per office worker in 1975. ZONING NEW YORK CITY, *supra* note 42, at 11. The number of workers given in the text was calculated using the 157 square feet per employee figure.

160. *See* p. 360 *supra*, on the Custom House transfer, which was never consummated, and Dissenting Report of Commissioner Beverly Moss Spatt, *supra* note 120, at 3282, for the number of new office workers which its unused development rights represent.

161. A wide variety of preservation devices has been developed. *See, e.g.*, R. MONTAGUE & T. WRENN, PLANNING FOR PRESERVATION (Am. Soc'y of Planning Officials 1964); J. MORRISON, HISTORIC PRESERVATION (2d ed. 1965); Wolfe, *Conservation of Historic Buildings and Areas—Legal Techniques*, in 2 ABA SECTION ON REAL PROP., PROBATE & TRUST LAW, PROCEEDINGS at 18 (1963); Turnbull, *Aesthetic Zoning*, 7 WAKE FOREST L. REV. 230 (1971); Comment, *Legal Methods of Historic Preservation*, 19 BUFFALO L. REV. 611 (1970); Note, *The Police Power, Eminent Domain and the Preservation of Historic Property*, 63 COLUM. L. REV. 708 (1963); Comment, *Aesthetic Zoning: Preservation of Historic Areas*, 29 FORDHAM L. REV. 729 (1961); Special Issue, *Historic Preservation*, 36 LAW & CONTEMP. PROB. 309-444 (1971); Comment, *Landmark Preservation Laws: Compensation for Temporary Taking*, 35 U. CHI. L. REV. 362 (1968).

It has been argued that the New York City Landmarks Preservation Law, discussed at pp. 350-51 *supra*, "enables the city's Landmark Commission to exert considerably greater leverage in dealing with landmark owners than commissions in other cities enjoy." Costonis, *supra* note 4, at 581-82 n.30. However well-founded, this observation is no argument for the adoption of a zoning device such as development rights transfer if its employment compounds the congestion, pollution, and general aggravation of living and working in the central city.

Although the National Trust for Historic Preservation does not maintain a list of those cities permitting development rights transfer from landmarks, a search of the Trust's legal archives revealed no cities which authorized transfer other than San Francisco and New York. Letter from Roger Holt, Assistant for Legal Services, Department of Field Services, National Trust for Historic Preservation, to author, Mar. 10, 1972, on file at *Yale Law Journal*. San Francisco's law permits the transfer of a landmark's total unused development rights to adjacent parcels. SAN FRANCISCO, CALIF., PLANNING CODE § 122.4(b). But a published discussion of this provision does not reveal how often it has been used. Svirsky, *San Francisco: The Downtown Development Bonus System*, in THE NEW ZONING, *supra* note 56, at 139, 152.

162. On the depressed market for office space in several major cities, see note 154 *supra*. It seems likely that part of this unrentable floor space may have been developed through other FAR bonus devices, so that the bonus technique and the development rights transfer technique work at cross-purposes. Indeed, this seems to have been precisely the result in New York. *See* note 155 *supra*. For a comprehensive survey of the numerous bonus incentive zoning techniques employed in several major American cities, see M. BROOKS, BONUS PROVISIONS IN CENTRAL CITY AREAS (Am. Soc'y of Planning Officials, Planning Advisory Service Report No. 257, 1970).

163. In the first published version of what became the "Chicago Plan," Professor Costonis wrote of "the problem of super-density":

Transfers under the proposal must be carefully meshed with the municipality's planning and zoning standards. *Prevailing bulk limitations reflect or, at least, should reflect a careful assessment of the city's space needs and the capacity of its public services to handle the demands of the projected densities.* Addition or rearrangement of bulk threatens to upset this assessment . . . .

Transfers should be permitted only within the highest density commercial and residential zoning districts. *Public services and facilities are most plentiful in these districts and will not suffer overloads from the marginal density increases resulting from the program.*

J. Costonis & J. Shlaes, Development Rights Transfers: A Solution to Chicago's Landmarks Dilemma 7, May 13, 1971 (Chicago Chapter Foundation of the American Institute of Architects National Trust for Historic Preservation) (emphasis added). Certainly Costonis and Shlaes are correct in asserting that bulk limitations should reflect an intelligent assessment of a municipality's needs for space and services. But their claim that such facilities are most plentiful "within the highest density commercial and residential zoning districts" is simply not true in New York, and remains unsubstantiated with regard to other major American cities in either the jointly-authored study or the later Costonis article.

164. Randall, *The Question of Size: A Re-Approach to the Study of Zoning*, 54 ARCH. FORUM 117 (1931).

165. Costonis, *supra* note 4, at 629-30. This same attitude is apparent in a recent publication of the Department of City Planning in New York:

The changes in bulk called for in our proposals would still keep the areas involved well within the theoretical zoned capacity of the 1961 Zoning Resolution, and many lots affected would only be built with the number of units originally envisioned because they would merely be exempted from stringent technical regulations which had precluded development. Thus, the intent of the 1961 zoning in matching density with existing and planned facilities would be followed.

INFILL ZONING, *supra* note 131, at 9.

Yet when these proposed changes in bulk were announced, they provoked great opposition in the affected neighborhoods precisely because current population densities had *not* been matched "with existing and planned facilities." *See* N.Y. Times, Feb. 13, 1972, at 50, col. 1.

166. Letter from Edwin Friedman, *supra* note 42.

As A Method of Preserving Landmarks
The New York Plan: Transfers
to Adjacent Properties

From Euclid to Ramapo:
New Directions
in Land Development Controls

DAVID H. ELLIOTT
Chairman, New York City Planning Commission

NORMAN MARCUS
Counsel, New York City Planning Commission

IF city planners are to succeed in shaping the growth and development of modern American cities, they must regulate the use of land in far more affirmative ways than they were able to achieve with their traditional zoning ordinances. Land use regulations have historically been designed to prevent harm, *e.g.*, to separate incompatible uses, to limit density and scale of particular neighborhoods, to prohibit or restrict development where public services are unavailable and to protect adjoining parcels from invasions of their light and air. These regulations, based on single lot development, are not concerned with how a section of the city actually works, *i.e.*, what positive relationships between single lot development in a unique area should be encouraged—whether office workers have room to walk on the sidewalk or can get into a subway entrance. As general rules, single lot regulations tend to codify minimal standards. They encourage inexpensive and often inadequate solutions to circulation problems and amenity needs. Traditional zoning has thus helped turn the concentration of activities that is essential to the success of a city into congestion.

In our view, government should intervene in the development process, creating zoning and other techniques that will encourage and even coerce private investment to make the city a more pleasant and efficient place in which to live and work. Public steps will still have to be taken in certain situations to prevent development where necessary. Accentuating the positive does not mean eliminating the negative in all cases.

New York City has developed and refined a series of tools to shape the nature of private development. The techniques that have been used raise interesting questions about the legitimate extent of government control and about the nature of new interests in land that have been created. It is the purpose of this article to explore the legal aspects of some of these questions as well as to explore the use of zoning as a creative device for eliciting public benefit from private development.[1] . . .

Any city where land scarcity pushes land values to the point they have reached in Manhattan's central business district will be interested in exploring the extent to which development rights transfers afford the means of preserving low-density landmarks and recreational islands essential to the livability of a metropolis. After a brief presentation of the central concept, examples from New York City's experience will be discussed with particular attention paid to the mandatory development rights transfer imposed on the owner of the Tudor City Parks.

The development potential of a lot is defined by zoning controls. New York City's Zoning Resolution allows a certain height, bulk and density for structures on each lot, proportionate to the size of the lot and appropriate to its location. Where an underdeveloped lot is occupied by landmarks or private parks FAR controls in high-density areas provide every incentive to the owner of such a lot to demolish the present use and rebuild to the allowable FAR maximum.

Traditional zoning ordinances do not permit transfer of unused development rights to non-contiguous lots. Such conveyances are regarded as contrary to the prevailing notions about the need for uniformity of controls in a given area. It is felt that the essential interrelationship of zoning density controls to street width, transit access, school seats, and other objects of planning concern could not survive indiscriminate transferability of unused development rights between widely spaced parcels. The unit of development control chosen by most ordinances was the zoning lot. Had a different unit of control been chosen as its basis—perhaps a block basis, or a square mile basis—there would have been no bias against wider area transferability of development potential. A block-by-block control can achieve density objectives as successfully as a lot-by-lot approach.[60]

It became necessary to find another location for the unused development potential of socially beneficial lots if the present desirable underdevelopment was to be retained. The three development rights transfer schemes discussed below all solved this problem. In the case of Amster Yard, the valuable unused development rights are transferred to a contiguous adjacent lot. In the case of the South Street Seaport, transfer may be made to designated non-contiguous lots within a radius of a few blocks.

In the case of the Tudor City private parks, their development rights are transferred out of the immediate vicinity to the adjacent midtown Manhattan business district.

1. *Next Door: Amster Yard*

Amster Yard is a 19th century collection of small residential structures and stores in Midtown Manhattan.[61] A logical outgrowth of the courts' gradual acceptance of "aesthetic zoning" as an extension of the police power[62] has been the demand for the preservation of landmark buildings like Amster Yard and historic districts. Early efforts in this area relied primarily on the use of private capital for the acquisition of threatened buildings. It was not until 1956 that the New York State legislature passed enabling legislation for the designation of landmarks and historical districts.[63] Nine years later, the City responded with its Landmarks Preservation Law[64] and the creation of the Landmarks Preservation Commission.

Landmark officials were still faced with the problem of finding a way to make zoning regulations work for, rather than against, landmarks. In areas zoned for high density development, small landmark structures like Amster Yard are ripe for demolition and redevelopment.[65] A technique was needed to fine tune the municipality's police power so that it would neither ride roughshod over the property rights of the landmark owners nor force the City to become ultimately bankrupt rather than face the destruction of its cherished heritage.

The City's solution was to offer the landmark owner the option to sell the development rights from a landmark and transfer them to an eligible receiving lot in the form of a developmental floor area bonus for such lot.[66] This innovation differed from the approach adopted in the special districts in two ways. First, the floor area bonus mechanism was being used to save pre-existing bricks and mortar threatened with demolition. Second, the development rights were being transferred across zoning lot lines, rather than being generated on the zoning lot by new development which itself contained a desirable amenity or uneconomic use.

Traditionally, the New York City Zoning Resolution has permitted the transfer of development rights between two contiguous zoning lots which are in the same ownership. Structures on such lots can be held in fee ownership or through a long-term lease arrangement.[67] In 1968, a zoning amendment was adopted which permitted the landmark's development rights to be transferred to a non-contiguous lot.[68]

In effect, the development rights transfer was used to add rentable floor space to a new development contiguous to or across the street from the low height and unique character of the landmark. The rationale for this approach was founded in traditional land regulation theory: the contiguous or across-the-street lot benefits from the low landmark in terms of light and air and the City preserves part of its heritage.

Saving a landmark from the wrecker's ball does not ensure its preservation. The 1968 amendment while requiring a program for continuing maintenance does not, however, favor one particular solution to the problem. In some cases, a historic structure can be made self-supporting either by virtue of tourist fees or profitable commercial or residential use.[69] In 1970, the City recommended that income from a $100,000 trust fund be applied to the maintenance of the 19th century Amster Yard, a privately owned series of homes, stores and interior garden.[70] The owner of this landmark proposed to sell a portion of his unused development rights to a contiguous parcel on Third Avenue, where an office building was going to be built. This private transaction was consummated and blessed by the City which made sure that the facade of the new building would be compatible with that of the smaller landmark structure.[71]

2. *Within the Immediate Vicinity: South Street Seaport*

An even more ambitious development rights transfer scheme involved the transfer of air rights within an urban renewal area.[72] The purpose of the Special South Street Seaport District was to make it possible to preserve and restore a number of approximately 200 year old historic buildings from the Fulton Fish Market in Lower Manhattan while accommodating, at the same time, the construction plans of the developers.

The Special District contains a preservation area and a redevelopment area.[73] In accordance with the detailed urban renewal plan, the low-scale of the Seaport will be retained by transferring development rights above the low buildings to specified neighboring locations for commercial development. All of the floor area potential not exhausted by the old structures[74] may be shifted onto specified parcels within the district.

In addition to conveyances to specified redevelopment lots, conveyance to middlemen was authorized, as well as subsequent conveyance in a chain that was required to end on one of the specified redevelopment lots. The attempt was to make the development rights as marketable as possible. An early sale would mean an early start on the historic building renovation. In effect, a bank of development rights was authorized, under the immediate management of private individuals, whose ultimate disposition was directed by the City in the Special South Street Seaport District zoning legislation.[75]

3. Outside the Immediate Vicinity: Tudor City Parks

Adjacent to Manhattan's densely populated Central Business District a small patch of green can bring to passersby a welcome sense of escape from monolithic skyscrapers and the cacophony of the City streets. In many respects, the small park is more important as an amenity than a landmark building or a shopping arcade. In the past, a few public-spirited citizens have seen fit to donate such urban oases to the City,[76] but such demonstrations of generosity are rare. The recently enacted "Special Park District" amendment to the Zoning Resolution[77] will ensure the preservation as public parks of existing private parks without cost to the City through a development rights transfer system.

The impetus for this proposal came from the plan announced by a developer to build on two small private parks that he had acquired as part of the Tudor City complex on Manhattan's east side. Local residents, however, urged the City to save the forty-year old parks which are valued at more than three million dollars. The land costs precluded purchase of the parks by the City. Instead, the Planning Commission took the unusual step of scheduling a public hearing to outline five different development strategies.[78] The final option, the creation of a special park district prohibiting development on designated parks and mandating transfer of development rights therefrom, was the one ultimately approved.[79]

The "P" District provisions could add a number of privately-owned parks, in addition to those at Tudor City, to a public classification. The legislation will also accord the same transfer rights to privately-owned land in the Midtown core which has been mapped as a public park, but has not as yet been acquired.[80] The zoning amendment stipulates that all such areas must meet uniform standards and be properly maintained. It will thereby enable the City to add new parks within this high land value area without adding to its capital or expense budgets.

The question that legal scholars must address themselves to is how far may the police power be extended in a regulation of this type without encroaching upon constitutionally protected property rights.[81] The Special Park District proposal would seem a logical extension of the municipality's general police power:

a. The provision of open space and parkland for City inhabitants falls within the scope of the "general welfare" requirement.[82]

b. The forced dedication of land for park and recreational purposes has been upheld by the courts as within the police power.[83]

c. The case of the owner of a private park can be readily distinguished from that of the owner of a revenue-producing facility,[84] where the courts will be more disposed to find that a purported regulation amounts to a "taking" for which just compensation must be paid.

d. The special needs of New York City add credence to the "public purpose" rationale of the regulations. The Supreme Court itself has indicated that the zoning power of municipalities increases as their size and problems increase. In *Euclid*, the court said that "a regulatory zoning" ordinance, which would be clearly valid as applied to the great cities, might be clearly invalid as applied to rural communities.[85]

e. The Special District calls for the preservation of an existing use, rather than a dedication of land for use in the future by an indeterminate group of people. Such innovative techniques of land regulation have found great receptivity in the courts, especially where the regulations' rationality is supported by a firm comprehensive planning basis.[86]

f. The Special "P" District would serve to provide amenities to the public without further threatening the liquidity of the City's fiscal resources. "The economic and physical well-being of the municipality and its inhabitants, both governmental and personal, depends on the ability to furnish the necessary governmental services without at the same time bringing about a confiscatory tax levy."[87]

g. The use of the City's eminent domain power is neither a justifiable nor viable alternative in terms of fiscal policy. First, the protection of economic position—the most salient effect of the constitutional prohibition against uncompensated takings—is not compromised by the Park District proposal. Given the provision allowing the transfer of development rights, the proposal would not take from the owner of a granting lot the economic benefit of his property; it would merely direct him to exploit his property's development potential in a way that, while perhaps unorthodox, would nevertheless be economically beneficial. Second, the City's shortage of funds would preclude or seriously delay any attempt to acquire and maintain private parks.[88]

NOTES

1. Zoning admittedly has minimal impact in areas where private investment is unprofitable. In these areas the City has relied most heavily on its capital budget and eminent domain urban renewal powers which have traditionally employed use and design parcel controls in the public interest which were individualized to reflect the needs of a particular neighborhood.

60. N. Marcus, *Air Rights Transfers in New York City*, 36 LAW & CONTEMP. PROB. 372-79 (1971).

61. Amster Yard is located on a through-block property east of Third Avenue between 49th and 50th Streets.

62. People v. Stover, 12 N.Y.2d 462, 191 N.E.2d 272, 240 N.Y.S.2d 734 (1963), *appeal dismissed*, 375 U.S. 42 (1963). (Ordinance prohibiting clotheslines from yards abutting a street was upheld as a valid exercise of police power in order to preserve the residential appearance of the area.)

63. LAWS OF NEW YORK of 1956, ch. 216 § 1, now N.Y. GEN MUNIC. LAW § 96(a) (McKinney Supp. 1972). *See*, J. J. Loflin, *Zoning and Historic Districts in New York City*, 36 LAW & CONTEMP. PROB. 363, 364 (1971). The passage of this law (the Bard Act) empowered the City to:

provide, for places, buildings, structures, works of art, and other objects having a special character or special historical or aesthetic interest or value, special conditions or regulations for their protection, enhancement, perpetuation or use, which may include appropriate and reasonable control of the use or appearance of neighboring private property within public view, or both. In any such instance such measures, if adopted in the exercise of the police power, shall be reasonable and appropriate to the purpose, or if constituting a taking of private property shall provide for due compensation. . . .

64. NEW YORK CITY ADMINISTRATIVE CODE, ch. 8-A, § 205-1.0 *et seq.* (Supp. 1970).

65. Many of the four- and five-story midtown landmarks are located in zones which could accommodate residential or commercial structures many times their size.

66. N. Marcus, *Air Rights Transfers in New York City*, *supra* note 60, at 374.

67. "For the purposes of this definition, ownership of a zoning lot shall be deemed to include a lease of not less than 50 years duration, with an option to renew such lease so as to provide a total lease of not less than 75 years duration." ZONING RESOLUTION § 12-10 (definition of "zoning lot").

68. ZONING RESOLUTION § 74-79 *et seq.*

69. Examples include Boston's Old City Hall, now thriving as a private office building, and Ghiradelli Square in San Francisco, where a former candy factory is now a stunning multi-level complex of boutiques and public open spaces. For other examples, *see generally* PROGRESSIVE ARCH., Nov. 1972.

70. NEW YORK CITY PLANNING COMMISSION REP. CP-21236 (July 20, 1970).

71. N. Marcus, *Air Rights Transfers in New York City*, *supra* note 60, at 376.

72. Special South Street Seaport District, ZONING RESOLUTIONS § 89-00 *et seq.*

73. *Id.* § 89-02, 89-05. Preservation areas are designated as granting lots; redevelopment areas are designated as receiving lots.

74. These landmark buildings were rezoned for a bulk of FAR 10.

75. *Cf.* Costonis, *The Chicago Plan: Incentive Zoning and the Preservation of Urban Landmarks*, 85 HARV. L. REV. 574 (1972).

76. Two examples are Paley Park at 53rd Street near Madison Avenue and Green-acre Park at 51st Street between Second and Third Avenues.

77. ZONING RESOLUTION § 91-00 *et seq.* An interesting question is posed by the existence of a security interest in the designated park. The instrument establishing the terms and conditions of such security interest should be amended to encumber the development rights with the same security interest as had attached to the designated park.

78. a. The City could do nothing and allow two towers under existing traditional zoning.

   b. Zoning and mapping changes could be granted permitting development of a 46-story tower on a platform spanning 42nd Street.

   c. The tower could be built on the northern park, which would be replaced by a new park on a bridge over 42nd Street.

   d. Two towers would replace the existing private parks, but a new park would be created on a deck over 42nd Street.

   e. Creation of a special park district.

Innovative Proposals for Tudor City Parks, City Planning News, Sept. 19, 1972. *See also* N.Y. Times, Dec. 18, 1972, at 38, col. 2 (editorial).

79. "It was a rare outburst at a City Planning Commission hearing—the audience standing up and applauding the Commissioners after a vote. 'I wish I could kiss all of you', said one elderly woman, while her neighbors in the Tudor City complex . . . talked happily about their victory." Freiberg, *2 Parks Saved in Tudor City,* N.Y. Post, Nov. 9, 1972, at 11, col. 1.

The "Special Park District" which may be located anywhere from 38th to 60th Streets, river to river, will require owners of designated existing private parks to sell or transfer their allowable development rights from the designated park to other parcels within the district between Third and Eighth Avenues. Owners of parcels receiving the development rights may have their FAR increased by as much as 20 percent, if they have a ground area of at least 30,000 square feet and are in a commercial district with a FAR of 15. Parcels within the Special Fifth Avenue and Theater Districts are ineligible as receiving lots because of public policy against competing with objectives of incentive zoning in those districts. ZONING RESOLUTION § 91-00 *et seq.*

80. An existing mapped park in private ownership on Tenth Avenue could qualify under this provision.

81. *See* Pennsylvania Coal Co. v. Mahon, 260 U.S. 393 (1922).

82. *E.g.,* Gorieb v. Fox, 274 U.S. 603 (1927). It is hard to see any controlling differ-ence between regulations which require the lot owner to leave open areas at the sides and rear of his house and limit the extent of his use of the space above his lot and a regulation which requires him to set his building a reasonable distance back from the street. Each interferes in the same way, if not the same extent, with the owner's right of dominion over his property. All rest for their justification upon the same reasons which have arisen in recent times as a result of the great increase and con-centration of population in urban communities and the vast changes in the extent and complexity of the problems of modern city life. *See also* HAAR at 404-05.

83. Ayres v. City Council of Los Angeles, 34 Cal. 2d 31, 207 P.2d 1 (1949) (require-ment of a ten-foot strip of land for tree and shrub planting purposes); In re Lake Secor Development Co., 252 N.Y.S. 809 (Sup. Ct. 1931) (neighborhood playgrounds or other recreation uses required within the subdivision); Jenad Inc. v. Village of Scars-dale, 18 N.Y.2d 78, 218 N.E.2d 673, 271 N.Y.S.2d 955 (1966).

84. Vernon Park Realty Inc. v. City of Mount Vernon, 307 N.Y. 493, 121 N.E.2d 517 (1954).

As A Method for Preserving Open Space: The New Jersey Proposal

Transfer of Development Rights: New Concept in Land Use Management

B. BUDD CHAVOOSHIAN
Land Use Specialist,
Rutgers University

THOMAS NORMAN, ESQ.
Institute of Environmental Studies,
Rutgers University

GEORGE H. NIESWAND
Associate Professor,
Rutgers University

In March, 1972 B. Budd Chavooshian and Dr. George H. Nieswand initiated the research and study of the Transfer of Development Rights (TDR) principle as a land-use control device to preserve farmlands and other critical land resources. Thomas Norman, Esq. shortly joined them to provide legal analysis and services. The Division of State and Regional Planning of the New Jersey Department of Community Affairs took an early interest and participated in the research activities. Subsequently, funds were provided by the New Jersey Open Space Policy Commission to develop fully the TDR concept and draft a legislative proposal. A small group of specialists from related disciplines was invited to serve on an advisory committee (see end of following article) to assist them in this research effort which was completed about May, 1973. In addition, Chavooshian and Nieswand, assisted by research intern Teuvo M. Airola who was working with the research team, developed a gaming device to investigate some of the problems and issues of the TDR concept. In view of the general interest expressed in the game, a manual for conducting the game has been published.

The following article describes the TDR concept as it was developed by this effort. However, the main focus and thrust of this research was the legislative proposal, which provided the research vehicle to analyze policy issues and substantive approaches and answer constitutional, legal, and administrative questions. A final report and the legislative proposal were submitted to the Open Space Policy Commission and the New Jersey Department of Community Affairs, and this article was published and given wide distribution in order to receive as great a feed-back as possible. It was agreed that for obvious reasons the legislative proposal would not be included in that publication nor would it be given immediate general distribution. The complete text of the legislative proposal is included at the end of the following article.

The publication received considerable attention throughout the country and in such countries as England, Australia, and New Zealand. The notion of transferring development rights as a device to preserve open space was of particular interest to the British since they had previously attempted to nationalize development rights. As further evidence of interest in this unique land-use management tool the article was reprinted by the Urban Land Institute, The Urban and Regional Development Center of the University of Florida, and the New Jersey Federation of Planning Officials.

We are pleased by the increasing interest in TDR, which reinforces our original belief that it is a valid land-use control device to preserve critical open spaces. We commend the Center for Urban Policy Research for publishing this edited reader which should aid in furthering the understanding of and dialogue on this unique land-use device.

THE NEW LAND USE CONCEPT

How can we protect critical natural areas, preserve open space, and ensure a high quality of life, yet at the same time accommodate the legitimate development demands of a growing society?

Whatever course is taken, it won't be easy! The purpose of this article is to describe a new concept of land use controls which holds the promise of achieving this seemingly impossible objective. It is called *transfer of development rights* (TDR). This is an uncomplicated idea—yet very different from centuries old traditional laws governing land ownership and development.

THE UNLIMITED LAND SYNDROME

American attitudes toward real property were inherited from the English land-tenure system and were strengthened during colonial times when there seemed to be unlimited land available. As expressed, for example, in the Northwest Ordinances of 1787, the central idea was ownership of land in "fee simple," which meant ownership that confers upon the owner the right to do anything he wants with his land except what is prohibited by local, state, and federal governments. In a sense land was treated as an unlimited commodity as abundant as air and water.

Once the early settler purchased title to his land, he had a free hand to farm it, mine it, build houses or stores on it, or simply hold it as an investment. However, as urbanization increased, the freedom to build as one desired without limitations was substantially restricted by zoning and planning under the exercise of the police powers. Today, the increased awareness of present and possible environmental problems is adding other restrictions to the development process and is further narrowing that unlimited freedom to develop, once so closely associated with land ownership.

THE NEED FOR ACTION

Land is modern man's most precious natural resource and its wise use is imperative. A highly developed, technological society ought to possess and enjoy an environment of the highest quality, but until very recently, land-use policies dictated by economic, political, and social (or perhaps antisocial) considerations have insensitively and irresponsibly squandered the land. For the most part an environment has been created that is not worthy of modern man's intelligence and highly advanced technology.

Generally, it is realized that open space provides aesthetic, psychological, and social values in the form of scenic landscapes, rolling and wooded hills, farmlands, stream valleys, flood plains, protected aquifer recharge areas, marshes, meadows, and historic sites. Yet rarely have these areas been retained and protected for their treasured and essential qualities in the planning, zoning, and development of a community. This is a strange paradox, although there are some signs now that limited open-space preservation is being recognized and dealt with in various ways, such as wetlands and flood-plain protection laws, coastal zoning, state land-use guidelines, and open-space purchase programs.

THE PROBLEMS OF ZONING

The basic technique used to guide the preliminary stages of development is conventional zoning which finds its basis for authority in a power not suited to protect open space and natural resources. Occasionally, the judicious application of geologic, physiographic, and hydrologic data sometimes did produce zoning classifications and densities that were less damaging to the natural environment than was random development.

However, in general little if any of the essential natural resources are preserved. The courts often find that zoning regulations intended to preserve large areas of land are unduly restrictive, confiscatory, and therefore, unconstitutional. Moreover, conventional zoning cannot and did not preserve natural environmental qualities; at its very best it could only provide for the harmonious and efficient development of *all* the land. Under zoning land is considered a commodity programmed to be developed for some appropriate use, a notion entirely consistent with our frontier heritage.

To overcome this shortcoming in zoning new concepts were developed to preserve some open space, such as the "greenbelt" concept borrowed from the "garden cities" principle established by the British. The outstanding example is Radburn, in Bergen County, New Jersey. Other techniques such as clustering, density zoning, performance zoning, floor-area-ratio, and planned unit development (PUD) were prompted by the housing boom of the fifties and sixties which permitted municipalities to explore and experiment with techniques to preserve some open space, rather than have entire tracts developed on a lot-by-lot basis. Cluster zoning—essentially the Radburn principle—was discussed extensively but used infrequently.[1] Planned unit development, a more sophisticated version of cluster zoning, is currently receiving greater attention in New Jersey.[2] The main thrust of all these devices and mechanisms was to preserve some open space and give relief from the typical monotonous sprawl development created by conventional zoning.

However, since these devices are generally applied to small areas and are usually an option to the existing lot-by-lot subdivision process within a municipality, the best to be achieved is some minimal break in an otherwise monotonous development. Haphazard, noncontiguous, scattered open space generally is the result. This is not necessarily bad or undesirable, but it does not protect the large areas of open space, such as farmlands, steep and wooded slopes, and aquifer recharge areas, that are necessary if the water and air supply is to be free from serious pollution as the population increases.

Of critical importance for the 1970's is an environmental balance that will ensure health and safety, retain open and productive land for water and air quality, and give psychological relief from the continuous sprawl of the megalopolis. The challenge is to accomplish this without creating so-called wipeout conditions for some landowners while creating windfalls for others—to adopt a land use control policy that balances legitimate development needs with valid environmental concerns in a positive, rational, and equitable manner.

PLANNING AND DEVELOPMENT RIGHTS

Almost any small town or city newspaper can provide a lengthy chronicle of battles waged over land use. In many cases, an individual property owner may wish to maximize the value of his investment, but his neighbors feel that development and the concomitant loss of open space threatens the desirability of their community as a place to live.

Besides the basic constitutional question of individual property rights and due process, development raises the plus of increased taxes for hard pressed municipalities against the minus of possibly making the community a less desirable place to live.

The transfer of development rights is a new technique to help solve this fundamental dilemma without violating basic rights and due process as guaranteed under the Constitution. It combines planning with certain aspects of property law.

The basic process is initiated when the municipality designates an area of open space and prohibits development therein, and the residential development potential in that area is transferred to another district or districts where the municipality determines that development is feasible.

Landowners in the preserved areas, who will continue to own their land, may sell their rights to further development to other landowners or builders who wish to develop those areas in which development is agreed on.

Transfer of development rights helps a community plan its growth. The net effect is the preservation of environmentally important areas with equitable compensation for the owners. There is no cost to the taxpayers since no acquisition by government is involved, and at the same time, the housing needs of a growing population can continue to be met.

CURRENT USE OF THE TDR TECHNIQUE

One of the first, if not *the* first, to suggest TDR as a technique to preserve open spaces was Gerald D. Lloyd.[3] Perhaps because it was too new an idea and too different from traditional property ownership and development laws, Lloyd's suggestion was not seriously pursued or developed into a workable form.

Almost 10 years later a technique of this type was adopted in New York City.[4] It allows air rights (one form of development right) to be tranferred from districts where strict height limitations are set (similar to open areas that are to be kept open) to districts where new higher height limitations are permitted. Since land values in New York are extremely high, the builders' incentive to purchase air rights is very great. The City of Chicago has been considering the adoption of a similar but more comprehensive TDR approach to preserve historic buildings as proposed by Professor John J. Costonis of the University of Illinois Law School.[5] A very limited TDR ordinance has been adopted in Washington, D.C.

Another example is Southampton Township in Suffolk County, Long Island which has adopted a zoning ordinance with an optional transfer of development rights to preserve prime agricultural lands.[6] Farmers are given the option of developing entire tracts under conventional zoning or of clustering development with in an area covering between 20 and 40 percent of the entire tract.

This resembles cluster zoning, but in certain cases farmers can transfer the development potential (rights) of their lands to another tract in a different district where a higher density is permitted. The farmland would then be placed in a municipal land trust and held as farmland in perpetuity. The farmer could continue to farm and pay a nominal annual rent, all the while benefiting from the development taking place on the off-site tract.

The Southampton ordinance is the first to apply the concept of transferring development rights offsite, but due to its voluntary nature, it does not assure the preservation of farmland.

The tiny community of St. George in Vermont, under the leadership of Armand Beliveau, has adopted the TDR technique to preserve its rural characteristics and set the basis for a rational growth and development plan.[7]

The first state legislation to create districts within which development rights would be transferred was introduced by Senator William Goodman in the Maryland Senate in January 1972.[8] Essentially the bill provides for the designation of planning districts where development would be permitted. Landowners would receive development rights in proportion to the amount of land owned, measured as a percentage of total acreage in the district.

These development rights *must* be purchased by builders, since *no* building would be permitted unless sufficient rights had been obtained. This in turn would guarantee a specified amount of open space. The value of the development rights would be determined by market conditions, but local officials would set the open space requirement.

Finally, Montgomery County in Maryland has a new ordinance which provides for the transfer of development rights for certain selected purposes. Several municipalities in New Jersey, Pennsylvania, and Virginia are currently considering the adoption of several variations of TDR.

NEW JERSEY'S RECOGNITION OF THE NEW APPROACH

Proposed legislation from New York City, Southampton, and Maryland came to the authors' attention in early 1972. At this time there was emerging a greater recognition of the enormous development pressures on New Jersey and the consequent impact on the rate of land so committed.

Land values were beginning to soar. Over 1.2 million acres of the state's 4.2 million acres were already developed. It was estimated at the time that most of the remaining usable land would be committed to development by the year 2000. The most vulnerable land in this context is agricultural which, unlike swamps, marshes, or steep slopes, requires minimum site preparation and construction costs.

Also, in many cases agricultural lands consist of large tracts under single ownership and are very attractive to large-scale builders. Experience indicates that this is especially true in New Jersey. Therefore, the main thrust of a transfer-of-development rights proposal could be to preserve prime agricultural lands and woodlands, although TDR is essentially a technique to preserve any open space lands.

Cook College and Cooperative Extension Service of Rutgers University have in recent years initiated research and programs in land use and resource management, especially with a view to preserving prime agricultural lands. At the same time the state had created the Blueprint Commission of the Future of Agriculture in New Jersey which explored ways to preserve agriculture in the state.

The objective of these groups was to develop more rational land use control techniques and to preserve agricultural land, not merely for the production of food and its contribution to the economy, but to guarantee open space to ensure the health and safety of citizens in the most densely populated state in the nation. Research is indicating that strategically located areas of agricultural lands and woodlands in an urban setting not only provide open space, with all its aesthetic values, but also provide a psychological uplift and an ecological balance. Furthermore, by keeping open large land areas, normal development can occur in a less sprawling pattern and costs of services such as utilities, schools, roads, and other transportation facilities can be reduced to some extent. Moreover, and perhaps most important, our legacy to future generations would not be a completely developed state where the only choices are living with past mistakes or creating open space at an extremely high economic, social, and political cost. Rather, we would leave to future generations the option of doing what their needs dictate with preserved agricultural lands.

It was in this context of urgency and need that efforts were initiated almost 3 years ago in applied research on the concept of TDR which resulted in a legislative proposal currently being considered by the state.

THE NEW LAND USE MANAGEMENT CONCEPT:
HOW IT WORKS

A development right is basically a creature of property law. It is one of the numerous rights included in the "fee simple" ownership of real estate. A mineral right (the right to mine and remove minerals from the land), an air right (the right to utilize the air space above the land's surface), and the right to travel across another person's property are examples of landownership rights. A development right is the right that permits the owner to build upon or develop his land; in an urbanizing region it constitutes great economic value and is usually the owner's most valuable right.

All landownership rights are subject to reasonable regulation under the police power and are also subject to the governmental power of eminent domain. Rights to landownership may be separated from other rights and regulated by the government or sold by the owner and transferred separately.

For example, a landowner may sell his mineral rights or air rights and still retain ownership and use of the land surface. A common example involves the owner's sale of an access easement to a public utility so that utility lines can be established and maintained on the owner's property. Similarly, an owner may sell all of his rights to develop his land and these rights may be bought and sold by persons other than the owner, who still retains the ownership to the land.

The transfer of development rights concept, as developed by the authors, is essentially a system is created that identifies the right to develop and creates a market for such development rights. Under this proposed system an overlay on the current zoning is created wherein a zoning district is established for preservation of open space. In this district all development other than farming or low intensity recreation use is essentially prohibited. The residential development potential of the zoning district before its open space designation is calculated as follows: for each residential dwelling unit eliminated in such a preservation district, a substituted dwelling unit is added to a developable district in the community. In other words, the residential development potential of the preserved area is transferred to other districts in the community which can accommodate the higher densities without causing environmental damage or creating incompatible land-use patterns, or putting heavy strains upon existing infrastructure. Development right certificates equal in number to the total dwelling units eliminated in the preserved district are distributed to the landowners in that district on the basis of the ratio of the value of each tract in relation to the total land value of the preserved district. To build a substituted dwelling in the developable part of town, a development right, as well as the appropriate zoning, is required.

Thus, a builder who proposes to construct at a higher density based on the new capacity or density resulting from the establishment of the preserved area must also purchase development rights equal in number to the increased density and at a price arrived at through the bargaining process of the marketplace. The builder has the right to develop at the lower density permitted by the previous zoning regulations, but he cannot build the higher densities unless he has development rights. Finally the continued market-ability of the development rights is insured by adequate "incentive zoning" in the developable districts. In other words, for this system to remain valid and functional there must always be a market for the development rights. Otherwise, there would be no place to transfer them, and the entire system could become invalidated and inoperative. Such a situation would occur if a builder chose not to build at the new permitted higher density, thereby creating a surplus of development rights equal to the number he could have used and for which there is no longer a market. In such an event the municipality would be required to rezone in such a manner that a market for all outstanding development rights is maintained.

Thus, by the use of the TDR technique critical natural environmental resources such as prime agricultural lands, aquifer recharge areas, floodplains, wetlands, and woodlands are preserved at no cost to local taxpayers.

THE STEPS INVOLVED IN CREATING
A TDR ZONING ORDINANCE

1. In the proposed municipal enabling legislation the first step toward implementing this system involves specific indentification of the areas to preserved. It must be an area(s) residentially zoned and substantially unimproved land consisting mainly of farmland, woodland, aquifer recharge areas, flood plains, steep slopes, or marshes, etc. The preserved area(s) must correspond to the community's master plan so that the area(s) essentially represents the product of a well-thought-out, rational planning scheme for orderly growth and development for the community.

2. Once the preserved district is designated, its residential development capacity or potential under the current zoning must be calculated by the local

government, converted into development rights, and then distributed to the property owners in the preserved district. This is done on the assumption that a development right is equal to each dwelling unit eliminated, so that the total number of development rights distributed in the preserved district must equal the total number of eliminated dwelling units for the entire preserved district. This total represents the development potential of the preserved area.

3. Each owner then receives development rights on the basis of the value of his tract in relation to the value of all the land in the preserved district. This method of distribution is employed so that the particular location and other characteristics of each tract are taken into consideration since some may have a market value higher than others.

4. The next step is the creation of a market which will give "value" to development rights. To accomplish this, the municipality must designate other districts in which a new and higher density development will be permitted if accompanied by development rights. The total permitted increased in density in the district will depend on the number of outstanding development rights issued as a result of the designation of the preserved district.

The actual increase in residential density over and above the former zoning maximum is the incentive which should attract a willing buyer of development rights. The specific increase for any one acre can only be established in light of the facts and conditions in each municipality. In some cases medium-density multiple-family zones may be designated. However, it may very well be that in certain instances single family residential dwellings on small parcels will be enacted, especially in areas where it is desirable to do so from a marketing and planning perspective. In any event, planning and zoning for the higher permitted densities must be based on sound planning principles to avoid incompatible land use patterns and undue strains upon the natural environment and infrastructure.

Moreover, whatever new density requirements are established in whatever location, the overall result must be a new zoning district where it is more desirable to build with development rights primarily because it is more profitable for the builder. In short, the new densities permitted must in fact create the incentive.

5. Finally, the proposal ensures the continued marketability of development rights. The incentive to purchase development rights must be perpetuated until all outstanding rights are utilized in actual development. Since building proposals that conform to the former zoning can be approved without development rights as a prerequisite, it is possible to have a surplus of development rights. If this should occur and more development rights were to exist than land upon which they could be utilized, it would then become the responsibility of the designated governmental body to rezone another district in which development rights could be used (that is, to reestablish the market for development rights and "incentive zoning"). Again, the rezoning would have to be made in accordance with the master plan in order to reflect sound planning principles.

At each critical step in the process, public hearings must be held with proper notice to landowners in the preserved areas as well as to all other affected parties. Appeals to the courts of all decisions will be provided for and the general tenets of procedural due process of law must be observed throughout the implementation of the program.

TAXATION OF DEVELOPMENT RIGHTS

Even assuming that a development right is personal property, it would be taxed in a manner similar to real property. For assessment purposes the initial value of a development right would equal the difference between the assessed value of the land for agricultural or lesser purposes and the assessed value of the land for development. The first sale of development rights in the open market would then be used to establish the assessed value of development rights in the future. The land in the preserved area is taxed as real property although it is assessed at its farmland or lesser value. Under this approach there is no change in the payment of taxes by the various taxpayers in the governmental jurisdiction.

GENERAL LEGAL IMPLICATIONS

Any form of police power regulation that results in virtually total economic loss is potentially assailable as a taking of property without just compensation and is in violation of the federal and state constitutions, not withstanding the benefits for society as a whole. In an urban state like New Jersey where land is extremely valuable because of its actual or speculative potential for high density development, restriction of use to open space and agricultural pursuits would result in a sharp economic loss. The issue raised is whether the economic loss to the property owner, which admittedly is great, can be justified in light of the benefits gained for society. To date, in New Jersey, the courts have very clearly stated that such a loss is a burden too great to be carried by a few landowners for the benefit of the general population. Development rights are intended to redress the landowner for his loss and therefore serve as a form of compensation.

Development rights are clearly valuable in an urban area where virtually all forms of development, whether of high, medium, or low density, are in great demand in the marketplace. However, even in this seller's market, development rights are not intended as exact compensation as employed in the legal sense as under eminent domain. They are rather a substituted form of development potential given to the property owner to reduce the severity of the impact of the police power regulation which restricts the use of his land. However, it does not stop here. The severity of the police power restriction must also be reviewed against the benefit to the public.

An examination of the benefits to be gained through the retention of productive open space in an area of vigorous economic growth has taken on new meaning. Generally, the argument for the preservation of open space has been based on an aesthetic notion that we must preserve our scenic areas. Certainly this is important, although not so critical as to justify very restrictive zoning regulations. However, we are now discovering that the wise, productive, and beneficial use of open space is essential in maintaining an ecological harmony, in improving the quality of air and water and in promoting the psychological well-being of the population. Open-space breaks in an otherwise endless stretch of subdivisions are becoming imperative. Pollution in many areas of New Jersey is almost an accepted condition of life. We know that if the population continues to increase all of these problems will be intensified and will endanger the basic health and safety of the community. This recognition of the health and safety aspects of open space preservation must be clearly documented and accorded considerable weight in the judicial balancing process.

SOME PLANNING IMPLICATIONS

The primary objective of the transfer of development rights as proposed here is the preservation of open space. However, the impact of this technique on the planning process cannot be ignored. More predictability, which is essential to effective planning, is promoted since all open-space designations are identified and permanently locked in the master plan and in zoning regulations. Also, the number of people who can live in the community is more clearly identified through the emphasis on the density requirements necessary to guarantee value for development rights. In addition, in many instances water supply can be predicted more accurately since the aquifers and recharge areas will be protected in the open areas, and to a major extent, the total population can be related to the water supply. Once approximate total density is established, better judgments relating to the planning and construction of capital improvements can be accomplished because districts where development is permissible can be very effectively planned on a comprehensive scale and related to the tracts of permanently preserved open space. In this process the locations of more intense development are identified and public services and facilities can be geared to them.

Another important aspect of development rights is the probable interest and participation in the planning process of many citizens within the community. Many will have development rights to protect and will be very interested in the process which gives these rights value.

CONTINUING RESEARCH

With funds from Title V of the Rural Development Act of 1972, a demonstration project is currently being conducted in South Brunswick Township, Middlesex County, New Jersey. The purpose of the project is to demonstrate, under simulated conditions working with Township officials and citizen groups, how a TDR zoning ordinance would be drafted. The project is in the early stages of delineation of preserved areas which will probably include prime agricultural lands, woodlands, aquifer recharge areas, swamps, and floodplains. Criteria, standards and methods for delineation are being developed. The project is scheduled for completion by July 1, 1975; if it is successful the next two years will be devoted, again under simulated conditions, to testing the manner in which the marketplace responds to this new marketable commodity.

THE TDR GAME

As a consequence of the relative complexity of the TDR concept, a gaming approach was used to investigate some of the problems and issues inherent to the process. The TDR game, itself, actually went through an evolutionary process which paralleled the development of a TDR legislative proposal for which the game was used as a research tool.

There is currently a tremendous amount of interest, both within New Jersey and nationally, in the TDR process, and the game is being made available to facilitate an understanding of the concept and to promote additional research on it. It is anticipated that if TDR legislation is passed the game could be used as an educational and research device in conjunction with the legislation, both in formal educational settings as well as with governmental units and citizen groups who will be involved in TDR programs.

To make the game easily available to individuals or groups interested in pursuing TDR as either a researcher or educator, a manual is being published which should be printed shortly.

A LEGISLATIVE PROPOSAL

For a period of about 10 months a small committee of specialists working with the authors conducted an extensive and intensive review of this revolutionary new land-use control concept. At the same time the authors spoke before many groups and organizations to get questions, reactions, and a general feed-back. This information was reviewed and analyzed by the committee. To the best of the committee's ability every critical element and principle of this new device was thoroughly analyzed, resulting in a legislative proposal which is considered to be valid and workable. It would not have been possible to produce this document in a short period of time without the intensive dedication of this small, highly motivated group of qualified specialists. The legislative proposal[9] drafted for New Jersey owes its existence and early emergence into the New Jersey land-use scene to the following:

Teuvo M. Airola, resident intern, Rutgers, The State University

Richard Binetsky, chief, Bureau of Regional Planning, Division of State and Regional Planning, New Jersey Department of Community Affairs

B. Budd Chavooshian, land-use specialist, Cooperative Extension Service, Cook College, Rutgers, The State University

Richard Ginman, director, Division of State and Regional Planning, New Jersey Department of Community Affairs

Thomas Hall, Eagleton Institute, Rutgers, The State University

James Jager, Esq., Division of State and Regional Planning, New Jersey Department of Community Affairs

Dr. George H. Nieswand, associate professor of environmental systems analysis, Department of Environmental Resources, Cook College, Rutgers, The State University

Thomas Norman, Esq., legal consultant and staff director of committee effort

Dr. Ernest C. Reock, Jr., director, Bureau of Government Research, Rutgers, The State University

Dr. Jerome Rose, professor of urban planning, Livingston College, Rutgers; Editor-in-Chief, *Real Estate Law Journal*

ACKNOWLEDGMENTS

The authors wish to acknowledge with deep thanks and appreciation Mr. John A. Waddington, chairman of the New Jersey Commission on Open Space Policy, and Mr. Sidney L. Willis, the Commission's secretary who is also assistant commissioner of the New Jersey Department of Community Affairs. Without their support and encouragement this work on TDR would not have been possible. The advice and assistance of the staff of the Division of State and Regional Planning and other members of the New Jersey Department of Community Affairs in the very early period of this research project was an extremely valuable and significant contribution. The general support of the Blueprint Commission for the Future of Agriculture in New Jersey also provided essential encouragement to proceed with the detailed research. Most important, the author wishes to thank Dean Charles E. Hess of Cook College, Rutgers—The State University, and Dr. John L. Gerwig, director of the Cooperative Extension Service of Cook College, Rutgers—The State University, for their unqualified support and approval of this research project.

LEGISLATIVE PROPOSAL:
THE OPEN SPACE PRESERVATION ACT

An Act to enable municipalities to preserve farmland, woodland and open space as part of the planning process and to provide a system for the transfer of development rights.

WHEREAS, vigorous economic growth has caused New Jersey to become the most densely populated state in the nation and has resulted in the loss of much of the state's farmland and woodland which represents New Jersey's primary source of open space lands; and

WHEREAS, the wise, productive and beneficial use of farmland and woodland is essential to preserve areas of ecological value, improve the quality of air, land and water resources, protect and maintain the psychological well being of citizens of New Jersey through the preservation of open space wedges and to ensure economic stability; and

WHEREAS, in many municipalities of this state all of the remaining farmland and woodland are in imminent danger of loss to sprawl development because such land is easily and profitably developed; and

WHEREAS, the decisions of the courts of this state have questioned the validity of laws restricting the use of land to agricultural or woodland use without some form of compensation; and

WHEREAS, the creation of districts for the natural preservation of farmland and woodland as part of the planning process will result in promotion of the health, safety and general welfare and the distribution of development rights to the individual property owners in such districts will reduce substantially the burden otherwise suffered by such landowners;

NOW, THEREFORE, BE IT ENACTED by the Senate and General Assembly of the State of New Jersey:

1. Title. This Act shall be known and cited as "The Open Space Preservation Act".

2. Purposes of the Act. It is the purpose of this act to enable municipalities to preserve undeveloped farmlands and woodlands as a strategic resource for food production and to provide New Jersey residents with a ready access to wholesome, locally produced fruit and vegetables; to ensure the productive use of open space in a manner which is consistent with sound environmental objectives; to retain agriculture and thereby contribute in a significant way to the employment of New Jersey residents; to retain irreplaceable areas of open space as a visual and psychological relief from the sprawl of urbanization; to protect and enhance the air quality through the retention of plant life for the regeneration of life-sustaining oxygen; to promote a system of open space buffers to serve as wind breakers and sound absorbers to reduce the noise and pollution of an urban environment, and to stabilize and reduce the severity of climatic fluctuations; and to ensure and protect the health, safety and general welfare of the residents of this state.

3. Definitions.

   a. "Agricultural use" means substantially undeveloped land devoted to the production of plants and animals useful to man, including but not limited to: forages and sod crops; grains and feed crops; dairy animals and dairy products; poultry and poultry products; livestock, including the breeding and grazing of any or all of such animals; bees and apiary products; fur animals; trees and forest products; fruits of all kinds; vegetables; nursery, floral ornamental and greenhouse products; and other similar uses and activities.

   b. "Aquifer recharge area" means an area exceptionally well suited for absorbing water from precipitation and streamflow and transmitting it to an aquifer.

   c. "Board of Adjustment" means the municipal zoning board of adjustment established pursuant to R.S. 40:55-30 et seq.

   d. "Conservation use" means any conservation activity which leaves the land essentially undeveloped and unimproved.

   e. "Development right" refers to the right set forth in section 7 of this act.

   f. "Exercise of a development right" means the submission of a development right to the designated municipal official in conjunction with an application for development approval.

   g. "Farmland" means land being used for agricultural purposes or substantially undeveloped land included in the categories of Class I, Class II and Class III soil classifications of the Soil Conservation Service of the United States Department of Agriculture.

   h. "Flood plain" means land subject to regulation pursuant to the laws of 1962, c. 19 as amended.

   i. "Governing body" means the chief legislative body of the municipality.

   j. "Land of steep slope" means land of a slope of not less than 25 percent.

   k. "Master plan" means the master plan prescribed in the Laws of 1953, c. 433.

   l. "Marsh" means low, spongy land generally saturated with moisture and having persistent poor natural drainage. Marsh shall also include the term "swamp."

m. "Planning board" means the municipal planning board established pursuant to the Laws of 1953, c. 433.

n. "Municipality" means any city, borough, town, township or village.

o. "Public hearing" means a hearing with public notice given in a manner prescribed in Revised Statutes 40:55-34, et seq., for hearings on amendments to a zoning ordinance. The said notice of the hearing shall contain a brief description of the property involved, its location, and a concise statement of the matters to be heard.

p. "Recreation use" means a recreational activity which leaves the land essentially undeveloped and unimproved.

q. "State agency" means any department, instrumentality, authority, agency or jurisdiction created by the State of New Jersey.

r. "Substantially undeveloped" means any parcel or area of land essentially unimproved except for such buildings, structures, streets and other improvements that are incidental to the use of the land for agriculture, recreation or conservation, provided that such land is essentially not developed according to minimum density standards of the zoning ordinance.

s. "Woodland" means substantially undeveloped land consisting primarily of trees and capable of maintaining tree growth.

4. Grant of Power. The power of zoning granted by the provisions in the Revised Statutes 40:55-30 et seq., shall include the power to provide for open space preservation districts wherein the use of land may be restricted to agriculture, conservation or recreation or any combination thereof and only such buildings or structures which are incidental to the permitted land uses shall be constructed. Any municipality may by ordinance amend its zoning regulations to provide for an open space preservation district, subject to the provisions of this act.

The enactment of an ordinance or amendment thereto pursuant to the powers granted herein shall be in accordance with the procedure required for the adoption of an amendment to the zoning ordinance as provided in Revised Statutes 40:55-34 and R.S. 40:49-2, as amended.

5. Open Space Preservation District.

a. The governing body may create an open space preservation district of such numbers, shapes and areas as it may deem necessary to carry out the purposes of this act, provided that (i) all land in each district is substantially undeveloped farmland, woodland, floodplain, aquifer recharge area, swamp, marsh, or land of steep slope, and that farmland or woodland, or a combination thereof shall constitute more than sixty percent of all the land in the open space preservation district; and, (ii) the location of each district is consistent with and corresponds to the master plan of the municipality; and, (iii) the aggregate size of the districts bear a reasonable relationship to the present and future patterns of population growth set forth in the zoning ordinance and master plan; and, (iv) the land in each district is not less than twenty-five contiguous acres.

b. Land zoned exclusively for any non-residential use at the time of the adoption of an ordinance pursuant to this act shall not be included in an open space preservation district.

c. Any nonconforming use of structure existing in the open space preservation district at the time of adoption thereof may be continued, and in the event of partial destruction of such nonconforming use or structure it may be restored or repaired.

d. Subject to subsections (e) and (f) of this section, all proposals for the establishment, construction or erection of a use, building, or structure in an open space preservation district shall be made to the planning board for review and recommendation upon public hearing and shall be submitted to the governing body for approval after favorable referral by the planning board.

e. Land within the open space preservation district may be subdivided pursuant to the Laws of 1953, c. 432, only for the purpose of transferring ownership of the subdivided parcel or parcels and a residential dwelling unit may be constructed on the subdivided parcel if it contains at least twenty-five acres.

f. A variance for a use of land not otherwise permitted in an open space preservation district may be granted by the governing body after favorable referral by the planning board to a state agency only for a development proposal which is reasonably necessary to protect public health or safety and no practical alternative to the proposed development is available. Otherwise, no variance for a change of use or zoning amendment shall be approved to permit development in an open space preservation district other than for uses which conform to the provisions of section 4 of this act.

6. Development Rights.

a. The ordinance creating an open space preservation district shall also provide for the establishment and distribution of certificates of development rights by the municipality and the transferability of certificates of development rights by the owners of land in the open space preservation district and shall further provide that an increase in the density of the development hereinafter provided for in section 9 shall not be permitted unless the applicant therefore possesses ownership of the required number of certificates of development rights.

b. Certificates of development rights, issued by the municipality subject to the provisions of this act, shall be recorded in the office of the County Clerk of the county in which the municipality is located. The sale and transfer of certificates of development rights shall be regulated in the same manner as the sale and transfer of real property. The exercise of a certificate of development right pursuant to section 9 (b) herein together with the issuance of building permits therefore shall cause the certificate of development right to attach to and merge with the development and in that event such certificate of development right to attach to and merge with the development and in that event such certificate of development right or rights shall be cancelled by the municipal official designated for that purpose. Notice of cancellation shall be given by the municipality within fifteen days of the exercise of the certificate of development right to the county clerk for the purpose of recording the cancellation of the certificate of development right.

7. Establishment of Development Rights. The planning board upon public hearing with personal notice to all owners of land in the proposed open space preservation district shall recommend to the governing body for their adoption the total number of certificates of development rights for distribution to all owners of property in the proposed open space preservation district as part of the adoption of such a district. Such determination by the planning board shall be made on the basis of one certificate of development right for each residential dwelling unit permitted in the open space preservation district as a matter of right in the zoning ordinance as of the date of the public hearing required by this section.

The total number of certificates of development rights shall be equal to and deemed to represent the full and total developmental potential of all undeveloped real property in the open space preservation district pursuant to the zoning regulations controlling development therein.

Any owner of property in the open space preservation district may appeal any determination made under this section to the Law Division of the Superior Court.

8. Distribution of Residential Development Rights.

a. The total number of certificates of development rights determined pursuant to section 7 herein shall be distributed in accordance with subsection (b) of this section to all owners of land in the open space preservation district. For purposes of distribution of certificates of development rights ownership of land shall be determined as of the date of the adoption of the ordinance creating the open space preservation district.

b. To provide a just and equitable distribution of certificates of development rights the number of such certificates distributed to an individual property owner shall be equal to a percentage calculated by comparing the market value of the individual's property to the market value of all property in the open space preservation district on the date of adoption of the open space preservation district.

To implement this section, the planning board shall review the assessed value of all property in the open space preservation district in order to establish market value on an equalized basis for the purpose of ensuring just distribution of certificates of development rights. The planning board shall hold a special hearing with personal notice to all owners of property in the proposed open space preservation district in order to review the appraisal and review such action as it deems necessary to ensure the just distribution of development rights.

9. Marketability of Residential Development Rights.

a. To create an incentive for the purchase of development rights, the governing body, by amendment to the zoning ordinance, shall designate specific zoning districts wherein the permissable residential dwelling unit density shall be increased beyond the density otherwise permitted under the zoning regulations in effect at the date of adoption of the open space preservation district. The overall result of such an increase in density must be a zoning district wherein there is greater incentive to develop with certificates of development rights than without such certificates.

b. Development at such higher densities shall be permitted as a matter of right if the applicant proposing such higher density possesses ownership of development rights certificates that are equal in number to the increase in dwelling unit density above the number of dwelling units permitted under the zoning regulations in effect on the date of adoption of the open space preservation district.

c. Development proposals which are consistent with the residential density requirements of the zoning regulations in effect on the date of adoption of the open space preservation district may be approved at such lower density without the requirement of certificates of development rights. However, if development proposals are approved at the lower density and as a result thereof an imbalance is created whereby the number of uncancelled certificates of development rights exceeds the amount of undeveloped land upon which certificates of development rights may be exercised, the governing body, in that event, within ninety days of the approval which caused the imbalance, shall amend the zoning ordinance to rectify the imbalance in order to maintain the marketability of the outstanding development rights certificates.

   d. In any zoning district building permits based on an increase in the residential density occasioned by the approval of a variance granted pursuant to R.S. 40:55-39 shall not be issued unless the applicant therefore possesses ownership of certificates of development rights in a number equal to the increase in residential dwelling units beyond the density otherwise permitted under the zoning regulations in effect at the date of the application for the variance.

10. Invalid Action. Any action taken under the authority of this act which defeats the purposes of this act or causes an unreasonable burden upon any landowner is invalid and void and may be remedied by the exercise of such legal or equitable relief as may be deemed necessary to effectuate the purposes of this act.

11. Taxation.

   a. Subject to subsection (c) of this section, certificates of development rights shall be taxed in the same manner as real property is taxed and the assessed value of each uncancelled certificate of development right at the time of the adoption of an open space preservation district shall be equal to the difference between the aggregate value of the land for agricultural purposes and the aggregate value of the land for purposes of development as divided by the total number of uncancelled certificates of development rights. Thereafter, such value shall be determined on the basis of current sales of certificates of development rights in the particular jurisdiction.

   b. Land in the open space preservation district shall be assessed at its agricultural value.

   c. Certificates of development rights issued to landowners of parcels in the open space preservation district shall be exempt from taxation if said parcels were qualified for farmland assessment pursuant to the Farmland Assessment Act, L. 1964, C. 48, as amended, at the time of the adoption of the open space preservation district, and shall continue to be exempt until such time as the certificates of development rights are transferred by said owners to a third party. At the time of transfer by the said owner the rollback provision of the Farmland Assessment Act, L. 1964, C. 48, as amended, shall apply.

12. Effective date. This act shall become effective 12 months after enactment thereof and during the said 12 month period the Division of State and Regional Planning in the Department of Community Affairs shall conduct such studies as may be necessary in order to prepare manuals, model ordinances, suggested rules and regulations or other similar studies that will aid and assist municipalities in the adoption and implementation of the powers granted herein. An appropriation of $200,000.00 is authorized for this purpose.

NOTES

1. One exception is Village Green in Hillsborough Township, Somerset County, New Jersey.

2. Examples of PUDs in New Jersey include Twin Rivers in Mercer County, Panther Valley in Warren County and Pine Run in Camden County.

3. Gerald D. Lloyd, *Transferable Density in Connection With Density Zoning*, Urban Land Institute Technical Bulletin No. 40, 1961.

4. Section 74-79 *et seq.*, *Transfer of Development Rights from Landmark Sites of New York City*, New York Zoning Resolution, Revised 5/21/70.

5. John J. Costonis, *The Chicago Plan: Incentive Zoning and the Preservation of Urban Landmarks*, 85 Harvard Law Review 574; also John J. Costonis, *Development Rights Transfer: Exploratory Essay*, 83 Yale Law Journal 74; also John J. Costonis, *Space Adrift*, University of Illinois Press, Urbana, Illinois.

6. Section 2-40-30, *Agricultural Overlay District*, of Zoning Ordinance No. 26 of 1972, of the Town of Southampton, Suffolk County, New York.

7. Susan Andrews, *St. George Slays His Second Dragon*, Chittenden, 1971.

8. S. 254, Senate of Maryland; introduced, read first time and referred to Committee on Economic Affairs, January 20, 1972.

9. See appended copy of "Legislative Proposal: The Open Space Preservation Act."

As A Method of Preserving Open Space: The New Jersey Proposal

A Proposal for the Separation and Marketability of Development Rights as a Technique to Preserve Open Space

JEROME G. ROSE

The first legislative attempt to create a comprehensive system in which the marketability and transfer of development rights are used to regulate land use was introduced in the Maryland Senate in 1972 by State Senator William Goodman.[62] At the same time, in New Jersey, a committee made up of Rutgers University faculty and members of the New Jersey Department of Community Affairs were independently engaged in a similar project.[63] The provisions set forth below are excerpts, *with modifications* of the legislative proposal that emerged from that committee.[64] This draft does not purport to be a complete or final draft of a legislative proposal. It is designed primarily as a device to draw attention to the possibilities for the use of the concept and to the problems which require solution.

Summary of the Legislative Proposal[65]

The proposed legislation seeks to utilize the separability and transferability of development rights as the basis of a technique to induce owners of undeveloped land to preserve their land in open space. The owners of preserved open space are compensated for their deprivation of use by the sale of development rights to developers of other land in the jurisdiction. To make these sales possible, it is necessary to establish a system that creates a market for development rights in which owners of developable land must buy development rights from owners of preserved open space land as a prerequisite for development.

The legislation is designed to create such a market in the following manner:

(1) Each local government would prepare a land-use plan that specifies the percentage of remaining undeveloped land in the jurisdiction and that designates the land to remain undeveloped as preserved open space land. The land-use plan would also designate the land to be developed and would specify the uses to which the developable land may be put. A zoning law would be enacted or amended to implement this plan.

(2) The planning board of each local government would prescribe the number of development rights required for each housing unit to be developed. On the basis of this numerical assignment, the planning board would then compute the number of development rights required to develop the jurisdiction in accordance with the land-use plan. The local government would issue certificates of development rights (ownership of which would be recorded) in the exact amount so determined.

(3) Every owner of preserved open space land would receive certificates of development rights in an amount that represents the percentage of assessed value of his undeveloped land to the total assessed value of all undeveloped land in the jurisdiction.

(4) An owner of developable land, who desires to develop his land more intensively (e.g., apartments instead of single family residence) would have to buy additional development rights, on the open market, from those who have acquired such rights from either original distribution or subsequent purchase.

(5) Thus, owners of preserved open space would be able to sell their development rights to owners of developable land (or real estate brokers or speculators). In return for the compensation derived from this sale, owners of preserved open space land will have sold their rights to develop their land in the future. Their land will thus be preserved in open space and the owners will have been compensated without any capital costs to government.

(6) Development rights will be subject to ad valorem property taxation as a component of the total assessed value of the developable real property in the jurisdiction.

Legislative Provisions With Commentary

Grant of Power to Local Government

The power of zoning granted by the provisions in [State Enabling Legislation] shall include the power to provide for open space preservation districts wherein the use of land may be restricted to agriculture, conservation or recreation or any combination thereof and only such buildings or structures which are incidental to the permitted land uses and approved by the Planning Board shall be constructed.

Any municipality may by ordinance amend its zoning regulations to provide for an open space preservation district, subject to the provisions of this act. The enactment of an ordinance or amendment thereto pursuant to the powers granted herein shall be in accordance with the procedure required for the adoption of an amendment to the zoning ordinance as provided in [applicable provision of State Enabling Legislation.]

Commentary:

This legislation does not disturb the existing allocation of the power of land-use regulation to local governments. Some members of the committee urged that regulating authority be vested in a state agency rather than in local governments. However, the limited political feasibility of approval of this proposal was the primary reason for retaining local control. The last paragraph seeks to retain the existing procedure in most states by which the Planning Board participates in the process for amending the zoning ordinance.

Creation of Open Space Preservation Districts

(a) *The governing body may create an open space preservation district of such numbers, shapes and areas as it may deem necessary to carry out the purposes of this act, provided that (i) all land in each district is substantially undeveloped farmland, woodland, flood plain, swamp, marsh, or land of steep slope, and that farmland or woodland, or a combination thereof shall constitute more than 60 percent of all the land in the open space preservation district; (ii) the location of each district is consistent with and corresponds to the master plan of the municipality; (iii) the aggregate size of the districts bears a reasonable relationship to the present and future patterns of population growth set forth in the zoning ordinance and master plan; and, (iv) the land in each district is not less than 25 contiguous acres.*

Commentary:

Subsection (a) makes it clear that the open-space preservation plan must be based upon the municipal master plan with particular reference to studies of future population projections and topographical, soil and other land use studies. In the process of computing the amount of land required to meet various municipal needs and designation of land most appropriate to meet those needs, land will be designated for open-space preservation. To avoid the designation of open-space districts too small to be effective, a minimum size of 25 contiguous acres is prescribed. The land in any open space preservation district may be comprised of any combination of the enumerated types of undeveloped land but must contain at least 60 percent farmland, woodland, or a combination thereof. The purpose of this provision is to preserve land that might otherwise be developed in addition to swamp, marsh, flood plain, and other land of limited utility for development.

(b) *Land zoned exclusively for commercial, industrial or other nonresidential use at the time of the adoption of an ordinance pursuant to this act shall not be included in an open-space preservation district.*

Commentary:

Subsection (b) is intended to exclude land zoned for commercial or industrial uses from open-space preservation districts. There are two reasons for this exclusion. The primary reason is based upon the committee's determination to limit the application of the program to *residential* development. The committee concluded that, if development rights are issued for commercial and industrial development, the program would become too complex to administer. The second reason for the exclusion of commercial and industrial property is that land zoned for those purposes may be too expensive or otherwise inappropriate for open space preservation. The committee was mindful of the fact that some municipalities zone unrealistically large proportions of undeveloped land for commercial and industrial uses as an extra-legal technique of retarding residential development.[66] In this case, a realistic rezoning of the areas will be required before adopting an ordinance pursuant to the provisions of this act.

(c) *Any nonconforming use or structure existing in the open-*

space preservation district at the time of adoption thereof may be continued and in the event of partial destruction of such non-conforming use or structure it may be restored or repaired.

Commentary:

Subsection (c) is intended to particularly protect the right of farmers and others who have existing structures that do not conform to the restricted use on open-space preservation land.

(d) *Subject to subsections (e) and (f) of this section, all proposals for the construction or enlargement of a building, or other structure in an open-space preservation district shall be made to the planning board for review and recommendation after a public hearing and shall be submitted to the governing body for approval after favorable referral by the planning board.*

Commentary:

Subsection (d) is intended to require all proposals for construction in open-space preservation districts to be subjected to the scrutiny of the planning board and the governing body. It is contemplated that farm residences, agricultural buildings, stables, and other structures not inconsistent with open-space preservation will be permitted, but only with the approval of both governmental bodies.

(e) *Land within the open space preservation district may be subdivided pursuant to [Subdivision Enabling Legislation] only for the purpose of transferring ownership of the subdivided parcel for farming purposes and a residential dwelling may be constructed on the subdivided parcel only if the parcel contains at least 25 acres.*

Commentary:

Subsection (e) is intended to restrict the subdivision of land in open-space preservation districts. The only exception permitted is subdivision of farmland into a parcel of not less than 25 acres. This exception was made to accommodate the practice of some farmers to subdivide their land among children.

(f) *A variance for a use of land not otherwise permitted in an open-space preservation district may be granted by the governing body after favorable referral by the local planning board and by the appropriate state agency only for a development proposal which is reasonably necessary to protect public health or safety and no practical alternative to the proposed development is available. Otherwise no variance for a change of use or zoning amendment shall be approved to permit development in an open space preservation district other than for uses which conform to the provisions of Section 1 of this act.*

Commentary:

Subsection (f) transfers the power to grant a variance in an open-space preservation district from the zoning board to the governing body, which in turn must obtain the approval from both the planning board and the appropriate state agency. This provision is intended to protect the integrity of the program from the kind of influences often exerted upon zoning boards.

Certificates of Development Rights

(a) *The ordinance creating an open-space preservation district shall also provide for the establishment and distribution of certificates of development rights by the municipality and the transferability of certificates of development rights by the owners of land in the open-space preservation district and shall further provide that an increase in the density of the development hereinafter provided for in Section (b) shall not be permitted unless the applicant therefor submits for cancellation the required number of certificates of development rights.*

Commentary:

This subsection authorizes the creation of an innovative legal instrument never used before, i.e., the certificate of development rights. Certificates will be inscribed in specific denominations and will be transferable by endorsement and registration as provided in Subsection (b). Certificates will be issued to owners of land designated for open space. Owners of developable land will have to purchase these certificates to increase the density of development of their land. Thus, both a supply of and demand for certificates is created.

(b) *Certificates of development rights, issued by the municipality pursuant to the provisions of this act, shall be recorded in the office of the County Clerk of the county in which the municipality is located. The sale and transfer of certificates of development rights shall be regulated and recorded in the same manner as the sale and transfer of real property. Upon exercise of certificate of development right pursuant to Section 6(b) herein and upon the issuance of a building permit therefor, the certificate of development right shall be cancelled by the municipal official designated for that purpose. Notice of cancellation shall be given by said municipal official to the County Clerk, who shall record the cancellation of the certificates.*

Commentary:

This subsection authorizes the creation of a recording system for certificates of development rights similar to the recording system for other instruments of real estate conveyancing. When an owner of land designated for open space sells his certificates to an owner of developable land (or to anyone else, such as a broker or speculator), the transfer will be recorded by the county clerk. When the development rights are used to obtain a building permit, the certificates are cancelled. When all the authorized certificates are cancelled, the remaining owners of developable land will be limited to the restricted use designated in the zoning ordinance, i.e., single-family residences. These constraints will tend to keep the certificates marketable as long as there is demand for residential development at increased densities. The market value of development rights will respond to the same economic forces as the market value of developable residential land. If an owner of development rights holds out for too high a price, the owners of developable land will tend to buy the rights from someone else or will use their land for single-family residences.

Establishment of Development Rights

(a) *The planning board, after public hearing with personal notice to all owners of land in the proposed open-space preservation districts, shall recommend to the governing body for adoption the total number of units of development rights for distribution to all owners of property in the proposed open-space preservation districts.*

Distribution of Residential Development Rights

(a) *The total number of certificates of development rights determined pursuant to section 4 herein shall be distributed in ac-*

cordance with subsection (b) of this section to all owners of land in the open space preservation district. For purposes of distribution of certificates of development rights ownership of land shall be determined as of the date of the adoption of the ordinance creating the open space preservation district.

Commentary:

This provision calls for the distribution of the development rights to the owners of open-space land. The certificates of development rights they receive provide the compensation for their loss of the right to develop their land. The right to receive development rights vests at the time of adoption of the local ordinance. As a result, when enactment of a development rights ordinance is anticipated the market value of open-space land will reflect the value of the development rights attached to it.

(b) *To provide a just and equitable distribution of certificates of development rights the number of such certificates distributed to an individual property owner shall be equal to a percentage calculated by comparing the market value of the individual's property to the market value of all property in the open-space preservation district on the date of adoption of the open space preservation district.*

Commentary:

This subsection provides the method of allocation of the previously determined total of development rights in the jurisdiction to the owners of open-space land. Each owner is entitled to the same proportion of the total number of development rights as the value of his open space land bears to the total value of all land designated for open-space preservation. This method of allocation is based upon the recognition that acreage alone is an insufficient basis of allocation of development rights because some land has greater value than other land because of its development potential prior to adoption of the development rights ordinance. Under this provision, the owner of the more valuable land will receive a greater proportion of the total number of development rights.

(c) *To implement this section, the planning board shall review the assessed value of all property in the open-space preservation district in order to establish market value on an equalized basis for the purpose of ensuring just distribution of certificates of de-*

velopment rights. The planning board shall hold special hearings with personal notice to all owners of property in the proposed open space preservation district to review all appraisals and consider such objections as may be presented, and shall take such action as it deems necessary to ensure the just distribution of development rights.

Commentary:

This subsection is intended to provide an open procedure to assure a fair distribution of development rights among owners of open-space land. Notice of all appraisals of land in the open space preservation districts will be given to all owners of open space land. Open hearings on the issue of value will allow each owner to compare the assessed value of his property with the assessed value of all other open space land.

(d) *Any owner of property in the open space preservation district may appeal any determination made under this section to the [appropriate court].*

Commentary:

This subsection provides a judicial remedy for owners of open-space land who feel aggrieved by the allocation of development rights.

Marketability of Residential Development Rights

(a) *To create an incentive for the purchase of development rights, the governing body, by amendment to the zoning ordinance, shall designate specific zoning districts wherein the permissible residential dwelling-unit density may be increased to a specified range of densities. Such zoning districts shall be designated for use and densities consistent with the master plan to create a greater incentive to develop land in such districts with certificates of development rights than without such certificates.*

Commentary:

This subsection provides for the designation of zoning districts in which higher densities will be permitted if the owner acquires development rights. Increased density is to be authorized only (1) where such density would be appropriate as determined by the land-use plan and (2) where there would be market demand for development at higher densities. The existence of this economic incentive is critically important because, unless there is a market for housing at higher densities in the district so designated therefor, there will be no market for the development rights and no compensation for the owners of land preserved for open space. On the other hand, if there is no market for housing at higher densities anywhere in the jurisdiction, then the claim of compensation by owners of open space land is probably equally remote and premature.

(b) *Development of prescribed higher densities shall be permitted as a matter of right if the applicant proposing such higher density owns development rights certificates in an amount equal in number to the increase in dwelling unit density above the number of dwelling units permitted under the zoning regulations.*

Commentary:

This is the provision that authorizes higher densities in designated districts to the extent permitted by the zoning ordinance if the owner has a sufficient number of development rights for the increased density. This provision presupposes the existence of height and bulk regulations in other sections of the zoning ordinance to the extent that such regulations are necessary to prevent overcrowding of the area and overutilization of neighborhood facilities.

(c) *Development proposals consistent with the residential density requirements of the zoning regulations may be approved at such lower density without the requirements of certificates of development rights. However, if development proposals are approved at the lower density and as a result thereof an imbalance is created whereby the number of uncancelled certificates of development rights exceeds the amount of undeveloped land upon which certificates of development rights may be exercised, the governing body may amend the zoning ordinance to rectify the imbalance to maintain the marketability of the outstanding development rights certificates.*

Commentary:

The first sentence of this subsection authorizes the development of land in developable districts at the lower authorized density. For example, an owner of an acre of land on which one residential unit per acre is permitted may build that one unit without the use of development rights. This provision is designed to overcome objection to the plan by owners of developable land who are content with that restricted use. An owner of developable land has a number of choices: (1) He can build in accordance with the lower authorized density. (2) He can purchase development rights and build at a higher density. (3) He can sell his land to others for development at higher densities.

The last sentence of this paragraph is intended to deal with the unlikely possibility that most owners of developable land will act against their economic self-interest and develop their land at the lower density in spite of market demand for more intensive use of their land. In this event, owners of open-space land would not be compensated because the demand for their development rights requires the existence of land developable at higher densities. Under these circumstances, the governing body is authorized to designate additional districts of developable land for which the development rights may be used to meet a projected housing need and the market demand based thereon.

(d) *No variance for residential use at increased densities shall be granted pursuant to [appropriate section of state enabling legislation] unless the applicant provides evidence of ownership of certificates of development rights in an amount sufficient to authorize a higher density under the provisions of this act. No building permit shall be issued upon such variances unless the requisite number of certificates of development rights are attached to said application for cancellation.*

Commentary:

This provision is designed to protect the integrity of the plan from derogation by the variance procedure. Without this provision, the entire plan could be frustrated by use variances for residential development. A use variance for residential units, under this provision, can be issued only if the applicant owns a sufficient number of development rights and is prepared to surrender them for cancellation when application is made for a building permit.

Taxation

(a) *Certificates of development rights shall be taxed in the same manner as real property is taxed. The assessed value of each uncancelled certificate, in the year of adoption of a development rights ordinance, shall be equal to the difference between the aggregate value of all undeveloped land zoned for restricted residential use and the aggregate value of said land if developed with the use of all development rights issued, divided by the total number of development rights issued. Thereafter, current sales, of certificates of development rights in that jurisdiction shall constitute evidence of market value for tax assessment purposes.*

Commentary:

This subsection provides the basic guidelines for the taxation of development rights. Because they represent a substantial part of the value of undeveloped land, development rights are to be taxed as real property. When the ordinance is first enacted, the aggregate value of all outstanding development rights will be the difference between the value of all residential land if fully developed with development rights and the value of the same land for restricted residential development. This is illustrated by the following example:

	Aggregate value of the land only
200 acres developed with 1,000 residential units (with development rights)	$5,000,000
200 acres developed with 200 residential units (restricted use)	1,000,000
Value of 800 development rights	$4,000,000
Value of 1 development right	$ 5,000

The underlying assumption of this calculation is that an owner would be willing to pay for a development right an amount of money equal to the increment in value of the land resulting from the use of that development right (in the above illustration, $5,000). As soon as a market for development rights is established in the jurisdiction, actual sales will provide evidence of value for assessment purposes.

(b) *Land in the open-space preservation district shall be assessed at its value for agricultural or other open space use.*

Commentary:

This subsection gives effect to the fact that, once the development right is removed from the land in open-space preservation districts, the value of that land is limited to its agricultural or other open-space use.

(c) *Tax exemption—DELETED.*

Commentary:

The original draft of the proposed New Jersey legislation contains a provision exempting development rights from taxation if issued to and held by an owner of land qualified for tax exemption under the New Jersey Farmland Assessment Act. This provision is not recommended because these tax exemption (1) would tend to discourage the marketability of development rights while held by farmers; (2) would impose an unnecessary tax burden on other taxpayers; and (3) would give an unjustified advantage to owners of farmland who may thereby continue to use the land for farm purposes and reap the advantages of increasing value of development rights without corresponding tax liability.

Effective date

This act shall become effective 12 months after enactment thereof and during the said 12-month period the [appropriate state agency] shall conduct such studies as may be necessary to prepare model ordinances, suggested rules and regulations and other studies that will assist municipalities in the adoption and implementation of the powers granted herein. An appropriation of [$ - - - - - - - - - -] is authorized for this purpose.

Commentary:

The last provision conveys the unanimous opinion of the members of the drafting committee that there are still undiscovered implications and effects of this proposal that require additional investigation and study.

NOTES

62 S. 254, Senate of Maryland; introduced, read first time and referred to the Committee on Economic Affairs, January, 1972.

63 Members of this committee were: T. Airola, R. Binetsky, R. Ginman, T. Hall, J. Jager, T. Norman, E. Reoch and J. Rose.

64 Many of the provisions set forth herein contain modifications made by this author and may not be in accord with the corresponding provisions in

the final draft submitted by the committee. For a more detailed report of the work of this committee, *see* B. Chavooshian and T. Norman, Transfer of Development Rights: A New Concept in Land Use Management (Mimeo, .Leaflet No. 492, Cooperative Extension Service, Cook College, Rutgers University, 1973).

65 *See* Rose, "Proposed Development Rights Legislation Can Change the Name of the Land Investment Game," 1 Real Estate L. J. 276 (1973).

66 *See* Cutler, "Legal and Illegal Methods for Controlling Community Growth on the Urban Fringe," 3 Wisc. L. Rev. 370 (1961).

As A Method of Preserving Fragile Ecological Resources:
The Puerto Rican Plan

The Puerto Rican Plan:
Environmental Protection Through
Development Rights Transfer

JOHN J. COSTONIS
Professor of Law
University of Illinois

ROBERT S. DEVOY
Real Estate Research Corporation

The dilemma of environmental preservation in Puerto Rico is two-pronged, reflecting inadequacies of public finance and of regulation of development in the island's natural areas. The relationship between the two is intimate: wary of the fiscal implications of stringent regulation, Puerto Rico too often chooses to regulate inadequately or not to regulate at all.

Lawyers are wont to describe the dilemma as pitting government's police power against its power of eminent domain, the former extending to the noncompensated restriction of private land use in the public interest and the latter entailing mandatory public acquisition of private property upon payment of "just compensation." At some point—inherently difficult to fix—public restrictions on environmentally sensitive land exceed the police power's ambit, setting the stage for the landowner's claim that compensation is constitutionally compelled.

But the dilemma's ramifications go far beyond the law and touch as well on troublesome political, public finance and administrative questions. Writ large, the issue is how shall Puerto Rico's finite land base, including its natural areas, be allocated consistently with the competing claims, public and private, now being asserted against it for residential, industrial, agricultural and capital improvements uses? Insistence upon the protection of private property rights has already been mentioned and, indeed, is the chief concern of this study. No less important in terms of ultimate land use patterns, however, are the claims of the island's various public agencies reflected, for example, in site inventories for new industry or proposed highway rights of way.

Severe public encroachments upon private land use may trigger justifiable demands for compensation that far outstrip the meager funds available through conventional public finance sources. Lacking these funds, public agencies, such as the Planning Board, have been reluctant to hold the line on environmentally objectionable projects even when constitutional grounds for possible compensation have been marginal or dubious. The compensation stalemate accounts in large measure for the absence of thoughtful, comprehensive and effective resource protection programs today in Puerto Rico. Without a strengthened development control system, the attrition of the island's natural areas will proceed apace.

2. The Study

The purpose of this study is to examine the contribution that development rights transfer promises for the island's lagging resource protection effort. In proposing the technique, we assume that Puerto Rico's environmental dilemma is largely, though certainly not exclusively, a product of the tension between the desire of private landowners to convert ecologically sensitive sites from low- to high-density and the conflicting attempt by government to prevent this conversion, typically without compensation. Obviously, the same site cannot support both a nature preserve, let us say, and a high density condominium development. And since conventional wisdom posits that the development potential or "development rights" of a site may be used *only* on that site, it makes an either/or choice inevitable.

Development rights transfer breaks the linkage between particular land and its development rights. It permits the transfer of those rights from land in "Protected Environmental Zones" (PEZs) to sites in "transfer districts" where greater density not only will be unobjectionable in environmental terms but will actually facilitate the implementation of the island's other comprehensive planning objectives. In freeing the bottled-up development rights for sale and use in transfer districts, development rights transfer avoids the either/or dilemma because it both protects the threatened resource and enables the owner of the restricted site to recoup the economic potential represented by the site's otherwise frozen development potential....

THE PUERTO RICO PLAN: ITS STRUCTURE AND LEGAL CHARACTER

1. An Overview

The Puerto Rico Plan includes four basic components:

1. preparing an inventory of PEZs and tailoring regulations to the special requirements of each PEZ;

2. identifying transfer districts and the development premiums that purchasers of transferred rights will enjoy;

3. administering the Environmental Trust Fund, including both receipt of

payments for development rights and pay-outs for condemnation awards and other expenses of the program; and

4. review and, where appropriate, settlement of claims of aggrieved PEZ landowners through monetary awards, liberalization of PEZ regulations, or other means.

The following summary of the Plan's over-all functioning illustrates how these components are related. With the assistance of an intergovernmental advisory group, the Planning Board would prepare an inventory of Puerto Rico's known environmentally sensitive areas, designate them as PEZs and prescribe criteria and related procedures for designating other areas in the future. This inventory and the policies guiding natural area protection would become a part of the master plan. The board would then promulgate regulations prescribing the kinds and intensities of the development that would be permitted within the PEZs. It would again be aided by other public agencies, and would impose development moratoria, where appropriate, to gain the time needed to prepare the regulations. Flatly prohibited would be development injuring the unique features of a PEZ—be they the dinoflagellates of the Phosphorescent Bay or the "haystacks" of the Karst area. Other types of development would be allowed if consistent with overlapping regulations of other agencies, exemplified by the water or air quality standards of the Environmental Quality Board. Regulating the PEZ in this manner would protect the resource yet minimize governmental interference with private ownership. Permitting a broad range of alternative uses short of those threatening environmental harm, moreover, would eliminate the "taking" objection to the Plan's application in many cases and it would reduce the amount of compensation found to be due in others.

Property owners within a PEZ would be permitted to challenge Planning Board rejections of their development applications as incompatible with PEZ regulations. Their contention that the regulations deny them a reasonable return on their land would be heard by an appropriate appeals board properly constituted for this purpose. Standards to guide landowners, the board, and, should the latter's ruling be challenged, the courts in assessing the reasonable return issue would be set forth in regulations prescribing the appeals procedure. The board of appeals' disposition of specific petitions would, of course, depend upon the persuasiveness of the complainant's showing on the reasonable return issue, as well as on the independent views of the board's staff.

A determination that a reasonable return is not prevented by the PEZ regulations would be subject to judicial review on the record made in the administrative proceedings. A contrary conclusion could result in one of three forms of relief: 1) compensation proportioned to the complainant's loss as fixed by the board; 2) liberalization of the regulation, through a variance or otherwise, sufficient to cure the taking objection; or 3) an agreement between the board and the applicant on some other alternative, such as a land swap utilizing the offices of the Land Administration. Under the first and third alternatives, the Land Administration, on behalf of the board, would acquire either the fee or a less-than-fee interest in the affected parcel as appropriate. Acquisition of a less-than-fee interest would entitle the landowner to a reduction in real estate taxes reflecting the depreciated value of his parcel. It would also obligate him to convey a "conservation restriction" to the Commonwealth, stripping from his parcel in perpetuity the development rights associated with development that conflicts with the PEZ regulations. The board would opt for the second alternative only after obtaining the Planning Board's assessment of the probable impact of the liberalized permission upon the PEZ resource.

Acquisition costs and related Plan expenses would be covered by an Environmental Trust Fund, administered by the Land Administration. Sale by that body of the development rights of parcels within PEZs would constitute the Fund's principal asset; other sources, such as Commonwealth appropriations, gifts, or federal grants would provide ancillary monies.

Development rights would be sold for use on parcels within transfer districts mapped beforehand by the Planning Board. Two kinds of criteria—economic and planning—would govern the selection of transfer districts and of development premiums within them. To insure that the Puerto Rico Plan enhances rather than erodes sound planning for the island, the board would permit transfers only to areas where greater density is presently or imminently desirable. Examples of such areas might be the underdeveloped sections of Puerto Rico's cities or metropolitan fringe locations to which the board wishes to channel population in coming years. And to prevent design abuse and overloads on public services and facilities, the board must also rigorously control the amount of the premium allowable on parcels within the districts. If the premium is increased density units per acre in an urbanization, for example, the increases should be subject to prescribed ceilings fixed after thorough review of the planning consequences of intensified development.

The market for new construction within areas tabbed as transfer districts must also be scrutinized. Without market demand, of course, developers in these districts will have no incentive to purchase the transferred rights. Similarly, market conditions must be examined in deciding what the content of the development premiums should be in specific districts. In some cases, premiums of increased residential density units per acre or commercial or office space will be appropriate; in others, the premium could be more flexible use controls or assembly of fragmented landholdings by the Land Administration on behalf of developers seeking to construct large-scale projects.

Zoning within transfer districts will be two-tiered if the development premium is computed in terms of density. All district landowners will be authorized specific residual densities as of right; only development rights purchasers, however, will be permitted to exceed the residual zoning or to enjoy whatever other form of development premiums is available. To illustrate: an urban area could be zoned to permit 50 density units per acre, the residual zoning. Upon the Planning Board's determination that planning and market criteria warrant further densities of, let us say, 8 density units per acre, developers opting to purchase the right to this premium would be authorized to build 58 density units per acre. The price paid for the premium would either be set in the open market pursuant to public bid procedures supervised by the Land Administration or determined by direct negotiations between developers and that body.

As summarized, the Plan promises to improve resource protection efforts on the island in six key respects. First, it safeguards natural areas without calling for drastic inroads upon constitutional principles or for governmental initiatives that are politically infeasible. Landowners within PEZs will be duly compensated for the curtailment of their legitimate development prerogatives. Developers within transfer districts, in turn, will receive an effective quid pro quo for their contributions to the Environmental Trust Fund—namely, the development premiums prescribed in the two-tiered regulatory system applicable within the districts.

Second, the Commonwealth can recoup for public benefit an appropriate measure of the values that it creates in privately held land. Our interviewees universally conceded that this objective is not now satisfactorily achieved by any of the recoupment mechanisms presently used in Puerto Rico, including real estate taxation, special assessment, or land banking. By treating the developmental potential of land within transfer districts as in part a community resource, the Plan allows the Commonwealth to share in the gains resulting from general community growth and public investment in the island's physical and service infrastructure. Compensation paid to landowners within PEZs will be discounted to eliminate windfalls attributable to these factors. Marginal downward revisions in the residual densities authorized in transfer districts will afford the funds required for these awards. Unrealistic demands upon the island's overburdened conventional revenue sources are therefore avoided, and the Commonwealth's entitlement to what land economists in Puerto Rico and elsewhere have long regarded as the "unearned increment" in private land is recognized.

Third, the Plan tempers the windfall/wipe-out effect that so often attends stringent regulation of private land use. Instead of wiping out owners of restricted resources in the PEZs, it accords them fair treatment. And the windfall of increased land values accruing to landowners within transfer districts due to these restrictions and the more general factors previously identified are reduced by the amounts required to deal fairly with PEZ claimants.

Fourth, the Plan shifts the cost of resource protection to the land development process where it properly belongs. For most of this century the costs, or what economists call the "negative externalities," of land development were poorly grasped. By exposing these costs to full view, the heightened environmental consciousness of recent years has sparked dramatic reforms, such as the Environmental Impact Statement requirement of the

National Environmental Policy Act, as well as a general recognition that land development is itself a primary agent of environmental despoliation. The Plan builds upon that recognition by charging these costs to the development process through the Environmental Trust Fund, much as the Highway Trust Fund charges the users of highways with the costs of the construction and maintenance.

Fifth, the Plan makes visible the long- and short-term costs and benefits of natural area protection. Much of the uneasiness aroused by existing environmental measures traces to their failure to make clear to government and the private sector what they will cost and how they will be financed. Government does not wish to become ensnared in open-ended programs that far outstrip its resources; landowners fear the capricious destruction of the investment that their land represents. The Plan responds to these concerns by detailing the magnitude of the resource protection effort and by creating a realistic mechanism to fund it. Constraints upon the Plan's ambit in the form of competing claims upon areas potentially designatable as PEZs and of the amount of income generated through development rights sales can be knowledgeably assessed as experience with the Plan grows. Greater familiarity with the Plan's operation, moreover, should assist the island in resolving what now unnecessarily appear as irreconcilable conflicts between its economic growth and environmental quality needs.

Finally, the Plan can serve as a catalyst to an improved development control system for the island. The inclusion of a natural area inventory as a component of the master plan has been mentioned. But the Plan also offers opportunities for achieving the various land use goals associated with channeling density and population to appropriate locations on the island. Examples include mapping transfer districts to encourage intensified development in the underdeveloped sections of Puerto Rico's cities or compact urbanization patterns along the metropolitan fringe. Other opportunities will emerge as experience with the Plan develops and as the Planning Board becomes adept in coordinating its use with other facets of the board's comprehensive planning process. . . .

THE TRANSFER OF DEVELOPMENT RIGHTS

1. Alternative Transfer Models

Two kinds of development rights transfers—one, literal, and the other, more metaphorical—must be distinguished in order to place the Puerto Rico Plan in context. The Chicago Plan for safeguarding urban landmarks illustrates the literal variety. Under this plan, unused office space allotted to downtown landmark sites is transferred for use in office buildings going up on other downtown sites. Development rights can literally be said to be "transferred" under this approach for three reasons. First, the rights are transferred in kind; the office space deducted from the landmark site appears as additional office space on the transferee site. Second, the amount of transferable development rights equals the difference between the *total* quantity of development rights authorized for the landmark site by existing zoning and the quantity of development rights actually used on the landmark site. Third, transfers are made on a one-to-one basis—from *this* landmark site to *that* transferee site or group of sites.

Development rights are transferred somewhat more metaphorically under the second model, exemplified by the Puerto Rico Plan itself. The shift appears in a comparison of the Puerto Rico and Chicago Plans in the foregoing three respects. First, rights are not transferred in kind under the Puerto Rico Plan. Transfers will not take place from office site to office site each within a few blocks of the other as under the Chicago Plan, but from rain forest or baylands to downtown San Juan or metropolitan Ponce. What the Puerto Rico Plan actually contemplates is the transfer of the *dollar* equivalent of the PEZ site's development rights, as validated by an administrative body. Because the PEZ landowner incurs a $75,000 loss, let us say, the purchaser or purchasers of his development rights receive a development premium of equivalent value but one which may translate into additional height, bulk, tower coverage, uses or whatever other trade-off the Planning Board fixes for the pertinent transfer district.

Second, something less than the full quotient of the development rights that might have been assigned to the PEZ site is transferable. This amount, it will be recalled, is determined by subtracting the development rights associated with the PEZ residual use from the rights associated with the reasonable beneficial use. In practical effect, therefore, the Puerto Rico Plan may be somewhat less generous than the Chicago Plan, a result attributable to the unzoned status of most of the lands likely to be designated as PEZs.

Finally, the Chicago Plan's one-to-one relationship between specific transferor or transferee sites is de-emphasized in the Puerto Rico Plan. The latter is comparable to the former in the respect that the total amount of additional development rights releasable in the transfer districts will strictly correlate with the development rights losses suffered at the PEZ sites. So long as the Environmental Trust Fund's debits and credits equalize at the end of each accounting period, however, no special effort will be made to link up specific development rights sold in transfer districts with the sites in PEZs from which those rights might be said to have originated. As discussed below, the shift in emphasis is largely a consequence of centralizing all transfer transactions in the Commonwealth rather than permitting PEZ landowners themselves to engage in such transactions.

2. Administration

The most prominent candidates to administer development rights sales in Puerto Rico are the Planning Board and the Land Administration. Supporting the former are the board's related functions, including PEZ administration, transfer district designation, and selection of the premiums to which development rights purchasers will be entitled. Most important, perhaps, is the board's responsibility to fix ceilings on the use of these premiums to prevent planning abuse, a responsibility that it could most effectively oversee on a transaction-by-transaction basis.

Despite these considerations, we recommend that the Land Administration conduct the development rights exchanges. Unlike the board, the Land Administration already possesses vast statutory powers to transfer property on behalf of the Commonwealth. Illustrative is its power under Section 7(b-1) of the Land Administration Act to:

> sell, whenever it may deem it necessary and desirable, lands or any interest therein, at such price as it may consider reasonable in order to . . . fulfill any of the purposes of this act.

Its powers to transfer property are corrollaries to its equally broad powers, previously noted, to acquire property and to pursue the island's environmental betterment. Given its various acquisition responsibilities under the Plan, whether at the direction of the administrative appeals board or otherwise, the Land Administration would seem the logical agency to sell off the development rights associated with these acquisitions in order to replenish the Environmental Trust Fund from time to time.

Further, the Land Administration's sophistication in the buying and selling of real estate and in related fiscal management responsibilities is unmatched by the Planning Board at the present time. The latter, it is true, does collect developer fees under the Neighborhood Facilities Program of Regulation No. 9 as well as channelization fees for the public contribution to waterway improvements; its staff, moreover, could be expanded to include the real estate professionals required to conduct development rights sales. But the general consensus of interviewees, including Planning Board officials themselves, ran so strongly against vesting the board with major fiscal duties under the Plan that we think it more advisable to stay with the Land Administration.

Also significant are the variety of subsidiary functions the Land Administration will be called upon to perform under the Plan. Land swaps with PEZ property owners and land assembly on behalf of developers in transfer districts have previously been noted as examples. Others undoubtedly will emerge as experience with the Plan grows. Centralizing the development rights sales function in the Land Administration would substantially increase its leverage and its opportunities in performing these subsidiary, but crucially important functions as well.

How will the Land Administration conduct the sales? Basically subject to two kinds of constraints. One will be the safeguards fixed by the Planning Board in the pertinent transfer district zoning regulations to prevent design abuse. If, for example, that zoning authorizes a premium of an additional two density units per acre, the Land Administration may sell no more than that amount. Clearly, it will have to coordinate closely with the board to insure compliance with the premium ceilings; the Land Administration can be expected, moreover, to actively assist the board both in selecting the premiums and in assessing how proposed ceilings on their use will affect their marketability. Cooperation will also be necessary to devise a system of documentation that informs Permit Bureau officials, mortgagees and other interested parties of the premiums that the Land Administration has sold.

The second set of constraints concerns the manner in which development rights are sold. The Land Administration Act expressly and implicitly permits a variety of methods, including public auction, sale to invited bidders, and negotiated sale at whatever price the Land Administration believes will best advance the purposes of the act (which, derivatively, incorporate the goals of the Puerto Rico Plan). In choosing among these methods, the Land Administration should strive to increase the resources of the Environmental Trust Fund as much as possible. Flexibility ought to be the keynote. If the premium being sold is attractive to developers generally and poses minimum design risks (e.g., the addition of two additional density units in urbanizations residually zoned for ten density units per acre), open public auction seems appropriate. If, on the other hand, a substantial block of development rights is being sold for use in a large-scale project on behalf of which the Land Administration is also lending its land assembly powers, a negotiated sale is in order. Once again, experience under the Plan will prove invaluable in concretizing policies and procedures that can only be sketched broadly in this study.

3. Transfers Between Private Landowners

Under the Chicago Plan, landmark owners receive the option either of selling their development rights to other private landowners or of obtaining compensation from the municipality, which may in turn resell the rights. Other development rights transfer programs, such as those proposed in Fairfax County, Virginia and in New Jersey, go further, envisaging no sales by government at all. Yet the Puerto Rico Plan, as described so far, excludes any mention of development rights transfers directly between PEZ and transfer district landowners. Why?

For reasons tracing to differences between the Plan and these other proposals as well as to the advisability of caution in the early stages of the Plan's implementation. Unlike the Puerto Rico Plan, the other proposals allocate discrete, easily determinable quanta of development rights to all transferor parcels and permit what essentially are transfers in kind within a tightly controlled planning framework. Government's functions under these proposals are two-fold: validator of transactions between private sector participants, and protector through its zoning authority of the market for development rights. Numerous advantages flow from this limited role. Both the government's financial risks and opportunities for official corruption and favoritism are decidedly reduced. Political and ideological opposition to the entry of government into the real estate market is assuaged. Development rights will become negotiable commodities much like stock certificates, futures contracts, or taxi medallions. And because of their negotiability, development rights rather than dollars may ultimately become the medium in which just compensation is paid.

These advantages are attractive indeed and, we hope, will eventually accrue to the Commonwealth under the Puerto Rico Plan. But voids in present understanding of and experience with the Plan's economic and planning consequences added to its greater complexity relative to other development rights transfer proposals advise that the power to transfer development rights lie only with the Land Administration initially. There will be opportunity enough to extend that power to the private sector should the results of its more restricted use so warrant.

As A Primary System of Land Use Regulation: The Maryland Proposal

Descriptive Information on Transfer of Development Rights, Accompanying Proposed Legislation

WILLIAM J. GOODMAN
Senator, Maryland State Legislature

The increasing land values in the fringe areas surrounding large metropolitan areas, combined with mounting pressures for more intense development have raised the sensitive issue of how to control "urban sprawl" and conserve open spaces, without denying local jurisdictions of their tax-based means of support.

Conventional means of control are not working effectively, and as population and urbanization increase, developmental pressures on privately held uncommitted land will become overwhelming.

New trends in land-use controls have emerged over the past decade that will, in some form or another, continue to be used for some years to come. Their principal features include averaging land-use intensity over relatively extensive districts, averaging diversified uses across a district and conservation of open spaces for recreational and other public interest uses. Several different types of innovative devices have been proposed to implement and extend these ideas. Examples which have seen some acceptance include cluster zoning, mixed and single use planned unit development zones, developmental districts large enough to be "new towns" or corridor cities. These concepts usually find application only in newly developing urban fringe areas, however, and really are not acceptable in an area already partially developed.

One new device that has created a lot of controversy recently in the State of Maryland calls for the creation of an entire new set of property interests, to be called "developmental rights". These rights would be marketable interests, similar to traditional mineral rights which all property owners have.

The development rights concept, as introduced to the Maryland Senate, would work in the following manner:

1. Counties would draw up master plans which specify the percentage of remaining undeveloped land to be developed, and where development must take place.

2. Counties will then assign developmental rights to all land owners for two categories of development: commercial and residential. The number of

rights given to each owner will be proportional to his property as a percentage of all land in the county, and all rights may be transferred or sold.

3. Developers must acquire a given number of rights per housing or commercial unit (to be established by the county planning commission).

4. No developer will originally own enough rights to build on all of his own land, he must buy additional rights, on an open market, from other land owners. Then, and only then, may he build.

5. Having sold their rights, farmers and other owners of open land will forfeit any chance to build commercial or residential developments in the future. This same constraint applies to heirs or transferees, and thus open spaces will be guaranteed.

6. If any landowner successfully petitions for an enlargement of the developable percentage of the plan, new rights will be allotted to all other holders of rights, proportionate to their existing rights, and a developer must therefore deal with them before he can build on the newly opened land. The holders may protect their own investments by refusing to sell their rights.

7. Agricultural and some outdoor recreational developments will not require rights, nor will land purchased by the county for schools, libraries, parks, fire and police stations and hospitals. Since these lands will escape the competition for developmental rights, their cost will remain relatively low.

This proposal has numerous features, all of which will tend to, either directly or otherwise, slow and eventually bring to a halt the spreading mass development which so many of our large cities have been surrounded by.

Among its strongest features is the effect that this proposal will have upon the disastrous speculation in land which has sent prices, taxes, and the cost of public services skyrocketing throughout the country. The plan also creates many disincentives to urban sprawl, and it may lead farmers, homeowners, county governments and even developers to oppose, by democratic methods, continued subdivision growth. The concept of developmental rights would also protect ecologically valuable (and vulnerable) zones from development, and it also strengthens the ability of counties to provide adequate schools, parks and public services for their residents.

Above all, developmental rights would wipe out the strongest legal barrier to the protection of open spaces. The courts have consistently held that a local government cannot prevent a private property owner from cutting down his forests or draining his swamp unless he is adequately compensated. If he is given developmental rights which he can sell, he will get his compensation while his county gets its open space.

With all the strong features presented above, it is difficult to see any faults with the plan, however several potential problems do become apparent after analysis of the proposal. Three become readily apparent on second reading of the plan: harmonizing the scheme with the state planning enabling acts, creating developmental rights as property, and using the rights as a basis for taxation.

The proposal, as described, will probably not run contrary to most state enabling acts, and suitable legislative strategy could be employed to make specific amendments where necessary. Some innovative regulatory schemes have been attacked as being preferential to special interests, but most courts have sustained them as supporting the public safety, health, morals and general welfare (the basic purposes of the enabling act).

Establishment of development rights as property creates no major problems, except as to the form that the rights should take. The Maryland proposal creates a set of new property interests, transferrable like any other, and this seems to be the best of the proposed possible forms (which have included various covenants to the land, easements, and municipal corporations established as dominant tenant).

Taxation of developmental rights can easily be achieved by using the rights as a basis for property classification, although in some states this may require constitutional amendment. This type of classification has been challenged in several states as being violative of uniformity clauses but has been uniformly upheld. Kentucky, Minnesota, Montana, Ohio, Virginia and West Virginia presently have property classification systems in effect, into which developmental rights could easily be fitted.

The Maryland plan, if adopted during the 1972 legislative session, will become the first development rights concept to be implemented in the United States. Excellent master development plans have been developed and adopted in many jurisdictions, but because of a basic weakness, they tend to deteriorate rapidly. A few land owners are given windfalls when their land is, by hook or by crook, designated for high density use. This is then followed by all other property owners requesting "just one little amendment" to the master plan, and eventually the entire plan is gone.

Some alternative to the master planning scheme must be implemented soon, before all available land is developed. HUD figures released recently indicate that each new single-family home built in the United States costs the public an estimated $17,000 in capital outlays for services. Any single unit home built in Maryland that costs less than $80,000 to construct, does not create a tax base sufficient to pay for its capital outlays. Therefore, the citizens who now live in the counties are forced, through increased taxes, to subsidize these new developments.

Recently, Palo Alto, California concluded that it would be more advantageous to purchase all the remaining open space rather than to permit development. Of the 22 different development plans considered, none yielded a positive net cash benefit.

Similar studies have been conducted in the San Francisco Bay area and other rapidly developing areas of the country, and the same conclusions are being reached after thorough study.

Fairfax County, Virginia has recently discovered that it loses over five and one half million dollars in net capital cost for every 7,000 new residents. This is another example of present residents being shortchanged for the illusory advantages of rapid single unit residential growth.

To permit this type of development to continue is to virtually give the key to the county treasury to the developers. Neither the state or the counties can afford to subsidize this type of loss, and it is only by controlling developments that the citizens' tax dollars can be applied for the benefit of existing residents.

It is hoped that the Maryland legislature will have enough foresight (as well as insight) to see that the proposal for the creation of developmental rights is passed during the 1972 session. If nothing else can have any impact, the last stated fiscal argument should be of sufficient weight of itself to convince them, and if it is passed, observers across the country will watch with a great deal of interest.

As A Primary System of Land Use Regulation: The Maryland Proposal

Maryland Senate Bill
No. 254 1972

AN ACT to add new Sections 10.01 through 10.09, inclusive, to Article 66B of the Annotated Code of Maryland (1970 Replacement Volume), title "Zoning and Planning," to follow immediately after Section 9.01 thereof, and to be under the new subtitle "Land Use Planning Districts"; to repeal Section 7.03 of said Article, Code and title, subtitle "General Provisions"; to repeal and re-enact, with amendments, Section 59-1 (a) of the Code of Public Local Laws of Prince George's County (1963 Edition, being Article 17 of the Code of Public Local Laws of Maryland), title "Prince George's County," subtitle "Park and Planning Commission," and Section 70-l of the Code of Public Local Laws of Montgomery County (1965 Edition, being Article 16 of the Code of Public Local Laws of Maryland), title "Montgomery County," subtitle "Maryland-National Capital Park and Planning Commission," to provide for the creation of land use planning districts, to require a master plan for each land use planning district, to establish rules and regulations governing the development rights of individual property owners within each land use planning district, and to remove the restriction that Article 66B is not applicable to chartered counties in order to bring all counties in the State and Baltimore City under uniform provisions.

WHEREAS, In many political subdivisions of the State of Maryland much of the lands have been lost or despoiled by the loss of open space, sprawl development, strip zoning, sewerage pollution, stream siltation and faltering transportation systems; and

WHEREAS, This unwise use and development often adversely affects the public safety, health and welfare of the present and future citizens of the State of Maryland by creating economic hardships, by the destruction of the natural resources, and by the disturbance of the ecological balance of the State; and

WHEREAS, The existing policies of the State, aimed at encouraging economic stability, the preservation of areas of ecological value, and the improvement of the quality of air, land and water resources, need to be supplemented; and

WHEREAS, The existing planning and land use control measures available to local public agencies within the State are not sufficient to deter damage to the public health, safety, welfare, and economic stability; and

WHEREAS, The apportionment of development rights to individual property owners will result in widespread citizen involvement in the land use planning districts and will encourage the pooling of rights for the purposes of developing and/or redeveloping the most desirable type of improvements in the most desirable locations and will insure maximum community support in carrying out State policies and eliminate arbitrary economic hardships; now, therefore,

SECTION 1. Be it enacted by the General Assembly of Maryland, That new Sections 10.01 through 10.09, inclusive, be and they are hereby added to Article 66B of the Annotated Code of Maryland (1970 Replacement Volume), title "Zoning and Planning" to follow immediately after Section 9.01 thereof and to be under the new subtitle, "Land Use Planning Districts"; that Section 7.03 of said Article, Code and title, be and it is hereby repealed; and all to read as follows:

LAND USE PLANNING DISTRICTS

10.01 Definitions

(a) "Agricultural use" means lands which are devoted to farming, forestry or open spaces.

(b) "Commercial category" means any use which materially affects the existing condition or use of any land or improvement which is not included within the definitions of "agricultural use" or "residential category" or "public service use" or "public use" as defined in Section 9.01 of this subtitle.

(c) "Commission" means a planning commission created by a political subdivision empowered to make, adopt, amend, extend, add to or execute a plan as provided in Article 66B, or as authorized by Chapter 780 of the Laws of 1959.

(d) "Development" means activity involving filling or removing of soil or new construction or expansions or additions or a change in use of existing improvements within a residential or commercial category.

(e) "Development right" means a percentage of interest in a category of rights to development hereafter referred to as "right".

(f) "District" means land use planning district.

(g) "Geographic value" means the value of a development right based on the percentage of the land area within the district it represents.

(h) "Improvement" means the filling or removing of soil, or new construction, or expansions or additions to existing improvements.

(i) "Jurisdiction" means the territory of a county or municipal corporation within which its powers may be exercised.

(j) "Land use planning district" means an area identified in a master plan, by metes and bounds, in which development rights are required prior to construction of any residential or commercial improvement, hereafter referred to as the "district".

(k) "Local legislative body" means the elected body of a political subdivision, whether known as county commissioner, or county council, city, town, or village council, or similar terms.

(l) "Master plan" means the adopted policies, statements, goals, and interrelated plans for private and public land use, transportation, utilities and community facilities documented in texts and maps which include all districts within the political subdivision.

(m) "Person" means any natural person, fiduciary, partnership, joint stock company, unincorporated association or society, or municipal or political subdivisions or other corporation of any character whatsoever.

(n) "Political subdivision" includes Baltimore City, any county of the State, and any municipal corporation with the authority to adopt master plans.

(o) "Public service company" means any public or private company that is regulated by the Maryland Public Service Commission; or any company which owns and/or operates a water or sewage treatment facility.

(p) "Public service use" means buildings used to house or store material, equipment, apparatus, devices used or to be used by a public service company in providing the service except buildings used primarily for administrative purposes.

(q) "Public use" means any improvement made by the State, a political subdivision or municipality not intended to be leased or rented primarily for residential and/or commercial use.

(r) "Residential category" means any use which materially affects the existing condition or use of any land or improvement used for single or multiple family dwellings.

(s) "Regulation" means any rule of general or specific applicability and future effect by an agency of State of local government, including any map or plan.

(t) "Right" means development right.

10.02 Grant of Power to Commission

(a) The commission shall divide the political subdivision into districts of such number, shape and area as may be deemed best suited to carry out the purpose of this subtitle.

(b) The commission shall promulgate rules and regulations governing the percentage of land which may be developed, designate locations, determine the geographic value of the rights, and determine the number of rights required to develop each type of improvement and/or use within each category in a manner that will accomplish the objectives of this subtitle within each district.

10.03 Planning

(a) It shall be the function and duty of the commission in each political subdivision to make and adopt a master plan made up of a district or districts for the entire political subdivision no later than January 1, 1974.

(b) Any political subdivision which has an existing master plan adopted before the effective date of this Act, shall only be required to divide the plan into districts and issue residential and commercial rights in accordance with the provisions in subsection 9.07 of this subtitle.

(c) The commission may consider existing land uses in the preparation of a district.

(d) The commission may, from time to time, amend the district.

(e) Each district shall be designed to carry out the purposes of this subtitle and shall include, among other things, the percentage of private land which may be developed, the designated locations, the total number of rights and their geographic value in each category.

10.04 Procedure for Adoption of a District Plan

(a) The commission shall adopt each district by a single resolution.

(b) The adoption of the district or amendment shall be by resolution of the commission carried by the affirmative votes of not less than a majority of all members of the commission.

(c) The resolution shall refer expressly to the maps and descriptive material and other matter intended by the commission to form the whole part of the district, and the action taken shall be recorded on the map and descriptive material and other matter by the identifying signature of the chairman and/or secretary of the commission.

(d) An attested copy of the district or part thereof shall be certified to the local legislative body and to the clerk of the court in the county or Baltimore City.

10.05 Legal Status of Official Plan

(a) Whenever the commission shall have adopted a district, no further development shall take place within the district until the location, character and extent thereof shall have been submitted to and approved by the commission.

(b) In case of disapproval, the commission shall communicate its reason to the local legislative body which shall have the power to overrule such disapproval by a recorded vote of not less than two-thirds of its entire membership. Failure of the local legislative body to act within sixty days from and after the date of the official submission shall be deemed a concurrence of the actions of the commission.

10.06 Procedure of the Local Legislative Body

(a) The local legislative body shall schedule a hearing within sixty days after receiving an attested copy of a district plan from the commission.

(b) The local legislative body shall make available to any land owner within the district not less than thirty days prior to the date set for hearing, the proposed rules and regulations as well as the proposed allocation of rights for each category of land use within the district.

(c) The local legislative body shall cause notice of the hearing to be published at least two times not more than thirty days and not fewer than ten days before the date set for hearing in a newspaper or newspapers published within and having a general circulation in the district.

(d) The local legislative body, after considering the testimony given at the hearing and any other facts which may be pertinent and after considering the rights of affected property owners and the purposes of this subtitle, shall establish by order the total number of rights in each category and the rules and regulations applicable.

(e) A copy of the order, together with a copy of the map of the district showing the boundary lines, shall be filed in the land records of the county or Baltimore City.

10.07 Development Rights

(a) After the adoption of the district, the local legislative body shall apportion all rights on a geographic value basis to all land owners within the district as shown in the land records of the county or Baltimore City except that the political subdivisions shall receive all rights to State-owned lands intended for public use within the districts.

(b) When rights are apportioned within a district and an improvement or improvements exist, all the rights of the owner in that category shall be attached to the improvement or improvements and cannot be sold or transferred separately.

(c) No additional rights shall be required for any improvement existing at the time of adoption.

(d) An owner of an improvement may request at any time the release of rights that are in excess of the number required for such improvement or improvements.

(e) Residential rights and commercial rights are separate and distinct categories and shall be recorded as such in the land records of the county or Baltimore City.

(f) No person shall be issued a permit for development unless he possesses title to such land and the number of such rights as required by the district.

(g) The sale or transfer of rights shall be regulated by the Maryland Real Estate Commission.

(h) Rights cannot be transferred between districts.

(i) All agricultural development, public service uses, public uses, and such types of private outdoor recreational development as approved by the State Planning Department are exempt from the provisions of this subsection.

10.08 Changes

(a) In order to make application for an alternate location of development, the applicant shall possess title to the land included in such proposed change and/or changes and shall also possess all rights required to implement the proposed change and/or changes to the plan. The designation of an alternate location of development does not constitute an increase in development within the plan but only an optional location.

(b) In order to make application for an increase in the number of rights within a district, the applicant shall hold title to land and rights within the district.

(c) In considering the merits of an application for an amendment, the local legislative body shall review the district and determine how the amendment would affect the implementation of this subtitle.

(d) Upon the determination that the number of rights to residential and/or commercial development within a district shall be increased, the additional rights shall accrue to all those persons holding rights within that category of development as recorded in the land records on the date the amendment is adopted.

(e) When an amendment is adopted, the local legislative body shall record in the record the justification for the change.

10.09 Application of Administrative Procedure Act

The Administrative Procedure Act shall apply to all hearings, judicial review, and appeals except where specific subject matter is provided by the subtitle.

SEC. 2. And be it further enacted, That Section 59-1 (a) of the Code of Public Local Laws of Prince George's County (1963 Edition, being Article 17 of the Code of Public Local Laws of Maryland), title "Prince George's County," subtitle "Park and Planning Commission," be and it is hereby repealed and re-enacted, with amendments, to read as follows:

59-1.

(a) The Maryland-National Capital Park and Planning Commission is continued as a body corporate, to have and exercise the powers, duties, and functions provided in this subtitle and in Article 66B of the Annotated Code of Maryland. It is the same agency as that with the same name created by Chapter 448 of the Acts of the General Assembly of Maryland of 1927, as subsequently amended from time to time. Hereafter in this subtitle it may be referred to as "the commission" or as "commission."

SEC. 3. And be it further enacted, That Section 70-1 of the Code of Public Local Laws of Montgomery County (1965 Edition, being Article 16 of the Code of Public Local Laws of Maryland), title "Montgomery County," subtitle "Maryland-National Capital Park and Planning Commission," be and it is hereby repealed and re-enacted, with amendments, to read as follows:

70-1.

The Maryland-National Capital Park and Planning Commission is continued as a body corporate, to have and exercise the powers, duties, and functions provided in this chapter and in Article 66B of the Annotated Code of Maryland. It is the same agency as that with the same name created by Chapter 448 of the Acts of the General Assembly of Maryland of 1927, as subsequently amended from time to time. Hereinafter in this chapter it may be referred to as "the commission" or as "commission."

SEC. 4. And be it further enacted, That if any provisions of this Act or the application thereof to any person or circumstance is held invalid for any reason, such invalidity shall not affect the other provisions or any other application of this Act which can be given effect without the invalid provisions or application, and to this end, all the provisions of this Act are hereby declared to be severable.

SEC. 5. And be it further enacted, That this Act shall take effect July 1, 1972.

As A Primary System of Land Use Regulation: The Fairfax County, Virginia Proposal

Transferable Development Rights: An Idea Whose Time Has Come

AUDREY MOORE
Supervisor, Annandale District
Fairfax County, Virginia

TDR—WHAT IS IT?

Transferable Development Rights is a substitute for zoning which allows for limits on the use of land, in accordance with a plan, while providing equal compensation to all landowners for their share in future development potential provided by the plan. It provides for the separation of land value and development values, grants more protection to the public interest against environmentally and financially unsound land use and development, while affording greater safeguards to the property rights of the non-speculative property owner. The "windfall/wipeout"[6] syndrome, created by government regulation of use, is therefore diminished.

TDR is an idea whose time has come. It is born out of the specific necessity to provide equal protection and fair compensation to all individuals, where the rationing of land uses is necessary to safeguard human needs. Rather than government deciding a community's lifestyle, the TDR proposal offered here reflects the philosophy that under a free market, mistakes in the use of land, potentially harmful to the future, will be lessened provided adverse economic incentives are removed.

However, my philosophy may not be one that others share. For example, it is important to note that other approaches, such as the one by Senator William Goodman of Maryland, assume and perhaps rightly so, that the principle will work equally as well where use of land is more specifically designated and where developers are encouraged to provide certain lifestyles through economic incentives in the requirements for rights.[7]

The Basic Principles of TDR

1. Separation of land and use of land for purposes of regulation.

2. Equal compensation for all landowners for development potential of a plan at no cost to the public.

3. Taxation of property by use, while keeping to the standard of fair market value for assessment purposes.

4. Provision for purchase of land for public facilities at minimum cost.

5. Elimination of lengthy procedures involved in government approval of development.

6. Provision of economic mechanism for total approach to population distribution.

Basic Procedure in Brief

1. The community will adopt a comprehensive master plan which will, among other goals, establish the total number of residents projected to live in an area and the total number of commercial/industrial needs projected for that area.

2. The community would determine how many development rights are required for each kind of residential and commercial/industrial development. Public facility use, farm use, conservation and recreation use and utility lines will require no rights.

3. The government will assign each property owner of record his rights in direct proportion to the number of acres of land owned, subtracting any development that may exist or development rights considered by the community to have vested.

4. To initiate development, the landowner will file with his site plan or subdivision plan, transferable rights equal to what is required for that development.

Frequently Asked Questions

Does this plan replace zoning?
    Yes.

Why do zoning procedures demand replacement?
    Because they do not work and are not fair.

 Is this idea constitutional?
    Yes. The courts have held zoning constitutional and this idea would simply implement the purpose for which zoning was established.

Would state legislation be necessary?

Yes, for full implementation. Modified approaches could be adopted without state legislation.

What about existing vested rights?
All land having received certain approvals will be entitled to transferable development rights. NO RIGHTS ALREADY APPROVED WHICH ARE CONSIDERED VESTED WILL BE TAKEN AWAY.

What about the effect on taxation?
Farmers and rural people would be taxed on USE rather than potential use of land. Market value would become the use value. Development rights are a separate property from the land. The system would be much more equitable.

How would development be timed?
In the same way it should be timed now. With a capital improvement program and requirements for adequate public facilities at the time of site and subdivision filing.

Is this complicated?
No. Zoning is complicated. The unfamiliar concept of having property rights separate from the land is the *one* difficulty. Once that concept is understood, the problems disappear.

Won't this system change the whole economic system?
No. Transferable Development Rights will not affect existing development or existing vested rights. It will make for a more sensible taxation system. It will make possible, for the first time, the implementations of plans. Attorneys will have plenty to do. Brokers will not only be selling land but also development rights. The builder and developers' lives will be much less complicated with no zonings to be obtained. Local officials will no longer spend countless hours in drawn out rezoning procedures. Most unhappy will be the land speculator who has already heavily invested in a piece of land, based on expectations of zoning from the elected body.

Would this system set a limit on growth?
No. It would simply be a more effective system for addressing total density, total use, total need for public facilities and total impact on the environment. There would be a built-in mechanism for increasing growth.

Why should a piece of marginal land receive the same credits as more easily buildable land?
Because all land is buildable and eventually, given enough economic pressure, it will be developed. Obviously, the buildable ground, intrinsically, will be worth more than marginal land.

TRANSFERABLE DEVELOPMENT RIGHTS—
PROCEDURES FOR FULL IMPLEMENTATION

A. Adoption Procedures

1. *Required State Legislation*

To allow for full use of this system, the Standard Code would require such substantive amendment as to make alteration of existing state law impractical. A new, proposed statute should incorporate the following features:

a. The requirement that basic comprehensive plan features, such as projected population, should be accomplished by referendum of the people.

b. A statement that the regulation of land as separate from the development rights in land is permissable.

c. A definition of development rights as constituting all shares of future development in the planned area; negotiable and freely transferable from one person to another; and precluding the possibility of their subjection to real property taxation.

d. The stipulation of that level of approval at which rights, for the purpose of distribution, are considered vested.

e. Permission to freeze assessments, for a limited time and only if necessary, for the purpose of providing a stable assessment base upon which to project revenues.

f. Provision to require referendum of basic elements for plan amendment.

2. *Local Plan Adoption*

a. The governing body will prepare a comprehensive plan, establishing the total anticipated population for the area, the total anticipated commercial and industrial use, land needed for public facilities, conservation, farmland, open space, etc., much the same as is presently done, except that more consideration would be given to:

(1). Waste absorption capacity of water and air

(2). Water supply

(3). The number of persons who can live in the area without undue congestion and adverse effect on health

(4). The need for jobs within reasonable commuting distance and the need for commercial/industrial tax base

(5). The need for working farmland

(6). The existing development

(7). The existing vested rights (which will not be taken away)

(8). The character of the land, i.e., slope, soil, hydrology

b. TDR calls for reform in implementation, not planning. All property holders will be compensated equally under this system, thus diminishing political pressures to design the plan to the advantage of the landowners.

The following specific features of TDR planning may differ from plan elements and procedures of today:

(1). Adoption by Referendum. Even under intense market pressures, plan implementation is assured. Therefore, adoption of the basic components of the plan should be accomplished by referendum.

(2). Density. Total planned population should be sub-set in neighborhood maximums, avoiding specific tract designations. This sub-designation is necessary to prevent congestion. However, if the density designations are detailed too specifically, the economic equity features of this plan will be diminished.

(3). Commercial and Industrial. The need for commercial and industrial square footage will be determined as in the past, on needs of projected population. Because of the lag in market demand for these uses, however, they call for specific site designations.

(4). Public Facilities. Size and location of public facilities should be easily projected. A financial program for construction must be included.

3. *Procedures under Site and Subdivision Ordinances—Proposed Amendments*

Elimination of the zoning approval process does not mean that development can automatically be processed, even if such development is in accordance with a general plan, with sufficient rights submitted. Certain set-back and height requirements would still be mandatory, differing somewhat from today's standards. The periphery of development must not be affected by inflicting damaging elements, e.g. diminishing light, air, etc. The availability of adequate public facilities must be assured. To avoid abuses, this provision should be specific and very carefully drafted. A requirement that, in no case, will development create an adverse environmental impact to neighbors and the general public should be explicit in the ordinance. These are the features of transferable development rights Subdivision/Site Plan Ordinance:

a. Incorporated in the Site and Subdivision Ordinance, rather than the Zoning Ordinance, would be permitted categories of development and their required number of rights. Commercial and industrial rights would be apportioned on the basis of square footage, and residential rights would be apportioned on the basis of dwelling units. Other uses would require site plan but no rights submission. These would include: farm, conservation and recreation, utility and public facilities.

b. Requirement that development proposal be in accordance with plan.

c. Definition of minimum adequate public facilities which must be available to serve development for plan approval.

d. Maximum emission standards for noise, light, and odors when near or adjacent to residential or certain commercial uses.

e. Requirements for land buffering and screening between certain uses and related to light and noise and height.

4. *Amendment to Law Governing Occupancy*

Before issuance of occupancy permit, development rights certificates must be recorded.

5. *Establishment and Assignment of Development Rights*
   a. Definition: Development rights are those portions of land ownership consisting of all rights to develop the land by the construction of improvements, excluding only open space uses such as agriculture, timber or recreation. Development rights may have become vested by exercise through construction of improvements or by prior approval of the community through

zoning. On assignment to particular parcels of their share of development rights, those rights not previously exercised will be made freely transferable from one person to another, separated from the particular parcel without action by the governing body and not subject to real property taxation until exercised. Development rights may be assigned in the form of negotiable instruments so as to render them more freely transferable by making absolute the power of the holder to exercise the development rights through filing a site plan anywhere in the planned area.

b. Categories: Three categories of development rights should be sufficient to meet planned objectives for private development by analogy with present major zoning classifications:

(1). DDR: Density Development Rights, in terms of dwelling units.

(2). CDR: Commercial Development Rights, in terms of square footage, including all private facilities supporting residential functions.

(3). IDR: Industrial Development Rights, in terms of square footage, including offices and other employment activities.

c. Determination of Rights Available for Assignment: In each category of rights, the development plan states the total dwelling units or square feet to be developed. Because some rights would be considered to be already vested, by development or by zoning consistent with the plan, these vested rights must be subtracted from total planned development to figure the new rights available for distribution. For example, if a small community planned a total of one million industrial square footage (IDR's) and one hundred thousand square feet of industrial space was already built, only 900,000 IDR's would remain for assignment at the time development rights were established.

Development rights vested by development would not need further recognition until the development is torn down, at which time the rights again become transferable. Zoning, as it stands at the time of establishment of development rights would be presumed honored and made transferable to other parcels. If the community discovered, in preparing its plan for total development, that it was already overzoned, the indicated down-zonings could be executed in preliminary action, so that the question of the vesting of certain prior zonings could be determined without threatening the overall planned limits.

d. Distribution by Acreage, Not Market Value: The available rights
    would then be assigned pro rata to every acre in the planned
    area. As noted above, the determination of market value is too
    vague and subject to improper pressure to base such an
    important right as development. Furthermore, although some
    acres are obviously more buildable than others, any effort to
    create sub-areas of differential development rights would end in
    the same unworkable governmental arbitrariness that has made
    the zoning district concept a failure.

e. Assignment of Rights to Particular Parcels: If a community
    established development rights when only agricultural develop-
    ment had occurred, it would be simple to divide total planned
    development by total acres in the planned area, giving the per
    acre average, and assign each parcel an amount of development
    rights equal to its number of acres times the per acre average.

    However, the development rights of some parcels will
    normally have been exercised by construction of improvements.
    No new rights will be assigned these parcels. For example, if the
    average commercial development rights (CDR's) are 500 square
    feet per acre, 500 CDR's would be assigned to every acre in the
    planned area except those already occupied by shopping centers,
    stores, gas stations or the like.

    The Density Development Rights (DDR's) are likely to
    require a more complicated preliminary calculation. This is
    because some parcels have already exercised more than the
    average per acre DDR's. Thus, the surplus DDR's of all such
    parcels must be subtracted from the new rights to be assigned, in
    order to figure the new average per acre DDR's, from which new
    rights can be assigned each parcel.

    The example which follows assumes a planned area of
    10,000 acres, for which a population of 100,000 is planned,
    which at 3.3 persons per dwelling unit would produce a total of
    30,000 dwelling units.

Area of Zone	Vested Zoning	Committed Dwelling Units
7,500 acres	at 1 dwelling unit per acre	7,500
2,100 acres	at 2.5 dwelling units per acre	5,250
300 acres	at 5 dwelling units per acre	1,500
100 acres	at 20 dwelling units per acre	2,000
		16,250
10,000 acres	avg. 3 dwelling units per acre =	30,000
	Uncommitted	13,750

It appears that the 5 dwelling units per acre zone and the 20 dwelling units per acre zone will not receive any new DDR's, because they are already over the planned 3 dwelling units per acre average. Therefore, the 13,750 uncommitted DDR's will be assigned to parcels in the 1 dwelling unit per acre zone and the 2.5 dwelling units per acre zone. The new average for these zones will therefore consist of the 12,750 committed dwelling units in those zones (7,500 + 5,250), plus the 13,750 uncommitted DDR's, divided by the 9,600 acres in the present 1 dwelling unit per acre and 2.5 dwelling units per acre zones. ($X = 26,500$, divided by 9,600 = 2,760).

In the foregoing example, therefore, each parcel in the old one dwelling unit per acre zone will receive an additional 1.76 dwelling unit per acre; and each parcel in the old 2.5 dwelling units per acre zone will receive an additional 0.26 dwelling units per acre. Total planned development of 30,000 will therefore be fully assigned at 9,600 acres at 2.76 dwelling units per acre (26,500) plus 300 acres at five dwelling units per acre (1500) plus 100 acres at 20 dwelling units per acre (2,000).

f. Assignment Mechanism: Not only the newly assigned development rights (13,750) in the above example, but also any unexercised but vested rights are to be rendered transferable. Therefore, a parcel by parcel search is necessary to figure how many of the rights assignable to the parcel are represented by construction in place. The amount of building permitted by old zoning and not yet built will be assigned as TDR's. For example, if a 10 acre parcel in the 20 dwelling units per acre zone has only a 100 unit garden apartment on it now, the owner will be assigned his remaining 100 TDR's. In effect, the community has already granted this owner this share of total planned development which the community now regards as vested for reasons it thought wise at the time of the original zoning.

A listing will therefore be prepared, from real property records, of each parcel, its owner's recorded address and the number of TDR's to be assigned. From this list, a preliminary notice—say 30 days—should be sent to allow the owner to correct any error, such as an overstatement of dwelling units in place or an understatement of units vested by old zoning. The allowance of occasional appeals will not make enough difference to require recomputation of uncommitted units. At the close of the notice period, an indication will be recorded in the registry of deeds, in the chain of title of each parcel, stating that development rights for the parcel have been rendered transferable under the TDR Ordinance. This warning to the purchasers of the land will have the same effect as an open space easement prohibiting development.

Although the TDR's could be maintained in a separate registry, consisting of the listing for notice purposes as corrected, the TDR's will be more saleable if certificates are actually prepared and mailed, one for each of the three categories of TDR's entitling the holder to development under the Ordinance. The certificate will be surrendered for cancellation at site plan submission for any parcel in the planned area. If the holder of a TDR certificate desires to sell only part of his rights, his first certificate can be cancelled and two new ones issued in the proper amounts. At this point, development rights will be fully established, independent of real property ownership. They will be fully transferable without action by the local governing body.

g. Summary: First, planned average development must be adjusted downward to a new average development to take account of previously committed rights in excess of the planned average. Second, the number of unexercised vested rights and newly assigned rights for each parcel must be figured and preliminary notice given. Finally, the chain of title of each parcel must be marked subject to the Transferable Development Rights Ordinance and certificates for the TDR's mailed to owners of record. Thereafter, the local governing body is not involved in the sale of development rights until a site plan for the exercise of a certain number of rights is presented.

B. Revision Procedure

The following features would be a part of any comprehensive plan amendment: 1. Any revision of the comprehensive plan would require a referendum of the people; 2. There will be no rights distribution without a revision of the comprehensive plan; and 3. Additional development rights will be distributed to *existing rights holders only*, similar to a stock split. There will surely come a time when there will be a desire within the community to increase density or allow for additional commercial or industrial expansion. A revision of the total plan would be necessary, with adoption. To strengthen and protect the free market, rights must be protected from dilution of value. They should be divided only among holders of rights.

TRANSFERABLE DEVELOPMENT RIGHTS—
PROCEDURES FOR MODIFIED IMPLEMENTATION

The need for total reform is especially urgent, given the relatively imminent transfer of the power to regulate, combined with the evils of the present zoning system. Given the lack of public understanding, the political clout that special interests will, no doubt, generate in opposition and even more importantly, the dearth of informed and concerted research on the whole concept, however, it is much more realistic to strive for at least partial implementation.

Precedent has been established for modified approaches.

Three communities have adopted modified versions of TDR for the preservation of historic sites and for the preservation of farmland. New York City[8] and Washington, D.C.,[9] have allowed the use of this concept to preserve historic sites. The Town of Southampton, Long Island, adopted an Agricultural Overlay District in May of 1972, allowing for the transfer of rights in farmland to a Residential Planned Community.[10]

The Southampton Ordinance allows for the transfer of rights *offsite*, while in New York City and Washington, D.C., the transfer was accomplished from adjacent sites. Chicago, Illinois is also considering offsite transfer to preserve historic sites; however, this proposal involves government regulation to a greater extent in the rights transfer.[11]

The following is a proposal, containing principles needed for partial implementation, which I presented to Fairfax County in September, 1973. It is being considered in connection with the county's new Planned Land Use System.

> Fairfax County would limit all residential construction to a maximum of ten units an acre in all multifamily zoning districts. Each zoning district would allow, however, a particular higher density on one site, requiring open space equal to the difference; such open space to be located either adjacent to the site or elsewhere in Fairfax County.
>
> For example, if a zoning district now allowed 40 units an acre, it could be changed to allow 40 units an acre to be built on one site, with the three acre requirement to be met, either adjacent to the site or separated from it. Criteria for the acceptance of the "cluster" land would be established on the basis of suitability for recreation purposes for use of the residents of the proposed development or for land suited for agriculture, flood plains, or steep slopes.[12]

Land and/or rights might be dedicated to the county, thus allowing land to be retained for the particular use of residents, allowing farms to operate, or providing for commercial recreation, all with a minimal tax burden.

By allowing the developer the option of retaining use of the land for the benefit of the residents of the proposed development, the argument that this regulation is a special requirement on a few for the benefit of the public at large can be overcome.

The contention that the constitutional requirement for equal protection is violated by requiring only proposed development of higher than 10 units an acre development to provide land preservation could be countered with the argument that such developments have a special congestive impact that lesser densities do not impose.

The primary legal obstacle is the question of exclusion, and I am assuming, hopefully, that 10 units an acre development would not be declared exclusionary in Fairfax County. The courts are beginning to recognize the needs of humanity which can only be met through preservation. By having open space and farm produce located nearby, the poor would benefit more than the rich. The courts should recognize the inherent injustice of requiring higher densities to prevent economic exclusion of classes of people without allowing corresponding municipal control over the price of housing.

NOTES

Note: Footnotes 1 through 5 were deleted in editing.

6. School of Law, University of California, Press Release, September, 1973. "Windfalls and Wipeouts: The Quiet Undoing of Land Use Controls."

7. Senator William Goodman, Senate of Maryland. No. 730, February 15, 1973.

8. City of New York Administration, Special Permits, New York Zoning Resolution Section 74-79, corrected 4/20/72, *Transfer of Development Rights from Landmark Sites.*

9. *The Washington Post*, editorial, "Landmark Decisions"—Washington, D.C. Zoning Orders 83 and 81, February 9, 1974.

10. Town of Southampton, Long Island, *Agricultural Overlay District*, Section 2-40-30-01, Section 2-40-30-02, Section 2-40-30-03.

11. "The Chicago Plan: Incentive Zoning and the Preservation of Urban Landmarks" by John J. Costonis, *Harvard Law Review*, Vol. 85, No. 3, January, 1972.

12. "Proposed Changes in Zoning Codes" by Audrey Moore, presented to the Fairfax County Board of Supervisors, September 10, 1973.

As A Primary System of Land Use Regulation: The Sonoma County Proposal

The Potential for Density Transfer in Sonoma County

THE SONOMA COUNTY PLANNING BOARD
Sonoma County, California

Density transfer is being studied in a number of areas of the country in an effort to discover if this practice might offer a solution to the problems of urban sprawl. Historically zoning alone has not provided permanent open space in the form of agricultural lands. And even those families who have wanted to remain in farming have been forced by high taxes to sell out for development. Often they have been richly rewarded financially, but the development has leapfrogged in many cases and despoiled neighboring farms.

The theory of density transfer has been written up extensively by a group at Rutgers State University, New Brunswick, New Jersey.[1] They discuss "density transfer" as a method for preserving desired open areas in "Open Space Preserves" with appropriate compensation to owners. Legislation for this purpose has been proposed in both Maryland and New Jersey. However, to date there is no known area where density transfer has been tried except as applied to floodway lands in Columbus, Ohio and Southampton Township (Long Island) to preserve prime agricultural lands.

In Sonoma County density transfer has been expounded by Supervisors Bob Theiller and Ig Vella as a method to create a greenbelt with equity to all owners involved. (This is separate from a proposed system of ranchettes to assure rural amenity outside urban areas.) The open areas would be protected in perpetuity from development other than for farming by sale of "development rights." The owners would be compensated for this curtailed future development by reduced taxes and payment for the difference in market value as farm land and its value if it had remained in farm use but with development potential. This payment would be financed by a "development rights tax" on lands within the "urban services" area of a city or community. The tax would be collected when applications are made for rezoning to a "higher" or denser use or annexation to a city.

This pilot study is an attempt to apply the principles of density transfer to an area just west of Santa Rosa. It involves a land use survey both inside and outside the City of Santa Rosa's "urban services" line as proposed for approval of the Local Agency Formation Commission. Existing city and county zoning has been considered as well as proposals for future land use in the city's 1967 General Plan. A land use inventory has been made and the potential for development calculated for parcels within and without the "urban services" line. The study also identifies several alternate methods of determining densities for transfer. These include application of the method described in New Jersey's Bill. (The Maryland method has not yet been evaluated. A copy of their legislation has just been received and the LAFC and planning staffs have had other commitments.)

THE STUDY AREA

The area west of Highway 101 to the Laguna de Santa Rosa and between Guerneville Road on the north and Highway 12 on the south is the subject of this pilot study. It comprises almost 14 square miles of which perhaps one-fifth is "flood-prone" according to the 1971 USGS Santa Rosa and Sebastopol maps. By "flood-prone" is meant that in any one year there is a one-in-a-hundred chance of flooding. Most of these lands are already in flood plain zoning which precludes residential development.[2] (See Map 1 for study boundaries and existing land use.)

Santa Rosa city limits in the pilot area are irregular, extending to Fulton Road in the south half of the pilot area and to approximately 1000 feet westerly of Marlow Road in some other sections. There are eight "islands" or "peninsulas" practically surrounded by City of Santa Rosa lands within the study area. These comprise about 430 acres excluding streets and channels and are only partially developed. Two of these have over one-third of their area designated "flood-prone" on the USGS maps, but it is considered that since they are close-in to town it will be economically feasible for developers to provide channels and structures to take care of storm waters. These two areas have not been placed in flood zoning.

The city's urban services boundary at this writing has been tentatively set as approximately one large parcel deep west of Fulton Road. Within this boundary there remain the eight island and peninsular areas which will have further development and be subject to a "development rights tax" under a proposed density transfer plan. There also remains a large area west of the city limits comprising almost 530 acres from which the development rights tax would be collected at time of development (or annexation or rezoning).

SCOPE OF THE STUDY

After inventory of zoning and land use, analysis has consisted of consideration of what development will probably take place under the 1967 Santa Rosa General Plan and possible modifications. (A future LAFC study proposes more detailed analysis of housing and land values.)

Inside the Urban Services Line

The nine areas inside the urban services boundary have been analyzed as to how many "density units" will probably be required for full development. The "development rights tax" proposed would be in proportion to the number of density units which would be needed. For example, if there are ten acres of agricultural land and someone would desire to rezone for apartments at 13 units per acre, he would be taxed on the basis of needing 10 acres x 13 or 130 "density units." The money from his development rights tax would then be used to purchase "development rights" from farm lands in the outlying areas.

The residential units have been easier to calculate than possible "density units" which would be needed for commercial and industrial development. These latter have been estimated from a formula based on a Trip Generation Guide, "A Fundamental Traffic Model," California Division of Highways, 2nd Edition, April 1967. This formula is predicated on the assumption that residential units, commercial, professional and industrial uses have a commonality of trip generation properties which reflect congestion and urban service needs.

The formulas below are based on estimates tailored to the Santa Rosa area:

                                                          No. trip ends per gross acre
Assume 8-13 dwelling units per gross acre generate 80
          Commercial uses generate 200
          Professional offices generate 100
          Industry generates 80

where x, y, z equal the number of "density units" to be required for a use other than residential.

1) *The proportion for commercial uses is:*

$$\frac{8 \text{ residential density units}}{80 \text{ trip ends per acre}} = \frac{x}{200 \text{ trip ends for commercial}}$$

$80x = 1600$

x = 20 density units required per gross acre in commercial uses.

2) *The proportion for professional offices is:*

$$\frac{8 \text{ residential density units}}{80 \text{ trip ends per acre}} = \frac{y}{100 \text{ trip ends for offices}}$$

$80y = 800$

y = 10 density units required per gross acre in professional offices.

3) *The proportion for industrial uses is:*

$$\frac{8 \text{ residential density units}}{80 \text{ trip ends}} = \frac{z}{80 \text{ trip ends for industry}}$$

$80z = 640$

z = 8 density units per gross acre in industrial uses.

In the application of the New Jersey method, no consideration would be given to the above formulas since a development rights tax in that state is proposed only for residential development. However, in calculating for other alternatives, a development rights tax is required as a condition of all forms of development. It is considered that to meet the criteria of fairness and equal treatment, all development should be taxed.

Outside the Urban Services Area

These lands comprise the beautiful western plain lands extending down to the Laguna. There are some dairy lands and they are dotted with Valley oaks. Included are the Country Club Estates and other more rural-looking communities of comparatively small parcels. Some have been prematurely developed in that the parcels are not large enough to permit septic systems to function well over existing hardpan. In some cases maintenance has not been efficient.

In calculating what potential development rights there will be available for sale, we can immediately eliminate the parcels that are entirely within the flood zone (F-1). They have no development rights at all. Those parcels with some land in the "F-2" zone or in other agricultural zones would have some potential development rights available.

The New Jersey method includes *all* essentially undeveloped lands in agriculture, wetlands, woodlands, etc. Those lands that are partially in the flood zone by this method would have all acreage included and "certificates" of development rights issued to all lands in an "open space preservation district." The ratio of "certificates" apportioned would reflect the assessor's appraisal based on location, flooding and other factors. In the alternative methods the "F-1" acreage would be eliminated from each parcel in calculating development rights (density units) which could be sold from the outlying area.

It should be understood that the acreages used in the pilot study are careful estimates and nothing more. Aerial photos (1971) were used to determine the amount of developable land; windshield surveys were used in the areas inside the urban services line. The several alternative methods for calculating the number of development rights (density units) available from the outlying area are these:

A. The New Jersey method. This is based on the following formula, with existing zoning frozen, solving for x the unknown:

$$\frac{x \text{ no. certificates for a particular parcel}}{\text{total no. of certificates issued in open space preserve}} \text{ equals } \frac{\text{cash value of that parcel—land only}}{\text{cash value of all land in the open space preserve}}$$

B. Exchange of one development right (density unit) in the outlying area for one needed inside the urban services boundary, based on existing zoning frozen in the outlying area. Modifications of this method would allow the same calculation of potential density units, but with immediate rezoning of all greenbelt lands to larger minimum size parcels, as 5, 10 or 40 acres.

C. Division of the outlying area into three development bands, each having a different ratio of exchange based on the present-worth-of-a-future-dollar with 7 percent discount rate used. The interior band would be assumed developable within 10 years, the next in 20 years and the third in 30 years. Values would be .5083, .2584 and .1314:1 respectively, and development rights in the outlying area would be required at these ratios to each density unit needed in the urban services area.[3]

CALCULATION OF DENSITY UNITS NEEDED

The following is a detailed calculation of net density units which will be needed in the nine areas *inside the urban services boundary*. They are indicated as Areas 1, 2, 3, 4, 5 and 5A, 6, 7 and 8.

Calculations under two methods require that a development rights tax be applied where zoning changes are needed for commercial, offices, industry and residential uses. Thus if General Plan studies show ultimate development of any of these types, additional density units will be required. The New Jersey method differs in that density units are never required for commercial or industrial development. . . .

CALCULATION OF "CERTIFICATES" OF DEVELOPMENT RIGHTS IN OPEN SPACE PRESERVE

An arbitrary decision has been made that an Open Space Preserve should consist of at least 25 acres.[4] Several or many contiguous parcels can be combined with individual plots as small as 5 acres in size. Parcels within a preserve should be essentially undeveloped with maximum coverage written into enabling legislation.

For a proposed Open Space Preserve within the pilot area, all parcels of less than 5 acres have been eliminated. Also parcels completely within the "F-1" (Flood Plain) zone would have no development rights under Sonoma County zoning. Lands within commercial zones and zoned for "R-1" are also eliminated from the preserve even though some are in parcels larger than 5 acres. *This leaves about 3000 acres suitable for inclusion in an Open Space Preserve*.

It is questionable whether all this area should be placed in a preserve at the outset. The literature suggests that an adequate amount of land be placed in an Open Space Preserve initially to take care of expected demand for density units inside the urban services boundary for several years. Then at a later date additional areas can be added to the preserve as demand increases.[5]

The following pages include calculations of potential "certificates" of development rights which might be available for purchase with development tax moneys. A summary of the acreages from which they are calculated, by present zoning, is shown in this table:

Estimated Gross Acres

In "AE" (Exclusive Agriculture Zone) where
owners may wish to convert to permanent open
space and sell development rights 500

In "AS-B4" (Potential 1-acre minimum parcel size) 2,125

In "AS-B5" (7-acre minimum); some larger parcels
could be recombined and divided 105

In "R-R" (2 d.u. per acre permitted without sewers) 280

3,010

Use 3,000 acres

There remains, of course, the question of whether property owners should be paid for development rights in agricultural areas that do not "perk." Would the county be justified in paying money for a development right where none exists for this reason? At what point should "perk" tests be required and who would pay for same? It is recommended that the seller of development rights be charged with the responsibility of proving that he has some for sale.

The New Jersey Method

The proposed New Jersey legislation would issue "certificates" of development rights (in proportion to assessor's "cash value") to all lands in an Open Space Preserve.[6] Wetlands, woodlands and agricultural lands, essentially undeveloped, are included and it is presumed there exist some development rights to sell.

Under Sonoma County zoning, lands entirely within the "F-1" district are precluded from development. However, using the New Jersey method those parcels partially within the "F-1" zone would have their total acreage included with the assessor's "cash value" reflecting less value due to flooding. Thus in addition to the estimated 3000 acres from which development rights might be purchased using methods B and C, another 900± acres would be included which are the portions of parcels in the "F-1" zone.

The first step in this method is calculation of an estimated assessor's "cash value" of land within the preserve area. Based on selected representative values of various size parcels in the pilot area, the cash value of Open Space Preserve lands is assumed to be $6,176,000.

It is probable under the New Jersey method that approximately 2900 density units will be needed ultimately for development inside the urban service line. For the purposes of this study an arbitrary decision has been made to issue 4000 "certificates" of development rights to parcels in the Open Space Preserve in calculations for applying this particular method.[7]

It is possible to figure the number of "certificates" issuable to each parcel, according to the New Jersey method, by this formula. Solve for x, the unknown.

x/parcel's land value = 4000/$6,176,000 (land value at total preserve)

The above, of course, is of interest only to an individual owner. The object of this study is to discover the macro effect.

It is not feasible to predict how fast development will come within the urban services boundary. Nor is it possible to predict how many outer-area property owners will decide to forego sale of development rights and hold their land speculatively. However, it is possible to describe what may happen.

Under the New Jersey plan the "certificates" would be taxed in the same manner as real property. Initially the value of each unsold certificate would be equal to the difference between the aggregate value of the land for agricultural purposes and the aggregate value of the land for development purposes as divided by the total number of unsold certificates of development. "Thereafter, such value shall be determined on the basis of current sales . . . in the particular jurisdiction."[8]

At this writing it is impossible to know how the market would establish a price for "certificates" of development rights. It is thought that with a period of slow building activity in the county there would be relatively low demand. With increased building activity there should be increased demand, and increased sale prices for certificates. Also it is not known how many owners would be willing to sell.

In summary of the New Jersey plan, *to satisfy the ultimate demand for approximately 2900 density units, 4000 "certificates" of development rights in an Open Space Preserve area could be issued.* Probably these would be issued in increments with additional areas added to the preserve as needed.

One-for-one Exchange of Density Units

By this method existing zoning is frozen. Then an estimate is made of how many development rights (density units) might be available in areas outside the urban services line. Such areas, essentially open and 25 acres or more, would be designated as an Open Space Preserve. Parcels inside the preserve could be 5 acres or larger.

It is estimated there are approximately 3000 acres available for the Open Space Preserve which would have development rights to sell. Industrial and commercially zoned lands have been excluded. "F-1" lands that lie within the preserve have no development rights that could be sold. It is thought owners of "AE" zoned land may like to convert and ultimately sell development rights. Thus "AE" zoned 500 gross acres + "AS-B4" zoned 2125 acres all @ 1 d.u. per acre (net of roads):

$$2625 \div 1.13 \text{ ac. (.13 for roadway)} = 2833 \text{ density units}$$

In "R-R" @ 2 d.u. per acre without sewers;
280 gross acres:

$$280 \div 1.13 \text{ ac. x 2} \qquad\qquad = 495 \text{ density units}$$

In "AS-B5" @ 1 d.u. per 7 ac. minimum:

$$105 \text{ ac.} \div 7 \qquad\qquad = 15 \text{ density units}$$
(some parcels might be recombined)

$$\overline{}$$
$$2833$$

minus 2% estimated existing density
units already used[9] -57 density units

$$\overline{}$$
2776 development rights
(density units)

Use 2775

Since approximately 3600 density units will ultimately be needed inside the urban services line, there is obvious imbalance.[10] To correct this, a multiplier of 1.44 could be applied so that a total of 4000 certificates of development rights could be issued to the owners of parcels in the Open Space Preserve area.

Several modifications of this method could rezone land in the Open Space Preserve to some particular minimum parcel size. Ten, twenty or forty acre minimum size agricultural parcels would make farming more economically productive and preserve the greenbelt character of the land to a greater degree. Owners would still be assigned the same potential number of density units as under the previous 1-acre minimum zoning. Some legal parcels of nonconforming size would remain in the preserve.

Division of the Outlying Area into Concentric Bands

Use of this method would be based on the premise that closer-in lands are apt to develop sooner than farther-out lands.

Based on a table giving the present-worth-of-a-dollar to be received in the future, relatively different values are assigned to three zones between the urban services boundary and the Laguna.

> *1st Zone*, from urban services boundary west to Irwin Lane and northerly extension thereof, assumed developable within ten years. Assign value of 0.5083 of one development right per acre.

> *2nd Zone*, from Irwin Lane and extension to Willowside Road and southerly extension thereof, assumed developable within 20 years. Assign 0.2584 of one development right per acre.

> *3rd Zone*, from Willowside Road and extension to the Laguna, assumed developable within 30 years. Assign 0.1314 of one development right per acre.[11]

The above would result in an estimated unweighted average value of 0.3 development rights per acre in the outlying area.

With an estimated 3010 acres of lands having development rights (calculated by Method B), 3010 x 0.3 (average) would give 903. To this a multiplier of 4.42 could be applied which would result in approximately 4000 "certificates" of development rights being available to satisfy a need for 3600 net units within the urban services line.

It would be advisable to designate priorities for these areas, so that in the first years of the program some contiguous development rights could be acquired. It should be decided whether a band of open space would best be assembled just east of the Laguna, or considerably farther east nearer to the urban services line, as a first priority.

Summary

Of the three methods described above, Method C is deemed to be the most equitable in one respect because it assigns higher values (more "certificates" per acre) to parcels closer in. It would seem logical these development rights would be of greater value than those of lands farther away from Santa Rosa.

Method C might be more difficult to administer because there could be objections from the public because of establishment of two arbitrary lines between zones.[12] Also this method depends on issuing "certificates" according to a relationship between a particular parcel's assessor's "cash value" of land and that for the entire preserve. Because of the time lag in reappraisals, this value is not an exact one. However, establishing a uniform minimum parcel size would eliminate some objections to present zoning boundaries. A minimum 5 or 10 acre parcel size would dispense with some of the objections encountered now that two different regulations on each side of a zoning line may be unfair and arbitrary.

CONCLUSIONS

While the pilot study area consists of almost 14 square miles, approximately one-fifth lies within the "F-1" (Flood Plain) zone which precludes residential development.

Within the 14 square miles approximately 9 square miles lie outside (west) of the City of Santa Rosa's proposed urban services line. More than one-third of this area is flood-prone, according to the 1971 USGS map.

An Open Space Preserve: For purposes of establishing an Open Space Preserve west of the urban services line, these lands are eliminated:

a) Parcels of less than 5 acres

b) Parcels in commercial or industrial use or zoning.

This leaves an estimated 4100+ acres for inclusion in the Preserve with approximately 1100 acres of this in "F-1" zoning. Almost 300 acres of the flood-prone lands consists of parcels with no portion in zoning other than "F-1". These, under Sonoma County zoning, would have no development rights as such.

It might be desirable to establish two other Open Space Preserve areas inside the City of Santa Rosa's proposed urban services line. Two areas fairly close-in would be especially desirable, namely north and south of Donahue Road, and near Dutton and West Third Streets. These lands are agricultural lands highly visible from Highway 12 and are of sufficient size to provide good vistas.

Development Inside the Urban Services Line: Since present Santa Rosa policy embraces the philosophy of compact growth, maximum densities from the General Plan were used in the pilot study.

Over 500 acres are available for development between western city boundaries and the proposed urban services line somewhat west of Fulton Road. In addition there are island and peninsular areas east of western city boundaries which comprise over 400 acres. For development of these areas approximately 3600 potential density units (development rights) would be required from outlying areas.[13] The amount of money per unit for a "development tax" has not been considered in this report. It would depend on estimates of amounts needed to buy development rights in the outlying area plus sufficient funds to administer the program. The proposed LAFCO study will address these problems.

Recommendations

A combination of the B and C methods for calculating "certificates" of development rights in an Open Space Preserve is recommended. Method B using a 10-acre minimum parcel size throughout the preserve would prevent the further division of land into small parcels. It would have another beneficial effect in that people will cease to think of these lands as so many potential one-acre sites. However, there should be citizen input before any proposed rezoning for this purpose is undertaken.

Plan C could be combined with the 10-acre minimum. Thus property-owners who in the past have been taxed more because of a close-in location could expect to receive relatively more from sale of development rights. Application of the present-value-of-a-future-dollar table based on estimated 10, 20 and 30 year potential for development (@ a 7 percent rate) would be more equitable than a one-for-one trade.

It is also recommended that sellers of development rights pay for "perk" tests to establish that they have rights to sell.

The above are aspects of a plan for obtaining permanent open space in "Open Space Preserves." The lands could be preserved in perpetuity by agreement between cities and the county. And through tax reduction there is provision for a just form of compensation to owners who forego development. Hopefully it would enhance both city and county areas as better places to live and would give stability to the county's development policies.

NOTES

1. See Chavooshian, B. Budd & Thomas Norman, "Transfer of Development Rights" in December 1973 *Urban Land* and "From the Legislature: Development Rights Device for Land Use Control" by Jerome Rose in the Winter 1973 issue of *Real Estate Law Journal*.

2. Construction of the Warm Springs Dam may reduce the size of areas now zoned "F-1."

3. p. 490, Table A-3, Frederick E. Case, *Real Estate*, Allyn & Bacon, Inc., Boston, 1962.

4. The New Jersey proposed legislation uses this minimum size, which would seem to be a suitable one to preserve vistas.

5. See Sec. 9(e) TDR No. 4, New Jersey (ibid).

6. See Appendix E for text of the proposed New Jersey legislation. (Deleted in editing.)

7. It is considered advisable to have more "certificates" available for sale than will be needed for close-in development, since some owners may not elect to sell development rights at all.

8. See Section 11, Appendix E, proposed New Jersey legislation. (Deleted in editing.)

9. Estimate from visual inspection of parcels 5 acres in size and larger in Open Space Preserve areas.

10. By all but the New Jersey method, additional density units are needed for commercial and industrial uses where rezoning is required. The New Jersey method would need only 2900 additional density units.

11. Estimates are based on Table A3, p. 47, Case (ibid), using a 7 percent interest rate.

12. Interview with Floyd Morgan, Assessor III, County of Sonoma.

13. The New Jersey method would require only 2900 density units because none would be required for commercial and industrial development.

As A Method of Encouraging the Construction of Moderate and Low Income Housing

**Building Zone Ordinance,
No. 26, May 1972**

*TOWN OF SOUTHAMPTON
Suffolk County, New York*

2-10-10   <u>General</u>

Within any Residence District, a building, structure, lot or land shall be used only for one of
the uses indicated in Section 2-10-50 Residence
Districts - Table of Use Regulations for the specific District in which it is located on the Zoning Map, and in accordance with the particular
classification of that use in that District.
Further, any such building, structure, lot or
land shall only be utilized in conformance with
the provisions of Section 2-10-60 Residence
Districts - Table of Dimensional Regulations.
In addition, such uses shall also comply with all
other applicable provisions of this Ordinance.

2-10-20   <u>Transfer of Permitted Residential Development
Rights</u>

2-10-20.01   These provisions are enacted to implement the
Town of Southampton Master Plan of 1970 by providing the means of achieving elements of the Community Planning Objectives with reference to natural resources, population, utilities and housing,
and more particularly, to do so while maintaining
the overall ratio established between population
capacity at ultimate community development and
the safe yield of the fresh ground water reservoir within the Town of Southampton's territorial
limits. Further, land from which the development
rights are to be transferred must have such
characteristics that their permanent open space
preservation will fulfill one of the following
objectives:

    (a)   Porous moraine soils, found in the CR-80
District, will be retained for the purpose
of maximizing ground water recharge while
lessening potential pollution of these
ground waters by individual sewerage disposal
systems.

    (b)   Soils, found in the Agricultural Overlay
District and conforming to United States

Soil Conservation Service capability Classes I and II, will be retained for permanent agricultural use.

(c) Tidal wetlands, as defined in this Ordinance and their immediate upland environments will be retained for their ecological benefits and held in permanent open space use.

(d) Lands, found in an area designated by the Town's Master Plan of 1970 for a greenbelt park system or for an individual park, beach or public recreation area, will be retained for such open space use.

2-10-20.02   In pursuit of these purposes the Town Board of the Town of Southampton may from time to time authorize by ordinance the transfer of permitted residential development rights from one parcel of land to another parcel of land within the same school district where such authorization shall be found to be beneficial to the town through serving to implement the Master Plan of 1970 and to be in accordance with the provisions of this Section.

2-10-20.03   Procedure:

(a) An applicant for the transfer of permitted residential development rights shall present documentation satisfactory to the Town Board indicating:

(1) the location, land area and related residential development rights permitted under the applicable provisions of this Ordinance which the applicant proposes to transfer

(2) the location and land area of the site to which such rights are to be transferred, the projected total number of dwelling units that would result on the site from such a transfer and a statement of the character of the projected housing development

(3) a presentation as to the reasonable and beneficial results anticipated from the authorization applied for with respect to the implementation of the Master Plan of 1970

(b) If the Town Board decides to consider the applicant's proposal, it shall proceed in the same manner as provided in Section 7-40 for amending this Ordinance, except that the fee for such application shall be $250.00

(c) The Planning Board report to the Town Board shall consider all aspects of the proposal, particularly that of the degree to which the proposal implements the Master Plan of 1970

(d)   Upon favorable review by the Town Board, such
      an application shall be approved subject to
      completion of the following actions:

      (1)   approval by the Planning Board of a de-
            tailed site development plan for the
            property to which the development rights
            are to be transferred and a recommenda-
            tion with regard to the disposition of
            the property from whence the development
            rights were transferred

      (2)   execution of an instrument legally
            sufficient both in form and content to
            effect such transfer and the transmittal
            of the fee title for the property from
            which the development rights are to be
            transferred to the Town of Southampton
            or such other governmental agency as
            the town shall designate for use as
            permanent open space

      (3)   filing copies of the executed legal in-
            strument in the office of the Town
            Clerk, the Planning Board, the Building
            Inspector and with the County Clerk as
            a notice of such transfer incorporated
            in the deeds of each property affected
            by the transfer. Such instrument shall
            specifically set forth the rights trans-
            ferred and the resultant total residen-
            tial development rights in each property

      (4)   such other requirements as the Town Board
            shall establish.

2-10-20.04   General Standards:

(a)   Districts in which an increase in the
      number of dwelling units may be permitted
      shall be restricted to those listed
      hereinafter, and for each district speci-
      fied, the number of dwelling units permitted
      shall not exceed the following.

      (1)   When proposed for transfer to an R-60
            or CR-60 District, the number of dwell-
            ing units shall not exceed the number
            which would be permitted in an R-40
            or CR-40 District.

      (2)   When proposed for transfer to an R-40
            or CR-40 District, the number of dwell-
            ing units shall not exceed the number
            which would be permitted in an R-20
            District.

      (3)   When proposed for transfer to an R-20
            District designated by the Town's
            Master Plan of 1970 as an appropriate
            location for multi-family housing, the
            number of dwelling units shall not
            exceed eight (8) per gross acre and the
            Table of Use and Dimensional Regulations
            for the MF-44 District shall apply.

(b)   The site, to which the transfer of development rights is proposed, shall be no less,
than 20 acres in any R-60, R-40, CR-60 or
CR-40 District; and no less than five (5)
acres when proposed for a site conforming
to 2-10-20.04 (a-3).

(c)   All yard requirements of the more restrictive
district found along the perimeter of the
site shall apply to perimeter yards on the
site to which the transfer of development
rights is proposed.

(d)   At no time shall the total number of dwelling
units in multiple dwellings, authorized by
this procedure or any other means, in a hamlet area exceed 5 percent of the total number of dwelling units of all types in such
hamlet as determined by the Planning Board
for the then current year.

(e)   The hamlet areas, referred to in 2-10-20.04,
(d) will be those which the planning board
delineates with reference to the Master Plan
of 1970 and subsequent amendments, and
computations shall be based on available
housing, land use and population data found
therein.

(f)   Nothing in this Section shall abrogate the
requirements of other codes and regulations,
including the Town of Southampton Subdivision
Regulations, when they are applicable.

2-10-30   Increased Residential Development Density to
Establish Low and Lower Middle Income Housing
Inventory

2-10-30.01   Since there is a limited supply of standard housing
available at purchase prices or rentals commensurate with the incomes of low or lower middle
income residents in the Southampton Community,
these provisions are enacted to implement the
Town of Southampton Master Plan of 1970's Community Planning Objective with reference to encouraging a wide variety of housing types and,
more particularly, to help make possible purchase
and rental costs in keeping with the financial
means of the town's residents who have low or
lower middle incomes.

2-10-30.02   In pursuit of this purpose, the Town Board of the
Town of Southampton may from time to time authorize
by ordinance an increase in residential development density where it shall be found that a bona
fide non-profit corporation guarantees to develop
and maintain the resultant housing at a purchase
price or rental cost within the low or lower
middle income housing market in accordance with
a contractual agreement between said non-profit
corporation and the town; and further that such
authorization shall be found to be beneficial
to the town through serving to implement the
Master Plan of 1970.

2-10-30.03 Procedure:

(a) An applicant for increased residential de-
     velopment density, under this Section, shall
     present documentation satisfactory to the
     Town Board indicating:

     (1) location, land area, proposed re-
          sidential density, and general de-
          velopment concept and physical charac-
          teristics of the development

     (2) organizational characteristics, legal
          basis and financial status of the non-
          profit corporation sponsoring the pro-
          posed housing

     (3) projected development costs, the resultant
          capital and operating costs, the detailed
          elements of the purchase price or ren-
          tal costs to be charged and the proposed
          income limitations to be placed on owners
          or tenants

     (4) details of any program whereby such owners
          or tenants may acquire equity in housing
          without changing the future market value
          of the proposed housing units and any proposals
          to overcome economic hardship for those even-
          tually moving out of the proposed non-profit
          housing

     (5) the instrument or instruments by which
          the objectives of this program are to
          be guided and enforced legally

     (6) a presentation as to the reasonable
          and beneficial results anticipated from
          the authorization applied for with res-
          pect to the implementation of the Master
          Plan of 1970.

(b) If the Town Board decides to consider the
     applicant's proposal, it shall proceed in the
     same manner as provided in Section 7-40 for
     amending this Ordinance, except that the fee
     for such application shall be $250.00

(c) The Planning Board report to the Town Board
     shall consider all aspects of the proposal,
     particularly that of the degree to which the
     proposal implements the Master Plan of 1970

(d) Upon favorable review by the Town Board, such
     an application shall be approved subject to
     completion of the following actions:

     (1) approval by the Planning Board of a de-
          tailed site development plan for the
          property.

     (2) execution of an instrument legally suffi-
          cient both in form and content to effect
          the purposes of these provisions

        (3)   filing copies of the executed legal in-
strument in the office of the Municipal
Clerk, the Planning Board, the Building
Inspector and with the County Clerk as
a notice of such instrument incorporated
in the deeds of each property affected
by the instrument. Such instrument shall
be specific as to the right of the Town
of Southampton to enforce its provisions
with reference to owner or tenant incomes and the non-profit character of
the project

        (4)   such other requirements as the Town
Board shall establish.

2-10-30.04   General Standards:

        (a)   At no time shall the total number of dwelling
units in such low or lower middle income
dwellings, authorized by this procedure or
any other means, in a hamlet area exceed
four percent of the total number of dwelling
units of all types occupied year around in
such hamlet as determined by the Planning
Board for the then current year

        (b)   The resultant number of dwelling units per
gross acre of land on the development site
shall not exceed 12 units. In all other
respects the provisions of the Table of Use
and Dimensional Regulations for the MF-44
District shall apply

        (c)   Nothing contained in this Section shall abro-
gate the requirements of other codes and regulations, including the Town of Southampton
Subdivision Regulations, where they are applicable; however, nothing in this Section shall
preclude the use of prefabricated housing
units where the construction quality of such
units is officially approved under the New
York State Building Code.

2-10-40   **Planned Residential Development**

These provisions are enacted to implement the Town
of Southampton Master Plan of 1970 by providing the
means of achieving elements of the Community Planning Objectives with reference to natural resources,
population, utilities and housing, and more particularly, to do so while maintaining the overall ratio
established between population capacity at ultimate
community development and the safe yield of the fresh
ground water reservoir within the Town of Southampton's
territorial limits.

2-10-40.01   In pursuit of these purposes the Town Board of the
Town of Southampton authorizes and empowers the Planning Board, simultaneously with the approval of a
plat or plats, to modify applicable provisions of
this Ordinance, pursuant to the provisions of Section
281 of Article 16 of The Town Law, where such authorization shall be found to be beneficial to the town
through serving to implement the Master Plan of 1970

and to be in accordance with the provisions of this
Section.

2-10-40.02   Procedure:

(a)   An applicant for planned residential development
      shall make direct application to the Planning
      Board pursuant to said Board's requirements as
      set forth in the Subdivision Regulations of the
      Town of Southampton.

2-10-40.03   General Standards:

(a)   An overall development plan shall be presented
      showing the use or uses proposed, including
      dimensions indicating the areas set aside for
      each use, and the locations of all structures,
      parking spaces, and rights-of-way or driveways,
      and the provision for community sewer and water
      service facilities.

(b)   Residential dwelling units may be in one-family,
      two-family, or multiple dwelling structures;
      provided that the total number of dwelling units
      shall not exceed the permitted number allowable
      under the residential use district for districts
      in which the site is located unless a transfer
      of development rights from other land holdings
      are a part of this plan and conform to the pro-
      visions of Section 2-10-20; and further provided
      that the minimum yard provisions, and in the
      case of a multiple dwelling, the minimum
      spacing between buildings, shall be not less
      than those required:

      (1)   in an R-10 Residence District for a one-
            family and two-family dwelling.

      (2)   in an MF-44 Residence District for a
            multiple dwelling.

(c)   Open space or common land resulting from the
      planned residential development design shall
      only be used for private or municipal recrea-
      tion, including natural park land, and for
      agriculture when found in the Agricultural
      Overlay District. Such land shall only
      be owned by a non-profit corporation or
      trust or shall be offered for dedication to
      the Town of Southampton or other public agency
      for the same uses; but in any case of a non-
      profit corporation or trust, a pre-established
      offer of dedication shall be filed with the
      Town for acceptance if such non-profit corpora-
      tion or trust were ever discontinued or failed
      to maintain the private recreation use,
      natural park or agricultural land.

(d)   The proposed planned residential development
      shall comply with all other applicable re-
      quirements of the town with respect
      to land development.

(e)   In a CR-60 or CR-40 District, a limited area
      for neighborhood convenience shops may be part
      of the planned residential development plan
      provided that its size shall be regulated so
      as to serve only the residents of the planned
      residential development; serve no less than 100
      units of housing; be no closer than two miles
      from an existing business district; and shall
      not be constructed until the entire residential
      portion of the plan is completed.

(f)   In the MHS District, a mobile home subdivision
      may be considered as a dwelling type in a
      planned residential development provided that
      it meets the requirements of (a) through (e),
      except for the explicit minimum yard and build-
      ing spacing called for in (1) and (2) of item
      (b) and further, that:

      (1)   the mobile home subdivision shall be
            licensed by the Town and comply with all
            the requirements of the mobile home
            subdivision ordinance.

      (2)   the site area shall be not less than 20
            acres.

      (3)   a proposed development plan prepared by
            a licensed professional engineer, shall
            be submitted for the entire site.

As A Method of Encouraging the Construction of Moderate and Low Income Housing

The Mandatory Percentage of Moderately Priced Dwelling (MPMPD) Ordinance Is The Latest Technique of Inclusionary Zoning

JEROME G. ROSE

At the same time that most suburban communities are utilizing various techniques of exclusionary zoning, such as large lot districts, minimum floor space requirements, apartment restrictions, controlled sequential development, etc.,[1] a few local governments have adopted a new statutory technique that seeks to provide housing for low- and moderate-income families within the community. It is not clear whether the statute is a response to recent judicial admonitions that municipal planning and zoning must provide for a balanced community[2] or to the combined political pressure of newlyweds, empty-nesters, local employers, and those who, for idealistic reasons, seek a more balanced socioeconomic mix in the community. Whatever the reason, the Mandatory Percentage of Moderately Priced Dwelling (MPMPD) ordinance is now a fact of life that should be noted and understood by the real estate industry.

An MPMPD ordinance has been adopted by Fairfax County (Virginia) and Montgomery County (Maryland)[3] and it is being studied by other local governmental agencies, including the Regional Planning Board of Princeton (New Jersey), as a possible method of overcoming the high costs of construction that are putting unsubsidized housing beyond the reach of low- and moderate-income families.

Purpose of the MPMPD Ordinance

The Montgomery County Council found, and the MPMPD legislation recites,[4] that a severe housing problem existed within the county due to an inadequate supply of housing for residents with low and moderate incomes. Studies had shown that there was a rapid increase in the number of residents of, or approaching, retirement age, who either had reduced or fixed incomes; that there was a growing proportion of young adults of modest means forming new households; and that there were numerous employees of government, commerce, and industry within the county whose services were necessary to support the existing and expanding economic base of the county. The supply of moderately priced housing was inadequate to meet the needs of these people. Consequently, many of those working within the county had to commute from outside the county to their places of employment, thereby overtaxing existing roads and transportation facilities and significantly contributing to air and noise pollution.

The Montgomery County Council found that approximately one-third of the county's projected labor force over the next ten years would require moderately priced dwelling units. In spite of this need, the concurrent high level of demand for higher profit potential luxury housing discouraged developers from offering a more diversified range of housing. The Council also determined that the private sector is best equipped and has the necessary resources and expertise to provide moderate-income housing. The only problem was the high cost of land and construction which reduced the profit incentives to build such moderately priced housing. This led the Council to conclude that private developers could be persuaded to build moderately priced housing if they were given adequate profit incentives by permitting greater zoning density

and by relaxing some building and subdivision regulations.

The underlying principle of the MPMPD statute is simple: Give a housing developer a bonus in terms of zoning density and the relaxation of building code requirements in return for his agreement to build a proportion of the units within the range of the moderate-income (or low-income) market. Although the principle is simple, the administration of the program is complicated and there are numerous unresolved legal issues.

Administrative Problems

To administer an MPMPD program it will be necessary to posit policy decisions and establish guidelines to resolve the following issues:

(1) What percentage of the total number of units built must be allocated to the moderate- (or low-) income market?

(2) What range of tenant or purchaser incomes should the mandatory percentage be designed to meet?

(3) What kind of administrative mechanism is necessary to adjust rents to changing economic circumstances?

(4) If dwelling units are to be sold, what mechanisms are necessary to retain the economic advantages for future purchasers?

• *The mandatory percentage.* There are at least two different views for determining the mandatory percentage of low and moderate units. Pragmatists would probably urge that the percentage be based upon market and economic studies to determine the extent to which the developer may effectively pass on the increased costs of subsidizing the lower priced units and the extent to which the market for the higher priced units would be adversely affected by the presence of lower income occupants. Idealists would urge that the mandatory percentage be based upon housing need or the goal of an "ideal" socioeconomic mix within the community. Whatever percentage is adopted would, very likely, reflect a compromise between the two points of view.

• *The range of income.* Determining this issue will also involve reconciling a number of divergent viewpoints. Pragmatists will argue that the program can succeed only if the market for the higher priced units is maintained. Consequently, they will urge that only the moderate income market be serviced by the program. Idealists will urge that at least some percentage of units be made available to low-income families. If such families cannot be serviced by subsidizing part of the rent, they will urge that some units be offered to the local housing authority under one of the federal public housing leasing programs.

• *Administration of rent regulation.* Administration of the program must be assigned to a governmental agency with authority to adjust rents. Such adjustment is

necessary to achieve the objectives of the program and at the same time to enable the landlord to obtain a fair return on investment. Changing costs of maintenance and fluctuating market demand for higher priced units will require rental adjustments for the subsidized units. The need for continual rent regulation is probably, from the developer's point of view, one of the most serious objections to the program. Zoning density bonuses and the easing of building code standards will have to be substantial to overcome the burdens of rent negotiations with a governmental agency that is subject to increasing political influence of tenant organizations.

• *Administration of sales regulation.* If the developer agrees to build townhouses or condominiums instead of rental housing, then the MPMPD program will continue to achieve its objectives, if, but only if, each purchaser of a subsidized unit, when he sells, is required to sell at a price that is within the means of low- or moderate-income purchasers. This means that purchasers of subsidized units may have to relinquish all, or part, of the appreciated value of the dwelling when it is sold. Thus, a government agency will have the task of developing principles and administering a program which establishes unit selling prices and selects qualified purchasers.

Legal Problems:
The Need for Enabling Legislation

MPMPD ordinances face two

serious legal problems—(1) questions of statutory authorization and (2) questions of constitutional validity. In the short history of this program, the first ordinance of its kind was challenged and found to be invalid on both counts. In *The Board of Supervisors of Fairfax County v. DeGroff Enterprises, Inc.*,[5] the Virginia Supreme Court held invalid a Fairfax County ordinance that required a developer of fifty or more dwelling units to commit himself, before site plan approval, to build at least 15 percent of dwelling units as low- and moderate-income housing. The court held that the ordinance exceeds the authority granted to the local governing body by the enabling act because it is directed to *socioeconomic objectives* rather than *physical characteristics* authorized by the state statute. Furthermore, the court said, the ordinance is invalid because it requires the developer or owner to rent or sell 15 percent of the dwelling units at rental or sale *prices not fixed by a free market.* Such a scheme, the court held, violates the state constitutional provision that no property be taken or damaged for public purpose without just compensation.

In spite of this initial setback, proponents of MPMPD ordinances argue that these ordinances will be upheld in those jurisdictions where the courts have held that the validity of a zoning ordinance depends upon its ability to "promote the general welfare." [6] They argue that these courts will hold that the "general welfare" requirement imposes the obligation upon munic-ipalities to provide for a variety of housing choices. Consequently, it is argued, the courts will determine that not only is the MPMPD ordinance within the scope of zoning enabling legislation, but there is an affirmative duty on the part of local governments to adopt techniques such as MPMPD to provide that housing choice.

In those states that adopt the reasoning of the *Fairfax County* decision, enabling legislation will be necessary. But in either case, the proponents urge, the MPMPD ordinance is alive and well, and gathering support for the next onslaught upon the citadel of suburban zoning practices.

NOTES

[1] See Rose, "New Directions in Planning Law: A Review of the 1972-1973 Judicial Decisions," 40 J. Amer. Inst. Planners — (July 1974).

[2] See Rose, "The Courts and the Balanced Community: Recent Trends in New Jersey Zoning Law," 39 J. Amer. Inst. Planners 265 (July 1973).

[3] For an excellent analysis of the Montgomery County, Maryland legislation see The Potomac Institute, Inc., Memorandum 73-11, Nov. 28, 1973.

[4] Montgomery County Code, Chapter 25A, title, "Housing, Moderately Priced," (1973).

[5] 214 Va. 235, 198 S.E.2d 600 (1973).

[6] E.g., New Jersey, Pennsylvania.

As A Method of Regulating the Location and Timing of Community Growth

Precedent-Setting Swap in Vermont

LEONARD U. WILSON
Senior Planning Associate,
Robert Burley Associates
Waitsfield, Vermont

Vermont expects a continued steady increase in seasonal and residential development with its accompanying demands for space and facilities. The challenge is to accommodate this growth in new development that is compatible with the environmental quality, the existing landscape and the settlement characteristics of the state. There is limited space suitable for intensive residential, commercial, industrial and recreational uses, and planning and control are therefore essential. Vermont is discovering that the legal and planning techniques needed to properly manage the tempo and pattern of settlement are yet to be developed.

The town of St. George is undertaking an innovative community design that may provide some clues to the components of growth control policy. St. George is 2,304 acres of Vermont geography. It's a town without a school, post office, town hall, gas station or store. St. George, however, is on the outer fringe of the rapidly sprawling Burlington urban area and has been subject to growth pressures that have threatened a total conversion of the town from rural to low-grade suburbia.

Located 10 miles southeast of Burlington, the state's largest and most prosperous city, St. George is in the path of spillover. Expansion in Burlington and its eight satellite towns with a population of over 87,500 has been haphazard with congested suburban shopping centers, waffle-styled subdivisions and choked throughways. St. George has begun to experience this urban impact, and its population jumped from 108 in 1960 to 477 in 1970.

The people of St. George decided to welcome and plan for orderly growth. They have adopted the objective of balanced social and economic development through a new community concept. In May 1970 the people voted to buy 48 acres of land on which a town center could be built, and the state's architects and planners were invited to enter a competition for the design of a new community. Robert Burley Associates of Waitsfield submitted the winning scheme. The concept was subsequently incorporated in a revision of the official town plan and thus becomes the basis for detailed planning and preparation for development. The town has adopted a plan that creates a compact village where expected further growth will be focused. The fulcrum of the plan is a parcel of land which the town has purchased in the area where it has been determined that growth will concentrate. This parcel will become the center of a projected village with commercial, public, residential and, perhaps, industrial elements.

The town will use the leverage of the control of this land to persuade developers to participate in the community project on the town's terms. To achieve the objective of concentrating settlement and preserving the rural character of most of the rest of St. George, the town may oblige a developer to transfer to the town development rights purchased from owners outside the project area in exchange for the opportunity to develop in the core village area. For example, a developer wishing to construct 20 units of housing in the village area would have to purchase 20 acres of land zoned at one family to the acre elsewhere in St. George and transfer his acquired right of 20 units of housing to the project area. The 20 acres from which the rights were transferred will remain open land in perpetuity or until the town releases it to meet future needs. The land will be taxed only at its value as undevelopable land.

St. George resident Armand Beliveau first conceived the use of development rights transfer as a means of implementing the community plan. Involved in local and regional planning, he learned by experience that the greatest hindrance to good planning and land use control in rural Vermont is the hostility of landowners who fear that zoning regulations will limit, if not eliminate, fair profits from the sale or development of land.

Beliveau sought a way of providing compensation for impaired property values at no cost to the municipality. He recognized the planning possibilities for the town if it were able to zone vast areas as agricultural or open with no complaints from landowners because they were compensated. Planning for growth and implementation could truly be accomplished to the advantage of the majority.

Beliveau's concept is based upon the separability of the *intrinsic value* of land from its *potential development* value.

The latter could be established for one parcel but then transferred to another parcel. An oversimplified example of the formula is: Smith owns 100 acres of abandoned hill farm. A density of one dwelling unit on two acres has been established as reasonable and equitable. Smith, therefore, owns 50 development rights or "credits" plus 100 acres of land. The area, however, has been zoned 20-acre agricultural reserve based on growth and development policies of the town. Smith can sell up to 50 development rights and keep the land for nondevelopment uses or sell both land and credits. However, only a maximum of five developments rights can be exercised on Smith's land; the other 45 must be used somewhere else in town.

A 20-acre piece of land owned by Jones is located in the village area where concentrated development is regarded as appropriate. Although it is zoned for four families to the acre, it has a development credit value of only one unit per acre to maintain a reasonable and equitable balance among all town landowners. With only 20 credits available with the land, Jones must purchase an additional 60 to realize the full development value of his property. This, of course, creates demand for Smith's development rights and, therefore, he receives compensation for them.

A portion of the property tax is assigned to the "development rights," and a portion stays with the land (intrinsic value). Once development rights are sold or transferred the property is taxable at only its intrinsic value which is much lower. The town does not lose the total taxable value since the development rights are still taxable. Once development rights are sold from the land, the nondevelopability of the land is made part of the deed. Development rights are transferred by the same procedure as deed transfers. Development rights could be sold by Smith as he saw fit.

The town, therefore, can direct development according to town growth policies in the town plan. The region could also direct development between towns according to a regional plan. The state might also use this concept to distribute growth throughout the state, if so desired.

The number of development rights may be limited to fit a growth time of five years. Rights could accumulate at an annual rate as a means of fixing future growth rate or the number of development rights could be reassessed every five years with increases proportioned out to original holders of development rights.

A simplified form of the Beliveau concept has been adopted as the basic land strategy in the St. George project. The number of development rights assigned to each property equals the number of houses that could be built on the property under present zoning. That is to say, 20 acres in a zone which requires two acres for a dwelling unit would have 10 rights available for transfer to the development area.

Further implementation of the transfer concept is contemplated when the actual building of the new community begins. The planners intend to propose a rezoning of the town to greatly reduce densities with the provision that the present number of development rights remain with each property. Property owners will be further restricted in the intensity of use of their land but will be compensated by the sale of their unusable rights.

Under this scheme the economic and environmental advantages of concentrated development and open space preservation can be achieved within the framework of established community growth and location objectives. Moreover, the concept of the transfer of development rights points the way to the resolution of the problem of compensating landowners for property rights otherwise impaired by control.

With the help of grants from the State of Vermont and the New England Regional Commission, the St. George community development project is moving forward. Negotiations are underway, and private developers are indicating an interest in participation. The physical program and plan for the project were developed by the Burley firm, which has been retained as project consultant.

Taken a couple of steps further than in St. George, the concept could become the basis of a zoning system that rewarded all landowners equitably whether or not their land was designated for development. Lawyers who have looked at the concept see no fundamental legal impediments but acknowledge that a substantial amount of complex legal analysis would have to be done before the system could be made operational on a large scale. □

As A Method of Regulating the Location and Timing of Community Growth

Controlling the Location and Timing of Development by the Distribution of Marketable Development Rights

KEVIN LYNCH
Professor of Urban Studies
Massachusetts Institute of Technology

Assuming that local control of the rate of development may be desirable in some situations, this essay proposes a mechanism for controlling that rate. After setting a desirable general rate, as well as the locations in which development is to be retarded or encouraged, a local government would issue the number of development rights each year which equals the rate of growth desired. These rights are distributed to landowners in proportion to their land holdings and may be transferred, bought, and sold. They may be used at any location in the region, subject to established density limits. The issuing agency may hold one block of rights to be used to encourage development in specified areas, or as a subsidy for low-income housing, or for other types of explicitly defined and socially desirable development.

The control of private land development in rapidly urbanizing areas suffers from certain well-known weaknesses, which zoning and subdivision regulations only partially overcome, or even accentuate. Chief among these weaknesses are the rigidity of comprehensive zoning; its inability to control rate in step with the provision of public services; the inequities inherent in zoning land at different densities, which also accentuates the imperfections inherent in the land market; the sudden profits to be made at a change of zoning, and thus the pressures of political influence and corruption; the inability to prevent development entirely in some area without outright and costly purchase of land, as well as the legal questions raised when densities are set very low; the use of land controls for social exclusion; and the focus on "ultimate" levels of development rather than the crucial rate of growth. Moreover, if a control over growth rate is actually attempted, there then arise some very sticky problems of rationing.

An equitable annual distribution of development rights to all landowners by a local government might circumvent *some* of these difficulties. We will not discuss the serious social and economic problems raised by growth rate control in general. Our discussion is limited to the description and analysis of one particular mechanism which might be used to accomplish that control.

One development right would be a permission (subject to other normal development controls) to build so many square feet of structure on any location in the area, or perhaps to build one dwelling unit, if residential growth were the key problem. This right would be good for five (or ten or . . .) years from the date of issue. It could be bought or sold on the private market, and used at any location where building were permissible, but with some limits on the distance over which it could be transferred (i.e., "good only in the Town of X", or "may be transferred to locations no more than y miles from the land to which originally issued").

A local government would make two political determinations: one as to the desired locations for development, and the other as to the rate of growth. The first would be a more stable decision, and would locate desirable densities and uses by zone, including areas where further development was prohibited and others where it was strongly encouraged. This is normal zoning, except that development can now be prohibited in certain areas without outright confiscation. Moreover, since development rights themselves are equitably shared, locational density can be manipulated more sharply with less political - pressure, opportunity for corruption, or charges of inequity.

The desired rate of development would be reset on a more frequent basis, perhaps annually, perhaps for longer periods. Or, to combine public flexibility with private predictability, the rate might be set annually for that year which is three to five years in the future. For example, if it were a question of controlling residential growth, a local government might determine that it could reasonably handle N new dwellings per year in the coming three to five year period. There would necessarily be limits on this power to set the rate, particularly if it is to be exercised by a local authority. It would have to be shown (to a state authority, or to a court if challenged) that this proposed rate bore some reasonable relation to past growth and to public purpose, to ecological and social constraints, and that it was tied to the planned and budgeted expansion of public services. Moreover, a supervisory body, like the state, might require that the rate include a certain number of rights assignable only to low cost dwelling units, so that local rate control could not be used to exclude a fair share of the regional need for low cost housing. Some portion of the total development rights (call it W) could be withheld in public hands, later to be given or sold to developers of low cost housing, or to developers in locations where it is a stated public purpose to stimulate growth. All these hedges on the rate-setting power are not unlike the legal and state restraints imposed on local zoning today. Nevertheless, the locality retains a better chance to manage its growth from year to year.

Once the growth rate of N units per year is set, and the number of W units per year to be withheld in public hands, then the amount to be distributed, $N - W$, is divided by the total number of acres, A, in the locality. A fractional development right, $(N - W)/A$, is then issued to each land owner for each acre he owns, counted to the nearest acre. It might be issued to him when he pays his annual property tax, to simplify administration, and as a further incentive to pay. He might also receive one right for each existing unit on his land which he demolishes or which is destroyed, although in some situations this could put a premium on the destruction of old, but sound low-cost housing.

(Note: It may seem more logical to distribute rights in new growth according to the development potential of land holdings. Under this rule, a town would calculate the maximum number of dwellings allowable on any tract according to its zoning rules, and subtract those already built to give those which could legally be added. The owner would then share in the total pool of rights according to the proportion of his potential new dwellings to the total town potential. Areas fully built up would receive no rights, and areas zoned for low densities would receive few.

We argue for a distribution based solely on acreage for reasons in addition to administrative simplicity. We intend to equalize the costs and benefits of development, as far as they are due to public regulation rather than to characteristics inherent in the land. We hope thereby to improve equity; to take some of the heat, and chance of windfall profit, from zoning changes; to separate rights of development from those of land use as far as possible; to permit public zoning of areas to a zero or a very low density without a taking; and to give some of the value of development to landowners who cannot share in it but who must share in its costs via their taxes. Thus we advocate a simple distribution in proportion to land area owned.)

The holder of such rights now has several options. He may lose the rights or destroy them, either because of carelessness or because he is motivated to retard development in the region, even at some cost to himself 'Thus some leakage of usable rights may always be expected. He may hold the rights, and accumulate enough to build on his own land, as permitted by the locational zoning. He may buy additional rights from others, so he can build at a greater density (again, if so permitted at his location). He may hold or buy up rights in order to speculate in them, although speculation will be difficult due to the time limits imposed on the rights, their widespread ownership, and the block of rights withheld by the local government. Finally, a land owner may sell his rights to someone who wishes to use them in another location or to a developer buying for future use on land not yet purchased. Since the rights are interchangeable, and of equal value, it should be possible to organize an orderly local market for them.

The local authority, meanwhile, may sell its withheld rights, W, to developers in particular locations to stimulate development there, or grant (or be compelled to grant) them to developers of low cost housing as a subsidy. The accumulation and release of such rights might also become a normal secondary function for a regional or state land bank, and so be used to stimulate metropolitan growth in desired directions or to break the suburban exclusionary ring. The land bank, in effect, would have a special power to speculate in rights. The use of rights by the state in this way might logically be tied to state subsidies to localities, for the expansion of public services.

In effect, we propose that the right of development be separated from the right of land ownership, except that ownership is the source of an annual grant of generalized development rights. The development right is now made transferable, marketable, and subject to regulation in time as well as in space. Thus the community has a much more effective and yet flexible way of coordinating public and private investment, and can do so with less injustice to particular land owners. At the same time, part of the rights in land now enter a freer and more rational market, conferring greater flexibility on the developer. The right to develop is a right given to all owners equally, once a feasible total quantity is set, and not a right which can be partially and unequally confiscated by variable zoning rules.

Neither the separation of the development right, nor the control of development rate, are new ideas. Great Britain nationalized all development rights in 1947. But this required a gigantic task of assessing the value of such rights throughout the nation, their purchase, and then the detailed burden of passing on each proposed new development. Development rights have already been transferred at a small scale in the regulation of historic sites in New York City and in Chicago. (See J.J. Costonis, *Space Adrift*, Urbana, University of Illinois Press, 1974.) In 1970, a group at M.I.T. proposed a state-wide market in development rights in Massachusetts, in their publication, "Urban Development Policies." A bill to establish transferrable development rights has been drafted in Maryland.

But the control of development *rate* has been linked to none of these recommendations. Control of the rate of growth has long been a subject of planning discussion, and recently towns such as Ramapo, New York, have instituted controls of this kind, tied to public investment plans and a rather elaborate set of "points" assigned to proposed development schemes. Linking development rights and rate control in an organized system seems to be a new possibility.

Many questions arise, of course. There might be administrative difficulties. But since rights are easily calculated, could be issued when taxes are paid, and could be an actual instrument which is later deposited by a developer when requesting a building permit, the difficulties do not seem to be very large. Other ways of rationing a limited amount of development—such as a lottery, a policy of first come first served, an auction, or a distribution based on development merit (as in Petaluma)—are either more complicated, more unjust, politically more tender, or less subject to public control. Someone would have to organize the local market in rights, however, and this might be a problem in a small town.

The courts might consider the scheme a confiscation of existing rights in land without compensation. But once the control of rate is accepted (and this is the key point which is not discussed here), then the distribution of rights based on ownership is perhaps the most equitable means that can be devised, with a lottery as a second choice. To the accepted concept of public control of density in space, we are adding the control of density in time. It must be subject to the same test of reasonableness, however. It is true that a development right cannot entirely compensate for the loss of any absolute right to build. But it spreads the loss, and softens the blow of restrictive zoning, since the owner is at least left with marketable rights, as well as the right to use his land without building on it. As a result, courts may take a more lenient view of low density or agricultural zoning in this situation.

The proposal might be considered an unfair redistribution of land values, since owners of inaccessible or unusable land get as many rights as the owners of "ripe" land. But the owner of the unusable land is still unable to market it, and this may be reinforced by the enactment of "non-development" zones. Differential market values still reside in the variable qualities of the land itself, which cannot be moved about. We have already argued for some equalization of development benefits.

The setting of the development rate, of course, would now be a high political act, similar to the setting of the tax rate. But, especially if it is directly linked to budgets for the expansion of public services, it probably should become so. Since the rate is set year by year, mistakes can be corrected fairly rapidly. The fluctuation in the market price of rights will in itself be a useful index.

A local government might consider *selling* the rights, instead of granting them, at a price which would compensate it for the additional public costs of private development. But this is a more radical shift in taxation, and might more easily be considered confiscatory by the courts. Moreover, the markets in rights will then become less responsive. However, a community might be justified in selling some of its withheld rights at a level consistent with the cost of servicing higher densities. Thus all owners are given the right to undertake moderate growth, but more intense growth must be paid for at its social cost.

The spatial "clustering" of new development, which has many advantages, can now only be encouraged where land ownerships are very extensive. The development right proposal would allow this to happen even where ownership was fragmented, since zones of concentration can be mapped which may only build up as rights are drained away from surrounding owners, or, more loosely, high densities might be allowed anywhere in certain general areas, provided that all or a proportion of the development rights had been drawn from land within a close-in radius.

So far, the proposal has been discussed as it would apply to local government. It might be even more useful at the regional level, where some collective authority would set growth rates for the region, or for its sectors, linked to regional development budgets and to regional policies for the location and timing of growth and the opening of social and economic opportunity. Public service costs might be supplemented in the various towns according to the number of rights used there. Moreover, the market in rights would now be large enough to be organized more easily.

The proposal has been keyed to urbanizing areas. Might it also be used in some form in "mature" developed areas, where renewal or intensification of use is contemplated? Could the use of rights not only have a time limit, but the rights themselves in some cases be time-limited? That is, could development rights be leased instead of sold or granted? At first look, these ideas seem to have some useful features. What might be some of the unanticipated consequences?

As A Method of Avoiding
the Windfalls and Wipeouts Syndrome

Windfalls and Wipeouts

DONALD G. HAGMAN
University of California, Berkeley

INTRODUCTION

Governments build public works projects and enact regulations. In the wake of such activity, some property owners are fortuitously visited with enormous increases in land value—they are the windfallers. Meanwhile, and equally by chance, other landowners suffer substantial losses in value—they are wiped out by governmental activity.

Examples may help. Consider landowner Jones who bought a parcel of property in 1965 for $5,000. In 1973 a station for a new subway is located on adjacent property, and the city rezones his property from single-family to multiple-family high-rise. Without lifting a finger, Jones' property may now be worth $500,000.

Meanwhile, consider landowner Smith, who bought a similar parcel in 1965 for $5,000. The city acquires an adjacent parcel for a garbage incinerator and subsequently, having discovered that Smith's land is a habitat for a rare insect, rezones his land from single-family residential to a conservancy district, which leaves Smith with virtually no use of his property. Smith's property is now worth $500.

Would it be fairer to devise mechanisms for recapturing Jones' windfall in part in order to mitigate Smith's wipeout? It might be prudent to devise those mechanisms soon, for the tough environmental regulation of recent years has magnified the inequity problem and led to other counterproductive behavior; and those who have been visited with disproportionate burdens in the name of a better environment are striking back, with justice as their clarion call. . . .

TECHNIQUES

There are several mechanisms which have been utilized or might be considered as windfall-recapture or anti-wipeout devices.

Special Assessments

The special assessment is the first in time of the American devices. Whether it was so at all times or places, it was certainly true in some in the past that developers merely drew lines on a map and sold off chunks of land. They did not consider it their responsibility to provide public facilities. At times, government used its general revenues to put in these facilities and thus make the lands utilizable. Perhaps the tradition of government so doing grew out of the pioneer spirit where one pioneer or settlement furnished the economic base for assisting the next.

But when government puts in the infrastructure and pays for it with general revenues, the newly developed area enjoys enormous increases in value. With those public facilities in place, it increases in value considerably. So if the burden of putting those facilities in is on others, the owners of the developable area enjoy a windfall. Because there is a windfall, the notion that the infrastructure for new development should be at the expense of the existing community has been waning, and the special assessment was the first device generally applied to the task of imposing the infrastructure costs on the new development itself.

Under a special assessment, land (not building) is assessed up to its pro rata cost of the project, e.g., a street, and up to the amount of benefit received. Typically, the existing community picks up part of the cost; typically, the amount of the assessment is nowhere near the amount of benefit received; typically, special assessments are utilized for only local improvements.

The special assessment reached its peak use in the 1920's. In the great depression, landowners did not pay off the special assessments because much land became valueless. As a result, the bonds funded by assessments and sold to pay for the improvements became valueless. While local governments did not always stand behind this debt, their credit was nevertheless impaired.

During the depression, properties were even abandoned for property taxes, let alone for the typically higher special assessment burdens, and where communities had allowed subdivision without the provision of improvements, they inherited the worst possible tax-abandoned situations—subdivisions with a checkerboard of unimproved lots, some owned by a variety of people, some owned by the original developer, and many "inherited" by the local government because of tax abandonment.

Ever since the bad experience with special assessments during the 1930's, they have not been the principal means used in America to impose the infrastructure costs on new development. But before considering the other devices, note an example of how special assessments might be used.

It is well known that when a fixed-rail mass transit system is built, land values increase dramatically around the stations. The owners of nearby land enjoy a windfall. There is little reason in theory, however, which would preclude use of a special assessment to recapture these increases in value. The funds raised could be used to help pay for the mass transit system or for other public purposes. Indeed, assuming that the plan of the community was to encourage intense development around mass transit stops, the high tax on land would help force intense development.

Subdivision Permission Exactions

With the demise of the special assessment as a windfall-recapture device, local governments turned to subdivision exactions as a means of loading the infrastructure cost of new development on the new development itself. In order to divide land and sell it nowadays, it is generally necessary to obtain subdivision permission from a local government. Before giving its final permission, the local government will require the developer to dedicate land for streets and parks and perhaps school sites; improve the streets; put in utilities such as sewer and water. Over the years local governments have imposed increasingly onerous exactions by way of dedication and improvement. Ferocious legal battles have been waged. Perhaps 90 percent of the case law and legal commentaries on subdivision deals with the exaction question. The war was won by local governments. While it is not yet everywhere clear, I think that ultimately a developer can legally be required to put in all public improvements required by the subdivision, the only limit perhaps being that the requirements laid on the new development cannot be greater than the benefits the new development receives from the improvements. Note the similarity to the limitation on special assessments.

The main advantage of the subdivision exaction scheme is that it assures the building of public improvements before the subdivided land is sold, rather than afterward. A major disadvantage is the bargaining that takes place and the shopping around by developers who try to find communities which are still willing to subsidize new development from the wealth of the existing community.

Subdivision Fees

Just as special assessments begat subdivision dedication and improvement requirements, these requirements begat a variant subdivision exaction—fees in lieu of dedication and improvement. For example, rather than require a subdivider to dedicate a park out of his land, he might be required to pay a fee in lieu thereof, which fee the local government would use with others to provide a park in some other location. Great legal battles were fought over this concept as well, for the direct relationship between the improvement and the subdivision was lost. But we are now to the point where it should be clear that if the park benefits the subdivision burdened by the fee, it need not be located within the subdivision—we are almost to the point that the fee is proper as a realization that the new development should pay something to buy into the existing community infrastructure.

Development Permission Exactions

It should be noted, at this point, that while the exaction system began with subdivision, it has now spread to all development permissions—rezonings, zoning variances, special use permits and even building permits. While still loosely associated with the need for infrastructure that the new development will generate, the relationship is tenuous. Particularly if it is a fee, the exaction begins to look very much like a charge for development permission. When applied to a rezoning, for example, it looks like an upzoning tax—a windfall-recapture device which has been suggested by such as Marion Clawson.

Development Taxes

The genealogy is complete when one considers another device that grew out of subdivision fees. Developer resistance to ever-increasing subdivision exactions led to enactment of state laws constraining the use of exactions. Cities were thwarted in their ever-growing tendency to impose all the governmental costs of new development on the development itself.

Therefore, local governments tried an end run. It was successful in California where cities have general power to impose business license taxes to raise revenue. A liquor license, for example, is an expensive license in many communities because it is used as a revenue raiser. So cities in California began imposing business license taxes on developers measured by, e.g., how many bedrooms were constructed by the developer. Thus, if a developer built a project with 1,000 units having 3,000 bedrooms and the tax was $1,000 per bedroom, the developer's tax would yield $3,000,000. That will buy a lot of street, park, sewer, water, school, etc. improvements. Indeed, since a business license tax goes into the general fund, there is no requirement that it be spent for those purposes. It could be used to pay salaries of policemen. A California court upheld the tax idea in 1971 and it has swept the state, many cities adopting the idea. Subdivision exactions could become a passé subject as the new license fee on developers, or developers' tax or impact tax comes to be accepted. And it was rejected by courts in Arizona and Florida; meanwhile, the Nevada legislature authorized it—in lieu of using subdivision exactions.

Capital Gains Tax

Though it did not evolve out of the continuum I have been describing, the capital gains tax is a windfall-recapture device of sorts. The opportunity to deduct capital losses is an anti-wipeout device. But the capital gain tax is not justified on the grounds that government should recapture some of the gains caused by it or others in the community. The capital gains tax is justified because realized gain is income, and there are federal and state income taxes in this country. To say the capital gains tax is a windfall-recapture device is to say that an income tax is a windfall-recapture device, which it is only in a very broad sense. But the capital gains tax does not distinguish between real and personal property and, thus far, this paper is addressed only to windfalls and wipeouts to landowners. Moreover, few if any local governments have capital gains taxes; yet it is their public works projects or their regulations which cause many of the windfalls and wipeouts.

Still, capital gains taxes might be affirmatively considered as a windfall-recapture device. It has often been argued that capital gains should be taxed at ordinary income rates. The argument can be made especially vigorously as to land, which often gains in value directly by governmental activity. The State of Vermont, concerned with rapid turnover of land by out-of-state speculators, investors, and developers, enacted a special additional capital gains tax on land sales only in 1972. New Zealand enacted such a law in 1973 and the English Conservative Government, sensitive about their long failure to recapture "betterment," proposed to do so in late 1973 with a stiff capital gains tax on land.

Transfer Taxes

Remember the documentary stamp tax the federal government used to impose of $.55 per $500 of the sales price of real estate. States and localities have taken over that tax, now abandoned by the federal government. The tax might be used more broadly so that a tax bite of more substantial amounts is levied every time property changes hands. Of course, in its traditional form it is not a windfall-recapture device. For example, property may sell for less than it was bought for, but the tax would still be due. Nevertheless, one could imagine a transfer tax which would apply only if there was a gain and was measured by the gain. So defined, it begins to look much like a capital gains tax.

Unearned Increment Tax

An unearned increment tax is another leading device for windfall-recapture, but it has never been tried in the United States, so far as I have been able to discern. It bears similarities to the special assessment and to the capital gains tax. The notion is that land increases in value due to public activity and private activity of others. As a result, there is an *unearned* increment which might be recaptured on such taxable events as sale or transfer or—to distinguish it from the capital gains tax—at the time development permission is obtained, or at the time permission is utilized, or even after a period of years if no other taxable event occurs. It also differs from the capital gains tax in that a concept of capital loss may not be included—it is a one-way street—there is no compensation for unearned decrement. It is also limited to land, which distinguishes it from the capital gains tax. It may have a provision for adjusting for inflation, that is, the increment may be measured only in real increase terms. It differs from a special assessment in that there is no need to form a special assessment district and make an assessment for benefit-producing improvement. And benefit is not measured in anticipation, as in the case of the special assessment, but at a taxable event. Moreover, it could be used to recapture benefits flowing from other than public improvements. Public regulatory activities, e.g., rezonings, or other private activity in the vicinity, could cause a recapturable increment.

The unearned increment tax gets good marks from many economists, though it comes in many varieties and is difficult either to endorse or condemn. The English tried it in the Land Commission Act 1967. Called the betterment levy, it was repealed by the Conservative Government when it came to power in 1970, though its merits were probably greater than the previous English experiment with recapturing land-value increments, which will be described later. The State of New South Wales, Australia, enacted a Land Development Contribution Law in 1970, an unearned increment tax, but both political parties came to agree in 1973 that it should be repealed. It is therefore surprising to see that New Zealand passed the Property Speculation Tax in 1973, which has some attributes of an unearned increment tax—the mere title of the Act suggests as much—though it also looks somewhat like a special capital gains tax on land.

Single Tax

The single tax is the last windfall-recapture device one might consider. Popularized by Henry George, it attracts converts as each new generation of students of tax policy consider the relation of taxation and land. It has never gone anywhere in this country and is not likely to go anywhere in the future. The notion of the single tax is that the only tax should be an annual property tax on land, excluding buildings. Those parcels of land which became more valuable because of public activity or other private activity would, of course, be assessed at a very high level reflective of their market value as contrasted with property which was not very valuable because of the absence of public and private value-causing activities in the environs.

As an annual tax, it differs from the others and might not be considered a windfall-recapture device. For example, assume that the property tax (now on land and buildings) is converted to a land value only tax. Effective property tax rates these days are about two percent, that is, the typical real property owner pays $2.00 every year for every $100 of market value of his property. Assume further that about half of the value of all property now in the property tax base is in improvements, which means that the property tax on land only would have to be levied at a $4.00 rate to raise the same amount of revenue as is now raised on both land and improvements. Suppose finally that a transit station is built in a neighborhood and that a parcel of property thereby increases in value from $10,000 to $110,000. The increment would be $100,000, but the *annual* tax would increase only from $400 to $4,400, only 4.4 percent of the total increase.

While one can make the illustration more sophisticated by considering capitalization of the tax in land value and discounting and the like, the point is a simple one, the land value tax does not recapture the increment at one time, as the others do. On the other hand, note that a special assessment does not typically do so either. While the assessment debt is created in one year, it is usually payable over a period of years. The difference is that the special assessment is fixed at one time, the land value tax varies as market value varies.

The main contribution of Henry George and the land value tax school of thought is the notion that private landowners have no right to the increase in value created by others, be the others private or public. That philosophical note underlies all of the windfall-recapture schemes.

WIPEOUT AVOIDANCE

Damage From Public Improvements

The story on wipeout avoidance is shorter. There are few techniques used in America, except in limited situations. Consider public improvements first. If a governmental entity acquires a site, of course, the landowner gets paid. That he should is not debatable. The federal and all state constitutions require it. We do not expect the landowner to absorb such wipeouts. Similarly, if only part of a site is acquired, the landowner not only receives compensation for the site, but usually receives damages to the remainder of his property caused by the acquisition. Thus, if half of one's property is acquired for a sewage treatment plant, the landowner gets paid for the property acquired and damages due to the fact that the remainder of his property is likely to be less valuable because of the sewage treatment plant acquisition.

However, generally speaking, the landowner whose property adjoins the sewer plant, no part of whose property is taken, but who may find his property value substantially affected, is wiped out. The government hardly ever pays in those situations. Of course, sometimes neighboring property is benefited as the result of acquisition. These windfalls are not recaptured under American practice.

The English call the externalities that flow from public acquisition "injurious affection," and in the Land Compensation Act 1973, lands adversely affected by public improvements, no part of which are taken, are entitled to compensation in some circumstances. It might be considered in America.

Damages in Nuisance

Nuisance law is a wipeout avoidance technique. Theoretically, if a neighbor uses land in a way which produces externalities, those landowners burdened by the externalities may be able to sue in nuisance. An injunction might be obtained against the use, but that is a rather drastic remedy, so damages are often allowed instead. In effect, the court permits the nuisance to continue but allows those landowners burdened by it to be paid by the nuisance-creator.

Nuisance law has not evolved significantly. One of the reasons is that governmental entities have been given a virtual monopoly over control of land use externalities through land use controls such as zoning. The assumption is that if a local government permits a particular use, the action can hardly constitute a nuisance. Similarly, courts are very loath to declare a governmental use of land a nuisance, though there has been some evolution of that relief as the courts become sensitized that governmental entities are the worst violators of environment.

Compensable Regulations

More is being heard these days about compensable regulations. I explain. One of the reasons few wipeout avoidance techniques have developed in America is that regulation of land has seldom been so severe as to cause a total or near total wipeout. Rather than sustain the regulation and require some compensation to be paid, courts have invalidated severe regulations. That is anti-wipeout protection by denying government its will, a topic not here relevant, since I am concerned with adjustments that permit government to act, not rules that prevent governmental action.

With the new environmentalism, however, regulations are now much tougher. Some courts have been willing to go along with the tougher regulations and, as a result, landowners have legislators discussing compensable regulations. Many other courts which would not sustain tough regulations would do so if some compensation were paid to the regulated landowner. The American Law Insitute is developing a Model Land Development Code which contains compensable regulation provisions.

Since noncompensatory regulations severely limiting use often turn out to be transitory, compensable regulations should involve a windfall-recapture provision. When the regulators change their mind and permit land to develop, the owners may gain a windfall. If the landowner has been compensated for the regulation, it would obviously be equitable to recapture the windfall when the regulator changes its mind and permits development.

WINDFALLS FOR WIPEOUTS

The most exciting techniques are those that simultaneously deal with the windfall and wipeout problems.

Zoning by Eminent Domain

Zoning by eminent domain is one such technique. The idea is over a half century old and stems from the early days of zoning, when it was unclear whether the courts would hold zoning by regulation valid. It was actually used in St. Paul and Minneapolis and Kansas City, where areas zoned by eminent domain still exist today. Interestingly, the technique also involves special assessments.

It works as follows. Assume an unzoned area or city. The city decides that certain areas should be used for commerce, other areas for residence, and yet others for industrial purposes. That constitutes the zoning feature. The eminent domain feature is that the city then acquires the development rights for all other purposes than those permitted under the zoning for the area. Landowners are paid damages to the extent that taking the development rights lowers values, thus wipeout is avoided. But, in that hypothetical city, since the zoning has just shifted values around, as is always the case with zoning, some property is worth more than it was before. The property worth more has received a benefit which is specially assessed—windfalls are thus recaptured and used to pay off damages. In short, windfalls for wipeouts.

Every time any zoning is changed, the benefit and the damage are measured and the transfer payments, if any, are made. Routinized and computerized, the system might be reasonably simple to administer. As actually applied in Minnesota and Missouri, the concept proved inflexible, but there is nothing inherent in the idea which requires such a result.

Development Rights Transfer

The windfalls for wipeouts technique presently getting the most attention is called development rights transfer. Consider an example of how it might work. A 2-story historic building is located in a central business district which is zoned for 50-story buildings. Noting a market for a new skyscraper, the owner of the historic building decides to tear it down and construct the large building. The city's historical society seeks foundation funds to acquire the historic site. That effort fails, and the city is asked to pass a zoning regulation requiring that the private landowner maintain the historic building. The city decides the proposed regulation would be unconstitutional, and the historic building is ultimately lost.

Under developmental rights transfer, however, the city could order the landlord to maintain the historic building, but, as compensation, would permit the landowner to sell his 48 stories of unused development rights to a neighbor, who can then build a 98-story building. These objectives are thereby accomplished:
—The landowner avoids a wipeout.
—The historic building is preserved.
—The overall permitted density of downtown goes unchanged.

The technique can be applied to other situations, e.g., marshland can be zoned so as to prevent all use, but the owners would be given development rights which could be used elsewhere or sold to others elsewhere who can then develop to higher than normal intensities.

Public Ownership

Finally, there are windfall-recapture and wipeout-avoidance devices about that involve public ownership of land or development rights therein. Obviously, if the government owns the land, there are no private windfalls or wipeouts from land ownership. But public ownership is outside the scope of matters considered in this paper. . . .

As A Method of Avoiding
the Windfalls and Wipeouts Syndrome

Saving Valued Spaces and Places
Through Development Rights Transfer

ELLIS GANS
Principal Planner
Marin County Planning Department
San Rafael, California

INADEQUACY OF CONVENTIONAL REGULATION

Public preservation of privately owned open space, agricultural land, historic sites, landmark buildings, and even marshes, is made doubly difficult by the "either/or" concept of land use and the pressure of private economic self-interest. We are used to thinking of public preservation in "either/or" terms: either the historic landmark is preserved or it is replaced by an economically more productive use. Either the open space or development.

Underlying the "either/or" dilemma is the force of private self-interest. Land is viewed as a commodity and the owner is entitled to get the most for it, subject to public regulation—usually considered an interference with the owner's freedom. Despite 50 years of zoning in America, the struggle between property owners and government continues with owners seeking to minimize the impact of public regulation on private economics.

Such struggle is not surprising since each side is operating on different values. Public regulation, zoning, and subdivision is based on the police power—the right of the public to protect its health, safety, morals, and general welfare. These values mean far less to private owners and developers than their own economic interests.[1] However, the police power does not consider private economics, nor does it include protection of the public's economic interests. Ideally, public regulation ought to minimize public costs and maximize public benefits resulting from private development.[2]

Because the public and private sectors are trying to maximize different values, they see each other as antagonists rather than as partners in community development. Public and private sectors work through complex regulatory procedures which do not adequately deal with the primary force shaping land use and development—private economic self-interest. More powerful than a thousand tornados, this force uproots old buildings, covers vast acreage of rich farm land with suburban sprawl, darkens the air, and pollutes the water. How to more effectively utilize this force for the public's welfare is the question. Zoning and subdivision controls are clearly not adequate.[3]

What is needed are techniques that appeal to the economic self-interest of all the parties involved; techniques that work with the market system not against it.[4] Two techniques that could be used are: transfer of development rights and a windfall tax (or as the British call it "a betterment charge."[5]). Although neither idea is new, they are not much used in America,[6] nor have they been used together.

This paper will explore the transfer of development rights (TDR) and windfall tax as they could be used in Marin County to preserve open space and agricultural lands, and to improve residential development.[7] TDR breaks the "either/or" dilemma of land use. It offers the owner an opportunity to continue a publicly desired use (such as agriculture, open space, historic building) while getting the same economic return as if he had developed.

TDR presents an essential alternative between regulation and public acquisition. It is not a panacea, but rather a supplement to existing techniques. TDR provides an economic option that will benefit the public and private sectors.

In rural areas, TDR can avoid the problems of randomly scattered small homesites (which often interfere with and gradually drive out agriculture) by applying the cluster idea to parcels under different ownership. Under a planned district zone the potential number of dwellings on a large parcel can be clustered in a small portion of the parcel. Clustering is a widely used example of TDR applied to land under common ownership.

WHAT IS TDR?

The ownership of land includes a number of rights such as: minerals, timber, water, air, and development. All of these rights can be sold separately from the land. The sale becomes a matter of public record.

The right to develop is conferred by zoning which stipulates the kind and number of permitted development. Zoning, of course, can be changed even without the landowner's consent.[8] Under existing zoning the quantity of permitted development may be greater than the amount actually on the land, in which case the owner could sell the excess number for use on another site. For instance if the zoning allowed 15 dwellings per acre and only 9 were on the ground, the owner could sell up to 6 units. When all 6 units were transferred, the owner would have zero development potential under the existing zoning.

Another example is a 600 acre ranch with A-60 zoning (one dwelling per 60 acres). If there were 2 existing residences, the rancher would have 8 unused development rights which could be transferred elsewhere. The number of acres associated with a single development right does not affect the TDR concept.

Development depends on the acquisition of two separate components:

land and permission to build a given number of units.[9] Because both are usually accomplished by land purchase, we don't think of them as different. With development rights transfer a separate market is created for the permission to build.

To facilitate the transition between the present and a time when TDR is a fully accepted part of the market, it would be best to allow an additional number of units above that provided by the base zoning.[10] Eventually it would be possible to buy and sell land without any development potential attached. Development rights would then be purchased separately as needed and to the extent allowed by zoning.

The TDR approach described in this paper will probably require state enabling legislation (at least in California).

HOW THE TDR PROCESS WORKS

Granting land

The TDR potential of any parcel is the number of dwellings permitted by zoning minus the number of existing units. Wherever there are unused development rights, any or all of them can be transferred from any parcel.[11] Although the transfer will usually be a sale from one owner to another, a noncash transfer could be made from one parcel to another when both are under the same owner. Anyone can purchase TDR's, and the price and means of financing would be decided by owner and purchaser.

Valuing TDR

The price of an improved (with road and utilities) building site varies depending on location, character of the land, aesthetics, etc. With the building site split into two separately marketable components (land and right to develop), thought was given to the feasibility of eventually holding TDR price level and allowing the land price to carry all of the difference due to amenity and location.[12] The advantages of a uniform price would be: easier and quicker to buy and sell TDR's; with all the speculative gain on raw land, overpriced land would drop in value. Furthermore, if county government had a sufficient supply of development rights on hand, there would be no point in TDR owners trading rights to others at higher prices or in hoarding, since a purchaser could get a lower price from the county. This is analogous to the time when for many years the U.S. Treasury had such a large stock of silver that it kept the price constant, since no one would buy for more or sell for less.

The argument against trying to keep TDR price level is that the land owners may not trust local government to be effective and either won't sell at the price offered, or may dump their rights at a high price which would probably be too high for developers and too expensive for the government.

During the phase-in of the TDR method, if TDR's don't offer land owners and developers the same economic return as they now get, they will not voluntarily participate. For this reason it is probably best (at least during the transition period) to allow a free market in TDR's. Even though this will impose a burden on developers who will have to shop around seeking the lowest TDR price. The probability of speculation in TDR's as with land should not be ignored. Since a new market is being created under government aegis, it would be most beneficial if speculation could be minimized.[13]

Receiving Land

Government specifically designates the precise area eligible to receive TDR's by means of an overlay (combining) zone.[14] The designation would be based on usual planning criteria[15] for higher than single family density.

The overlay zone can be used to implement the Marin County General Plan which shows medium and high density for certain areas. For TDR to work there must be an adequate supply and adequate demand. Regulating the demand may be the more difficult. One way is to down-zone[16] before instituting TDR method. This direct approach may encounter political opposition, since people dislike giving up even the promise of speculative gain. A more politic method is to leave the existing zoning alone[17] and only grant new up-zoning with TDR overlay zones.[18]

Eventually residential density could be permitted only with TDR's under a single zone. However, during the TDR transition period, when there is competition with existing conventional high density districts, it would be better to have two zones on the receiving land. The base zone would generally permit single family dwellings, the overlay zone would allow additional density only with TDR's. This gives the owner a development choice.

Under the base zoning the owner is in the same economic position as any other comparable owner. However, for the higher density permitted with TDR, the owner would get less than an owner of similar high density under conventional zoning. We shall call this difference between what the two owners would get a "windfall". How it is recouped for public purposes plays an important role in TDR, and will be discussed in the next section.

Using TDR an owner can get a little more for his land than under the base zoning. While he would naturally prefer to retain the "windfall" the loss of it will not discourage him from participating in TDR, if that is the only way he can get any increase. (Most everyone decries land speculation, while doing it whenever they have a chance. Since land is not portable, the owners can't escape regulation.)

Windfall Tax

A windfall tax is needed to make TDR economically more attractive compared with conventional high density zoning; to enable government to get quality development; and to recoup some of the public investment which made high density possible.

High density is economically feasible only because of considerable public and private investment in the surrounding area over a long period. The landowner awarded high density rezoning often obtains a windfall profit when the land is sold or developed,[19] yet his investment is small compared to the total.

Just because government has recouped little, if any, of this windfall until now is no reason to continue this practice. Because development rights transfer is a new way of doing business, it offers a new opportunity to recapture the windfall profits that TDR will create.[20] State enabling legislation would be needed to permit the county or cities to levy a windfall tax.

Instead of merely recouping past investment, some or all of the windfall tax could be used to assure developers more profit with TDR, than conventional high density zoning—if the developer provides a sufficient amount of amenities.[21] The lure of more profit will encourage more developers to use TDR, and better quality developments will benefit both the developer and the community. During phase-in of TDR when it is competing with a lot of land already zoned for high density, the best strategy may be to use the windfall tax to improve amenities rather than trying to maximize recoupement of past public investment. Naturally the cost of amenities required must be balanced against the amount of windfall tax rebated to the developer.

Development is community building. The public has an over-riding interest in how its physical plant is built and the long range consequences. Development should be regarded as a joint venture between local government and the private developer, where the developer receives a fair profit by doing a job for the community. Zoning has been an impediment to this concept because it is essentially negative: regulations and prohibitions; with increased density as the only incentive (and much of that profit going to the landowner not the developer). Too often the minimum standards in zoning became the maximum the market would provide, because there was no economic incentive. TDR is no panacea, but it does offer incentives and enables government to become a more active partner in community building.

As an example, consider a developer wanting to build 12 units on one acre. Land price for conventional R-3 zoning (12 units/acre) is $150,000; price for R-1 zoned land (4 units/acre) is $50,000. A transferred development right cost $5,000 apiece.[22] The developer buys 8 rights for $40,000.

Developer finds land, comparable to R-3, which has a base R-1 zone plus XR-2 overlay zone (8 units/acre only by TDR). The owner of this land being aware of the higher density would ideally want $150,000 in order to get the same return as the R-3 owner. However, the developer would not offer more than the R-3 price, less TDR cost[23] or $110,000 ($150,000 - 40,000); otherwise the developer would, for the same market and land quality, be better off buying the R-3 land.

The owner of the TDR zoned land, seeing that no one will offer more than $110,000 would probably accept.[24] The developer would face the same costs as for conventional R-3 except for the additional effort spent buying TDR's.

Without the windfall tax the developer would not be compensated for this extra time.

The windfall tax applies only to that part of the land price due to the TDR zoning. There would be no tax on the part due to the base zoning. Seller would pay the tax and would not be able to pass it on to purchaser, because purchaser would then find cheaper land elsewhere.[25] Experience will be needed to determine the optimal tax rate. In this paper we shall assume it lies between 50 to 80 percent.

Continuing with the above example, let's see how the windfall tax works. Developer bought the land for $110,000. Assuming a 75 percent windfall tax, the seller would get $50,000 + 25 percent of $60,000 or $65,000.[26] Local government gets $45,000.

If, for instance, half of the windfall tax were returned to the developer, his net cost would be $50,000 + $110,000 − $22,500, or $137,500. Compared to R-3 price of $150,000, this is a 14 percent savings. Were 90 percent of the windfall tax returned to the developer, his net cost would be $109,500—a savings of 27 percent. Should the land be sold at a lower price the windfall tax would be less, and so would the net cost to the developer. On the other hand, if the land sold at $150,000, seller would get $50,000 + 25 percent of $100,000, or $75,000. Government gets $75,000. If 90 percent of this was rebated to the developer, his net cost would be $122,500—a savings of 18 percent. These savings are not pure gravy; the developer would have to provide publicly desired amenities in order to get the rebate. With more amenities, the development might command a higher market price. However, by meeting the cost of these amenities through tax rebate, the developer can offer a better product at a lower price. Thus, the windfall tax can go a long way towards solving the problem of lower priced, but unimaginative, poorly constructed tract housing.

Local government will need to know development costs much more accurately in order to understand the developers' position. In addition government will need more economically knowledgeable staff and better monitoring of the real world in order to fine tune windfall tax and TDR supply and demand. There is the risk that government will give away more than necessary to achieve a given result. More sophisticated staff can reduce the risk.

The Transfer Process

Local government (the county in Marin's case) plays a key role by creating the demand, setting the windfall tax and by providing a market place. There are at least three different market roles for the county:

1. Broker. County keeps a file of willing buyers and sellers and charges a small fee for putting them in touch with each other. Buyers and sellers directly negotiate and set their own price. This role seems the most feasible during the phase-in period.

2. TDR purchaser. County buys TDR's in competition with other

purchasers. County would provide an ever-ready market. It would sell TDR's at auction or at fixed price. In the long run, this could stabilize price. State legislation needed for this option.

3. Exclusive market. All TDR's must be bought and sold through the county. In the long run this might be the best way to minimize speculation and insure adequate supply. Initially, it would require state legislation and does not appear very practical politically or economically during the TDR phase-in period.

Once a development right is sold off the granting land it should be immediately transferred to the receiving land and not left floating. If TDR were allowed to float off the land, it would cause uncertainty as to the availability of the supply and could encourage hoarding and speculation.

The county would certify that the transfer of rights from one land to another met all the requirements. The transfer document is a public record.[27] As soon as the transfer was made, the assessor's records would be changed to reflect the higher assessment on the receiving land and the lower assessment on the granting land.

In practice a developer would probably option the needed TDR's until the entire deal was ready to close, at which time the purchase and transfer would occur. One possible exception to the principle of not letting TDR's remain off the land is the case where a developer cannot continue a project after buying the land and TDR's. If the developer then had to sell the land and did not have another eligible for the TDR's available, the developer could put his TDR's in escrow with the county. He would be taxed on the TDR's as if they were still on the granting land.

Zoning is critical to the success of the TDR method. Zoning must be consistent and, preferably, not higher than current uses and needs require. A lot of land is over-zoned because the owners hoped for speculative gain. Once the TDR method is started, no more conventional high density residential zoning should be issued. The existing high density zoning should be allowed to remain unless it is clearly over-zoning.

When most of the privately held development rights have been transferred, government will have a choice: either grant private owners more TDR's by up-zoning, sell TDR's from public lands, or simply issue TDR's (not based on land) which developers would buy from government. The inequity of granting more windfalls to private owners and the political squabble over which governmental entity gets the TDR value from public lands leads to the conclusion that the third approach is probably best in the long run.

USING TDR IN MARIN

TDR can greatly help to carry out the Marin County Plan whose goals are to concentrate growth in the eastern third of the county, which is already urban and to keep the western, rural, two-thirds in agriculture and open space. There are four situations in which TDR can be used: rural to rural; rural to urban; urban to urban; and urban to rural. While the TDR method is the same in all four cases, the economics differ.[28]

Rural to Rural

In rural Marin (where people and cows aren't the best neighbors) TDR would enable development to be shifted with no increase in overall density. Rural sprawl would be avoided by concentrating development where it makes good sense in terms of topography, land use, and community values, instead of the economic desires of landowners. About 94 percent of Marin's agricultural lands are zoned A60 (number of acres per dwelling) with small amounts in A40, A30, A20, A10, and A5. Smaller lot sizes are permitted only in and around the villages.[29] Market prices run $800-1,200/acre and occasionally as low as $250/acre. Agricultural value $300-350/acre. At a net value of, say $600/acre, one development right in an A60 zone is $36,000 ($600 x 60) or in an A20 zone $12,000.

A rancher who needs cash or is reluctant to remain in agriculture has these development options:

1. Sell out (full fee sale)

2. Subdivide (develop with the number of units allowed)

3. Buy TDR for a larger development (assuming zoning permits)

4. Sell TDR without hope of future development rights

5. Sell TDR with expectation of being assigned more development rights in the future (say, 8-15 years)

In addition, the rancher can defer development, hold TDR for future speculative gain, sell out to another rancher or continue in business.

Profit maximization is useful in predicting economic behavior when all the costs and benefits can be expressed in dollars. However, such analysis is not adequate for small individual agriculturalists, because part of their benefits is a life style and sense of freedom which cannot be quantified. Family considerations, personal desires, and future expectations vary greatly among ranchers, so what seems sensible to one may not to another. Because there are so many intangibles, a farmer's decision to stay in agriculture, develop in whole or in part, or transfer development rights cannot be judged solely in terms of finances, as the following examples show. There are only about 80 active ranching families in Marin. To see whether TDR will meet their needs, it will probably be necessary to analyze each situation individually.

Ranchers now under Williamson Act agricultural preserve contracts are assessed on basis of the capitalized value of their agricultural income. Under an agricultural preserve contract, the owner technically has no development rights (since he agreed not to develop for 10 years). If the owner were to sell his rights, he would pay (under current law) a cancellation fee of 12½ percent of the market value of the TDR. Or the owner would receive only the "present worth" of those rights 10 years hence and would not renew the contract on the rights.[30] This technical problem is not yet resolved. It will require a change in state law. About 30 percent of Marin's agricultural acreage is not under contract. This is the land most susceptible to development pressure, so TDR method can still be applied.

To illustrate only the financial differences under A60 zoning between the five options, consider two ranchers A and B. Both have cattle grazing ranches and both are thinking of development instead of agriculture. Good land planning indicates that the total development from both owners should be clustered on parcel A. This can be encouraged by zoning a selected area P.C. (planned community) for the same total number of units as the zoning permits. Development can then be shifted within the P.C. subject to regular planning review. Administratively this seems like the simplest and best approach. Another way is to use an overlay zone which allows additional dwellings only with TDR.

Selling Out

The price of one development right at 60 acres each is $36,000 ($600 x 60). This maximum is usually achieved only if the owner sells out. If the rancher wants to continue in business and follow the other options, he will usually get less per development right because the value drops when less acreage is involved on the transferred site and overall density is not increased.[31]

Subdivide (develop with the number of units allowed)

Rancher A has 10 excess development rights (DR), which could be clustered on 10 acres. Rancher A could put in time and effort to do his own development or turn over the land at less profit to a developer. We assume the former for the sake of illustration.

Full market value if A sells out (11 x $36,000)	$396,000
Agricultural value of ranch after transferring 10 DR	
Value of 650 acres at $350/acre	$227,500
Equivalent value of A's house	36,000
	$263,500

Theoretical market value of 10 one acre sites
$396,000 − 263,500 = $132,500 ÷ 10 = $13,250/acre
"Real market" value for each improved site $8,000-15,000
    where improvements[32] cost $5,000-8,000
    and the land value per site ranges $3,000-7,000.

The closer the agricultural value is to the market value, the closer the theoretical site price will be to the "real" price.[33]

Buy TDR for a Larger Development

There are economics of scale that will increase a developer's profit with more units. Per site road costs drop. A package sewage plant may become cheaper than individual septic tanks. Engineering and survey costs per site drop. The financial advantages depend on the individual case.

Assuming a proper location this option offers benefits to the community, such as: support local retailers, enhance visual aesthetics, reduce traffic congestion and hazards, reduce encroachment on agriculture (e.g. dogs running loose).

Sell TDR Without Hope of Future Development Rights

After transferring development rights the owner would sign a deed restriction[34] stating there were no more (or only a certain number more) development rights under the existing zoning. When the per acre market and agricultural values were close, the price per development right would probably be close to that under the following option (sell with expectation of more). When values are further apart, the owner may want a higher price for the irrevocable loss of his rights. This may require some public subsidy such as reduced taxes over a period of years or cash payment by local government.

Except for possible difference in DR price, the assumptions under this option are similar to the following option.

Sell TDR With Expectation of More Development Rights in the Future

The carrying capacity of the land, utilities and public services usually allow for more dwellings per acre than the public thinks desirable. In eastern Marin many wish to stop the transition from suburban to urban density. The number of TDR to be created or settled is dependent on public opinion and desires of individual owners more than technical limitations (such as capacity of roads and sewers). Initial acceptance is the major hurdle for any new idea. Thus this option may be one of the most politically feasible during the phase-in of TDR.

After enjoying the proceeds of TDR now, an owner would have a chance to sell more again in some future time, if and when the zoning was changed. For instance, rancher B now has 15 excess DR under A60 zoning. Assume all are sold off. If after, say 10 years, the zoning was changed to A40, rancher B would then have 23 excess DR, which could be sold.[35] By offering owners the hope (not a promise) of future capital gain, more may be willing to sell their rights now and at a lower price. The waiting period can be written into the deed restriction. How long it should be will depend. A fixed period is easier to administer.[36]

The financial value of rancher B's development rights is:

Full value if B sells out ($600 x 960)	$576,000
Agricultural value of ranch after transferring DR	
Value of 900 acres at $350/acre	$315,000
Equivalent value of B's house	36,000
	$351,000

Theoretical market value of 15 DR's
$576,000 - 351,000 = $225,000 ÷ 15 = $15,000 each
"Real" market value of A's unimproved sites $3,000-7,000 each.

Assume A can sell improved sites at $10,000 each and with economics of scale (from B's TDR), the site improvement cost is $5,500. A could afford to offer B up to $4,500 per development right. A's "profit" comes from scale economics on his own site improvement costs. Some of the reasons why B might accept this offer are:

Agricultural operation is economically sound, owner intends to stay in business a long time.

Desire to keep the land undeveloped.

Concern that future owners might improperly develop.

Raise cash quickly when other sources not available.[37]

Take advantage of capital gains income tax.

Not want the burden of doing own development.

If B's land were farther away in a less desirable location, or was more difficult to develop, then the actual market value for such TDR's might be less than A's. Some price could be reached that would give B more for transferring than developing, and A would still make a profit.

In the above examples, the actual value of a TDR was less than its theoretical value. The theoretical value is still based on market prices that were established largely on the basis of A2 zoning. The lower density due to A60 zoning is expected to lower the market price, but there have not been enough sales yet to determine what this new price range will be.

In Marin, one of the barriers to those who would like to get into agriculture is the high market value of land. Speculative market value has gone way above agricultural value over a succession of owners in expectation of higher density and thus greater demand. If public pressure keeps local government from granting higher density, then it is hoped the speculative value will gradually be reduced over a succession of owners. Some owners may use such losses to offset other income on their taxes. Only with a consistent, long range government policy will market value approach agricultural value.

Urban to Urban

About a third of eastern Marin now designated for open space has a potential 3,000 TDR's.[38] With open space land averaging $1,700 per acre, one TDR might cost $17,000. The per unit cost of raw land for townhouses and apartments runs $3,000-6,000.

While these figures look unfavorable at present, in the future the value of townhouse and apartment sites is likely to rise, while the speculative value on open space lands may drop when government and the courts consistently support low density zoning. Should the TDR economics remain unfavorable (assuming these TDR's are permitted to transfer to rural areas), then public acquisition may be needed[39] since most of this open space has no agricultural value. Although there may be owners willing to accept a loss because of desire to preserve the land, offset other income on taxes, etc.

Urban to Rural

Initially this appears to be the most economically feasible, since TDR's are worth more in rural Marin, though rural Marin has about 5,000 TDR's under present zoning. Planning would like to transfer from rural to urban not vice versa. The county could prohibit transfers in the wrong direction, thus creating separate rural and urban TDR markets. The extent of this problem and what should be done is not known at this time.[40]

Rural to Urban

Transferring development rights from rural to urban Marin would be a good way to save marginal agricultural lands from development pressure. Economically this doesn't appear too practical (buying high, selling low), although there may be some owners wanting to stay in agriculture who, because they need immediate cash, may sell rights at a lower price.

During the TDR phase-in, the rural to urban transfer may require public subsidy. It appears that TDR price will generally be higher in rural than urban areas, because of the different acreage on the granting and receiving lands. In the long run, if a single price for TDR's was established, then this transfer direction would work.

While the rural to urban shift will not affect any taxing district which includes both granting and receiving lands, rural school and other local districts would find their tax base decreasing if there were enough out-of-area transfers.

Probably the most equitable solution would be for the county to slightly raise its property tax in order to pay an in-lieu fee to the districts when they are affected. With say a 10 year phase-out of the in-lieu, the districts would have ample time to readjust.

WHERE SHOULD TDR BE APPLIED

TDR should be used where high market prices are forcing agricultural land into development, for example, upper Lucas Valley, Nicasio, east shore of

Tomales Bay, and around Pt. Reyes Station. TDR could relieve development pressure on waterway conservation zones designated in the County General Plan.

In urban Marin, receiving lands for TDR would be those high density areas shown on the County General Plan. In rural Marin, TDR would mainly be used to cluster development outside the villages. Just where these clusters should be will require further study.

NEXT STEPS

Presentation of the TDR method and its application to the Marin County Planning Commission. If the Commission approves, staff will refine the idea through further discussion with county counsel, assessor, realtors, developers, lenders, etc. Then a presentation to the Board of Supervisors. If they concur, staff will work towards state enabling legislation.

As with any untried idea, there will be problems. So far they do not seem insoluble.

Development rights transfer is a potentially powerful tool for achieving a number of publicly desired goals. It is an idea whose time has come—and Marin County can be a pioneer in its development.

NOTES

1. The private owner has no mechanism (except regulation) for internalizing the costs and benefits of his development on the community's health, safety, and welfare. The owner's balance sheet reveals profits in terms of the costs the owner must bear directly. No wonder regulation is resisted when it introduces other costs which, if they cannot be passed on, will reduce profit.

2. This would include quantifiable economic impacts measured in dollars and qualitative impacts such as health, safety, aesthetics, open space, and general welfare. As yet, the techniques for measuring public economic impact, particularly at the local level are not adequately developed.

3. Too often the general public is unwilling to pay for what its conservationists want. Hence public acquisition of the land in toto or in part (easement) is rarely sufficient to accomplish all of the preservation deemed necessary.

Another less fiscally demanding method—compensable zoning—has not been used. For a brief description of land use, acquisition, and regulation methods, see Jerome Rose, "A Proposal for the Separation and Marketability of Development Rights as a Technique to Preserve Open Space", *Real Estate Law Journal*, Vol. 2 No. 3 (1974) pp. 635-642.

4. The trail of abandoned plans, discarded planners, and frustrated citizens who thought they could control local market forces by plans and regulations is ample evidence of the power of economic self-interest.

5. "Betterment" is the increase in land value due to public works or other improvements on or near the land. On the theory that the owner is receiving a windfall (in higher market value) from public investment, the public is entitled to recoup or tax all or part of this windfall.

6. Currently development rights transfer is used in Chicago and New York for historical building preservation, by enabling the owner of a landmark building to sell the difference between the total floor area of the building permitted by the zoning less that which is used by the landmark, for use on another site. Development rights transfer has been proposed for State of Maryland, and for St. George, Vt., see Leonard Wilson,

"Precedent-Setting Swap in Vermont", *AIA Journal*, March 1974, p. 51. The transfer method proposed for Puerto Rico comes closest to that suggested for Marin County. See John Costonis, "Development Rights Transfer: An Exploratory Essay", 83 *Yale Law Journal* (1973) p. 91-95.

7. TDR can be used for any type of development; Marin's concern is mainly residential, since it is an upper income bedroom suburb of San Francisco.

8. Owners do not normally have vested rights in a particular zoning. That is, they cannot claim that a change of zoning is taking away a potential profit. Only if an owner has made a significant investment under a given zoning, and that investment were to be significantly diminished as a result of a change in zoning, could the owner legitimately claim a vested right.

9. Road access and utilities are also necessary.

10. Lands designated to receive TDR's would have two zoning densities. The lower or base zone specifies the number allowed, the same as under the present system. An overlay or combining zone would specify additional units which could only be added by TDR's.

11. TDR gives owners a third choice in deciding what to do with their land: 1) hold on, do nothing; 2) sell or develop; or 3) TDR and keep the land.

12. It could be argued that since there is a difference in the capitalized value of an apartment unit, townhouse, expensive single family and inexpensive single family dwelling, this difference should be reflected in the price of TDR's and not attached only to the land. The capital value of different kinds of multiple family units is less than between multiple and single family. However, by keeping TDR prices nearly constant regardless of how used, land which lacks premium value because of location or quality will sell at lower price. Thus the speculative pressure on raw land can be reduced.

13. The idea of a purchase tax on TDR's does not appear feasible. If the tax were on the landowner selling the rights, he would then get less than if he were to develop himself (or sell to a developer). Were the tax on the purchaser of TDR's he would pay more than if he bought land already zoned for high density.

14. Combining zones are frequently used. Owner would not be taxed on potentially higher value due to overlay zone until it was actually used.

15. Such as adequacy of roads and utilities, suitable location, proximity to business, industry, schools, etc.

16. It is not uncommon for the zoning to permit more dwellings per acre than are on the ground. Down-zoning merely makes zoning reflect actual land use, rather than speculative use.

17. The existing land use density should be compared with that permitted by the zoning.

18. Up-zoning includes increasing the number of units permitted in a residential district, as well as changing from say an industrial or agricultural to a residential zone.

19. A simple example is where an owner is rezoned from R-1 (4 dwellings/acre) to R-3 (12 dwellings/acre) because a new shopping center was built across the street. The additional amount the owner can now get for the land is the "windfall".

20. In theory the windfall tax could be applied to any increase in density or even to rezonings that resulted in more profitable land use. Politically this is unlikely.

21. Such as a certain number of low and moderate price dwellings, more private usable open space per dwelling, better landscaping, better design, child care center, recreation facilities, etc.

22. This assumes that developers will be able to buy TDR's at economically feasible prices. TDR prices will vary considerably. The averages quoted here are only for illustration. However, if the TDR prices in rural and urban areas turn out to be signficantly higher than their value for multi-family dwellings, it may be possible in some cases to use part of the windfall tax to compensate the developer for the difference. A much better approach is to take steps to reduce the TDR price at the source.

23. Thus the market value of the XR-2 overlay zone could vary between $50,000 to $150,000. If TDR prices vary with the market, then so will the value of TDR overlay zones.

24. This is another reason for keeping TDR prices level. If they vary widely, owners might hold out waiting for a better offer which could only be done if the developer spends more time looking for the cheapest TDR available.

25. The windfall tax is a variation of Henry George's single land tax.

26. Both seller and purchaser would have to report sale price to local government. Since purchaser wants the largest rebate, he would not understate the price. Seller pays tax at time of sale. Purchaser gets rebate right away, thus minimizing his cash flow problem.

27. The county should also keep separate records to facilitate title search for the transferred rights. This should result in a lower service charge by the title insurance companies.

28. All costs used are only for illustration. Land prices vary greatly depending on location, appearance, proximity to utilities, ease of development, etc. Likewise site improvement costs will vary: usually higher in rural than urban areas. Figures quoted are within the ball park. Whether TDR works economically in each case will depend on the particulars.

29. Under existing zoning about 5,000 more units can be built now in rural Marin than are planned by 1990 (a total then of 5,300 units).

30. If there is a deed of trust or mortgage, the lender may claim a substantial share of the proceeds. This would pay off the mortgage quicker but would reduce the cash flow incentive. About half of Marin's ranches appear to be mortgaged now. The average mortgage is paid off in 5-8 years.

31. Usually when large acreage is subdivided, the aggregate value of all the small lots is much higher (even without counting site improvements) because of the increased number of development rights permitted.

32. Road, electricity brought to edge of property, survey, water line (if available) brought to property. Well and septic tank may or may not be included in this figure.

33. A20-A60 zoning was established in late 1972. There haven't been enough sales to say whether the zoning is reducing the market price as expected. Some knowledgeable realtors believe this will happen. Because of the variability of land quality, more sales are needed to establish a trend.

34. In the form of a deed of sale of the air rights in perpetuity.

35. From the public's view, this is akin to printing paper money. A little can be a good thing, too much is a disaster.

36. Less than 5 years is too short, the political pressure may be too intense, and the market may not adequately lower the DR price. Over 20 years is probably too long, except for young owners. A time range, say 8-15 years could be specified in the enabling legislation, leaving the exact period to be negotiated.

37. Banks and insurance companies base farm loans on the capitalized agricultural return. Development potential usually discounted heavily. Depending on the risk and other circumstances, these institutions might lend 55 to 80 percent of the agricultural value.

38. Based on the 10 acre per unit zoning being applied to the 30,000 acres designated for open space.

39. When geological and flood hazard zoning or allowing clustered development on large parcels are not sufficient to preserve open space.

40. Enabling legislation setting up TDR system should make provision for dealing with this. Instead of administrative prohibition, a transfer tax might be equally effective.

IV.
EVALUATION
OF THE
PROPOSALS

From A Psychological, Legal, and Administrative Perspective

Psychological, Legal,
and Administrative Problems of the Proposal
to Use the Transfer
of Development Rights as a Technique
to Preserve Open Space

JEROME G. ROSE

INTRODUCTION

The transfer of development rights (hereinafter referred to as "TDR") is the most innovative, imaginative, and potentially effective technique of land use control to be proposed since the introduction of zoning and subdivison regulations. TDR may be used to accomplish numerous and diverse planning goals and objectives beyond the scope of any other technique of land use control. It can provide more effective control of land use than zoning; it can assure economy and efficiency in the delivery of municipal services; it can protect agricultural land from the pressures of high taxation and development opportunities; it can preserve floodplains, woodlands and wetlands for ecological regeneration; it can be used to preserve historical and architectural landmarks in central cities; it can be used to provide public amenities in high density urban areas. And, TDR can do all of this and more, *without any direct cost to government*!

The proposal to use the transfer of development rights as a technique to preserve open space is an example of the great potential of this new concept. This proposal is the product of a committee made up of Rutgers University faculty and members of the New Jersey Department of Community Affairs.[1] It is designed to induce owners of undeveloped land to preserve their land in open space by compensating them by the sale of their development rights to developers of other land in the jurisdiction. To make such sales possible, this proposal establishes a system that creates a market for development rights in which owners of developable land must buy development rights from owners of preserved open space land as a prerequisite for higher density development. The proposal seeks to create such a market in the following manner:[2]

    1. Each local government would prepare a land use plan that specifies the

percentage of remaining undeveloped land in the jurisdiction and that designates the land to remain undeveloped as preserved open space land. The land use plan would also designate the land to be developed and would specify the uses to which the developable land may be put. A zoning law would be enacted or amended to implement this plan.

2. The planning board of each local government would prescribe the number of development rights required for each housing unit to be developed. On the basis of this numerical assignment, the planning board would then compute the number of development rights required to develop the jurisdiction in accordance with the land use plan. The local government would issue certificates of development rights (ownership of which would be recorded) in the exact amount so determined.

3. Every owner of preserved open space land would receive certificates of development rights in an amount that represents the percentage of assessed value of his undeveloped land to the total assessed value of all undeveloped land in the jurisdiction.

4. An owner of developable land, who desires to develop his land more intensively (e.g., apartments instead of single family residence) would have to buy additional development rights, on the open market, from those who have acquired such rights from either original distribution or subsequent purchase.

5. Thus, owners of preserved open space would be able to sell their development rights to owners of developable land (or real estate brokers or speculators). In return for the compensation derived from this sale, owners of preserved open space land will have sold their rights to develop their land in the future. Their land will thus be preserved in open space and the owners will have been compensated without any capital costs to the government.

6. Development rights will be subject to ad valorem property taxation as a component of the total assessed value of the developable real property in the jurisdiction.

The TDR proposal offers many advantages not available from any other technique of land use control: (1) unlike the exercise of the police power, the owners of land preserved in open space are compensated for the deprivation of the development value of their land; (2) unlike the exercise of the power of eminent domain, the property remains on the tax rolls and does not impose additional tax burdens upon the owners of other property within the jurisdiction; (3) the proposal is consistent with and functions in accordance with the market incentives of a free enterprise system; and (4) the proposal provides a technique for effective implementation of a rational system of land use allocation.

It is not surprising that a proposal that offers the promise of so many advantages also has its share of disadvantages. The TDR proposal does in fact have its share of psychological, legal, and administrative problems.

PSYCHOLOGICAL PROBLEMS: XENOPHOBIA

Xenophobia, defined as fear of a stranger, is an intellectual as well as a social pathology. The fear of the consequences of the introduction of a strange new concept into the body of property law is similar in many ways to the fear of the consequences of the introduction of a stranger into a community. In both cases, there may be a rational basis for concern about the unknown effect of a new variable upon the system. In both cases, the fear can be dissipated or confirmed by more information and a greater understanding of the alien element. In both cases, the passage of time is necessary to allay the latent qualms.

There is a rational basis for concern about the effect of the creation of a separate market and conveyance system for development rights. The legal system has been compared to a seamless web that responds in many directions to every tug and pull upon its fabric. No computer has yet been programmed to simulate the myriad consequences of a legal innovation upon the juridical system. Every proposal for change carries unknown risks; the risks can be minimized by limiting the scope of the modification from the established path. Anglo-American jurisprudence has been sustained for centuries by adherence to the principle of *stare decisis* and by reliance upon slow, tentative, incremental advances, followed by sufficient repose to measure and absorb the repercussions of each change before the next advance.

The psychological problem of the proposal for the transfer of development rights results from the fact that it comes on too strong. It comes on to the scene of well established land use controls with a boldness and a confidence that shatters the complacency and comfort of well-known truths and conventional wisdom. TDR calls into question many *a priori* principles. It defies classification into known categories; it raises anxieties about its impact upon cherished and settled doctrines upon which professional, proprietary, and pyschological stability is founded.

Before the TDR proposal can be adopted it will be necessary to abate this anxiety, to dispel this apprehension, to exorcise this fear of the unknown. These goals can be accomplished only by better understanding of the concept and by a greater knowledge of its consequences.

LEGAL PROBLEMS: *SUI GENERIS*

The legal issues raised by the TDR proposal illustrate the kinds of problems this new concept must face: the TDR proposal would have been so much easier to explain if it fit unambiguously into the definition of either the police power or the power of eminent domain.

More specifically, the issue is this: Is the TDR proposal like zoning or subdivision controls wherein the use of land is regulated to achieve the health, safety or welfare of the community? (i.e., Is it an exercise of the police power?) Or, is it more like the acquisition of land for a park where the land is *taken* from a private owner for a public use upon the payment of just compensation? (i.e., Is it an exercise of the power of eminent domain?)

One of the legal problems of the TDR concept is that it does not fit precisely into either category. It combines the characteristics of both. To use legal phraseology, it is *sui generis*; it is in a class by itself.

For example, it might well be argued that the restriction of the use of land to undeveloped open space use is only one small step beyond zoning for agricultural use, or large minimum size lot restriction and that the development of farmland, woodland, swamp or marshland or land of steep slope is "not a reasonable use of that land which is protected from police power regulation."[3] On the other hand it may be argued that such a restriction of use constitutes a taking of private property which would be invalid without the payment of just compensation.[4] The issue is further complicated by the debatable significance of the issuance of certificates of development rights to the owners of property restricted to open space use. Does the receipt of such certificates remove the harshness of the deprivation of use of the land by the owner to make the proposal a valid exercise of the police power? Or, does the acceptance of the certificates constitute a "payment" to fulfill the just compensation requirements of the *exercise of the eminent domain power*?

There are a number of technical legal principles that prevent a definitive affirmative answer to either question. It is difficult to maintain that the transfer of the development rights is a mere "regulation" of property. The underlying legal theory of the TDR proposal is that the right to develop is one component of the "bundle of rights" that comprises "title" to or "ownership" of land. This component of ownership is not merely regulated; it is separated out from the rest of the ownership and transferred away or "taken" from the owner. It may be compared to a taking of an easement or right of way over the owner's property. Such transfer or "taking" goes beyond police power regulation. It involves the exercise of the power of eminent domain.

On the other hand, if it is the power of eminent domain that is being exercised it is necessary to comply with the well established principles by which "just compensation" is defined: One such principle requires that compensation must be in *money*.[5] Statutes providing for payment by something other than money, such as warrants, or stocks or bonds have been held to be invalid.[6] Statutes providing for compensation by an award of other lands have been held invalid.[7] Another legal principle of eminent domain requires that just compensation be unconditional.[8] A third principle requires that the damages be definite and not based upon uncertain future events.[9] Still another principle requires that compensation be based upon the value of the property at the time of the taking, without regard to subsequent inflationary effects upon the property's value.[10]

These legal principles create problems because the TDR proposal is based upon the idea that the owner of land preserved in open space is compensated by the issuance of certificates of development rights that may not have an established ready market at the time of issuance but which will acquire a market and (presumably) increased value as the demand for development of "developable" land in the jurisdiction increases. Thus, the above principles are violated because: (1) the original compensation is by certificate rather than money; (2) its value relates to the potential of increased value of other land; (3) the compensation is conditioned upon the creation of a market for the certificates; and (4) the value of the certificates depends upon the value of right to develop other land at the time of the sale of the certificate rather than the value of the right to develop the owner's land at the time of the taking.

Although these technical legal problems are real and may not be dismissed summarily, nevertheless, they need not present insuperable obstacles to the validity of the TDR proposal. The technical requirements of just compensation were designed to protect an owner whose property is taken in a conventional and traditional eminent domain proceeding. In such cases the owner is deprived of use of and title to the property itself in an unequivocal and unconditional way and is entitled to an unequivocal and unconditional compensation. However, the TDR proposal is not a traditional eminent domain taking of the title and use of property. The owner retains title to and limited use of the property. He is deprived only of the right to develop, which right may not have ripened to a point where its value has become defined and unconditional. Time is usually in favor of the owner of the right to develop. Frequently, it is in his interest to postpone the determination of the value of his development right until some time in the future. The application of the traditional rules of just compensation requiring immediate and unconditional payment in money would be a disservice rather than a benefit to the owner of preserved open space. Because of this distinction, an informed and learned court would not feel constrained to a blind application of the traditional common law rules. The validity of the TDR proposal, when challenged for failure to meet the requirements of just compensation, may very well depend upon the ability of counsel to explain, and the ability of the court to understand, the unique nature of the TDR proposal.

ADMINISTRATIVE PROBLEMS:
PROFICIENCY AND INTEGRITY

The criticism to which the TDR proposal is most vulnerable is based upon the realization that the success of the program depends upon the proficiency of the planners and the integrity of the governing body responsible for its administration. To the extent to which either group falters, the program may be jeopardized.

The dependence upon the proficiency of the planning profession is particularly critical. The entire proposal is based upon the assumption that the owners of preserved open space land will be compensated for the deprivation of the use of their land by the sale of certificates of development rights to owners of developable land. This relationship is predictable in theory and workable in practice only to the extent that the planners' projection of future economic demand for land development is accurate and their designation of sites for specified land use is skillfully performed.

For example, a market for development rights will be created only if the owners of developable land find it more profitable to develop at higher densities with the use of development rights than at the lower densities permitted as of right. The assumption that more intensive development is more profitable and that this profit incentive will create a market for development rights appears to be a sound theoretical premise. However, its implementation in practice will depend upon the accuracy of the planners' quantitative projections of development demand and the skill with which designations of land use are made to meet that demand and at the same time fulfill the public need for open space. These determinations will require a measure of art as well as skill. The success of the program may well depend upon the planners' proficiency in this task.

Now, let us assume that the planner has performed his job well and submits his findings and recommendations to the governing body. That body of elected officials will be required to adopt a program that will have political as well as planning significance. Under our democratic system some degree of compromise of the planner's recommendations would not be unusual. The land designated for development at more intensive use will be given a potential for increased value in most cases. In other situations such land may have already increased in value based upon its development potential and in spite of its zoning restrictions to less intensive use. In all cases, there will be political pressures imposed upon the governing body to modify the planners' recommendations to enhance personal, rather than public, objectives.

It is very likely that the political pressures upon the governing body will tend to increase with the passage of time after the adoption of a TDR program. There are a number of reasons for this: first, the TDR program is different from all previously used land use control techniques. It will take a period of time after its adoption before people become sufficiently familiar with the concept to determine the course of action in their best personal interest. Second, under the TDR proposal the power of zoning boards to grant variances is severely restricted. Variances for a change of use in an open space district may be granted only by the governing body, with the recommendation of the planning board; variances for an increase in the density of development in developable districts may be granted only if the applicant acquires the requisite number of development rights. Third, as the community develops and the incentives for more intensive land development increase, the governing body will become the primary governmental tribunal in which relief from the restrictions of the TDR system is available.

The vulnerability of the TDR program to the vicissitudes of the local governing body is a formidable problem. The success of the program depends not only upon the skill and wisdom with which the land use plan is originally conceived but also depends upon a degree of assurance that the program will not be abandoned and that the underlying rules will not be changed along the way. It is generally agreed that the reason for the failure of the British Town and Country Planning Act of 1947, under which British government took over the development rights of all undeveloped land, is that landowners refused to develop their land or sell it in the belief that a Conservative government, when it returned to power would change the system. This prediction proved to be correct, and the British system of land use control through the use of development rights was, for the most part, abandoned.[11] A similar question will arise in any American jurisdiction that adopts a TDR program.

However, the fact that, under a democratic system the current legislature may, in the absence of constitutional restrictions, modify or repeal laws adopted by a prior legislature does not mean that new programs should not be adopted. The primary significance of the power of subsequent governing bodies to amend or repeal existing programs is the necessity of obtaining and maintaining widespread democratic support for the program. The TDR program has the potential for providing an effective technique for the rational allocation of the use of land to achieve public needs and at the same time provide property owners with a reasonable use of their land or fair compensation. However its ability to fulfill this potential will depend upon the ability of its advocates to garner sufficient support for its adoption and sustenance. This in turn will require patience, dedication and a willingness to adapt and modify the plan in response to the suggestions of both friendly and hostile critics. Time and the free marketplace of ideas will judge the merits of this proposal. Understanding, acceptance, and continuing approval by the electorate will determine its success.

NOTES

1. Members of this committee were: T. Airola, R. Binetsky, B. Chavooshian, R. Ginman, T. Hall, J. Jager, G. Nieswand, T. Norman, E. Reoch and J. Rose. The committee was aided by a prior proposal introduced in the Maryland Senate in 1972 by State Senator William Goodman, S. 254, Senate of Maryland.

2. See Rose, "Proposed Development Rights Legislation Can Change the Name of the Land Investment Game," 1 *Real Estate L.J.* 276 (1973).

3. E.g., Just v. Marinette County, 201 N.E.2d 761 (Wis. 1972).

4. E.g., Morris County Land Improvement Co. v. Parsippany Troy Hills Township, 40 N.J. 539, 193 A.2d 232 (1963).

5. See 27 *Am. Jur.* 2d Sec. 265; Nicholas on Eminent Domain, Sec. 8.2.

6. Martin v. Tylor, 4 N.D. 278, 60 N.W. 392 (0000).

7. Louisiana Power & Light Co. v. Lasseigne, 220 So.2d 462 (La., 1969); Gardiner v. Henderson, 103 Ariz. 420, 443 P.2d 416 (1968).

8. Keystone Associates v. Moerdler, 19 N.Y.2d 78, 224 N.E.2d 700 (1966).

9. See discussion in United States v. Westinghouse Electric & Manu. Co., 339 U.S. 261 (1950).

10. See United States v. 158.76 Acres of Land, 298 F.2d 559 (2nd Circ. Vt.) 92 A.L.R.2d 766; State, by Highway Commr. v. Gorga, 54 N.J.Super. 520, 149 A.2d 266 (1959).

11. See Rose, "A Proposal for the Separation and Marketability of Development Rights as a Technique to Preserve Open Space," 2 *Real Estate L.J.* 635, 642-645 (1974).

From A Psychological, Legal, and Administrative Perspective

The Chicago Plan: Incentive Zoning and the Preservation of Urban Landmarks

JOHN J. COSTONIS
Professor of Law
University of Illinois

Despite the economic feasibility and sound urban design features of the Chicago Plan, the prospect of a legal challenge may deter its acceptance by landmark owners, the real estate industry, and local government. A court test of the plan is likely to center upon three of its principal features: the condemnation of preservation restrictions, insofar as it makes possible the sale of development rights; the use of preservation restrictions to encumber landmark properties; and the authorization of greater floor area for development rights purchasers than for other property owners within the transfer district. Opponents of the proposal will contend that it violates the "public use" limitation on governmental power under the state and federal constitutions to condemn property because the acquisition of preservation restrictions is linked to a scheme of selling development rights on the private market. They will attack the use of preservation restrictions on various grounds: the most troublesome is that such restrictions are not recognized property interests and that their acquisition is not authorized by existing preservation enabling acts and ordinances. And they are likely to assert that nonuniform floor area allocations violate state zoning enabling legislation and deny equal protection and due process to property owners who do not purchase development rights.

A. *The Public Use Requirement*

If the Chicago Plan envisaged only the condemnation of an interest in landmark properties, no serious constitutional objection based on the public use requirement could be asserted against the Plan's employment of the condemnation power. The courts have repeatedly held that landmark preservation is a public use, in aid of which that power may be exercised.[94] Moreover, the objection that acquisition of less-than-fee interests fails to promote a public use because such interests are not susceptible to physical use or occupation by the public has also been discredited.[95] It is now recognized that visual enjoyment alone constitutes a sufficient use by the public to warrant condemnation.

But the Chicago Plan also authorizes municipalities to resell in the private market the development rights associated with the preservation restriction that it condemns in private properties. Because condemnation of the preservation restriction and resale of the associated development rights are connected steps in an integral scheme, opponents of the Chicago Plan may assert that it violates the public use requirement on two further grounds. First, it may be argued that, despite its claimed public objectives, the Plan in fact serves the interests of a distinct private group, namely development rights purchasers. Second, it may be argued that governmental action taken to recoup the costs of condemnation of the preservation restriction violates the public use requirement.

1. Private Benefit. — Without the active participation of private developers, the transfer proposal cannot succeed. To secure their support, it accords them preferential treatment by relaxing zoning restrictions to permit them to build more profitably than nonparticipants in the program. Hence, there is the possibility of an attack on grounds that the proposal serves private rather than public interests and that the use of eminent domain to this end is invalid. Similar charges are seen in cases dealing with governmental efforts to enlist private enterprise in programs designed to renew urban areas,[96] attract industry to depressed locations,[97] revitalize port and terminal facilities,[98] and secure the construction of parking facilities [99] and government buildings.[100]

This charge is a difficult one for the courts to handle. The dangers of improper private gain are often quite real. And, regrettably, favoritism or venality on the part of the public officials who administer these programs is not uncommon. But this century has witnessed a vast expansion of governmental responsibilities as a result of population growth and the population movement to the cities. The courts have responded by broadening earlier notions of the ambit of the public use concept and by according legislatures wide discretion in selecting means for meeting these responsibilities.[101] Moreover, the charge that a program, legislatively declared to be a public use, actually serves private interests requires courts to go behind the statute to peer into legislative motive and into the program's history and implementation. Few courts welcome these tasks.

Judicial discomfort in the face of these difficulties pervades the decisions that examine allegations of undue private gain. Four conclusions emerge from an examination of such cases. First, private gain, whether accruing to identified individuals [102] or to the private sector generally,[103] does not itself invalidate a program. Second, private gain must be justified by the benefits accruing to the public under the program.[104] Judicial tests of justification are crude and, in large measure, conclusory: some courts reason that private gain must be "incidental" or "subordinate" to the public gain;[105] others emphasize that the public gain must justify the risk sustained by the government in the program.[106] Third, each case turns very much on its own facts and the specific legislative framework within which the program operates. Fourth, and perhaps most important, allegations of undue private gain are rejected in the overwhelming majority of cases; they prevail only under circumstances of clearly disproportionate private gain.[107]

These conclusions augur well for the transfer proposal. That developers receive substantial benefits does not of itself taint the proposal. Authoritative recognition of landmark preservation as a public use is persuasive evidence that the public advantages of the proposal offset those benefits.[108] Moreover, the transfer proposal contains safeguards to insure that the benefits to private developers do not become the tail that wags the dog. Condemned development rights are credited to the municipal bank in an amount strictly calculated to reimburse the city for its condemnation costs. Besides, since developers will be expected to bid for the development rights on the open market, the value of these rights will be returned to the city in the form of cash payments from these developers.

2. Recoupment. — The second aspect of the public use limitation proscribes condemnation solely designed to recoup the cost of public programs or to add to the public fisc generally. It is on this basis, for example, that courts have frowned upon excess condemnation,[109] the acquisition of more land than is needed for a public project with the intent to resell the remainder at a profit after completion of the project. Needless to say, the recoupment objection has particular relevance to the transfer proposal: only by selling development rights acquired from nonparticipating landmark owners will a city be able to compensate them for their losses.

The courts have been no more comfortable with the recoupment objection than with the claim of undue private benefit. Again, the competing considerations are not easily reconciled. The key objection to recoupment concerns the propriety of utilizing eminent domain, one of the harshest of governmental powers, to fund public programs, rather than resorting to general tax revenues for this purpose. Municipal poverty, it is argued, does not justify such drastic interference with private ownership.[110]

For some, the objection is ideological:[111] government has no place in the private real estate market and thus should not be able to sell or lease portions of condemned property to private parties. For others, it rests on the practical consideration that government enjoys unfair advantages over the private real estate industry in any competition between the two.[112] Still others express misgivings about the wisdom of government becoming involved in high-risk ventures.[113] The final objection is the familiar one that opportunities for favoritism and corruption are heightened by public programs that return large sums of money to municipalities.[114] On the other hand, adherents of recoupment counter that expanding governmental responsibilities in this century have created demands for public funding that simply cannot be met out of general tax revenues.[115] Without recoupment of at least some ot these funds, they note, many programs of vital importance to public welfare would be gravely endangered.[116]

Caught between these opposing contentions, the courts have found uneasy refuge in the formula that recoupment objections will be overridden if the recoupment is but an "incidental" element of a program that furthers an independent public use.[117] This formula is first cousin to the judicial formula used to evaluate claims of undue private gain, both formulas approving the challenged feature if it rides piggyback on a recognized public use.[118] While both formulas are imprecise, they allow the judiciary to control the more egregious of legislative excesses. And both formulas result in the approval of the great majority of the programs to which they are applied.

Three groups of cases serve to illustrate judicial reluctance to invalidate the use of eminent domain because of a recoupment objection. The first concerns the propriety of selling a byproduct of property condemned for a public project,[119] best illustrated in litigation dealing with the sale of electricity from navigation improvement projects undertaken by federal and state agencies. Recoupment challenges to such sales have been decisively rejected.[120] In rejecting such challenges, the courts have pointed to three grounds for validating such sales: they enable public agencies to recapture the costs of public improvements;[121] they advance community welfare by making possible the fulfillment of vital public needs that would otherwise go unmet for lack of funds;[122] and they encourage the productive use of valuable resources.[123]

In the byproduct cases no portion of the condemned land is devoted to private uses. The recoupment question is more difficult in the second group of cases, which examine projects in which space in buildings erected on condemned land is leased to private firms to defray project costs. Such arrangements are common in highway, port, railroad terminal, governmental center, and parking projects.[124] Again, however, the courts generally find that recoupment of project costs through leasing arrangements with private firms is "incidental" to an overall public use.[125]

Certain factors stand out in the leasing cases which are relevant to the Chicago Plan. If the project cannot be carried on without recoupment or if it responds to a public need that private enterprise cannot or will not meet, the courts are likely to be sympathetic.[126] That the project involves government in competition with private enterprise is irrelevant provided that an independent public use is served by the endeavor.[127] Nor are the courts impressed with claims that a program is not financially feasible; they defer to legislative judgment on questions of program content and merit unless the program is patently unreasonable.[128] Similarly, they reject the oft-repeated charge that use of the eminent domain power in part for recoupment goals opens the way to "outside land speculation" and other abuses.[129] Should these abuses eventuate, they note, an appropriate remedy will lie in the courts. Otherwise, government, too, is entitled to exercise sound business judgment in the formulation and conduct of public programs.[130]

In the final group of cases, which deal with the recoupment objection in the context of urban renewal, the government's involvement with the condemned property is the most attenuated. In urban renewal programs, after the city has acquired and cleared the land, it resells it to private developers. Once again, however, the courts have overridden the recoupment objection. Public use of the land, these courts say, is achieved once the city has acquired and cleared it.[131] Its resale to private developers thereafter is but an "incidental" aspect of the urban renewal process, akin to, if not identical with, the general municipal practice of disposing of city property no longer needed for public purposes. Retention of the land, they note, would be poor municipal stewardship because resale enables the community to recapture much of its initial outlay and to return the land to productive use and to the tax rolls.[132]

Taken together, the three groups of cases indicate that the success of a recoupment challenge to the condemnation of preservation restrictions under the Chicago Plan is extremely unlikely, even though condemnation is connected with a scheme of selling development rights to fund the costs of condemnation. Like by-product sales, the transfer of development rights enables public agencies to recapture the costs of public improvements (the costs of preserving landmarks); to fulfill community needs that would go otherwise unmet (landmark preservation being impractical without the sale of development rights); and to ensure the productive use of valuable resources (the unused but authorized development rights of public and private landmarks otherwise being lost upon permanent designation).

The leasing cases reinforce this conclusion. They emphasize the legal irrelevancy of the fact that the sale of development rights may involve the city in competition with private enterprise if developers elect to purchase these rights rather than to acquire privately owned parcels in completing land assemblages. The leasing cases confirm that competition between government and the private sector is not legally objectionable so long as government enters the private marketplace in furtherance of a program that serves an independent public use. Questions concerning the financial feasibility of the Chicago Plan will also not be litigable under these precedents. Finally, charges that the Chicago Plan might involve a municipality in land speculation and other abuses will receive scant attention since the leasing cases establish that this question will be considered only if and at the time that such abuses eventuate.

The urban renewal cases offer further proof that, in and of itself, the recoupment feature of the Chicago Plan does not constitute a basis for the Plan's invalidation. Under the Plan the city retains a continuing interest in the landmark property in the form of a preservation restriction. Yet, in the urban renewal context, many courts have rejected the recoupment objection under a rationale that does not obligate the city to keep any interest whatsoever in the urban renewal tracts that it resells to private developers.[133]

B. The Preservation Restriction

The purchase or condemnation of preservation restrictions raises a host of legal problems that lack clear resolution in most states. Their range is suggested in *Pontiac Improvement Co. v. Board of Commissioners*,[134] a 1933 Ohio case that puzzled over a statute authorizing local governments to condemn the "fee or any lesser interest" in real estate. In *Pontiac*, the Cleveland Park Commission attempted to condemn the right to impose controls respecting drainage, construction, planting, and the like over the plaintiff's land, which adjoined a city park. The court invalidated the taking in a rather confused opinion that appears to reflect at least three concerns. One is the injustice to the plaintiff of taking a less-than-fee interest in his land, thereby leaving him with all of the responsibilities but few of the privileges of ownership.[135] The second is the novelty of the interest in question and, by implication, the vagueness of the statutory mandate on which the taking was premised. The court might have approved the taking had the interest fit within one of the traditional less-than-fee interests recognized at common law or had the authority for its acquisition been clearly spelled out in the statute. Third, its doubts on both counts led it to conclude that, whatever the nature of the interest, the statute failed to define the rights and obligations of the parties with sufficient clarity to be enforceable.[136]

Pontiac dealt not with a preservation restriction but with what would now be termed a "conservation" or "scenic easement." [137] The relation between the two types of interests, however, is sufficiently close that the concerns expressed in *Pontiac* provide a useful framework for an examination of the legal problems affecting the preservation restriction.

1. Acquisition in Fee. — *Pontiac*'s concern that a less-than-fee taking by itself is unfair to the landowner seems misplaced. It runs counter to the well-settled view that public authorities neither may nor should take a greater interest in or amount of land than the public use necessitates.[138] This view finds strong support in the policies that favor limiting outlays of public funds and minimizing governmental interference with private ownership.[139] *Pontiac*'s concern seems especially inapplicable to urban landmarks. Most of these buildings return amounts well in excess of their taxes and operating expenses. Thus, even after condemnation of a preservation restriction (with its concomitant tax reduction), the landmark should be able to operate at a profit.

However, in some cases landmarks will be unable to return a profit after condemnation of a preservation restriction. In these cases, leaving a landmark owner with what one commentator calls the "rump rights" [140] of ownership may raise questions of equity to the landmark owner. Structural unsoundness, advanced deterioration, or changes in the surrounding neighborhood may mean that acquisition of a preservation restriction will, in effect, saddle the owner with a white elephant. In such instances, the landmark commission should recommend that the city acquire the property in fee.

2. Acquisition of a Less-Than-Fee Interest. — The powers of purchase and eminent domain granted in many preservation acts are as imprecisely defined as those in the *Pontiac* statute.[141] Do these acts authorize the acquisition of a preservation restriction in landmark properties? As suggested above, that question can be answered affirmatively only if a court is prepared to conclude either that preservation restrictions fall within one of the less-than-fee interests recognized at common law or that the statutory language itself creates a novel property interest.

(a) *Traditional Interests*. — The first alternative assumes an extremely sympathetic court. Preservation restrictions do not easily assume the garb of easements, real covenants, or equitable servitudes, the relevant common law categories.[142] They are most often compared with negative easements,[143] which obligate a landowner to refrain from performing acts on his property that would otherwise be permitted as an incident of fee ownership. Landmark owners, for example, may not build in the airspace over their buildings nor may they demolish or significantly alter them. But negative easements have normally been restricted to the four types approved in the early English cases: easements for light, for air, for support of a building laterally or subjacently, and for the flow of an artificial stream.[144] Although resembling easements for light and air in its restriction against building above the landmark, a preservation restriction goes beyond the former in its controls over alteration and demolition.[145] In addition, some courts may not enforce negative easements that are not "appurtenant" to the benefited parcel, the dominant estate.[146] The appurtenancy requirement is satisfied only if the easement benefits the owner of that estate in the physical use and enjoyment of the land and was created expressly for the purpose of conferring that benefit.[147] If these requirements are not met, the easement will be deemed to be held "in gross." Municipal ownership of parcels that will qualify as "appurtenant" is likely to be infrequent unless the courts will so categorize city-owned properties within the general vicinity of a landmark or the publicly owned streets and alleys that border on it.[148] Even assuming that a jurisdiction approves negative easements in gross, moreover, the assignability of these interests has been questioned.[149]

It is even less likely that preservation restrictions will be enforceable as real covenants. Courts generally insist that these interests, too, must be appurtenant to a benefited dominant estate.[150] An additional requirement, privity of estate between the original promisor and promisee, dictates that the benefited and burdened parcels must initially have been in common ownership and that the burden must have been imposed on the latter parcel at the time the ownership was divided. Otherwise, the burden of the real covenant will not bind subsequent takers of the parcel.[151] Because few, if any, cases under the transfer proposal are likely to duplicate these rather specialized facts, it is doubtful whether a municipality will be able to enforce a preservation restriction against a successor of the owner who executed it. In addition, some jurisdictions balk at the enforcement of affirmative duties

in real covenants,[152] a qualification that could prove troublesome
if a municipality wished to include maintenance obligations in
the preservation restriction.[153]

Characterizing a preservation restriction as an equitable
servitude offers a more promising route than either of the previous alternatives. Equitable servitudes are not restricted to four
specific types as are negative easements, but may incorporate any
obligation that does not violate public policy.[154] No privity of
estate other than that provided by the agreement need exist between the landmark owner who executes it and the city in order
for the agreement to be effective against successors of the former.[155] Servitudes are enforceable by injunction [156] and may
include affirmative as well as negative obligations.[157] They must
reflect the intent to bind subsequent takers; [158] and the latter
must have notice of the agreement,[159] requirements easily satisfied by careful draftmanship and use of the deeds registry, respectively. But in many jurisdictions servitudes held in gross
are not enforceable against subsequent takers of the burdened
parcel [160] and may not be assignable as well.[161] So again, municipalities in these jurisdictions must be prepared to argue that
municipally owned property, whether adjacent to or nearby the
landmark property, will be directly benefited by enforcement of
the servitude.

The technicalities attending each of the common law interests
confuse the status of the preservation restriction under the common law. Though the courts in some jurisdictions may be willing
to enforce the preservation restriction under the rubric of one
of the foregoing interests, a preferable solution would seem to
lie in clarifying legislation.

(b) *Statutory Authorization.* — Whether statutory authorization to acquire an imprecisely defined, less-than-fee interest re-
lieves a municipality of the burdensome restrictions of the
common law rules is problematic. *Pontiac* suggests not. But an
opposite view, which may well have supplanted *Pontiac* in most
jurisdictions,[162] was tersely stated by then Chief Judge Holmes in
Newton v. Perry:

> [I]t is plain . . . that the purpose of the taking must fix the
> extent of the right. The right, whether it be called easement or
> by any other name, is statutory, and must be construed to be
> large enough to accomplish all that it has taken to do.[163]

The question is further confused by decisions that subsume
less-than-fee interests under one of the traditional categories even
though they clearly fail to meet the formal requirements of the
latter.[164]

State legislatures have grown uneasy with the dubious formalism of the common law and the ambiguity in the case reports. To facilitate highway beautification and open-space programs, many have expressly authorized state and local agencies to acquire "scenic easements," "development rights," and other novel less-than-fee interests.[165] Although the statutes fail to detail precisely what is intended by these labels, *Kamrowski v. State*,[166] which upheld a Wisconsin statute authorizing acquisition of "scenic easements" along the Great River Road, confirms the readiness of the judiciary to construe them most favorably to the public agency. Significantly, *Kamrowski* did not even mention the possible difficulties posed by the differences between the statutory easement and its common law cousin, but focused instead upon the compatibility of the statute with the public use requirement.

Of greater interest are statutes in three states [167] that accord express recognition to the preservation restrictions as an independent, valid less-than-fee interest. Directly addressing the difficulties outlined in this section, these statutes provide that preservation restrictions shall not be unenforceable because of lack of privity of estate or of ownership of benefited land. They also stress the assignability of preservation restrictions, even if held "in gross." Less elaborate statutes have also been passed [168] that modify the common law by recognizing "easements in gross," which are assignable and, if negative, not restricted to the four types known to the common law. By clarifying an intolerably opaque area of the law, both groups of statutes enable government and the private sector to participate in preservation and conservation programs confident that some hoary doctrine will not frustrate their reasonable expectations.

3. Indefiniteness. — The *Pontiac* court considered that the rights acquired by the park department were so indefinite as to be incapable either of valuation or of enforcement. The valuation objection does not seem well taken. Less-than-fee interests are condemned as a matter of course by government and public utilities. In these cases, a basic "before and after" theory of valuation is used that measures the value of the parcel with and without the encumbrance.[169] And, although "not simple," setting a price tag for preservation restrictions "by no means goes beyond techniques which are widely recognized in the field of real estate valuation." [170]

Nor is the court's skepticism concerning enforcement insuperable if the preservation restriction is properly drafted. In fact, with the increasing refinement of these instruments, indefiniteness no longer appears to be a serious problem. Typical preservation restrictions [171] detail the legal authority on which acquisition is premised, restrictions on use, maintenance obligations, duration, remedies, and miscellaneous matters. Public agencies and preservation societies carefully spell out the statutory basis for acquisition to emphasize that they are empowered to acquire the interest and that enforcement of the latter is consistent with sound public policy. Use restrictions are as varied as the character and setting of particular landmarks. They may include prohibitions against alteration or demolition, signs, subdivision of the landmark tract, addition of buildings to the site and specified uses of the landmark. Administrative provisions detail the procedures for obtaining approval for permitted modifications and for making periodic inspections of the premises to insure that the restrictions are being honored. Maintenance obligations are variously stated. Landmark owners may agree simply to keep their properties in good repair or they may undertake to comply with property maintenance standards that are incorporated by reference into the preservation restriction. In some instances, owners even commit themselves to restore the properties in accordance with detailed specifications and schedules.

Duration of the restriction may be in perpetuity or be limited to a number of years. The instruments underscore the intent of the parties that the benefits and burdens of the restriction shall run to their successors in interest. The remedies clause identifies who may sue for breach of the restriction and what relief may be obtained. Miscellaneous provisions may include anything from rights of first refusal to express disclaimers of rights of public access to the landmark. Surveys, line drawings, and photographs appear increasingly as appendices to preservation restrictions. They permit precise identification of prized interior or exterior features, such as paneling, fireplaces, and cornices.

Although most preservation restrictions relate to residential properties at the present time, they can be drawn just as effectively for downtown office and commercial buildings. Remedies and legislative authority clauses will be similar in the two cases. Use restrictions should prove simpler for downtown buildings because tract subdivision and the addition of new buildings are not serious problems. Continuation of office or commercial uses within these buildings, moreover, will not impair their status as landmarks. Controls over alteration will deal mostly with changes in the exterior facades of these buildings, an infrequent occurrence and one that is relatively easy to regulate.

The definition of proper maintenance standards is no different for downtown landmarks than for other centrally located office and commercial buildings. It is a routine responsibility for attorneys who represent the holders of mortgages on the latter structures and the tenants who occupy space in them under long-term leases. The task will be somewhat complicated, however, if the landmark commission's appraisal of a building reveals that restoration of the building or one or more of its characteristic features is in order. In those instances, the financial package that the commission proposes to the landmark owner may include sums for this work. If so, the nature of the restoration and any specific requirements regarding subsequent maintenance must be detailed in the restriction or in a related document, as the sense of the transaction dictates.

The most troublesome drafting problem is posed by the fact that many downtown office and commercial buildings have a limited economic life. The day may come, sooner for some landmarks than for others, when they can no longer meet debt service and operating costs as a result of increases in the latter and declining revenues. At that point, ownership for private profit obviously becomes impossible.

Among the potential solutions to this problem, three seem especially promising.[172] One is to project the costs and income curves of individual landmarks to arrive at a date in the future when those curves are likely to intersect. The owner of the landmark could be given the option at that date either of continuing to operate the building or of turning it over to the city. Acquisition costs then would be nominal because of the landmark site's lack of development potential and the further age of the building. The city could use the building for its own space needs or lease it to a suitable tenant who desires the prestige of a landmark location.[173] The second is to devise appropriate subsidies for landmark owners out of monies generated by the development rights bank. The third is to seek an institutional buyer, such as a college or other nonprofit organization, to acquire the building after its development rights have been transferred. Developers and speculators will probably not wish to retain the building after that point, and the buyer will be in a position to acquire it at a favorable price.

C. Development Rights Transfers

The Chicago Plan contemplates a two-level system of bulk zoning regulation — development rights purchasers are permitted to build larger structures than the other lot owners in a development rights transfer district. The legal issues inherent in this disparate treatment will be addressed in this section, examining, first, challenges based on the uniformity provisions of state zoning acts and the equal protection clauses of the federal and applicable state constitutions, and, second, objections grounded in issues of substantive due process.

1. "Uniformity" as a Statutory and Constitutional Restraint.
— The question whether application of a dual standard of bulk

regulation to lots within a transfer district denies uniform treatment to property owners within the district may be posed in either statutory or constitutional terms. The relevant statutory text is the requirement of most state zoning enabling acts that "[a]ll [zoning] regulations shall be uniform for each class or kind of buildings throughout each district." [174] The governing constitutional principle is the equal protection requirement of the federal [175] and applicable state constitutions.

As seen above,[176] the Chicago Plan could be implemented exclusively through a preservation enabling act. There are, however, compelling reasons for analyzing the legal issues inherent in the Plan's two-level system of bulk regulation through examining judicial interpretations of the uniformity requirement of state zoning enabling acts. In the first place, it is doubtful whether the preservation enabling legislation of any state,[177] Illinois excepted, authorizes the use of transfers as a means of safeguarding landmarks. Thus communities that wish to avoid the problem of securing amendments to that legislation must look to their zoning enabling acts as the basis for their power to authorize development rights transfers. Second, zoning precedents offer the most useful basis for predicting the likely judicial reaction to the transfer technique even if it is implemented under preservation enabling statutes. If transfers pass muster under zoning precedents, they would undoubtedly be valid under a properly drafted preservation statute as well. Finally, commentators are in general agreement that the statutory requirement of uniformity duplicates the constitutional requirement of equal protection.[178] Hence, if the transfers of development rights do not run afoul of the uniformity requirement, it would appear that these transfers would survive the equal protection challenge as well.

At first blush, the uniformity requirement seems to present an obstacle to the legality of the Chicago Plan: regulations for buildings within a development rights transfer district are not uniform in the sense that purchasers of development rights can build to greater bulk than other property owners within the district. This reading of the uniformity requirement, however, ignores the growing recognition of urban planners and municipal governments that in many cases the individual lot is not the appropriate unit of development control, and the corresponding willingness of the courts to interpret the uniformity requirement so as not to foreclose alternative planning methods.[179]

Virtually every major innovation in the land use field over the last fifteen years rejects the notion that individual lots must serve as the unit of development control.[180] Two of these innovations — density zoning and the special development district — are of particular relevance to the question whether development transfers conflict with the uniformity requirement: they provide the twin pillars upon which the development rights transfer element of the Chicago Plan is founded. Rejecting the individual lot as the unit of bulk control, density zoning [181] substitutes entire areas of the community in its place. It prescribes a maximum amount or range of bulk for an area as a whole, and permits developers to concentrate bulk there in accordance with flexible site planning or urban design criteria. Typically, density zones are overlay districts that include one or more traditional bulk zones within their boundaries. Developers may elect to build under the bulk regulations of the density zone or under those of the residual bulk zone.

The special development district [182] complements density zoning by particularizing the development goals that will guide the distribution or redistribution of bulk within a density zone. A special development district is established only after a municipality has evaluated the special functions or needs of the geographic area in question, and selected the goals that will channel development or redevelopment there. In most cases, these goals are incorporated into a detailed area plan that itself is coordinated with the community's comprehensive plan.

A development rights transfer district is, in effect, a special development district in which bulk is redistributed in accordance with the density zoning technique. It encompasses an area of the community that is unique because of the concentration there of many of the community's landmark buildings. The community's goal in establishing the transfer district, of course, is to safeguard the landmarks within the district from destruction. The detailed plan that the landmark and planning commissions draw up for the district is the product of exhaustive studies by both agencies that inventory the landmark buildings there, identify the boundaries within which transfers may be made, and coordinate bulk concentrations within the district with the community's overall development program. Bulk is allocated within the transfer district on an area-wide rather than lot-by-lot basis because landmark lots must remain underimproved while lots utilizing the transferred development rights must be allowed to exceed the bulk limitations that are prescribed for individual lots in the traditional bulk zones within the district. The regulations of the residual bulk zone are superseded when the local governing body approves development rights transfer authorizations recommended by the landmark commission.

Judicial reaction to challenges to density zoning measures under the uniformity requirement augur well for the Chicago Plan: no density zoning measure that has come before the courts to date has been invalidated on the ground that it denies uniform treatment to affected property owners.[183] Challenges to these measures have arisen in the context of two distinct applications of the density zoning technique: cluster zoning and planned unit development (PUD). Cluster zoning ordinances offer the developer a trade: if he agrees to devote a prescribed percentage of this tract to a community use, such as a park or a schoolground, he is authorized in return to build the same number of residential units on the remaining portion of his tract that he formerly could have built on the tract as a whole.[184] PUD ordinances go further by relaxing building type and use restrictions as well as area restrictions: single family, multifamily, and highrise units, and residential, commercial, and light industrial uses — all of which are segregated within separate districts under traditional zoning — often may be included within a single zone under these ordinances.[185]

The courts have expressly held that both types of ordinances will meet the uniformity requirement if they entitle all property owners within the cluster or PUD district to take advantage of the opportunity to develop their parcels in accordance with the flexible density, building type, or use requirements of these ordinances.[186] Rejecting a uniformity objection to a cluster ordinance, for example, a New Jersey appellate court held in *Chrinko v. South Brunswick Township Planning Board*[187] that the clustering technique "accomplishes uniformity because the option is open to all developers within a zoning district."[188] *Chrinko* echoes a number of earlier, nondensity zoning cases in emphasizing that the uniformity required by statute refers not to the end product of the development decisions within the district — in *Chrinko*, the minimum lot size of the dwellings actually constructed there — but to uniform application of the regulation to all landowners within the district.[189]

The same rationale appears in *Orinda Homeowners Committee v. Board of Supervisors*,[190] which upheld a PUD ordinance against a claim of nonuniform application of district regulations concerning building types:

> A residential planned unit development . . . does not conflict with [the uniformity provision] merely by reason of the fact that the units are not uniform, that is, they are not all single family dwellings and perhaps the multi-family units differ among themselves. [The uniformity provision] provides that the *regulations* shall be uniform for each class or kind of building or use of land throughout the zone. It does not state that the units must be alike even as to their character, whether single family or multi-family.[191]

The uniformity problem is somewhat more complicated than

the stated rationale in *Chrinko, Orinda* and related cases indicates because access to the benefits of cluster or PUD ordinances is normally limited to owners of sizeable parcels.[192] However, neither uniformity nor its constitutional equivalent, equal protection, would appear to be violated by the size criterion. Discriminations among the members of a regulated class are permissible if they can be reasonably grounded in the purpose of the underlying regulation.[193] Since the principal objective of both cluster and PUD ordinances is to promote large-scale developments of attractive design, limiting the benefits of these ordinances to developers with substantial land holdings would appear to meet this test.[194]

These density zoning precedents strongly indicate that the development rights transfer component of the Chicago Plan will not fall before the objection that it denies uniform treatment to lot owners within a transfer district. By providing for the disposal of development rights through appropriate public bidding and sale procedures, the Plan will insure that all district owners have access to the purchase and enjoyment of development rights. This is not to say, of course, that some lot owners may not enjoy greater advantages than others as a result of the Plan. The configuration of particular lots may be such that the acquisition of additional development rights would carry no economic benefit for their owners.[195] Since the demand for the rights will probably exceed the available supply at any given time,[196] many lot owners will lack the financial resources to acquire these rights at prevailing market prices. But these or similar impediments to practical as opposed to formal access attend any program in which surplus public property is disposed of by public sale and bidding procedures. Moreover, though the benefits of cluster and PUD zoning are limited to owners of large acreage, and thus possibly to a wealthier class of developers, this has not deterred judicial acceptance of these plans. A uniformity challenge to the Chicago Plan, based on the fact that the bidding technique for disposal of transfer rights favors wealthier bidders, would thus seem unlikely to succeed.

Finally, the Chicago Plan is likely to encounter even less judicial resistance under the uniformity requirement than PUD ordinances and other forms of innovative zoning that mix diverse building types and uses. Use zoning has traditionally proven more controversial than bulk zoning because of its more immediate impact upon surrounding property.[197] The increasing willingness of American courts to approve the mixture of uses and building types once thought incompatible [198] offers strong evidence that the marginal bulk adjustments permitted under the Chicago Plan will not be found offensive by the courts.

The Chicago Plan appears equally able to surmount any direct equal protection challenge to its transfer feature. Recent Supreme Court decisions have suggested that the mere fact that a law works to the disadvantage of less wealthy individuals does not call for more than a rational basis for the state's actions.[199] This basis is present in the Chicago Plan: by selling development rights at the highest possible price, the city maximizes the revenues it has available for the operation of its landmark preservation program.

Basing the development rights transfer component of the Chicago Plan on the density zoning precedents above carries the additional advantage of differentiating transfers from the traditional zoning variance. At first blush, the two may be confused because both enable their recipients to erect larger buildings than are permitted by the regulations of the bulk zone in which the buildings will be located. A court that identified a development rights transfer with a variance, however, would probably invalidate the transfer because transfer authorizations are not administered by the board of zoning appeals and are not granted on the basis of economic hardship, as required for variances by most zoning enabling acts.[200] But the right of the development rights purchaser to build to greater bulk originates in the bulk regulations applicable to the transfer district, and hence is substitutive of, rather than a variation from, the regulations of the traditional bulk zone. This right, moreover, is founded on the planning considerations that support density zoning generally, not on grounds of special hardship.

The transfer authorization and the variance are not wholly unrelated, however. The administration of variances by lay boards has been roundly condemned on all sides [201] because these boards, whether through incompetence or outright corruption, have freely granted variances with little regard for the statutory requirement of economic hardship. Municipalities that adopt the Chicago Plan can restore the variance to its proper role by requiring developers who seek bulk variances on spurious grounds to purchase development rights from landmark owners or from the municipal development rights bank.

2. *Substantive Due Process as a Constraint Upon Transfer Authorizations.* — Of the various obstacles to public and judicial acceptance of development rights transfer programs such as the Chicago Plan, none looms larger than the specter of urban design abuse that critics of these programs have raised. For example, Beverly Moss Spatt, as a member of the New York City Planning Commission, denounced that city's landmarks transfer program as a "gimmick" that "can only lead to an unplanned future — to chaos." [202]

The argument implicit in this charge cannot be easily dismissed. The greater bulk authorizations permitted for transferee sites under the program do appear to call into question the reasonableness either of the community's existing zoning plan or of the transfer program. If the existing zoning is sound, it may be claimed, relaxing bulk restrictions on transferee sites will overload public services and distort the urban landscape, thereby producing the planning chaos of which Mrs. Spatt warns. If it is too stringent, the proper course is to raise prevailing bulk limitations within the area generally and, in the process, to remove unwarranted public restrictions on the rights of property owners there. But, the argument proceeds, a program that retains existing bulk levels for most property owners while relaxing them for development rights purchasers sacrifices sound zoning and planning to short-term fiscal advantage. Hence, it is an arbitrary exercise of the police power, condemned under the due process clause of the fourteenth amendment.[203]

This argument fundamentally misconceives the process by which bulk levels are determined and the functions that they serve. As a result, it invests the numbers in the zoning code with an aura of scientific exactitude that is largely without foundation in fact. The precision that is attainable in setting bulk limitations in the downtown commercial and high-rise residential zones that will be included in transfer districts under the Chicago Plan turns upon the purposes that these limitations are designed to achieve. Among these purposes are the following: regulating population; insuring an adequate amount of light, air, and open space; rationing demands upon public services and facilities; and accommodating market demands for new office and residential space.[204]

The process by which these objectives are translated into numbers is among the most complex in the urban design field.[205] It proceeds on at least two levels: fact determination and political judgment. The facts that must be established or projected, such as the correlation of population increments with demands upon public facilities or the capacity of the market to absorb a stated amount of office space over a given period, are often elusive and inevitably tentative.[206] Political judgment must be exercised in selecting the desired development objectives for specific areas of the city and in resolving conflicts that may be inherent in these objectives. For example, the bulk levels that will satisfy demands for office space in a booming economy may clash with those that are thought appropriate for the particular city's aesthetic character.[207] Such clashes are unscrambled, not on the planner's slide rule, but in the political arena [208] and, in some instances, in public referenda as well.[209]

The specific bulk levels that emerge from this two-step process fall considerably short of Platonic absolutes, the slightest deviation from which threatens the dire planning consequences predicted by Mrs. Spatt.[210] Were it not for the risk of discriminatory official action,[211] in fact, it would be far less arbitrary to express bulk levels in terms of a *range* of integers rather than as *fixed* integers. [212] Whether office buildings in the downtown section of a major city are permitted to go to sixty-five rather than sixty-two stories, after all, is not an issue of great moment. What is critical, however, is that this range of stories — or its equivalent in terms of FAR's — accurately reflects the development objectives that the city seeks to achieve in its downtown section.

On the basis of this analysis, the charge that the Chicago Plan fosters arbitrary zoning should be rejected since the bulk increments allotted to development rights purchasers fall within a range that is defensible in planning terms. The reasonableness of deviations under the Chicago Plan from preexisting bulk regulations is not called into doubt by the presumed soundness of these regulations: the net increases, if any,[213] in overall density in the district under the Chicago Plan will not be enough to bring the overall density of the district outside that range originally decided upon, and the increases in bulk on individual transferee lots will not be arbitrary in planning terms.[214] The argument that builders who do not purchase development rights are suffering unconstitutional encroachments upon their right to develop their property is equally unsound. If all builders in the development rights district were allowed to exceed the original bulk restrictions, then the increase in bulk *would* exceed the range that had been previously decided upon.

There is good reason to believe that the courts will accept this analysis and uphold the Plan against the due process attack. Judicial approval of density zoning [215] implies acceptance of the principle that a community may prescribe multiple densities for individual lots as long as a sound planning rationale supports this decision. Moreover, the courts have traditionally accorded wide deference to legislative economic measures that are challenged on substantive due process grounds.[216] In the land use field, the American judiciary has proven especially responsive to the efforts of local governments to meet pressing development needs,[217] and, since 1926,[218] has approved a broad array of innovative measures that, like the Chicago Plan, promised to enhance community welfare.[219] In light of this fact, it seems most unlikely that the courts would undertake to second-guess either the wisdom or the arithmetic [220] of a community's transfer program if the latter is rooted in careful planning studies of the kind envisaged in the Chicago Plan.[221]

NOTES

[93] The misconception that zoning and the regulation of individual landmarks are indistinguishable manifestations of the police power probably results from the fact that early preservation ordinances focused almost exclusively on the regulation of historic districts. Historic districting may properly be viewed as a special case of zoning because of its area-wide focus. But a "zoning" measure that singles out an individual landmark property for severe bulk, use, and area restrictions not applicable to its neighbors generally would risk invalidation on spot zoning and equal protection grounds. *See also* note 36 *supra*. Further, while zoning establishes area-wide restrictions that may be varied only in cases of individual hardship, most preservation ordinances treat *all* formally designated landmarks as potential candidates for variances. Formal designation does not and is not intended to impose permanent landmark status on these properties. Rather, it continues under most ordinances only so long as the landmark owner consents or, under others, until the owner establishes that designation entails undue economic burdens. *See* p. 581 *supra*. It is for this reason that courts typically reject due process attacks on designation alone, but caution that designation and its attendant restrictions must be lifted upon a proper showing of economic deprivation. *See, e.g.*, Trustees of Sailor's Snug Harbor v. Platt, 53 Misc. 2d 933, 280 N.Y.S.2d 75 (Sup. Ct. 1967), *rev'd on other grounds*, 29 App. Div. 2d 376, 288 N.Y.S.2d 314 (1968); Manhattan Club v. Landmark Preservation Comm'n, 51 Misc. 2d 556, 273 N.Y.S.2d 848 (Sup. Ct. 1966); *cf.* State *ex rel.* Marbro Corp. v. Ramsey, 28 Ill. App. 2d 252, 171 N.E.2d 246 (1960); *In re* Opinion of the Justices, 33 Mass. 773, 128 N.E. 2d 557 (1955).

If individual landmarks could be regulated through the zoning power, the objectives of the Chicago Plan could be achieved largely by downzoning all landmark sites to the bulk of their present improvements. Measures akin to this technique were upheld in Rebman v. City of Springfield, 111 Ill. App. 2d 430, 250 N.E.2d 282 (1969) (downzoning of commercial area around President Lincoln's home to low density residential uses upheld), and underlie the "limited height district" provision of the New York Zoning Resolution. See NEW YORK, N.Y., ZONING RESOLUTION art. 1, ch. 1, § 11–121; art. 1, ch. 2, § 12–10 (1971) (strict height limits may be imposed throughout designated historic districts). Both examples, however, entail regulation of entire areas of a city, not of individual landmarks.

[94] *See, e.g.*, Roe v. Kansas *ex rel.* Smith, 278 U.S. 191 (1929); United States v. Gettysburg Elec. Ry., 160 U.S. 668 (1896); Barnidge v. United States, 101 F.2d 295 (8th Cir. 1939); United States v. Certain Parcels of Land, 99 F. Supp. 714 (E.D. Pa. 1951), *aff'd*, 215 F.2d 140 (3d Cir. 1954).

[95] *See, e.g.*, Kansas City v. Liebi, 298 Mo. 569, 252 S.W. 404 (1923); *In re* New York, 57 App. Div. 166, 173, 68 N.Y.S. 196, 200–01, *aff'd per curiam*, 167 N.Y. 624, 60 N.E. 1108 (1901); Kamrowski v. State, 31 Wis. 2d 256, 142 N.W.2d 793 (1966).

[96] *See, e.g.*, Belovsky v. Redevelopment Auth., 357 Pa. 329, 340, 54 A.2d 277, 282 (1947).

[97] *See, e.g.*, City of Frostburg v. Jenkins, 215 Md. 9, 16–17, 136 A.2d 852, 856 (1957); Basesore v. Hampden Indus. Dev. Auth., 433 Pa. 40, 50, 248 A.2d 212, 217 (1968).

[98] *See, e.g.,* People *ex rel.* Adamowski v. Chicago R.R. Terminal Auth., 14 Ill. 2d 230, 236, 151 N.E.2d 311, 315 (1958).

[99] *See, e.g.,* Poole v. City of Kankakee, 406 Ill. 521, 530, 94 N.E.2d 416, 421 (1950); Court St. Parking Co. v. Boston, 336 Mass. 224, 230, 143 N.E.2d 683, 687 (1957).

[100] *See, e.g.,* People *ex rel.* Adamowski v. Public Bldg. Comm'n, 11 Ill. 2d 125, 144, 142 N.E.2d 67, 77–78 (1957).

[101] *See, e.g.,* People *ex rel.* Adamowski v. Public Bldg. Comm'n, 11 Ill. 2d 125, 142 N.E.2d 67 (1957); Lerch v. Maryland Port Auth., 240 Md. 438, 214 A.2d 761 (1965); Court St. Parking Co. v. Boston, 336 Mass. 224, 143 N.E.2d 683 (1957).

[102] *See, e.g.,* Hanston v. Danville & W. Ry., 208 U.S. 598 (1908); Town of Steilacoom v. Thompson, 69 Wash. 2d 705, 419 P.2d 989 (1966).

[103] *See* cases cited notes 96–100 *supra.*

[104] *See* Note, *State Constitutional Limitations on the Power of Eminent Domain,* 77 HARV. L. REV. 717, 724–25 (1964); Note, *The 'Public Purpose' of Municipal Financing for Industrial Development,* 70 YALE L.J. 789, 796 (1961).

[105] *See, e.g.,* Papadinis v. City of Somerville, 331 Mass. 627, 632, 121 N.E.2d 714, 717 (1954); Denihan Enterprises, Inc. v. O'Dwyer, 302 N.Y. 451, 458, 99 N.E.2d 235, 238 (1951).

[106] *See* Price v. Philadelphia Parking Auth., 422 Pa. 317, 336, 221 A.2d 138, 149 (1966).

[107] *See, e.g.,* Shizas v. Detroit, 333 Mich. 44, 52 N.W.2d 589 (1952); Denihan Enterprises, Inc. v. O'Dwyer, 302 N.Y. 451, 99 N.E.2d 235 (1951); Price v. Philadelphia Parking Auth., 422 Pa. 317, 221 A.2d 138 (1966); Note, *State Constitutional Limitations on Eminent Domain, supra* note 104, at 724–25.

[108] *See* cases cited note 94 *supra.*

[109] *See* Cincinnati v. Vester, 33 F.2d 242 (6th Cir. 1929), *aff'd,* 281 U.S. 439 (1930); *cf.* Salisbury Land & Improvement Co. v. Commonwealth, 215 Mass. 371, 102 N.E. 619 (1913). *See generally* R. CUSHMAN, EXCESS CONDEMNATION (1917) [hereinafter cited as CUSHMAN]; Hodgman, *Air Rights and Public Finance: Public Use in a New Guise,* 42 S. CAL. L. REV. 625 (1969).

[110] *See, e.g.,* CUSHMAN 14–16.

[111] *See* Housing Auth. v. Johnson, 209 Ga. 560, 563, 74 S.E.2d 891, 894 (1953) (to permit eminent domain for urban renewal would "cut the very foundation from under the sacred right to own property").

[112] *See, e.g.,* Wilmington Parking Auth. v. Ranken, 34 Del. Ch. 439, 485, 105 A.2d 614, 640 (Sup. Ct. 1954) (dissenting opinion); Adams v. Housing Auth., 60 So. 2d 663, 668–69 (Fla. 1952); Courtesy Sandwich Shop, Inc. v. Port Auth., 12 N.Y. 2d 379, 398, 190 N.E.2d 402, 411, 240 N.Y.S.2d 1, 13–14 (1963) (Van Voorhis, J., dissenting).

[113] *See, e.g.,* Adams v. Housing Auth., 60 So. 2d 663, 670 (Fla. 1952) (characterizing urban renewal as a "gigantic real estate promotion"). After detailing the enormous losses of public monies suffered by European countries that utilized excess condemnation schemes in the 19th century, Cushman states that "[t]he first conclusion is that the risk of loss is too serious to warrant [the] adoption [of excess condemnation] as a method of municipal finance." CUSHMAN 212.

[114] *See, e.g.,* Pennsylvania Mut. Life Ins. Co. v. Philadelphia, 242 Pa. 47, 57–58, 88 A. 904, 908 (1913).

[115] *See, e.g.,* Wilmington Parking Auth. v. Ranken, 34 Del. Ch. 439, 461, 105 A.2d 614, 627 (Sup. Ct. 1954); *cf.* Haar & Hering, *supra* note 75; Hodgman *supra* note 109.

[116] *See* cases cited note 101 *supra.*

[117] *See, e.g.,* Kaukauna Water Power Co. v. Green Bay & Miss. Canal, 142

U.S. 254, 273 (1891); Wilmington Parking Auth. v. Ranken, 34 Del. Ch. 439, 450, 105 A.2d 614, 620–21 (Sup. Ct. 1954); Courtesy Sandwich Shop, Inc. v. Port Auth., 12 N.Y.2d 379, 390, 190 N.E.2d 402, 406, 240 N.Y.S.2d 1, 7 (1963).

[118] An examination of the opinions reveals that a court's willingness to label the recoupment feature "incidental" to the underlying purpose frequently turns upon its willingness to concede that the latter is indeed a public purpose. *Compare In re* Opinion of the Justices, 332 Mass. 769, 126 N.E.2d 795 (1955), *and* Hogue v. Port of Seattle, 54 Wash. 2d 799, 341 P.2d 171 (1959), *with* Lerch v. Maryland Port Auth., 240 Md. 438, 214 A.2d 761 (1965), *and* Atwood v. Willacy County Navigation Dist., 271 S.W.2d 137 (Tex. 1954), *appeal dismissed*, 350 U.S. 804 (1955). Especially illustrative of the mixing of the two issues is the dissenting opinion of Judge Van Voorhis in Courtesy Sandwich Shop, Inc. v. Port Auth., 12 N.Y.2d 379, 393, 190 N.E.2d 402, 407, 240 N.Y.S.2d 1, 9 (1963).

[119] *See, e.g.*, Ashwander v. TVA, 297 U.S. 288 (1936); Arizona v. California, 283 U.S. 423 (1931); United States v. Chandler-Dunbar Water Power Co., 229 U.S. 53 (1913); Kaukauna Water Power Co. v. Green Bay & Miss. Canal Co., 142 U.S. 254 (1891).

[120] *See* cases cited note 119.

[121] *See, e.g.*, United States v. Chandler-Dunbar Water Power Co., 229 U.S. 53, 72–73 (1913); Kaukauna Water Power Co. v. Green Bay & Miss. Canal Co., 142 U.S. 254, 273 (1891).

[122] *See, e.g.*, Ashwander v. TVA, 297 U.S. 288, 336–37 (1936); Kaukauna Water Power Co. v. Green Bay & Miss. Canal Co., 142 U.S. 254, 273 (1891).

[123] *Cf.* Ashwander v. TVA, 297 U.S. 288 (1936); Arizona v. California, 283 U.S. 423 (1931).

[124] *See, e.g.*, People *ex rel.* Adamowski v. Public Bldg. Comm'n, 11 Ill. 2d 125, 142 N.E.2d 67 (1957) (public buildings); Lerch v. Maryland Port Auth., 240 Md. 438, 214 A.2d 761 (1965) (port facilities); Court St. Parking Co. v. Boston, 336 Mass. 224, 143 N.E.2d 683 (1957) (parking facilities); Bush Terminal Co. v. New York, 282 N.Y. 306, 26 N.E.2d 269 (1940) (railroad terminal facilities).

[125] *See, e.g.*, Wilmington Parking Auth. v. Ranken, 34 Del. Ch. 439, 105 A.2d 614 (Sup. Ct. 1954) (lease of space in municipal parking facility); People *ex rel.* Adamowski v. Chicago R.R. Terminal Auth., 14 Ill. 2d 230, 151 N.E.2d 311 (1958) (lease of space in railroad terminal); *In re* Opinion of the Justices, 330 Mass. 713, 113 N.E.2d 452 (1953) (lease of space for restaurants and filling stations along highways). *But see* Shizas v. Detroit, 333 Mich. 44, 52 N.W.2d 589 (1952) (lease of space in parking facility invalid); Price v. Philadelphia Parking Auth., 422 Pa. 317, 221 A.2d 138 (1966) (same).

[126] *See* cases cited note 125 *supra*; *cf. In re* Slum Clearance, 331 Mich. 714, 50 N.W.2d 340 (1951).

[127] In his dissenting opinion in Courtesy Sandwich Shop, Inc. v. Port Auth., 12 N.Y.2d 379, 393, 190 N.E.2d 402, 407, 240 N.Y.S.2d 1, 9 (1963), Judge Van Voorhis warned that centralization of international trade firms in one governmentally sponsored center threatened to wreak havoc with New York City's private real estate market. However, private enterprise has no constitutionally protected immunity from competition by governmental agencies, *see, e.g.*, Green v. Frazier, 253 U.S. 233, 243 (1920); Poole v. City of Kankakee, 406 Ill. 521, 529, 94 N.E.2d 416, 420 (1950).

[128] *See, e.g.*, Wilmington Parking Auth. v. Ranken, 34 Del. Ch. 439, 448–49, 105 A.2d 614, 620 (Sup. Ct. 1954); Lerch v. Maryland Port Auth., 240 Md. 438, 449, 214 A.2d 761, 767 (1965).

[129] *See, e.g.*, People *ex rel.* Adamowski v. Public Bldg. Comm'n, 11 Ill. 2d 125, 144, 142 N.E.2d 67 (1957); People *ex rel.* Gutknecht v. Chicago, 3 Ill. 2d 539, 545, 121 N.E.2d 791, 795 (1954); Courtesy Sandwich Shop, Inc. v. Port Auth., 12

N.Y.2d 379, 391, 190 N.E.2d 402, 406, 240 N.Y.S.2d 1, 7 (1963).

[130] In United States *ex rel.* TVA v. Welch, 327 U.S. 546 (1946), the Supreme Court upheld the condemnation of a strip of land not directly included within a TVA project area against the claim that the TVA's sole motive in acquiring the land was to reduce project costs. The Court reasoned:

> The cost of public projects is a relevant element . . . . [T]he Government, just as anyone else, is not required to proceed oblivious to elements of costs. . . . And when serious problems are created by its public projects, the Government is not barred from making a common sense adjustment in the interests of all the public.

Id. at 554 (citations omitted). Numerous cases, both before and since, have expressly acknowledged that government may exercise its power of eminent domain in accordance with sound business judgment provided, of course, that a valid public use underlies the governmental program. *See, e.g.*, Old Dominion Land Co. v. United States, 269 U.S. 55, 66 (1925); Simmonds v. United States, 199 F.2d 305, 306 (9th Cir. 1952); Boston v. Talbot, 206 Mass. 82, 90, 91 N.E. 1014, 1016 (1910); *cf.* Brown v. United States, 263 U.S. 78 (1923).

[131] *See, e.g.*, People *ex rel.* Tuohy v. Chicago, 394 Ill. 477, 485, 68 N.E.2d 761, 766 (1946); Papadinis v. City of Somerville, 331 Mass. 627, 632, 121 N.E.2d 714, 717 (1954); Foeller v. Housing Auth., 198 Ore. 205, 241, 256 P.2d 752, 769 (1953). It should be noted, however, that a number of jurisdictions find that the public use requirement is satisfied whenever a government program serves a public purpose. *See, e.g.*, Gohld Realty Co. v. Hartford, 141 Conn. 135, 104 A.2d 365 (1954). These jurisdictions, therefore, would not even need to focus on the city's temporary occupancy of condemned land in considering the validity of an urban renewal program.

[132] *See, e.g.*, *In re* Slum Clearance, 331 Mich. 714, 722, 50 N.W.2d 340, 344 (1951).

[133] To be sure, all local governments sell urban renewal tracts subject to restrictive covenants that ensure that the urban redevelopment plan for the area will be accomplished. *Cf. Project Planning* ch. 2, at 1 (RHA No. 7207.1, 1969), in U.S. DEP'T OF HOUSING & URBAN DEVELOPMENT, URBAN RENEWAL HANDBOOK (1971). Some jurisdictions, in finding that urban renewal serves a public use, point to this factor. *See, e.g.*, Foeller v. Housing Auth., 198 Ore. 205, 256 P.2d 752 (1953). A significant number of other jurisdictions, however, find that a public use is achieved merely by the city's ownership of the urban renewal property during the period of clearance. *See, e.g.*, People *ex rel.* Tuohy v. Chicago, 394 Ill. 477, 485, 68 N.E.2d 761, 766 (1946).

[134] 104 Ohio St. 447, 135 N.E. 635 (1922). *See also* Albright v. Sussex County Lake & Park Comm'n, 71 N.J.L. 303, 57 A. 398 (Ct. Err. & App. 1904) (taking under statute authorizing acquisition of "rights of fishing common to all in freshwater lakes" held invalid).

[135] Pontiac Improvement Co. v. Board of Comm'rs, 104 Ohio St. 447, 456–57, 135 N.E. 635, 637–38 (1922).

[136] *Id.* at 463–64, 135 N.E. at 640. A further ground for the court's invalidation was its conclusion that the condemnation did not promote a public use. *Id.* at 459, 135 N.E. at 638. This conclusion seems clearly inapplicable to preservation restrictions, *see* p. 603 *supra*.

[137] The literature concerning this interest has been extensive in recent years. *See, e.g.*, BRENNEMAN; S. SIEGEL, THE LAW OF OPEN SPACE (1960); A. STRONG, OPEN SPACE FOR URBAN AMERICA (1965); W. WHYTE, SECURING OPEN SPACE FOR URBAN AMERICA: CONSERVATION EASEMENTS (Urban Land Institute, Technical Bull. No. 36, 1959); N. WILLIAMS, LAND ACQUISITION FOR OUTDOOR RECREATION — ANALYSIS OF SELECTED LEGAL PROBLEMS (Outdoor Recreation Resources Review Comm'n Study Report No. 16, 1962) [hereinafter cited as WILLIAMS];

Note, *Techniques for Preserving Open Spaces*, 75 HARV. L. REV. 1622 (1962);
Note, *Preservation of Open Spaces Through Scenic Easements and Greenbelt Zoning*, 12 STAN. L. REV. 638 (1960).

[138] *See, e.g.*, Miller v. Commissioners of Lincoln Park, 278 Ill. 400, 406, 116
N.E. 178, 181 (1917); 3 NICHOLS § 9.2 (3d rev. ed. 1965); WILLIAMS 46.

[139] 3 NICHOLS § 9.2 (3d rev. ed. 1965).

[140] WILLIAMS 48. In Professor Williams' view, a "policy of taking conservation
easements under the characteristic general statute is undesirable, potentially unfair, and legally dangerous." *Id.*

[141] *See, e.g.*, FLA. STAT. ANN. § 266.06 (1962) ("real property or rights or easements therein"); IND. ANN. STAT. § 48-9004(1) (Supp. 1971) ("any real estate").

[142] The discussion of this extremely complex topic is necessarily abbreviated in
this paper. More detailed analyses may be found in BRENNEMAN 20-64; WILLIAMS
37-55; Commonwealth of Massachusetts: Metropolitan Area Planning Council,
Massachusetts Open Space Law: Government's Influence Over Land Use Decisions,
4 Open Space and Recreation Program for Metropolitan Boston, April 1969, at
18-23, 140-56.

[143] *See, e.g.*, WHYTE, *supra* note 137, at 44-46; Comment, *Legal Methods of
Historic Preservation*, 19 BUFFALO L. REV. 611, 621 (1970). The easement category appears to be the one most readily invoked by courts when confronted with
a novel less-than-fee interest. *See, e.g.*, Buck v. City of Winona, 271 Minn. 145,
151, 135 N.W.2d 190, 194 (1965); Piper v. Ekern, 180 Wis. 586, 596, 194 N.W.
159, 163 (1923).

[144] *See* 2 AMERICAN LAW OF PROPERTY §§ 8.5, 9.12, 9.24 (A.J. Casner ed. 1952)
[hereinafter cited as AMERICAN LAW OF PROPERTY]; RESTATEMENT OF PROPERTY
§§ 450(e), 452 (1944). *But see* BRENNEMAN 23-24; WILLIAMS 49-50 & nn. 72-76.

[145] *See* pp. 618-19 *infra.*

[146] *See* 2 AMERICAN LAW OF PROPERTY § 8.2. *But see* WILLIAMS 51.

[147] *See* 2 AMERICAN LAW OF PROPERTY §§ 8.6, 9.8.

[148] *See* WILLIAMS 50.

[149] For accounts of the confused state of the law on this problem, *see, e.g.*,
BRENNEMAN 30; C. CLARK, REAL COVENANTS AND OTHER INTERESTS WHICH RUN
WITH LAND 67-79 (2d ed. 1947); Comment, *Assignability of Easements in Gross*,
32 YALE L.J. 813 (1923).

[150] *See, e.g.*, Young v. Cramer, 38 Cal. App. 2d 64, 100 P.2d 523 (1940); London County Council v. Allen, [1914] 3 K.B. 642. *But see* Neponsit Property Owners' Ass'n v. Emigrant Indus. Sav. Bank, 278 N.Y. 248, 15 N.E.2d 793 (1938). The
British National Trust, which typically acquires real covenants in historic properties, has secured legislation that eliminates the common law requirement that
it own nearby land as a condition to its right to enforce the benefit of the covenants. *See* National Trust Act, 1 Edw. 8 & 1 Geo. 6, c. lvii, § 8 (1937).

[151] *See, e.g.*, Hall v. Risley, 188 Ore. 69, 213 P.2d 818 (1950); BRENNEMAN
54. *But see* Nicholson v. 300 Broadway Realty Corp., 7 N.Y.2d 240, 164 N.E.2d
832, 196 N.Y.S.2d 945 (1959); CLARK, *supra* note 149, at 116-21.

[152] *See, e.g.*, Miller v. Clary, 210 N.Y. 127, 103 N.E. 1114 (1913); BRENNEMAN
57; Lloyd, *Enforcement of Affirmative Agreements Respecting the Use of Land,*
14 VA. L. REV. 419 (1928).

[153] *See* pp. 618-19 *infra.*

[154] BRENNEMAN 50-51, 55.

[155] *See, e.g.*, Trustees of Columbia College v. Lynch, 70 N.Y. 440 (1877); 2
AMERICAN LAW OF PROPERTY § 9.26; BRENNEMAN 56.

[156] BRENNEMAN 55. Real covenants, on the other hand, may only be enforced
in an action at law for damages. *Id.*

[157] *See* BRENNEMAN 57; Lloyd, *supra* note 152.

[158] *See* Mass. Open Space Law, *supra* note 142, at 148–49.

[159] *Id.* at 148.

[160] *See* 2 AMERICAN LAW OF PROPERTY § 9.32; BRENNEMAN 58. *But see* Van Sant v. Rose, 260 Ill. 401, 103 N.E. 194 (1913); Pratte v. Balatsos, 99 N.H. 430, 113 A.2d 492 (1955).

[161] *See* BRENNEMAN 59.

[162] *See, e.g.,* State *ex rel.* Ervin v. Jacksonville Expressway Auth., 139 So. 2d 135, 138 (Fla. 1962); Cornwell v. Central Ky. Natural Gas Co., 249 S.W.2d 531, 533 (Ky. Ct. App. 1952).

[163] 163 Mass. 319, 321, 39 N.E. 1032, 1032 (1895).

[164] *See, e.g.,* cases cited note 143 *supra*; Burger v. St. Paul, 241 Minn. 285, 64 N.W. 2d 73 (1954). *Burger* is of special interest to this article because it construes a statute that parallels the transfer proposal in enabling municipalities to zone by acquiring the development potential of parcels within "designated residential districts" in order to prevent them from being utilized for other than low-density, residential uses. *See* MINN. STAT. ANN. §§ 462.12–.14 (1963). In *Burger*, the court variously labeled the interest that the statute empowered communities to condemn an "easement," a "negative easement," a "reciprocal negative easement," a "restrictive covenant," and, for good measure, a "negative equitable easement." Burger v. St. Paul, *supra* at 293, 294, 297, 299, 64 N.W.2d at 78, 79, 80, 81. It did not discuss whether the common law formalities applicable to easements and real covenants were superseded by the statute notwithstanding the obvious differences between the interest acquired and the common law interests. Other cases construing the statute include State *ex rel.* Madsen v. Houghton, 182 Minn. 77, 233 N.W. 831 (1930); Summers v. Midland Co., 167 Minn. 453, 209 N.W. 323 (1926); State *ex rel.* Twin City Bldg. & Inv. Co. v. Houghton, 144 Minn. 1, 176 N.W. 159 (1920). Approving a similar zoning scheme, the Missouri Supreme Court labeled the interest acquired a "negative restriction." Kansas City v. Kindle, 446 S.W.2d 807, 813–14 (Mo. 1969). That court, too, ignored the common law problems associated with its characterization of the interest.

[165] *See, e.g.,* CAL. GOV'T CODE §§ 6950–54 (West 1966); MASS. ANN. LAWS ch. 92, § 79 (1969); WIS. STAT. ANN. § 23.30 (Supp. 1971).

[166] 31 Wis. 2d 256, 142 N.W.2d 793 (1966).

[167] *See* CONN. GEN. STAT. REV. P.A. No. 173, § 2 [Jan. 1971] Conn. Legis. Service No. 2 (May 16, 1971); ILL. REV. STAT. ch. 24, § 11–24.2–1A(2) (1971); MASS. GEN. LAWS ANN. ch. 184, § 32 (Supp. 1970).

In addition to curing the ambiguities of the common law in relation to preservation restrictions, the Massachusetts statute also provides for the recordation of these interests on a public tract index and suspends the operation of Massachusetts' marketable title and obsolete-restrictions legislation for any interest entered upon the index. *See* MASS. GEN. LAWS ANN. ch. 184, §§ 3, 33 (Supp. 1970).

[168] *See, e.g.,* MD. ANN. CODE art. 21, § 8 (1957); VA. CODE ANN. § 21.12 (Supp. 1971).

[169] For appraisal techniques used with respect to the acquisition of less-than-fee interests generally, *see, e.g.,* 4 NICHOLS § 12.4 (3d rev. ed. 1971); South v. Texas E. Transmission Co., 332 S.W.2d 442 (Tex. Civ. App. 1960). A useful analysis of the valuation techniques used in the acquisition of scenic easements along highways is found in DEPARTMENT OF TRANSPORTATION OF WISCONSIN, A MARKET STUDY OF PROPERTIES COVERED BY SCENIC EASEMENTS ALONG THE GREAT RIVER ROAD IN VERNON AND PIERCE COUNTIES (Special Report No. 5, 1967). Valuation of preservation restrictions is discussed in Chicago Report 11–15.

[170] Chicago Report 11.

[171] Instruments reviewed in compiling the outline in the text are those ac-

tually being used by the following organizations and institutions: Maryland Historic Trust; Historic Annapolis, Inc.; Historic Savannah Foundation; Ipswich (Mass.) Historic Trust; Cambridge (Mass.) Historic Trust; and the United States Dept. of the Interior. Useful guidelines and examples for use in drafting conservation and, derivatively, preservation restrictions may be found in BRENNE-MAN apps. II, IV; WHYTE, *supra* note 137, at 44–46, apps. A–H *passim*; WILLIAMS 53–55; Mass. Open Space Law, *supra* note 142, at app. 8.

[172] The Department of Housing and Urban Development has awarded a demonstration grant to the National Trust for Historic Preservation to examine the general applicability of the transfer proposal in the United States. A major concern of this broader study, which is being directed by the author of this article, is the problem of duration discussed in the text.

[173] Numerous illustrations of this possibility are recounted in *Dollars and Sense: Preservation Economics*, HIST. PRESERVATION, Apr.–June 1971, at 15. *See also* N.Y. Times, Aug. 12, 1971 at 1, col. 1, for an account of the plans to rent the Villard Houses, designated New York landmarks, to a "conservative commercial firm that will use and maintain them in a style befitting a landmark."

[174] ADVISORY COMMITTEE ON ZONING, DEP'T OF COMMERCE, A STANDARD STATE ZONING ENABLING ACT UNDER WHICH MUNICIPALITIES MAY ADOPT ZONING REGULATIONS § 2 (rev. ed. 1926).

[175] U.S. CONST. amend. XIV, § 1.

[176] *See* p. 601 *supra.*

[177] While not expressly authorizing municipalities to engage in such programs, the following state preservation enabling acts contain grants of power that may be of sufficient breadth to warrant such a construction. CAL. GOV'T CODE § 37361 (West 1968); N.M. STAT. ANN. § 14–21–4 (1968). A less affirmative but possibly useful basis for implementing the proposal might be found in the language of many state preservation enabling acts authorizing local preservation commissions to devise an "economically feasible plan" to safeguard threatened landmarks in private ownership. *See, e.g.,* MD. ANN. CODE art. 66B, § 8.09 (Interim Supp. 1970); MICH. COMP. LAWS ANN. § 399.205(4) (Supp. 1971).

[178] The chief draftsman of the Standard State Zoning Enabling Act has written that the purpose of the uniformity requirement is "to make it understood that all property situated alike shall be treated alike." E. BASSETT, ZONING 50 (1940). *See, e.g.,* Haar, *"In Accordance with a Comprehensive Plan,"* 68 HARV. L. REV. 1154, 1172 (1955). Significantly, the uniformity provision has most frequently been invoked in the spot-zoning context — where a small tract is zoned differently from its surrounding area. *See, e.g.,* Bartram v. Zoning Comm'n, 136 Conn. 89, 68 A.2d 308 (1949); Cassel v. Mayor & City Council, 195 Md. 348, 73 A.2d 486 (1950). Spot zoning, however, raises the statutory issue of conformity with a "comprehensive plan" and the constitutional issue of equal protection. *See* Haar, *supra.* It does not put in issue the statutory requirement of uniformity, which, by the terms of the zoning enabling act, relates only to the manner in which regulations are applied within the *same* zoning district.

[179] At least four factors account for the current disrepute, among land use scholars and local governments, of the premise that the individual lot should serve as the unit of development control. First, it hampers sound planning on a community-wide basis and promotes sterile design on individual sites. Second, it assumes that development still occurs on a lot-by-lot basis rather than on large landholdings, as in urban renewal areas and on the metropolitan fringe. Third, it fails to take account of the special needs and functions of a community's unique areas and to protect these areas from the destructive impact of private market decisions. Finally, it prevents communities from enhancing their amenity levels generally by means of incentive zoning programs such as those described in this

article. *See, e.g.,* E. LOVELACE & W. WEISMANTEL, DENSITY ZONING: ORGANIC ZONING: ORGANIC ZONING FOR PLANNED RESIDENTIAL DEVELOPMENT (Urban Land Institute, Technical Bull. No. 42, 1961); NEW ZONING *passim*; Goldston & Scheuer, *Zoning of Planned Residential Developments,* 73 HARV. L. REV. 241 (1959); *Symposium, Planned Unit Development,* 114 U. PA. L. REV. 1 (1965).

[180] Among these developments are expanded use of the variance and special exception, and innovations such as floating zones, cluster zones, planned unit developments, overlay districts, and special development districts. Accounts of the evolution of these techniques may be found in authorities cited note 179 *supra.*

[181] *See* authorities cited note 179 *supra.*

[182] For discussions of special development districts *see, e.g.,* Fonoroff, *Special Districts: A Departure from the Concept of Uniform Controls,* in NEW ZONING 82; Huxtable, *A Solid Dross City?,* N.Y. Times, Mar. 14, 1971, § 2, at 16, col. 5; Huxtable, *supra* note 13. Examples of special development districts include the New York Special Theater District, *see* note 10 *supra;* Fifth Avenue Retail District, *see* note 12 *supra;* and the Special Greenwich Street Development District, *see* note 13 *supra.*

[183] *See, e.g.,* Orinda Homeowners Comm. v. Board of Supervisors, 11 Cal. App. 3d 768, 90 Cal. Rptr. 88 (1970); Chrinko v. South Brunswick Tp. Planning Bd., 77 N.J. Super., 594, 187 A.2d 221 (L. Div. 1963), Cheney v. Village 2 at New Hope, Inc., 429 Pa. 626, 241 A.2d 81 (1968); *cf.* Millbrae Ass'n for Residential Survival v. City of Millbrae, 262 Cal. App. 2d 222, 242–43, 69 Cal. Rptr. 251, 265–66 (1968) (dictum).

The rock on which some density zoning ordinances have foundered has not been the uniformity objection but the challenge of improper delegation of legislative power. *See, e.g.,* Millbrae Ass'n for Residential Survival v. City of Millbrae, *supra;* Hiscox v. Levine, 31 Misc. 2d 151, 216 N.Y.S.2d 801 (Sup. Ct. 1961). *See generally* Krasnowiecki, *Planned Unit Development: A Challenge to Established Legal Theory and Practice of Land Use Control,* 114 U. PA. L. REV. 47 (1965); Mandelker, *Delegation of Power and Function in Zoning Administration,* 1963 WASH. L.Q. 60 (1963). Although the decisions are hardly consistent, *compare* Cheney v. Village 2 at New Hope, Inc., *supra, with* Hiscox v. Levine, *supra,* some courts have invalidated these measures on the ground that the regulation of bulk and area requirements on a district-wide basis is a legislative function that cannot be delegated to a planning commission, an administrative agency. *See, e.g.,* Millbrae Ass'n for Residential Survival v. City of Millbrae, *supra.*

Since the Chicago Plan vests approval for transfers in the local legislative body, rather than in the planning commission, it will be immune from delegation problems that have afflicted other density transfer measures.

[184] *See* URBAN LAND INSTITUTE, NEW APPROACHES TO RESIDENTIAL LAND DEVELOPMENT (Tech. Bull. No. 40, 1961); W. WHYTE, CLUSTER DEVELOPMENT (1964). Representative state and local cluster provisions are collected in W. WHYTE, *supra,* at apps. B & C.

[185] *See, e.g.,* Goldston & Scheuer, *supra* note 179, at 255–62 (1959); *Symposium, supra* note 179.

[186] *See, e.g.,* Orinda Homeowners Comm. v. Board of Supervisors, 11 Cal. App. 3d 768, 90 Cal. Rptr. 88 (1970); Chrinko v. South Brunswick Tp. Planning Bd., 77 N.J. Super. 594, 187 A.2d 221 (L. Div. 1963); Cheney v. Village 2 at New Hope, Inc., 429 Pa. 626, 241 A.2d 81 (1968).

[187] 77 N.J. Super. 594, 187 A.2d 221 (L. Div. 1963).

[188] *Id.* at 601, 187 A.2d at 225.

[189] *See, e.g.,* Greenpoint Sav. Bank v. Board of Zoning Appeals, 281 N.Y. 534, 540, 24 N.E.2d 319, 322 (1939), *appeal dismissed,* 309 U.S. 633 (1940); Mandis v. Gorski, 24 App. Div. 2d 181, 186, 265 N.Y.S.2d 210, 216 (1965).

[190] 11 Cal. App. 3d 768, 90 Cal. Rptr. 88 (1970).

[191] *Id.* at 773, 90 Cal. Rptr. at 90–91.

[192] *See, e.g., id.* (187 acres); Cheney v. Village 2 at New Hope, Inc., 429 Pa. 626, 241 A.2d 81 (1968) ("a large tract of land").

[193] *See, e.g.,* McGowan v. Maryland, 366 U.S. 420 (1961); Goesaert v. Cleary, 336 U.S. 106 (1949). More rigorous review has been applied when "fundamental interests" or "suspect classifications" are involved. *See Developments in the Law — Equal Protection,* 82 HARV. L. REV. 1065, 1087–1132 (1969). However, strict review does not appear to apply to wealth classifications by themselves. *See* p. 627 *infra.*

[194] Whether the uniformity provision is even applicable to bulk or area regulations is dubious. On its face, it appears to deal only with use restrictions. *See* p. 620 *supra. But see* IND. ANN. STAT. § 53–755(1) (1964):

> Regulations as to *height, area, bulk* and use of buildings and as to the area of *yards, courts* and *open spaces* shall be uniform for each class of buildings throughout each district. (Emphasis added.)

At least one court has held the uniformity requirement inapplicable to bulk restrictions. *See* Scrutton v. County of Sacramento, 275 Cal. App. 2d 412, 418, 79 Cal. Rptr. 872, 877 (1969). Numerous others have implied this result. *See, e.g.,* Rockhill v. Township of Chesterfield, 23 N.J. 117, 126, 128 A.2d 473, 478 (1957); Schmidt v. Board, 9 N.J. 405, 417, 88 A.2d 607, 612–13 (1952); Walker v. Elkin, 254 N.C. 85, 118 S.E.2d 1 (1961). These decisions appear to recognize that use zoning has a more immediate impact upon community welfare than bulk or area zoning. Hence, they do not insist that the latter secure mathematical uniformity, but seem willing to approve the flexible application of bulk or area regulations even in traditional bulk zones.

[195] As lot size decreases, higher construction becomes unprofitable because a substantial portion of a building's interior space must be given over to its elevator core and mechanical systems.

[196] *See* Chicago Report 16–19.

[197] *Cf.* Heyman, *Innovative Land Regulation and Comprehensive Planning,* in NEW ZONING 23.

[198] *See, e.g.,* Millbrae Ass'n for Residential Survival v. City of Millbrae, 262 Cal. App. 2d 222, 69 Cal. Rptr. 251 (1968); Hiscox v. Levine, 31 Misc. 2d 151, 216 N.Y.S.2d 801 (Sup. Ct. 1961).

[199] *See, e.g.,* James v. Valtierra, 402 U.S. 137 (1971); Dandridge v. Williams, 397 U.S. 471 (1970). *See* Coons, Clune & Sugarman, *Educational Opportunity: A Workable Constitutional Test for State Financial Structures,* 57 CALIF. L. REV. 305, 349 (1969).

An equal protection challenge to the Chicago Plan should be distinguished from equal protection challenges to government zoning practices that have the effect of pricing housing in a given community out of the reach of low-income groups. This practice, referred to as "exclusionary zoning," has aroused the increasing concern of commentators, *see, e.g.,* Note, *Exclusionary Zoning and Equal Protection,* 84 HARV. L. REV. 1645 (1971). Unlike exclusionary zoning, the Chicago Plan appears to have no differential impact on the housing of low-income groups.

[200] *See, e.g.,* ADVISORY COMMITTEE ON ZONING, DEP'T OF COMMERCE, *supra* note 174, § 7; CAL. GOV'T CODE § 65906 (West 1966).

[201] *See, e.g.,* R. BABCOCK, THE ZONING GAME 7 (1966); S. TOLL, ZONED AMERICAN 184 (1969); Dukeminier & Stapleton, *The Zoning Board of Adjustment: A Case Study in Misrule,* 50 KY. L.J. 273 (1962).

[202] Dissent from Resolution CP–21166 of the New York City Planning Commission to the Board of Estimate, May 13, 1970.

[203] *See, e.g.,* Village of Euclid v. Ambler Realty Co., 272 U.S. 365, 395 (1926)

(zoning ordinances are valid unless shown to be "clearly arbitrary and unreasonable"). One commentator has summarized the current content of the due process challenge to zoning regulations as follows:

> [W]here a zoning ordinance is challenged on the ground that it takes property without due process of law, [a court] will consider: (1) the impact of the restriction upon the land of the plaintiff (How serious is the deprivation attributable to the ordinance?); (2) the objective of the restriction (Is it intended to serve the public health, safety, morals, or the general welfare?); and (3) the reasonableness of the restriction (Do the means selected have a rational tendency to achieve the objective?).

Anderson, *A Comment on the Fine Line Between "Regulation" and "Taking,"* in NEW ZONING 66, 70. The due process challenge discussed in text relates primarily to the last consideration enumerated by Anderson.

[204] *See* authorities cited note 43 *supra.*

[205] Accounts of this process may be found in, *e.g.,* G. FORD, BUILDING HEIGHT, BULK AND FORM (Harvard City Planning Studies II, 1931); S. TOLL, *supra* note 201, at 161–66; Randall, *The Question of Size: A Re-approach to the Study of Zoning,* 54 ARCH. F. 117 (1931).

For excellent analyses of the process by which the City of San Francisco arrived at the bulk levels of its present zoning ordinance, see Ruth, *supra* note 69; Svirsky, *supra* note 6.

[206] *See* authorities cited notes 43 & 205 *supra.*

[207] Members of the real estate industry have expressed the view that contemporary zoning impairs downtown development by overemphasizing requirements of light, air, and open space in central areas. *See, e.g.,* OFFICES 280–81; *Air Rights* 497.

[208] *See* S. TOLL, *supra* note 201, *passim.*

[209] Objecting to the "Manhattanization" of their skyline resulting from increased bulk levels adopted in 1961, an organization of San Franciscans succeeded in having submitted to referendum a proposition that would have required specific voter approval of the construction of any building over six stories or 72 feet. The proposition was defeated. N.Y. Times, Nov. 4, 1971, at 36, col. 1.

[210] In an exhaustive examination of the problem of the optimum size of downtown structures, one commentator concluded:

> Conclusive quantitative proof of the desirability of these things [sunlight, air, etc.] is almost impossible, as is also the setting up of any unqualified standard for safety and well-being below which we should not go. The general indications would lead to the belief that, while sunlight, air, outlook, privacy, the avoidance of a sense of "shut-in-ness" and of actual congestion are highly desirable, we are not able to set up a minimum which, let us say, if curtailed by 10 per cent would spell disaster or if augmented by 10 per cent would spell relative happiness and prosperity.

Randall, *supra* note 205, at 117; *see* S. TOLL, *supra* note 201, at 137.

[211] Professor Mandelker has noted that "conventional lot regulations are utilized because they simplify the problems of control." Mandelker, *Reflections on the American System of Planning Controls: A Response to Professor Krasnowiecki,* 114 U. PA. L. REV. 98, 101 (1965).

[212] One interesting attempt at expressing density for individual parcels on the basis of a sliding scale of integers is the Land Use Intensity system described in Hanke, *Planned Unit Development and Land Use Intensity,* 114 U. PA. L. REV. 15, 22–30 (1965).

[213] *See* notes 71 & 72 *supra.*

[214] *See* p. 590 & note 55 *supra.*

[215] *See* cases cited note 183 *supra.*

[216] *See, e.g.,* West Coast Hotel v. Parrish, 300 U.S. 379 (1937); Nebbia v. New York, 291 U.S. 502 (1934).

[217] *See* Anderson, *supra* note 203, at 75; *cf.* D. HAGMAN, URBAN PLANNING AND LAND DEVELOPMENT CONTROL LAW 75–76 (1971); Heyman, *supra* note 197, at 40, 51–52.

[218] The United States Supreme Court upheld zoning as a constitutional exercise of the police power that year in Village of Euclid v. Ambler Realty Co., 272 U.S. 365 (1926). Prior to this decision, substantial conflict existed among the state courts concerning the constitutionality of zoning. *See* Cribbet, *Changing Concepts in the Law of Land Use*, 50 IOWA L. REV. 245, 257 (1967).

[219] *See, e.g.*, Orinda Homeowners Comm. v. Board of Supervisors, 11 Cal. App. 3d 768, 90 Cal. Rptr. 88 (Ct. App. 1970) (PUD zoning); Beall v. Montgomery County Council, 240 Md. 77, 212 A.2d 751 (1965) (floating zoning); Bucholz v. Omaha, 174 Neb. 862, 120 N.W.2d 270 (1963) (conditional zoning); Chrinko v. South Brunswick Tp. Planning Bd., 77 N.J. Super. 594, 187 A.2d 221 (L. Div. 1963) (cluster zoning).

[220] On the basis of an exhaustive review of bulk zoning decisions, one commentator has concluded that "[s]o far, courts have shown a healthy respect for the figures arrived at after careful research and planning." Note, *supra* note 43, at 512.

[221] The importance of thorough, well-documented planning studies in withstanding due process as well as equal protection and spot-zoning challenges to innovative measures has been stressed in a comprehensive analysis of incentive zoning measures prepared by Professor Heyman. *See* Heyman, *supra* note 197, *passim*. The recurring thesis of the Heyman study provides additional support for the position that the Chicago Plan will be upheld by the courts. As stated by Heyman:

> [The] courts should and will approve a flexible regulatory device where it is shown that its use sensibly relates to public objectives identified in advance in a planning process and is justified by a detailed explanation showing the actual relationship between the objective and the action.

Id. at 40.

From An Economic Perspective

Who Pays for Transfer
of Development Rights?

JARED B. SHLAES
Senior Vice President
Arthur Rubloff and Co.

The right to develop land as the landowner might wish
is no longer implicit in his ownership, if indeed it ever was.
Zoning and other external controls demonstrate the public
interest in development rights, which we still tend to think
of as private and property-specific. The growing need for
better public control over land use has forced a rethinking
of traditional views about the nature of real property,
which in turn has led us to perceive that development
rights are not only quasi-public, but also mobile in nature:
that they need not remain fixed to the soil, like trees, but
can be moved like seeds or saplings to some more
propitious location. Properly harnessed, this mobility
becomes a potent energy source for effective land-use
control in growing areas.

The transfer of development rights, or TDR as it has
come to be known, is not wholly new. Liberating but not
revolutionary, it has been put to work by the British for
more than 25 years. New York City has made use of it to
encourage the preservation of landmarks and open spaces
by allowing their owners to transfer density to adjacent
sites. But it is only since the 1971 publication of the
"Chicago Plan," which broke away from the adjacency
rule to allow transfers of development rights anywhere
within a designated zone and which provided a funding
mechanism, that TDR began to come of age in America. It
is now being widely discussed as a vehicle for the
preservation of landmarks, historic districts, and open
space and as a supplement to, and perhaps replacement
for, conventional zoning.

The time is thus ripe for us to examine the costs of
TDR and to ascertain who, if anyone, must pay them. We
can begin by attempting to define TDR operationally and
to describe its workings.

TDR is a system designed to permit the orderly
reallocation of density within a given district in a manner
which meets legitimate planning objectives without
placing unfair burdens on the property owner. It grows

out of existing zoning, which sets limits on the size and configuration of buildings allowed on any given property within a designated zone. Quite typically, these limits exceed those which would be required by existing older buildings and by open space uses. The difference between the density which would be allowed under existing zoning and that which actually exists on any given parcel of land, expressed in suitable units such as square feet of building area, constitutes the unused "development rights" of the property. It is these "development rights" which become the subject of the transfer.

The concept requires that these rights be made transferable on a limited basis within a designated transfer zone or zones, subject to suitable planning controls. Transfers occur either privately or through the intermediary of a public agency charged with this function and designated as a TDR trustee or bank. The preservation of open space or of landmark buildings or districts which are not built up to their zoning potential is then accomplished by taking away, either by negotiation or by an eminent domain process, existing rights to develop further those properties which are to be preserved.

Owners of such properties are compensated either by allowing them to transfer, in the private market, development rights equivalent in money to the economic loss sustained, or by outright purchase of the rights through the TDR agency. This agency pays for such purchases by reselling the rights as needed, subject to market demand and to local planning concerns. The property preserved is in effect encumbered with a preservation or open space easement which imposes appropriate constraints upon the owner and permits him to seek a corresponding assessment reduction. Overconcentration of density on the transferee site is prevented through planning controls, which may include a percentage limitation on permissible density increases.

The process is initiated through the passage of appropriate enabling legislation and the establishment of a suitable TDR agency, which can be funded in the beginning by donations of publicly or privately held development rights. Money from the sale of these rights can be used for acquisitions and administration.

Like the Indian rope trick, TDR can be self-supporting. As long as an adequate market exists for the sale of the rights at prices greater than their cost, the process funds itself. Market adequacy will vary among different communities as well as over time and will depend upon the size and character of the transfer zone, the rigidity of its zoning, and the demand for new development within its boundaries. Where these factors are favorable, as they tend to be in landmark and open space preservation, TDR

can cover administrative as well as preservation costs. In
*Development Rights Transfer: A Solution to Chicago's
Landmarks Dilemma* (Chicago Chapter Foundation of the
American Institute of Architects/National Trust for
Historic Preservation, 1971), John Costonis and I showed
that in the limited but difficult case of Chicago's landmark
office buildings TDR could be not only self-sustaining but
profitable. Careful designation of transfer zone boundaries
will insure an adequate market at sufficient prices in most
other cases where enough growth exists to make TDR
worth considering.

No loss of real estate tax revenue need result from TDR.
Any loss in assessed value occasioned by the separation of
development rights from the transferor site will be made
up, and perhaps more than made up, by new construction
elsewhere. Meanwhile the rights can be taxed as real
property while in transit.

It thus appears that TDR can be cost free in terms of its
impact on municipal finances and may indeed prove to be a
new source of funds for those jurisdictions which can make
use of it.

If the municipality doesn't pay the flute player, who
does? It has been variously argued in the literature and
elsewhere that the cost of TDR is borne by: the transferor
property owner, who loses some of his property rights
without compensation; the transferee property developer,
who must pay for the rights in addition to what he pays for
the property itself; the tenant or purchaser of the space
created by the transferee site; the transfer district, which
must bear the aesthetic cost of development more dense
than would otherwise be possible; and the general public,
which somehow must support the entire process. Let us
examine these possibilities one at a time.

In principle, TDR fully compensates the owner of the
transferor site for whatever economic rights he may lose as
a result of landmark or open space designation. It gives
him the option of either development rights, for his own
use or sale, equivalent to the rights which he loses as a
result of such designation, or cash in an equivalent
amount out of the TDR bank. This amount, which would
constitute just compensation in the eminent domain sense,
is fixed either by negotiation or by the courts pursuant to
an eminent domain proceeding. To the extent that the
owner loses all or part of his right to alter or demolish his
building, to develop his land, to mortgage or sell his
property, to drill for oil beneath its foundations, or to do
any of the other things implicit in his ownership, he is
compensated for that loss by the process. He may
complain, as do owners of condemned property elsewhere,
that he is being inconvenienced in ways left uncompen-

sated by the constitutional doctrine of just compensation; but he is left whole in economic terms. Thus it is not he who must pay the TDR piper, except perhaps in some sense unrelated to economics.

The developer of the transferee site must buy development rights from the bank, the transferor site owner, or an intermediary, if he wishes to develop the transferee site beyond the density permitted by its existing zoning. However, he is under no compulsion to buy these rights and is free to develop the transferee site to its zoning limits without any costs other than those associated with the purchase and development of a comparable property lying inside or outside the district. He will ordinarily purchase development rights only if it is cheaper for him than purchasing additional land. TDR is thus without cost to him.

By similar reasoning, the tenant or purchaser of the space created on the transferee site as a result of the transfer will pay no more for such space than he would pay for equivalent space either inside or outside the district. Whether the space is permitted by virtue of development rights or of additional land purchases is immaterial to him. He will not, and does not, pay the cost of TDR.

Neighbors will unquestionably grumble that TDR permits larger structures within their community than would otherwise be possible without a zoning change. Their complaints, however, are of questionable validity, since in the typical urban situation entire districts are massively overzoned to begin with. Few areas in our major cities are built up to anything approaching the densities permitted by zoning, nor could they be developed to such densities without choking their streets and their citizens. Thus the TDR process, which permits a slight overreach of permissible densities at specific locations under the supervision of planning authorities, in effect merely redistributes density within the district and can be discontinued, if desired, long before the ultimate permissible densities are approached. The greater precision offered to the planning authorities by TDR permits much more sophisticated development control than is made possible by zoning alone. The residents of the district presumably will benefit from this increased precision while retaining their right to oppose any specific transfer thought to be adverse.

It is difficult to find a sense in which the general public pays for TDR. Tax revenues are in no way diminished; landmarks and open spaces are preserved; and the community can benefit from improved planning. If properly administered, the process can be self-sustaining and even profitable in fiscal terms. Some will take the view that TDR impairs zoning and that this impairment constitutes a social cost. However, it remains to be shown that whatever benefits are conferred by zoning will be diminished in any way by TDR, since it supplements zoning as a planning tool and increases its flexibility and precision. These benefits should also offset social costs attached to the frictions, slippages, and mistakes which are bound to occur when TDR is first introduced.

While we have seen that, on the whole, developers, purchasers, tenants, and the public within the transfer district pay no share of TDR costs, there remains the possibility that the owners of properties located near transferor and transferee sites must bear some uncompensated burden. This possibility is real and merits further investigation.

The owner of property adjacent to the landmark or open space to be preserved may fail to realize the gains anticipated from new development on the transferor site. These gains may include additional business volume generated in his retail property or an increase in property value arising out of the stimulus provided by new construction nearby. However, since the development of the transferor site is ordinarily beyond the control of adjacent property owners and the benefits conferred thereby can hardly be treated as money in the bank by them, such losses are at best highly speculative. Against them must be weighed the advantages conferred by permanent adjacent open space or landmark amenities, which, in addition to pleasure, can sometimes confer business and investment benefits.

Properties adjoining the transferee site can conceivably be affected in several ways. The property owner may find that his neighbor has built a larger structure than would otherwise be possible on a nearby site, thereby reducing access to light, air, and view. Whether or not such damages are in reality greater than those which would have been produced by a building held within zoning limits may be a matter for expert opinion. However, any damages can be held to a minimum if reasonable planning controls govern the transfer. Certainly the owner of affected adjacent property should have a say in the review process. Should his arguments against the transfer not prevail, he may console himself with the hope that the additional new construction thus permitted will add to the value of his property or business.

Apart from problems which might be created by the excessive size of structures at the transferee site, the transfer process may have an effect on the speculative value of large and small property holdings within the transferee zone. This grows out of the fact that large land holdings in many areas, particularly downtown areas, tend to be worth more per square foot than small ones as a result of zoning bonuses and economies of scale. Thus, the tendency in such areas is for properties to be aggregated so that they can attain maximum value. Owners of small properties can look forward to seeing their holdings acquired by a land assembler willing to pay a high price, while the land assembler in turn can hope to buy out his smaller neighbors at discount prices.

TDR disturbs these expectations on both sides by permitting the land assembler to acquire development rights without equivalent land purchases and by permitting the landowners of at least some small properties to build with TDR structures which would have been impractical without them. The bargaining position of the small property owner is thus weakened vis-a-vis an adjacent land assembler, who now can look elsewhere for what he needs. However, by the same token, the small property owner has greater freedom to develop his property than he had before TDR. The owner of the larger holding may be said to have lost some of the advantage inherent in size, but at the same time he is less vulnerable to the extortions of his smaller neighbors than he would be without TDR.

Any losses sustained thus appear to be either speculative or offset by corresponding gains. While exceptions will occur, it seems safe to say that as a general rule it is not the owner of adjacent property who pays the cost of TDR. Similar arguments apply to the tenant or occupant.

The term "land development" is often a cover for the activities of individuals who purchase property, arrange for its rezoning to a higher density, and then sell or develop it to get the benefit of the resulting increase in property value. This activity would become significantly less popular under TDR, and its practitioners would suffer, as would those officials fortunate enough to have had a piece of the action. Against these losses, which many citizens would consider quite tolerable, there stands the view that TDR, as a substitute for more informal mechanisms of zoning adjustment, offers clear advantages to the public.

It has been suggested that transfer areas be downzoned in order to insure a market for development rights. Such a policy might result in property value losses which could be indirectly brought about by TDR, thus converting the rope trick into an effective noose. It would therefore seem unfair and unwise to engage in a general downzoning for TDR reasons alone. However, if such downzoning should occur, those property owners caught in the noose might properly blame TDR for their losses. It would seem preferable to avoid this problem by avoiding such downzoning.

There is no escaping, however, the need for reasonably rigid enforcement of zoning limits if TDR is to function at all smoothly. No one will purchase development rights if he can obtain an equivalent zoning adjustment without great cost or difficulty. In this sense all property owners within the transfer district may be said to bear whatever costs are induced by increases in the rigidity of zoning administration necessitated by TDR. They may also be said to reap the benefits of such rigidity, which include relative freedom from the abuses of administrative discretion which have characterized zoning in many communities.

If what we have said up to this point is correct, it seems clear that, once the zoning frame of reference is established, no one pays for TDR, with the possible exception of the zoning operator. For those who are familiar with the economic writings of Lord Keynes or with Alexander Hamilton's vision of the national debt as a basis for economic growth, this discovery should prove plausible as well as heartening. Indeed, like the Indian who first climbed a rope in the presence of passersby and was showered with coins for his pains, we may find that TDR confers blessings which far outweigh the cost of the rope. If the rope is free, as it seems to be, so much the better.

From A Practical Planning Perspective

Transferable Development Rights: An Idea Whose Time Has Come

AUDREY MOORE
Supervisor, Annandale District
Fairfax County, Virginia

THE ADVANTAGES
OF TRANSFERABLE DEVELOPMENT RIGHTS

A. Encouragement of Controlled and Timed Development.

The compensatory features of this system, combined with its beneficial effect on taxation equity, should allow for judicial support of community control for phased and timed staging of development. Moreover, it seems logical that without restraint, more orderly growth would occur naturally. Leapfrogging far out into the countryside, beyond community-provided urban or suburban services, would no longer be of financial advantage to the developer.

B. Separation of Exclusionary Argument from Allowable Density.

Under zoning, communities have been accused of deliberately writing zoning ordinances that are socio-economically exclusionary. In some cases, this has been the unstated purpose of large-lot zoning; however, in other instances, sincere motivation to protect the public from congestion, to provide for phased development, or to provide a beneficial environment has been the guiding force.

The dilemma of trying to decide which is the greater need: housing at a reasonable cost or environmental protection, has led, and will lead, to bitterness and strife among people who otherwise would be in agreement. The development industry has not failed to note or take advantage of this dilemma.

This predicament would be eliminated under the proposed TDR system. The exclusion argument would be limited to economics where it belongs. Furthermore, subsidies, at no cost to the public, would be available to reduce the cost of land for low-cost housing, through rights distribution to land owned by the government.

The poor, under TDR, would benefit far more than the rich. Fundamental to this approach is the philosophy that what is basic and essential to human life will be available to all people.

C. Compensatory System at No Cost to the Public.

Needs no explanation.

D. More Effective Comprehensive Planning—More Likely to be Implemented.

Heinlein said, "The greatest productive force is human selfishness."

A case study on a master plan revision would show that those individuals most directly benefiting financially from the configurations of the plan are those most intimately acquainted with the planners and lawmakers. Under TDR, comprehensive planning would better reflect the general public needs and aspirations. Without affecting the basic human need for overall control of development, gross density and gross use of land, fortunes can still be made and lost in speculation under TDR.

Furthermore, the reduction of the value of land itself will allow for more commonsense and generous use of land for buffering needs. Some land should not be used at all. Land, along major highways for instance, where use can only impede the flow of traffic or provide unhealthy surroundings for residents should be ruled out. A heavy stand of trees between otherwise incompatible uses can make good neighbors of disparate land utilization.

TDR would also allow for correction of past mistakes in zoning or otherwise vesting of rights in land. The zoning would be honored in the distribution of rights, but construction could take place in some other location. In Fairfax County, Virginia, for instance, in an area where traffic congestion is intense, over 100 acres of unused high-rise apartment zoning exists. TDR would allow those property owners to be compensated, but the density could be moved to a location where it could be accommodated.

E. Beneficial Effect on Taxation Equity

Payment of taxes only on services required, without changing market value as a basis for assessment is one of the most desirable effects of TDR. Special tax relief measures such as deferral taxation or preferential taxation would simply not be necessary. Market value would be based on the actual use of the land rather than its development potential, as is now the case. To the farmer near an urban area, the system would offer not only short-term, but long-term relief from the heavy burden of taxes which has driven many farmers off the land.

Market value is a relatively simple, understandable measure to apply in determining if taxation is being handled equitably. It should not be abandoned.

F. Publicly Owned Land Receives Development Rights

Along with all privately owned land, land owned by the government also receives its fair share of development rights. A community could use this to produce revenues or to provide a subsidy for land costs for low income housing. Judiciously used, this could provide a large subsidy at no cost to the public.

G. Public Facility Uses Would Not Require Development Rights

One of the greatest problems in the suburban fringe area is providing land for public facilities in sufficient quantity. Because of the character of the resident population (suburbanite and farmer/landowners), borrowing is the only fair way to meet these needs. Naturally, this arrangement limits the funds available for this purpose. In most jurisdictions, the actual practice today is to provide for the needs of existing population only, precluding the acquisition of land for future needs. Savings in the cost of land for public facilities is a major advantage of TDR. Nor will the landowner suffer since he may transfer title to the property to the government and keep the certificates for development rights. These rights may then be sold separately.

H. TDR Provides Mechanism to Project and Provide Public Facilities

With plan implementation a realistic possibility, accurate public facility requirements can be projected and met.

I. Economic Mechanism to Allow for Controls on Total Population and Use

This is neither a growth, nor a no-growth, proposal. It simply provides the mechanism for monitoring and controlling total planned growth. The system would allow for growth beyond that called for in the adopted master plan, but would require a new master plan with a new issuance of development rights.

J. Beneficial Effect on Integrity of Government Processes

In the Washington, D.C. area where the market is intense, there are all too many documented examples of corruption and bribery of officials involved in zoning. The area is not unique. It is naive to think that removing zoning to another level of government will reform the process. No matter at what level of government, one group of human beings, elected or appointed, must make decisions which may involve many millions of dollars and which may adversely affect human life irreparably. Corruption of planning and zoning officials goes far beyond planning and zoning. It corrodes the very fiber of government. The effects of bribery indictments and convictions in Fairfax County, Virginia, which occurred years ago, are still being felt today. To knowingly implant this system in state government is absolutely unconscionable. TDR provides the economic checks and balances to make land-use regulation work. It removes the temptation that zoning creates.

K. Advantages for Developers

The system provides more certainty. The rules are clear and precise. The personal factors involved in the approval process and the possibilities for favoritism are greatly reduced. The time and expense involved in obtaining zoning approval is avoided. Costs for land plus development rights should be roughly the same as the land would cost today, given time for the market to adjust. Many innovative architectural designs are precluded by the arbitrary bulk, height, and set-back regulations implicit in zoning regulations. The market would be allowed to operate more freely while still protecting what is fundamental to human life.

TDR allows the small builder to operate. Zoning has worked so poorly that the fashionable belief today in planning circles is that only through the big developer approach—the new town with single ownership and control of land—can sound land use goals be achieved. Land use must not be our only concern in devising control measures. Freedom of the individual and governmental integrity will be better served when more, rather than fewer, interests may participate.

L. Preservation of Open Space and Farmland

Much of the Class A farmland, needed for production of food for city residents, is located near these same cities. The value of development potential of this farmland precludes purchase of land or rights. Tax relief measures, such as tax deferral or preferential assessment have only a limited benefit, giving the public time to find a solution. TDR would allow for the preservation of open space and continued operation of farms at no cost to the public.

M. Suburban Governments Might Spend This Time on Issues Other Than Planning and Zoning.

Due to the needs of land control, many important problems of government never receive more than minimum attention by elected officials and staff of suburban areas where the pace of development is rapid. The time required to cope with overseeing land regulation in Fairfax County, Virginia does not lead to the best decision making, either in land regulation or other areas of governmental policy.

PROBLEMS WITH TRANSFERABLE DEVELOPMENT RIGHTS

A major problem with Transferable Development Rights, as it is here proposed, is that it still does not deal with the "Windfall/Wipeout" effect on land values created by government location of public facilities. To achieve the desired economic/equity result, a device must be found to return to the public its investment of funds for such public facilities as highway construction. Otherwise, there will be a bonanza for a few at the expense of the many. Public officials will still be tempted to sell their souls for a few miles of concrete. Special assessments and user fees are probably the answer. Transferable Development Rights should give legal support for consideration of the imposition of these special taxes.

Those individuals who have invested in land, with the expectation of future approvals, and who are not considered to have "vested rights" by a community, stand to lose. Some of these interests, it should be forewarned, are in a position to have tremendous influence over government decisions.

Suburbanites will be required to pay taxes on their actual use of services. While this may be equitable, they will undoubtedly not think so. In fact, any quick changeover could create a hardship. However, in most developing areas where suburbanites make up a majority of the residents, relatively little of the tax base (as opposed to the land area) will be undeveloped land. Improvements and the land on which these improvements sit will make up most of tax assessments. Either the ad hoc practice of the local assessments office has been to underassess open land or some form of special treatment for open land has been allowed by the municipality.

Government must continue to function. While it may not be necessary in all circumstances, the interim period while the market adjusts may require a freeze on assessments. A community which is primarily farmland will not require a freeze. A community where the tax base is for the most part composed of improvements should not require this temporary freeze, but this may be a problem and should be recognized.

If the community plans for too small a population, some smart speculators are going to make themselves very rich. The speculation itself will not affect the public or its environment, but it is a factor officials should be watching.

If the community plans for too many people, the community, at some time in the future will be faced with either impending congestion or having to buy the rights back at tremendous cost.

Economic disparaties in the costs of development may inadvertently be created by one jurisdiction which adopts this approach to land use control if the general market area contains more than one jurisdiction and the technique is not adopted throughout the general area. This is not a new situation. Governmental regulation on usury, lot sizes, water pollution and building codes have had profound impact on the market economics of the construction industry in the Washington, D.C. area, for example.

The major problem with TDR is the lack of public understanding. The general public does not understand the mechanisms of our present form of land regulation. They somehow have the impression that zoning protects them; that the key to reform is honest officials. Given that situation, it is difficult for the public to accept something different which requires some background knowledge of our present system. Those who know the present system all too well feel that they benefit and are threatened by the possibility of change. . . .